Capitalizing on College

Advance Praise for *Capitalizing on College*

"At a time of growing mistrust in the academy and burgeoning skepticism around the value of a college degree, Brown crafts a narrative that foregrounds untold stories of innovation and impact on college campuses. He brings needed clarity to the fundamental purposes of American higher education, showcasing the importance of strategic leaders whose commitment to access, equity, and excellence for all students transcends both the constraints of exigent financial circumstances and emerging threats to the mission, vision, and values foundational to our nation's diverse colleges and universities."

Lynn Pasquerella, president, American Association of Colleges and Universities

"*Capitalizing on College* is a must-read for scholars of organizations and education, as well as anyone employed in the US higher education sector. Brown offers a chilling account of the changing logics confronting colleges and universities that rely on tuition to function, and describes the strategies employed by administrators to keep the lights on when faced with declining tuition revenues. The attention to the sociopolitical and historical shifts in the US higher education sector allows the reader to better understand crises in higher education and current debates around topics like loan forgiveness. The book is masterfully written and offers vivid portrayals of the administrators responsible for developing new business models, finding new student segments, and generating novel sources of revenue."

Sarah A. Soule, Morgridge professor of organizational behavior, Sara Miller McCune director of the Center for Advanced Study in the Behavioral Sciences, Stanford University

"Like the Red Queen in *Alice in Wonderland*, schools without substantial endowments must run faster just to stay in the same place. *Capitalizing on College* identifies strategies colleges and universities have used to try to get off this treadmill. In an environment where every school aims to establish a competitive advantage, this book is essential reading for any university administrator."

Jay Barney, presidential professor of strategic management, Lassonde chair of social entrepreneurship, Eccles School of Business, The University of Utah

"Higher education is one of the few institutions in American society seen as a cornerstone for economic prosperity. In an era where students, employers, and public policy leaders alike are demanding schools deliver on this promise, great leadership and entrepreneurial nimbleness are needed now more than ever. Brown's book, which includes road-tested insights from a diverse group of higher education leaders, provides a path forward."

Gerard Robinson, professor of practice in public policy and law, University of Virginia; former secretary of education for Virginia

"In tackling the most pressing topics in contemporary higher education, Brown has done the essential and the unusual: rather than prescribe 'solutions' from the vantage of elites, he has instead talked with a wide range of college and university leaders to understand the nuances and complexities of decision making in our market-driven institutions. His awareness of the important role of mission-driven institutions in the higher education landscape is welcome, and his analysis is trenchant and insightful. This book is essential reading for those who care about higher education as an avenue to opportunity and transformation for our students, and indeed for our society."

Mary B. Marcy, president emerita, Dominican University of California; author, *The Small College Imperative*

Capitalizing on College

*How Higher Education Went From
Mission Driven to Margin Obsessed*

Joshua Travis Brown

OXFORD
UNIVERSITY PRESS

Oxford University Press is a department of the University of Oxford.
It furthers the University's objective of excellence in research, scholarship,
and education by publishing worldwide. Oxford is a registered trade mark of
Oxford University Press in the UK and in certain other countries.

Published in the United States of America by Oxford University Press
198 Madison Avenue, New York, NY 10016, United States of America.

© Joshua Travis Brown 2025

All rights reserved. No part of this publication may be reproduced, stored in a retrieval system, transmitted, used for text and data mining, or used for training artificial intelligence, in any form or by any means, without the prior permission in writing of Oxford University Press, or as expressly permitted by law, by license, or under terms agreed with the appropriate reprographics rights organization. Inquiries concerning reproduction outside the scope of the above should be sent to the Rights Department, Oxford University Press, at the address above

You must not circulate this work in any other form
and you must impose this same condition on any acquirer

CIP data is on file at the Library of Congress

ISBN 9780197780701
ISBN 9780197780718 (pbk.)

DOI: 10.1093/oso/9780197780701.001.0001

Paperback printed by Marquis, Canada

Hardback printed by Bridgeport National Bindery, Inc., United States of America

The manufacturer's authorised representative in the EU for product safety is Oxford University Press España S.A. of El Parque Empresarial San Fernando de Henares, Avenida de Castilla, 2 – 28830 Madrid (www.oup.es/en or product.safety@oup.com). OUP España S.A. also acts as importer into Spain of products made by the manufacturer.

For those faculty and staff at marginalized institutions who serve marginalized students, but whose stories are too often excluded from the national education narrative.

Contents

Acknowledgments   x

   Introduction: "We Have to Grow, or We're Going to Die"   1

1. The Traditional Strategy: "You Come . . . to a Tradition"   32
2. The Pioneer Strategy: "We Build With Adult Money"   79
3. The Network Strategy: "In Growth We Trust"   128
4. The Accelerated Strategy: "More Money Than God"   177
5. A Sector of Schools: "We're Here to Make Money"   227

   Outtakes: "These Are Things I Wish I Could Tell Somebody Someday"   259

Methodological Appendix: "I Am Probably Being Too Candid Here"   264
Bibliography   277
Index   285

Acknowledgments

I rarely begin reading any book with its introductory chapter or preface. One of my quirks is that I start by reading the acknowledgments of a book to understand "the story behind the story"—the account of persons hidden in its margins as well as the labyrinth of obstacles the author overcame. Such a tale is certainly the case with *Capitalizing on College*. It has taken a community of individuals more than 10 years to help me shape this book through two distinct periods—an era of research and an era of writing.

An Era of Research

I am indebted to those who supported me throughout my doctoral program at the University of Virginia. My committee members—Josipa Roksa, Derrick Alridge, Carol Anne Spreen, Mark Hamilton, and Patricia Thornton—pushed me to clarify that what I was seeing in my sample applied more broadly to higher education. Because I was working full-time through my doctoral program to pay for tuition, I likely might not have completed the program if not for the intellectual and emotional support of my writing group, "the Cone." Michele Darling, Megan Juelfs, Sarah Mosseri, and I committed to two ideas: "What was said in the Cone, stayed in the Cone" and "Everyone finishes." We fought side by side through some difficult circumstances but ensured in the end that four dissertations were completed.

I learned it was important to talk about early ideas with others. William Ocasio challenged my initial sample of institutions, noting they would bias my results. In the end, adhering to his methodological insights led me to discover a key finding—that there were different strategies behind margin capitalization. Monsignor Michael McCarron helped me understand the culture of an unfamiliar faith. Mitchell Stevens and Ari Kelman made the Stanford University community available by offering writing and presentation opportunities, which blossomed into a broader network of support with anthony lising antonio, Candice Thille, Mark Algee-Hewitt, Sarah Soule, and others at SCANCOR.

I discovered that when you write in coffee shops, they become an important part of your community. There were three coffee shop encouragers—Ritchie

McKay, Samuel Omotoye, and Erik Koroneos—whose optimistic early-morning words kept me inching forward in challenging periods. Many of the Starbucks baristas at Boonsbux—Sydney, Chris, John, Estephanie, Miranda, Jen, Ruth, and Meredith (among others)—were studying via ASU Online and experiencing firsthand what this book chronicles. They helped vet early research ideas. In trying to name the innovative financial practices I was seeing across the set of universities, I am grateful for the help of two savvy businesspersons, Leon Hill and Chris Kennedy, who helped me arrive at *margin capitalization*.

When my ideas needed testing among colleagues, Patricia Thornton urged me to choose a venue where people would come alongside my ideas to build them up rather, than a place where they would be criticized in a manner that tore them down. Her counsel led me to the European Group for Organizational Studies, where myriad minds influenced early versions of this work, including Angela Greco, Vern Glaser, Derrick Harmon, Hovig Tchalian, Luna Ansari, Fransisco Ramirez, Tatiana Fumasoli, Marc Ventresca, Grace Augustine, Harsh Jha, and Jeffrey Loewenstein.

This work would not have been possible without financial support from the National Science Foundation and Buckner W. Clay Endowment and research support from Alicia, Clint, Alex, Rachel, Victoria, Gabby T., Gabby G., and Irene. Most important, I am grateful for mentorship by Josipa Roksa and for the gift of time from Mark Hine during this era, without which these bound pages would merely be blank.

An Era of Writing

After trying unsuccessfully for 2 years to write a book in the same way I had been trained to write research articles, the journey through the writing labyrinth took a dramatic turn toward clarity and confidence thanks to Sarah Davidson, my running partner and Ironman triathlete. She helped me understand that the most skilled athletes in the world rely on coaches to help them achieve their goals, and oftentimes, differences in performance are psychological and could be attributed to the influence (or absence) of a coach. Her words compelled me to invest in myself midrace and find a coach to help me complete the literary marathon. Olson Pook took my raw writing elements and showed me how to use them in new and refined ways, some of which are described in the methodological appendix. This decision further transformed both me as an author and the book itself.

I believe it is important for new authors to walk the unfamiliar path of publishing with someone who has previously traversed the same road. I am grateful to Ilana Horwitz for offering countless insights rooted in experience. I reached out many times from confounding crossroads and in every instance she responded.

My Oxford writing group with Ariell Ahearn, Aoife Brophy, and Abrar Chaudhury—also affectionately known as Kaizen—provided the early-morning consistency and intellectual companionship necessary for the project. Through two fellowships, the University of Oxford community helped me experientially understand the role of elites for a book about marginalized colleges and universities. Adam Smith, Uta Balbier, Katy Long, and Hannah Greiving were beyond supportive throughout my year as fellow-in-residence at the Rothermere American Institute, while Susan James Relly and James Robson were generous collaborators as a fellow at the Center for Skills, Knowledge, and Organizational Performance.

Others in the writing era who deserve special acknowledgment include the baristas at Golf Park Coffee—Haylynn, Cole, Tanner, Al, Doug, Zoe, Aubrie, Annie, Theo, and Bren—who provided a safe space for writing during COVID lockdowns. Thanks to those who read my "shitty first drafts," including Kate Drezek McConnell, Morwari Zafar, Sondra Barringer, Jeremy Alexander, Jason Lawyer, and members of Kaizen and the Cone. The manuscript was snatched from the throes of bureaucratic hell thanks to the advocacy of Christian Steinmetz and Marcy Reedy. I am grateful for the serendipitous introduction to Sonal Patel because of our canceled flights. The clarity of the book's title is the result of her insistence and marketing genius. Similarly, the graphic design talent offered by Patrice Brown took the images in *Capitalizing on College* to the highest level of professionalism.

The support team at Oxford University Press provided indispensable guidance. My acquisitions editor, James Cook, believed in this work from the beginning and helped me navigate my entry into the publishing world. I am grateful for the generous comments of the anonymous reviewers who helped improve the clarity of the book.

This book exists because eight marginalized universities invited me to be part of their community for an extended period. The unnamed persons at these universities showed me firsthand the wonderful world that exists beyond elite institutions of higher education. In addition to the 150 leaders who shared their stories, more than 100 others offered unmatched hospitality, assisting with meals, tours, lodging, and scheduling. The librarians at each university guided me through archives in an attempt to portray their unique institutional history and culture accurately. Anonymity prohibits me from listing these persons, but their stories and acts of hospitality are the soul of *Capitalizing on College*.

Finally, I would like to thank my family, who offered relentless emotional support and encouragement across both eras. Specifically, Maddie Brown, thank you for your patience and forbearance, as you, more than anyone, understand the peculiar early-morning writing routine your father holds.

Introduction

"We Have to Grow, or We're Going to Die"

It was a common story, one I had heard repeated time and again in interviewing college administrators on their campuses. "Six months before I was hired, the university had taken on $140 million of debt," this particular chief financial officer began, describing the financial albatross he inherited. His school's leaders had turned to the textbook solution of increased enrollment growth but still could not steer their way clear of the looming financial crisis.

Like so many others, the leaders borrowed to give themselves time to solve a puzzle that was vexing schools across America—how to keep the lights on while providing an increasingly expensive product. As he explained to me,

> You need enrollment to get the funds to continue doing things. . . . So you grow, but then you need more classrooms, and you need more office space, and you need more faculty and you need more staff, and you just don't quite arrive.

The tried-and-true formula for schools like his was no longer working: "It is the middle of summer and we're down 250 students." What was worse in his eyes was how the university lacked financial alternatives and wound up recruiting poorer students simply to achieve enrollment growth. "If you look at family income, it went down by $10,000 for the incoming class," he noted. "A lot of schools have endowments . . . if we had that revenue stream to help feed scholarships, that would be huge!" But also like most colleges and universities, his school was tuition driven, and in line with many of his similarly positioned colleagues he was perplexed regarding a way forward: "What is the model? Schools increasing tuition 3% to 4% per year? That's just *not* going to work." He looked hard at me before summing up the puzzle facing these schools: "What is a school's strategy to exit this model?"

Complicating the puzzle for these schools was the fact that generating more revenue by raising the cost of tuition to resolve the crisis was seen as potentially leading to a deeper problem—undermining the mission.

Capitalizing on College. Joshua Travis Brown, Oxford University Press. © Joshua Travis Brown (2025).
DOI: 10.1093/oso/9780197780701.003.0001

The mission of most of these tuition-driven schools was to provide educational access to first-generation, underrepresented, and diverse student populations—a vision that for generations remained an integral part of the American promise of opportunity. The tuition-driven sector of higher education comprises a diverse array of institutional types that include women's, historically Black, Hispanic-serving, religious, vocational, regional, Tribal, and minority-serving institutions—schools that also attract educators committed to sustaining access: "I had no interest—zero interest—in going to an elite school," one provost stressed:

> I wanted to go to a place where their mission is to open doors to make lives better for a group of students that have the ability, but they might not otherwise have an opportunity if that group was not being served.

But as these leaders were painfully aware, passion does not fund educational opportunity: "At the end of the day you cannot have a mission without the resources to fulfill it," quipped another provost. The crisis vexed the administrators I spoke to who were struggling to resolve the tension. "It was so difficult, because you want to have those values and keep that culture," a vice president agonized, "but at the same time, from a business perspective, you need to make decisions that allow the university to continue. It's the old saying: 'No money, no mission.'"

The same tension plagued the chief financial officer I was speaking to. "With the economic changes in the state, the demographic changes, if we don't get another source of revenue going *fast* . . ." He paused, choosing his words carefully as he continued. "It's going to be a *struggle*. Those are the 'brutal facts.'" The executive turned and withdrew a bright red volume from his shelf. Handing it to me, he said, "It's just like Jim Collins says in his book *Good to Great*."[1] But what caught my eye was the book's subtitle: "Why Some Companies Make the Leap and Others Don't." The phrase spoke to the broader concerns of this volume—namely, how many mission-driven and tuition-driven institutions did attempt to "make the leap" to a new model and develop another source of revenue—and the surprising and unexpected outcomes that emerged as a result.

Over the course of 2 years and 150 interviews, I discovered four strategies—different attempts to bridge the financial chasm that looms large for most tuition-driven colleges and universities. In talking with everyone from faculty and staff to provosts and presidents, I observed a diverse array of institutions hard at work trying to find innovative new ways to fund their missions of educational access that aimed to keep open the doors of opportunity for those in society who need it most. The stories these leaders offered to me in the privacy of their offices stressed how the scarce availability of financial resources severely threatened educational access at these schools—and, for many, the survival of the institution itself. But understanding the crisis university administrators find themselves in and the various strategies they employed (and continue to employ) to solve the financial conundrum they face requires first stepping back and understanding the broader system and culture of higher education within which these institutions find themselves enmeshed.

A Story Eclipsed by Elites

There is a widespread understanding of what it means for a young person to "go to college" and a shared image regarding how a university campus is supposed to look. These deeply held norms originated with the storied residential "Oxbridge" tradition of elite European institutions whereby students—predominantly wealthy and male—embarked on a rite of passage in a communal university setting to live, dine, socialize, and learn.[2] When early American colleges adopted the same approach, it all but ensured future generations would see the educational path to a successful life along the same lines—a timeworn understanding of opportunity defined by elite institutions centered on the residential college experience. This traditional understanding of college has remained embedded in American society for centuries, shaping the intentions of individuals, institutions, and governments from one generation to the next.

Throughout this volume, I refer to this traditional residential model of higher education as the residential core. The residential core is often characterized by a sprawling, well-groomed pastoral campus dotted with stately structures situated about an academic quadrangle.[3] The costly facilities of the core include a well-resourced library, academic and administrative buildings, residence halls, student unions, athletic complexes, and dining halls. Teaching in the residential core relies on highly credentialed faculty to deliver in-person instruction to students who physically come to the campus. These features of the residential core serve as important signals of legitimacy that have customarily distinguished a college or university as "real" (rather than for-profit).[4]

Although the majority of American colleges and universities are not elite institutions but rather tuition-driven schools, their leaders emulate the elites for fear of losing their perceived legitimacy. The legitimating practices that elite institutions maintain are critical to grasp because they are the socially accepted practices that most institutions aspire to follow and are measured against. Most institutions of higher education continuously strive to become more prestigious, improve their brand, and climb within the widely publicized university rankings.[5] They also accordingly subscribe to the residential core model. An academic official at one of the schools examined in this volume stressed the lengths to which administrators are consumed with imitating elites:

> We're always comparing ourselves to Harvard or Yale. When something comes up that pushes against that—to recognize we are not—there is a visceral reaction to do whatever you have to do to save face, to make sure it is, "No, no, no! We are! We are!" There is a whole lot done to present this image when the reality is very different. A lot goes into continuing to prop up that image.

The practices of elite institutions function as powerful constraining frames that explain why many colleges and universities adopted similar practices and strategies over time (a process known to strategy scholars as isomorphism).[6] Simply put, in higher education conformity is king.

The Case of Endowments

The focus on elite institutions in the media has resulted in a skewed understanding of how the American system of higher education operates. As with society more broadly, the experiences of elites are rarely similar to those of the masses. For example, in higher education, looking at marginalized populations in elite institutions is not the same as studying them at their more common tuition-driven brethren.[7] Another area where tuition-driven colleges are substantially different from elite schools is in the widespread elite practice of maintaining an endowment to partially fund the expenses stemming from the residential core. The money in an endowment generates profitable interest revenues that are not taxed like the investments of other major organizations.[8] At elite institutions, the interest from endowments provides considerable annual revenue used to offset operating expenses (anywhere between approximately $500 million and $1.5 billion per school),[9] including subsidizing the gap between student tuition and the high cost of providing the in-person residential core student experience. The enormous endowments of elite institutions mean tuition comprises only around 25% of their overall revenue stream. But the situation is quite different at tuition-driven schools, which find themselves caught between the proverbial rock and a hard place—obligated to provide a similar residential core experience under the auspices of legitimacy, yet having to pay for it almost entirely with tuition dollars.

Another clear difference between elite and nonelite institutions is in the financial aid packages students receive. Marginalized populations at elite institutions are given scholarships and in-kind support from endowment revenues, effectively eliminating the need for student loans.[10] Quite the opposite happens at colleges with modest or no endowments, where the growth of student loans plays an outsized role in the strategies they adopt to pay for the residential core.

Endowments have come to underscore the substantial inequality that exists among institutions in the American system of higher education, separating the "haves" from the "have nots."[11] While many colleges and universities followed the example of elite institutions and created endowments in an attempt to defray the costs of the residential core, their meager revenues stand in marked contrast to those generated by elites, whose endowments are much larger. With 75% of all endowment assets nationally held by approximately 10% of institutions, the majority of American colleges and universities are left to rely on a single revenue source—student tuition.[12]

While imitating the trappings of elite colleges is common in higher education, lacking the financial resources to support the residential core forces most universities to be creative in how they achieve the goals of legitimacy. As one vice president remarked, "Higher education as a business has really been thrust into the milieu of consumerism." The university leaders interviewed for *Capitalizing on College* revealed that the vital financial resources needed to sustain the residential core experience for their undergraduates predominantly derived from innovatively securing more federal financial aid through increased student enrollment. These schools could not rely on endowments and wealthy alumni to support the residential core. Instead, as one vice president confessed in the most succinct terms, "We have to grow, or we're going to die."

Driven by Mission

While the identity of elite colleges and universities emphasizes the prestige they maintain, the identity of tuition-driven institutions is primarily underscored by their solitary source of income. Tuition-driven leaders are readily aware of this and respond by emphasizing their unique institutional mission as an equally important, if not more important, part of their identity. This aspect of the school's identity stems from the student population to which it seeks to provide educational access. These include colleges for women, colleges for men, religious institutions, and Hispanic-serving, historically Black, minority-serving, Tribal, vocational, and even regional institutions, among others. These schools possess rich histories, and many have remained at the frontier of access to American higher education since their founding. As one provost nostalgically put it, "They have been part of their local communities anywhere from 50 to some of them almost 200 years." In short, the unique educational missions of tuition-driven colleges and universities vary considerably, but they all broadly share a similar financial model.

Tuition-driven institutions operate within a revenue paradigm that one administrator described as a "stressed business model" informed by "a lot of anxiety about enrollment." Because the populations these schools serve lack generational wealth, most students pay for college through federal financial aid—making student loans the primary means of survival for these schools. One senior leader bluntly conveyed the reality they faced: "We could not function if it was not for the feds. If we did not have Pell Grants and Guaranteed Student Loans, half of our kids couldn't come to school." A tuition-driven school must take immediate action if its enrollment goals are not met: "Our operating budgets have to be sustained by our tuition ... if your enrollment goes down, your budgets all of a sudden have to reflect that," a cabinet official confessed. Any decrease in a given year necessitates that university executives avail themselves of cost-saving mechanisms to address the financial loss, including cutting programs, reducing employee benefits, eliminating student services, securing credit, and implementing efficiencies. As explained by another leader, the tuition-driven model is "very much a numbers game" that can be plainly understood as "numbers equal the money."

Enrollment at tuition-driven institutions is particularly susceptible to changes in the environment, which makes these schools "distinctly vulnerable" to "reversals of fortune."[13] Yet when confronted with financial challenges, the leaders of tuition-driven institutions possess limited options to generate new revenues, a predicament that vexes most executives, as one pointedly shared: "What do you do? All of a sudden, you're looking in the medicine cabinet of what can I actually grab onto that can help me meet the business objectives of enrollment?" To generate the revenues needed to sustain the institution, leaders continually applied the same "cure." They increase student tuition and student enrollment, using students as financial resources.

As a result of these persistent increases, administrators readily understood that (in the words of one department chair) "students come with dollar signs attached."

The Expanding Role of the Market

Prior to the 20th century, paying for higher education through grants and loans via federal financial aid did not exist. From the founding of colonial colleges in the 1600s extending to the Second World War in the mid-1900s, students who enrolled in American colleges were predominantly those of financial means who could afford to pay full tuition or worked in some capacity as a form of tuition payment.[14] Payments for tuition were received directly from resources immediately available to the enrolled students, but only covered a portion of the costs an institution incurred to provide an education to its students. The remaining costs were subsidized. For private institutions, costs were paid by benefactors or religious denominations, whereas state and federal governments financed the remaining costs for public institutions.[15]

In the middle of the 20th century, two seismic policy shifts occurred in the way individuals would pay for higher education. Following the Second World War, federal lawmakers "rewarded" American military personnel with a financial grant to attend college known as the GI Bill.[16] The GI Bill was a stark philosophical shift in financing the college experience because the money was tied to the enrolled student. Then, in 1958, Congress passed legislation known as the National Defense Education Act. The comprehensive legislation put forth a new indirect funding approach to finance the college experience using borrowed money. This was another radical philosophical shift in paying for college, since the individual and not the organization owned the debt. Financial liability was transferred from the school to the student, and the college experience was paid for with future rather than present money.

The two policy innovations of indirect funding and student loans fundamentally altered how all institutions could choose to strategically pursue new financial resources. Colleges and universities were no longer limited to direct funding provided by the state, supportive agencies, or students of means. By leveraging these two "portable market-driven mechanisms," tuition-driven institutions could pursue monetary resources associated with *any* person able to obtain federal financial aid.[17] To enroll a student was to secure federal money, and to enroll *more* students was to secure *more* federal money. Thus, the incentive "to grow our way out of problems" (as one administrator put it) was "hard-wired" into higher education, with momentous consequences to follow.

What immediately followed was seemingly miraculous—an explosive era of increased access and public support that became known as the golden age of American higher education. The enrollments of public and private institutions alike increased as new types of students, including veterans, women, and racial/ethnic minorities, pursued the opportunity to go to college and experience the coming-of-age traditions associated with the residential core. Many institutions reorganized their admissions, business, registrar, and other student service offices into large administrative divisions renamed *enrollment management* that quickly became the financial engines of many American institutions.[18] For a time, it seemed as if the market—deemed an effective social arbiter for allocating scarce financial resources efficiently—would offer a neoliberal solution to persistent worries about educational access.[19] This perspective was undergirded by a belief that a market approach empowered students with the opportunity to "shop" across institutions in search of educational savings and quality. Neoliberal paradigms also transformed student loan policies, with lawmakers creating variations of the guaranteed student loan that permitted private banks rather than the federal government to get into the game with government-subsidized low interest rates.[20]

Although leaders at tuition-driven schools expressed considerable unease with mounting levels of student debt, the reality is that the institutions they led were embedded in a broader regulatory system whereby students were the very mechanism through which federal financial resources were allocated. Within this engineered financial system, individual institutions retain hundreds of millions of dollars to spend at their discretion, while students are left shouldering the financial responsibility for the college experience decades into the future in the form of loans. With the tuition burden having predominantly shifted to individual students, there remained virtually no liability for institutions, as one academic administrator pointedly remarked: "These student loans are going up . . . but we've got our money." The dependence on federal financial aid created a tenuous situation where university leaders often disclosed they felt caught choosing between two seemingly dichotomous options—massive student debt, which was antithetical to their mission, or organizational survival. "People cannot come to college without student loans. A majority of our money comes from student loans to support us," an academic administrator lamented. "It's a vicious cycle that I don't know how to get out of."

The Strategic Turn to Innovation

Matters came to a head for many tuition-driven schools in the final decades of the 20th century, when the pressure to grow met a dramatic decline in the number of traditional college-age students, leading to increased competition among colleges for the shrinking pool of students. Nothing less than their reputation as a "real college" that offered a robust residential core experience was at stake. With limited financial resources to sustain themselves, their inability to subsidize the gap in operating costs created by tuition discounts with revenue from endowments meant that without a dramatic turnaround, many of these schools would be forced to close.

The narratives that follow examine the attempts by nonelite tuition-driven schools to find ways to pay for their residential core model—a model now increasingly stressed with the influx of new students as a result of embracing a mindset rooted in a system that rewarded resources through enrollment growth. Colleges turned to students for revenue, but the rub was that they still had to house and feed those students. As one academic chair confessed, "We're at capacity in terms of the physical space. I don't know what we're going to do with all these thousands more students that we're supposed to get. Where are we going to put them?" Growth, in other words, did not yield pure profit; in fact, it came with heavy costs. At certain enrollment junctures, new facilities needed to be built. Ironically, the resulting need for more buildings on campus further exacerbated the financial crisis the schools were facing—leading to even more pressure on schools to generate revenue and recruit more students.

To break free of this unsustainable cycle and obtain the financial resources they needed, tuition-driven institutions adapted their organizational form and innovated their educational programs to pursue nontraditional (i.e., non-residential) student enrollment markets—a type of innovation born of the need "to keep up with the Joneses," as described by one administrator. But the fear of being perceived as "illegitimate" restrained many institutions and their leaders in this pursuit, leading them to simultaneously attempt to appear to be "playing by the rules" (i.e., the norms established by elite institutions) so as not to jeopardize their established reputation. The tension between innovation and legitimacy is quite vividly felt by those schools that do not possess privileged positions within the collegiate hierarchy, as one vice president in the study emphasized:

> I think actualizing our vision is very possible, but it may not look like what we think the typical university looks like because that's just one way to carve out the

world. You can define excellence and value in a whole different way, and we need to leverage that piece and define our own sense of excellence and not how *US News & World Report* likes to define us. Because our mission isn't to do that in the first place.

The traditional norms in higher education maintained by elite institutions possess a powerful legitimating function that requires a compelling cause if a tuition-driven school is to forswear their influence to innovate and pursue a new path. University leaders at tuition-driven schools dealt with this tension by framing innovation as stemming from their institutional mission. "[The founders] came here in the 1800s on an ox-pulled cart and developed all this," one professor told me. "You don't think that was innovation? You don't think they were looking forward and responding to a need? I think we are *still* continuing that!"

The various institutional missions wedded a noble sense of purpose to forward thinking—in other words, they were cultures with a cause that legitimated innovation. As one dean explained, this blend of purpose and innovation strongly influenced how their leaders saw themselves and their institutions: "We see ourselves as being individuals that are innovative—individuals that like to think and dream outside the box." Backed by cultures that supported them in going beyond traditional bounds and formulating an "exit strategy" from the unsustainable cycle of growth that never quite covered the cost of the residential core, the leaders of the institutions examined in *Capitalizing on College* rejected the status quo and embraced various forms of entrepreneurialism in pursuit of nontraditional student enrollment growth.

Innovative Educational Products

It is often remarked that within higher education, tuition-driven schools innovate while elites legitimate. By changing how financial resources were distributed to institutions, policy makers also changed how financial resources were pursued by all institutions, regardless of type. In response, institutions began to develop dynamic and innovative "students-as-resources" strategies. For instance, some public institutions increased their financial margins by enrolling different types of students who paid a higher tuition rate,[21] whereas other public institutions achieved the same by recruiting poorer students who were eligible for larger amounts of student loans (and charging them more).[22] While all institutions adapted to the changing market context to secure vital financial resources, the competition was particularly intense for the vast numbers of tuition-driven institutions that were limited to a single source of revenue to sustain the organization.[23]

Faced with limited options, university leaders elected to expand student enrollments in different parts of the institution, which meant reconceiving the form of the institution and what it looked like. Tuition-driven leaders continued to grow their residential core, faithfully following the legitimating "best practices" that all colleges and universities pursued. But in addition to expanding the residential core, these institutions innovatively established periphery enrollment markets by offering new educational products to new groups of students to secure new avenues of indirect federal funding. Creating innovative products and processes was the crucial first step for these entrepreneurial schools to obtain the vital financial resources associated with nontraditional student enrollment growth.

These entrepreneurial schools were united in reconceiving how the institution and education might look if the classroom were not confined solely to the residential core. Leaders took what they had and redesigned their offerings into different formats to sell a fundamentally new type of educational experience. Innovations ranged from creating new products (which included degree programs, niche courses, certificates, badges, and microcredentials) to establishing new processes that generated entirely new "bundles" or "strings" of courses. These new products and processes in turn allowed leaders to develop new enrollment markets defined by student type, mode of delivery, and even class content, including adult learners, transfer students, international campuses, satellite sites, regional centers, online classes, vocational education, professional development courses, and degree completion requirements. The new periphery enrollment markets enabled universities to add new students without having to add the expensive physical infrastructure associated with the residential core.

Central to their innovative approach was the pressure exerted by time. Some schools took advantage of "first-mover" opportunities and focused on being first to establish a multisite system of satellite campuses in shopping malls, hotels, and military bases that made higher education accessible to new students. Other schools pursued saturation with speed to create a multitype system of campuses across the region, nation, and globe. And a select few unlocked the secret of scaling educational offerings in unprecedented ways, enabling leaders to swell their periphery enrollments to eclipse their residential enrollment 10-fold.

The consequences these leaders faced for choosing to jettison the normative approaches of the field were substantial, but their culture and mission braced them when they faced severe stigmatization. One senior administrator recalled just how tenuous it was when their school made its blind leap of faith into innovative but nontraditional educational products:

> That was a big step—it was a big risk to go adult education. At the time, that was sort of cutting edge. People were not doing it, and if you tried it people were going to criticize you for it. But that was a turning point that came from a level of courage and desire to try to do something different and be different.

The censure leaders encountered from other colleges and universities was only the first of many obstacles they faced. Yet going it alone also contributed to notable financial gains. As one leader recalled, "We were doing that when everyone else was dismissive of it, and it allowed us to make huge advances." As these advances accumulated, they provided opportunities for leaders to innovate in the financial realm with two altogether new practices—margin capitalization and margin philanthropy.

Innovative Financial Practices

Confronted with a particularly acute era of competition for students, tuition-driven leaders contended it was vital they transform their physical facilities to entice prospective residential students to enroll. As one vice president explained, facilities enabled leaders to remain competitive with traditional students and legitimize themselves as real institutions. Prospective residential students and parents used the campus aesthetic and its buildings to make inferences about the educational quality of the university: "If you have old, rundown buildings, parents are much less likely to send their students, because they think the child is not being properly taken care of here," one professor explained. "If the buildings look bad, what will be the quality of the teaching?" Armed with the marginal revenues from nontraditional students in periphery enrollment markets, university leaders did not just erect a building or two as a signal for prospective residential students. Rather, the entrepreneurial-minded leaders at the institutions examined in *Capitalizing on College* overhauled their residential core campuses in a transformational effort requiring both time and financial resources. Although the nontraditional students in their periphery enrollment markets did not experience the new and expensive state-of-the-art campus buildings, their tuition money paid for them.

Higher education institutions have customarily relied on capitalization approaches funded through donations or bonds to pay for new academic buildings, residence halls, and athletic facilities. But lacking the expansive donative networks available to elite institutions, leaders of the tuition-driven colleges and universities in this book innovatively turned to the financial resource that was available to them—student tuition and the indirect federal funding associated with each enrolled student—for capitalization. The periphery enrollment markets that leaders established provided these tuition-driven schools with marginal revenues (i.e., profits) because the cost of providing an education to students in the periphery was much lower given that it lacked the expensive amenities (i.e., residence halls, student lounges, athletic facilities, etc.) inherent in the residential core. The leaders used the marginal revenues generated in the periphery enrollment markets to fund the costs of the residential core—managing both the institution (i.e., operating expenses) and the construction of facilities for residential students (i.e., capital projects). I use the term *margin capitalization* to describe the innovative practice of utilizing alternative sources of revenue from periphery markets to address capitalization needs in the core market. As one leader put it bluntly, "Whenever we want to do something, we crank up enrollment."

In some instances, the margins from student tuition were large enough to not only finance the capitalization needs of an institution but also invest in financial accounts that in turn yielded additional revenues. As previously noted, elite institutions of higher education have traditionally strengthened their financial future by developing large savings and investment accounts known as endowments, a practice that generates tax-free interest revenues used to subsidize the costly expenses of the residential core. With large philanthropic donations concentrated among elite institutions, some tuition-driven leaders relied on entrepreneurial uses of student financial aid to significantly expand their endowments. I use the term *margin philanthropy* to describe an entrepreneurial form of growing the university endowment through the marginal revenues generated from student tuition heavily subsidized by student loans and government financial aid—a process whereby current students become the new philanthropists.

University leaders devised these innovative financial practices to address the same systemic crisis they all faced. With their institutions enmeshed in an engineered system that allocated funding based on market principles of efficiency and competition, they remained challenged as to how to secure financial resources without undermining institutional missions of access and affordability. But the pursuit of resources and growth was truly a double-edged sword. As an astute administrator noted, resources offered on the one hand the hope of strengthening the mission: "Once we get consistent and reliable enrollment numbers and some growth, then we are going to have more resources to support the objectives to live our mission, to distinguish us from competitors." But on the other hand, the pursuit of financial resources in the form of new enrollment markets caused concern that something important was being forsaken along the way. Repeatedly, I heard administrators admonishing themselves, echoing the words of one provost: "Do not lose the heart and the soul of the university—do not lose that mission."

The Choice of Colleges

With approximately 6,000 colleges and universities in the United States eligible to receive federal financial aid, selecting which institutions to visit and which leaders to interview regarding what was happening in higher education was a conscientious process.[24] When studying organizations, researchers often rely on the case selection method—choosing a set of representative institutions to highlight an event of interest as well as to reduce competing explanations of the event (what researchers commonly refer to as *noise*).[25] Honing in on a single institutional type reduced alternative explanations that differences among the schools could be attributed to their type. Among the myriad categories of tuition-driven institutions, I chose a single type that offered a rich array of approaches—the religious college.

Unbeknown to many, the religious college type represents the largest group of schools among the tuition-driven institutions, with over 900 institutions annually reporting they are religiously affiliated.[26] Historically, the American system of higher education has deep roots in religion. While most elite colleges and universities do not currently maintain a religious affiliation, many were founded during the colonial era to educate clergy (including the "Big Three": Harvard, Princeton, and Yale Universities).[27] In the era following the Civil War, American higher education experienced an explosion of newly established religious institutions led by the efforts of many denominations that were motivated to meet the educational needs of their region.[28] Numerous schools popped up where denominations were concentrated—Lutheran colleges dotted the Midwest, Mormon universities proliferated in the far West, Jesuit schools spread throughout the East, and Baptist institutions were scattered across the South.

For more than a century, the prevailing story of religious colleges has focused on serving marginalized students, a narrative that deliberately challenges the selectivity of elites by creating opportunity. For example, in the early 1900s when the Big Three and other elite schools formally established admissions processes to strategically limit the number of Jewish students,[29] religious schools like DePaul University conversely emphasized educational opportunity rather than elite exclusion. As one of the vice presidents in the study explained,

> When DePaul was formed, the Catholic bishop of Chicago at the time went to the Fathers and said, "We need a school for immigrants, because the University of Chicago and Northwestern will not take Catholics." The Fathers said to the bishop at the time, "We will open the school, but we take everybody. We will take all your Catholics, but we are taking *everybody*." And as a result, they had a huge Jewish alumni, they had a huge African American and minority alumni, because they took them back when nobody would take them.

Just as they accepted Jewish students in the past, in the early 21st century Catholic colleges are educating sizable numbers of Muslim students. As self-described "opportunity schools," religious colleges have made it possible for generations of students of every imaginable background to pursue their educational ambitions when they were excluded from elite institutions.

In serving students of need, religious colleges have customarily operated on the margin of financial need themselves. Like most tuition-driven institutions, religious colleges remain in continual tension between sustaining their mission and keeping costs affordable. In fact, the challenge of limited financial resources remains a perennial problem for most college and university leaders striving to uphold institutional missions, such as state schools promoting "the public good," historically Black colleges and universities offering "minority opportunity," women's colleges fostering "gender equality," and Tribal institutions providing "Indigenous access." Among these diverse institutional missions, I focused on religious colleges partly because the tension between purpose and profit is palpable, making market-oriented strategies easy to identify. As in most tuition-driven institutions, the leaders of religious colleges must leverage the market logic to secure the funding necessary to sustain their mission. However, religious colleges possess tenets about money that should seemingly offer leaders motivation to push back on extreme market practices that might undermine their educational mission. An impassioned provost put it well when he reiterated that purpose, not profit, was the underlying motivation of these institutions:

> This is hearts and minds, this is people's existence we are supposed to be serving... people will walk through hell for that! Nobody is going to walk through hell to make another 1% profit margin!

As I show in the chapters that follow, looking for extreme market practices in the religious college sector suggests that to the extent innovative educational products and financial practices may be happening there, they can happen anywhere within the nonprofit sector. And while the focus of this volume highlights the stories of these religious schools, the phenomenon of leveraging enrollment growth to secure greater financial resources is widespread, reaching even into elite institutions like Duke University, Vanderbilt University, Stanford University, and the University of Pennsylvania.[30]

Scattered from coast to coast, the geographic diversity of the eight religious colleges examined in *Capitalizing on College* mirrors the institutional diversity that serves as the backbone of the American postsecondary system. But even more important in selecting cases is choosing institutions that have different approaches toward the event of interest—in this instance, enrollment growth. The sizable number of religious colleges within the tuition-driven sector permits a wide opportunity from which to select institutions that vary in their student enrollment growth. Accordingly, I sampled institutions based on variations in their growth rate from 2000 to 2014, choosing one Catholic and one Protestant school that experienced high (more than 100%) and medium (61%–99%) to low (1%–60%) and negative (less than 0%) growth to construct a matched-pair design, leading to a sample of eight institutions. The selected schools also resembled institutions in other diverse sectors of higher education, including "aspiring Ivies," "flagships," "branch campuses," and "multiversities." (Greater detail regarding selection can be found in the methodological appendix).

There is one final reason for turning to tuition-driven religious schools. Considering the stories of nonelite institutions permits us to move beyond the hegemonic narrative that emphasizes the selectivity and endowments of elites to understand what is in fact a diverse story within American higher education—one that, when told, is more institutionally inclusive and representative of the experiences of many marginalized students.[31] Including the voices of leaders from nonelite institutions provides the opportunity to discover how different strategies for approaching market-based policies exist within the tuition-driven sector. It offers the chance to highlight multiple cultures and ways of seeing the world that do not readily accept the underlying assumptions of elite cultures. Indeed, the focus on elites and the resulting homogenous narrative toward colleges and universities has remained a ubiquitous and distorting force in American higher education—one pervasively felt by tuition-driven leaders themselves. As one president in the study put it,

> There is really a disappointing understanding as to what the higher education enterprise is, a kind of cavalier assumption that there is a one-size-fits-all

approach ... I just find the approach unnuanced. That institutions of every stripe can be lumped together and seen as having the same characteristics ... it is a disaster, in my view.

How Schools Strategized to Capitalize on College

Much has been said about tuition-driven institutions by scholars, journalists, and politicians,[32] but how do university leaders themselves talk about their experiences, challenges, and strategies? Policy makers contend that market-oriented policies create an environment where students are empowered with the choice to shop between schools, but how do these policies rooted in economic reasoning impact the leaders of these schools? More specifically, how do college and university leaders strategically generate the necessary funding in a competitive environment to provide access, and what do they do with the financial resources once the money associated with individual students has been obtained?

To bring the perspective of college and university leaders to the conversation, over the course of a year in the mid-2010s, I traveled to each of the eight selected universities. During my week-long campus visits, I interviewed numerous university leaders (between 18 and 21 individuals at each institution) to inquire about their organizational culture, educational innovation, resource allocation, future growth, and financial challenges. Every day on campus brought new interview experiences as I listened to executives and faculty transparently disclose stories of strategy, failure, growth, and anxiety from within the trusted confines of their own offices. I participated in admissions tours, dined at campus food courts, slept in residence halls, and scoured archives to truly understand each institution's culture.

By the time I concluded the final day of interviews and strolled the grounds of the last manicured academic quadrangle, over 150 university leaders from eight schools in eight states had shared personal accounts about their institutions and their relentless attempts to secure financial resources in a competitive, market-oriented environment. The descriptions were candid offerings from university decision-makers who included everyone from trustees and board members to chancellors, presidents, and provosts, from chief information and chief financial officers, to executive and division vice presidents, to deans, athletic directors, head coaches, and various levels of faculty from an array of academic programs. Their confidential narratives are the empirical data on which this book rests.

The pages that follow offer an untold story of innovation and impact in American higher education that has remained overshadowed by the narratives told by and about elite colleges and universities. To journey beyond the framework of elite universities, *Capitalizing on College* follows a path that uses money as a guidepost to chart a new course of understanding. As one vice president of finance in the study explained,

> We tell a lot of stories here to try to convey the [mission]. That has helped me in my job to understand it's not always about the dollars and cents. But likewise, the dollars and cents—they do tell a story. They tell a history. They tell how you prioritize.

Although this book follows the "dollars and cents," there are no budgets, no statistics, and no balance sheets of any kind. Instead, it relies on the stories of university leaders who pursued different strategies in the face of neoliberal economic policies to financially sustain their missions of educational access and opportunity. The strategies they adopted are similar to practices researchers have previously chronicled as characteristic of for-profit colleges and universities.[33] Yet, with both the nonprofit and the for-profit sectors of higher education built on the same policy foundation—one that allocates financial resources based on a market-oriented logic—shifting the focus from sectors to strategies highlights the extent to which institutions (regardless of their sector) rely on similar practices to secure financial resources. As the senior leaders candidly made clear, competition makes no distinction between non- and for-profit institutions, and every school is seeking enrollment at all costs.

Capitalizing on College is about locating financial margins in new markets to subsidize the expensive traditional residential model of education. Despite their embrace of different strategies to "grow the core" and achieve financial sustainability, leaders of these schools discovered that the pursuit of legitimacy via the practices of elite institutions in an environment that allocated resources based on competition created a financially volatile mix. Although attention to enrollment is paramount if a college or university is to survive, the issue is particularly vital for those who must sustain the high costs associated with a residential model of higher education.

By identifying multiple growth strategies, *Capitalizing on College* contributes to a body of knowledge known as organizational theory and strategic management, an area of inquiry that examines the actions an organization takes to carry out its mission.[34] The strategy perspective considers the methods that leaders employ to achieve organizational objectives as well as the decisions they make to take advantage of changing circumstances. By examining the discretionary judgment of actors, the strategy perspective aims to generate theories that assess the approaches taken to ensure the survival and success of an organization in competitive or changing contexts. Each of the main chapters of the book examines a different strategy—traditional, pioneer, network, and accelerated—developed by university leaders to financially sustain their residential core.

The Traditional Strategy

Not every institution in *Capitalizing on College* acted in entrepreneurial ways to establish innovative educational products and financial practices to address their enrollment challenge. Some attempted more "traditional" means of countering the shrinking number of typical college-aged students and increased competition as a result of economic reasoning. Chapter 1 lays out the traditional strategy and explains how leaders at two institutions—Boxborough College and Havertown College[35]—chose to implement the best practices of elite institutions by focusing on bolstering the prestige of their residential core and increasing endowment revenues to subsidize the expensive characteristics of the model. The university leaders of these aspiring Ivies pursued a "commitment to tradition" that had remained central to the Boxborough and Havertown heritage (Figure 1).

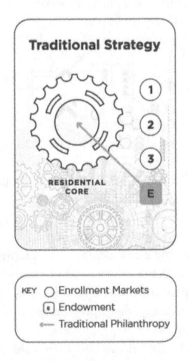

Figure 1 The Traditional Strategy for Sustaining the Core

At the turn of the 21st century, these two universities boasted the largest endowments in the study and leveraged traditional philanthropy to generate approximately $10 million annually in endowment revenue.[36] Leaders of these schools specifically attempted to strengthen the prestige of their university brands by establishing residential graduate programs in business, law, and healthcare. Decision-making and growth within the institutions were described as "deliberate" as opposed to "by the seat of your pants," and faculty stressed the need to "be patient" with the speed of the administrative processes within the university. But an emphasis on elite best practices proved no match to withstand the competition built into the broader system of higher education as it continually evolved.

Leaders discovered they could not rely on traditional philanthropy to simultaneously expand the endowment to subsidize the residential core operating gap *and* transform the residential campus to attract students. And inclusive decision-making processes lacked the speed to respond to changes in the enrollment environment brought on by increased competition and demographic changes. Ultimately, the traditional strategy proved ineffective at staving off the enrollment crises these schools faced. Once these schools were faced with the same kinds of financial pressures that drove innovation at entrepreneurial schools, they were ready to embrace and furthermore legitimate innovative educational options previously considered antithetical to their mission. Recognizing the failure, administrators concluded that their school had to pivot and "try to be creative and innovative in the offering of programs that are applicable to a changing world."

The Pioneer Strategy

Lacking the robust endowment revenues of elite institutions and the brand recognition of Havertown and Boxborough that might allow them to grow their endowments, the trio of institutions highlighted in Chapter 2—Lansdale University, Stoneham University, and the University of Malvern—embraced *value entrepreneurism.* They acted as "first movers" to establish a periphery enrollment market consistent with the value they placed on relationships, providing them with marginal tuition revenues to subsidize their residential core. While leaders at schools that embraced the traditional strategy expected students "to come" experience the prestige of place on the residential campus, leaders who adopted the pioneer strategy innovatively took "place" in new forms to populations of students previously excluded from the exclusive residential model (Figure 2).

Leaders at these schools held fast to their value entrepreneurism and established an array of satellite locations near their nontraditional student populations to allow for in-person learning in unconventional classrooms

Figure 2 The Pioneer Strategy for Sustaining the Core

that included shopping malls, high schools, hotel conference rooms, and military bases. "It's about us going and meeting students in smaller centers, a place that a state school could not go," one Stoneham professor observed. Their organizational form quickly metamorphosized from a single residential campus to a multisite fleet of campuses funneling marginal tuition revenues back to the flagship: "The money that got produced pretty much went to build this campus," one president told me from within the stately interior of the newly renovated administrative hall. But transformation came with stigmatization: the leaders of pioneer institutions routinely described a social ostracism associated with deviating from traditional enrollment norms and elite best practices in higher education.

These schools initially did not pursue certain periphery enrollment markets and limited their growth in others based on the value they attached to the relationships they sought to cultivate. But over time, leaders were challenged to maintain their first-mover advantage as competition from nearby colleges and universities increased and they were forced to defend against enrollment losses at both the flagship school and the fleet of campuses they established. Substantial increases in workload and cutbacks in resources undermined the ability of faculty to foster relationships and embody the values these schools relied on for their educational cachet. As a result, the pioneer strategy ultimately fell short. But administrators remained committed to their belief in innovation and were on the lookout for "the next thing" in periphery enrollment markets that would give them an altogether new first-mover advantage to financially sustain their residential core.

The Network Strategy

At one point, the financial circumstances for two institutions in *Capitalizing on College*—Pepperell University and the University of Winchendon—were so dire that senior administrators had developed strategic plans for closing rather than growing. In a last-ditch effort to save these schools, the university boards hired "turnaround" presidents who urged the institutions (like the schools that adopted the pioneer strategy) to "rely on enrollments rather than endowments." But in a departure from the pioneer strategy, the leaders profiled in Chapter 3 opted to simultaneously pursue multiple types of enrollment markets rather than a single one with multiple campuses—what I refer to as the network strategy. The efforts of the Pepperell and Winchendon leaders were rooted in their *social entrepreneurism*, which emphasized a "broad access-for-all" approach—and one that embraced programmatic diversity as a result (Figure 3).

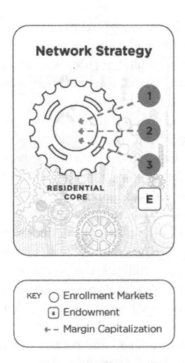

Figure 3 The Network Strategy for Sustaining the Core

Leaders at these schools emphasized speed to establish 8 to 10 new periphery enrollment markets across their regions, the nation, and even the world, wherein their institutions quickly became complex "multiversities" composed of a vast periphery network of enrollment markets viewed as multiple "legs" that financially supported the residential "tabletop." Instead of targeting just one peripheral market, such as adult education, Pepperell and Winchendon simultaneously pursued enrollment pools spanning adult education, international campuses, regional/branch campuses, online programs, vocational education, and professional development. Innovative ideas to expand into new markets were embraced rather than eschewed; as one president explained,

> You've got to be willing to stand up, you've got to be willing to lose your job. . . . This place was on its deathbed, and the board resurrected it. They've heard crazy ideas from me, but guess what? They seem to be working!

The aim of the network strategy was to function like a diversified portfolio of investment stocks whose gains and losses balance one another to reduce overall risk.

The network strategy focused on the relentless addition of new peripheral enrollment markets to strengthen marginal tuition revenues, but in doing so, leaders were confronted with the arduous task of maintaining a complex, ever-changing periphery that severely strained their human resource capacities. In their frenzy of creating new revenue-generating legs, leaders wound up adding what ultimately amounted to a second tabletop instead—an additional residential campus that required further subsidies. At the same time, increased competition with other institutions caused academic divisions within each school to compete with one another for the same students. When enrollments in multiple legs simultaneously declined, network leaders found themselves chasing what was ultimately an elusive formula for trying to scale operations in their most profitable enrollment markets to generate greater marginal tuition revenues.

The Accelerated Strategy

Chapter 4 reveals that one institution in *Capitalizing on College*—Ardmore University—was among a select group of schools that successfully unlocked the secret of taking higher education to scale. The university established a dominant periphery revenue source through online education that was rapidly scaled until the ratio of periphery students to residential students was 10 to 1. While leaders who embraced the network strategy focused on maximizing sources of growth, Ardmore's leaders focused on maximizing margin rates: "You're not going to make any money . . . unless you've got a certain scale," one leader pointedly explained. Because Ardmore had the greatest penchant for expansion, Ardmore leaders were compelled by their *cultural entrepreneurism* to "change the world"—and certainly led the way in changing higher education by embracing the accelerated strategy (Figure 4).

With decision-making processes and resources structurally centralized within the organization, administrators could (in the words of one) "control all decisions through a single pipe" en route to scaling the periphery online market while simultaneously holding costs flat. The financial rewards were remarkable, and the school embraced an approach that deliberately departed from the conventional higher education mindset. As one senior vice president boasted,

> We've been very, very smart about how we manage those cash reserves in a non-traditional way. We don't have an endowment way of thinking; we have more of the mentality of a for-profit investor.

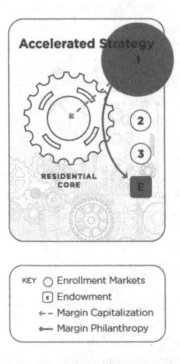

Figure 4 The Accelerated Strategy for Sustaining the Core

Whereas the practice of margin capitalization only postponed the financial crisis facing schools, the advent of margin philanthropy announced a strategy that seemingly offered the same kind of financial security that elites enjoyed with their massive endowments. In fact, this approach allowed Ardmore leaders to use marginal revenues from student tuition to not only realize a billion-dollar campus transformation (funded by margin capitalization) but also generate a billion-dollar endowment (funded by margin philanthropy).

Although Ardmore leaders had arrived at a lucrative self-sustaining strategy, they were keenly aware of the rampant competition and labored to maintain their enrollment advantage. Rather than passively waiting for innovation to arrive, Ardmore leaders imported innovative business practices directly from other industries in their attempt to create new margins from student tuition. The financial approach Ardmore adopted enabled its entrepreneurial leaders to unabashedly embrace market logic and create an altogether new model of funding a university using the sources of revenue available to them in innovative ways that departed from the norms of legitimacy. But in so doing, they also seemingly departed from their educational mission, arriving at a place where current students unwittingly generated hundreds of millions in marginal revenues annually as the "new philanthropists."

A Sector of Schools

While the four main chapters examine phenomena within a particular strategy, Chapter 5 offers a between-case comparison that examines phenomena across all tuition-driven school types. In doing so, it explains how the tuition-driven sector of schools collectively functions within a broader system of higher education designed on market principles of competition and choice. The principal emphasis on an economic style of allocation has brought about an upward drift toward increasingly innovative entrepreneurial practices just to remain competitive (Figure 5).

Federal policies rooted in a market logic compelled leaders at tuition-driven schools to seek new funding solutions in the ambiguous portions of the policies themselves where latent opportunities for interpretation existed. It was there that leaders discovered that "threshold" policies further incentivized institutions to recruit minoritized students to secure greater sums of federal money. But as they sought to remain competitive in the scramble for federal student loans, the schools in this sector also encountered challenges to their institutional identity. Ultimately, all schools in the study chose to "cannibalize their core" by replacing or blending key elements of in-person instruction and educational services inherent to the residential experience

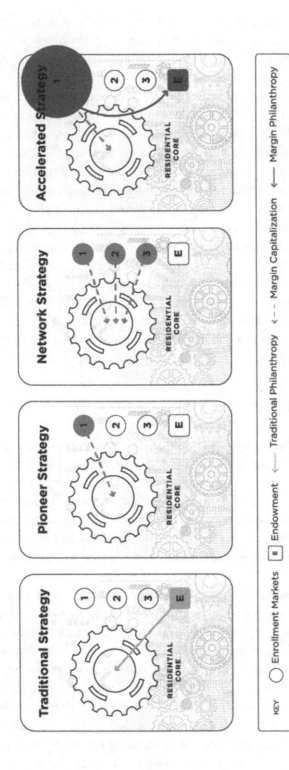

Figure 5 Revenue Sources for Sustaining the Core

with approaches developed in the periphery. The hybridization of the residential model by university leaders was aimed at further controlling costs and offsetting unsustainable revenues from their periphery enrollment market(s).

The concluding chapter underscores that ongoing policy debates and policy solutions that aim to solve the funding crisis in American higher education must address the strategically engineered system generating the crisis in the first place, especially because the findings reported in *Capitalizing on College* are projected to become even more acute. The competition among institutions to secure student enrollments will significantly increase over the next 2 decades given the precipitous decline in the number of traditional-aged college students forecast by demographers.[37] If state governments continue to withdraw public funding and wealthy philanthropists continue to concentrate their giving at elite institutions, the increased competition will only cause the market-oriented practices outlined in this book to rapidly accelerate in both degree and scope as they become commonplace for all but a few select institutions.

The Missing Middle

"Please do not hit record yet," the executive vice president said, as she motioned toward the recorder resting on the table between us. At her request, our interview had been rescheduled from a midday meeting at the university to an early-morning get-together at a local restaurant. After taking a moment to doctor her coffee and compose her thoughts, the administrator said she wanted to first explain the context of what she was about to say. Because we were the only guests seated before dawn, the diner felt as quiet as a confessional.

"In this administrative job," the executive vice president offered, "it is imperative that you establish what I call a personal 'Go to Hell Fund.'" She went on to explain that the money in this fund was a financial reserve set aside to permit a leader like herself to not remain beholden to their employer. If a predicament or professional impasse were to occur, the reserve would provide the administrator the financial cushion to stand by their convictions and quit (effectively telling their boss to "go to hell!"). She then confided that "as this job and the institution itself has changed, I have increasingly been tempted to use that fund."

In collecting her thoughts that morning at breakfast, the executive vice president explained she had been contemplating using her "Go to Hell Fund" in light of the university's recent addition of nondisclosure agreements to employee contracts. The addition was intended to give the university a further competitive advantage over its peers by prohibiting employees from sharing information about its innovative products and processes. But the executive vice president had been offering her services—partly through professional networks and partly through consulting opportunities—at significantly reduced rates or pro bono to less-resourced colleges and universities to help them gain a leg up in the face of the intense competition in higher education.

To her thinking, nondisclosure agreements were the latest in a series of market-oriented practices that prioritized competition over cooperation and money over mission. Visibly vexed, she explained it had become increasingly difficult to uphold a personal commitment to educational access and opportunity as her university became increasingly unrecognizable to her in appearance and mission. But in talking with her colleagues at other schools, she had begun to wonder whether this ongoing "battle" was not just a local institutional deformity and instead a systemic force altering the face of higher education.

The experience this executive vice president described is representative of the many stories I collected in talking with university leaders—what I have come to call "the missing middle." Most analyses of higher education policy and finance predominantly focus on the "bookend" crises—surging student debt on one end and diminishing state support on the other. By emphasizing the middle and "going inside" colleges and universities to offer the organizational perspective, *Capitalizing on College* sheds light on how leaders made sense of and responded to market-oriented policies while trying to maintain missions that emphasized educational access. This book not only highlights the strategies leaders adopted to financially sustain their organizations under the constraints of a sole source of revenue while trying to remain affordable. It also reveals the costs of those decisions on the leaders themselves and the impact these decisions had on the culture of the schools as a whole.

Having prefaced our interview, the executive vice president nodded to the tape recorder, and as I leaned over to hit the record button, I asked her the first in the series of questions I posed to everyone: "Can you describe what brought you to this university?" Her face lit up with a nostalgic grin. "Yeah, I can," she said, the smile growing even wider. "It was a '*who*,' not a '*what*.'" And like dozens of university leaders I had interviewed over the past year, she began her story by telling me about the joys of working in an institutional setting that transformed the lives of the students the elite schools had left behind.

Notes

1. Collins, J. (2001). *Good to great: Why some companies make the leap and others don't.* Harper Collins.
2. A term derived from the combination of Oxford and Cambridge Universities.
3. Stevens, M. L. (2007). *Creating a class: College admissions and the education of elites.* Harvard University Press.
4. Cottom, T. M. (2017). *Lower ed: The troubling rise of for-profit colleges in the new economy.* New Press.
5. Tuchman, G. (2009). *Wannabe U: Inside the corporate university.* University of Chicago Press.
6. DiMaggio, P. J., & Powell, W. W. (1983). The iron cage revisited: Institutional isomorphism and collective rationality in organizational fields. *American Sociological Review, 48*(2), 147–160; Suchman, M. C. (1995). Managing legitimacy: Strategic and institutional approaches. *Academy of Management Review, 20*(3), 571–610.
7. The minoritized experience at Harvard is documented in Jack, A. A. (2019). *The privileged poor: How elite colleges are failing disadvantaged students.* Harvard University Press; the minoritized experience at schools across California is documented in McDonough, P. M. (1997). *Choosing colleges: How social class and schools structure opportunity.* State University of New York Press.
8. The nonprofit designation is granted to institutions like hospitals, schools, foundations, religious organizations, theaters, and museums whose mission seeks to benefit the good of society.
9. *Endowment funds of the 120 degree-granting postsecondary institutions with the largest endowments, by rank order: Fiscal year 2020,* Digest of Education Statistics 2022. https://nces.ed.gov/programs/digest/d21/tables/dt21_333.90.asp
10. Stanford Afford offers free tuition to families making less than $150,000 and states, "We do not expect students to borrow to meet their need." Retrieved from https://admission.stanford.edu/afford/.
11. Eaton, C. (2022). *Bankers in the ivory tower: The troubling rise of financiers in US higher education.* University of Chicago Press.
12. Sherlock, M. F., Crandall-Hollick, M. L., Gravelle, J., & Stupak, J. M. (2015). *College and university endowments: Overview and tax policy options.* Congressional Research Service.
13. Taylor, B. J., & Cantwell, B. (2019). *Unequal higher education: Wealth, status, and student opportunity.* Rutgers University Press.
14. Tuskegee University (Alabama) and Hampton University (Virginia) are examples of institutions that historically provided a work–study option: Fort, E. (Ed.). (2013). *Survival of the historically Black colleges and universities: Making it happen.* Lexington Books.
15. Lucas, C. J. (2016). *American higher education: A history.* Springer; Rudolph, F. (2021). *The American college and university: A history.* Plunkett Lake Press.
16. Formally titled the Servicemen's Readjustment Act of 1944. See Duffy, E. A., & Goldberg, I. (1998). *Crafting a class: College admissions and financial aid, 1951–1994.* Princeton University Press.
17. Loss, C. P. (2012). *Between citizens and the state: The politics of American higher education in the 20th century* (p. 212). Princeton University Press.

18. Kraatz, M. S., Ventresca, M. J., & Deng, L. (2010). Precarious values and mundane innovations: Enrollment management in American liberal arts colleges. *Academy of Management Journal, 53*(6), 1521–1545.
19. Throughout this volume, I refer to this modern transformation of society using the terms economic reasoning, market logic, and neoliberalism interchangeably. See Berman, E. P. (2022). *Thinking like an economist: How efficiency replaced equality in US public policy.* Princeton University Press; Marglin, S. A. (2008). *The dismal science: How thinking like an economist undermines community.* Harvard University Press; Harvey, D. (2007). *A brief history of neoliberalism.* Oxford University Press; Brown, W. (2015). *Undoing the demos: Neoliberalism's stealth revolution.* MIT Press. For sources about the "market logic," see Thornton, P. H., Ocasio, W., & Lounsbury, M. (2012). *The institutional logics perspective: A new approach to culture, structure and process.* Oxford University Press.
20. Shermer, E. T. (2021). *Indentured students: How government-guaranteed loans left generations drowning in college debt.* Belknap Press of Harvard University.
21. Curs, B. R., & Jaquette, O. (2017). Crowded out? The effect of nonresident enrollment on resident access to public research universities. *Educational Evaluation and Policy Analysis, 39*(4), 644–669.
22. Hamilton, L. T., & Nielsen, K. (2021). *Broke: The racial consequences of underfunding public universities.* University of Chicago Press.
23. Dehne, G., & Small, C. (2006). The dilemma of the tuition-driven college. *Trusteeship, 5*(6): 13–18.
24. Figures provided by the Federal Student Aid Office. https://studentaid.gov/data-center/school.
25. Eisenhardt, K. M., & Graebner, M. E. (2007). Theory building from cases: Opportunities and challenges. *Academy of Management Journal, 50*(1), 25–32.
26. The "religious affiliation" classification is annually reported to the National Center for Education Statistics. By comparison, there are 570 Hispanic-serving institutions and 107 historically Black colleges and universities.
27. Marsden, G. M. (1996). *The soul of the American university: From Protestant establishment to established nonbelief.* Oxford University Press.
28. Gleason, P. (1967). American Catholic higher education: A historical perspective. In R. Hassenger (Ed.), *The shape of Catholic higher education* (pp. 182–220). Chicago University Press; Hughes, R. T., & Adrian, W. B. (1997). *Models for Christian higher education: Strategies for survival and success in the twenty-first century.* Wm. B. Eerdmans.
29. Karabel, J. (2005). *The chosen: The hidden history of admission and exclusion at Harvard, Yale, and Princeton.* Houghton Mifflin Harcourt.
30. Elite institutions commonly partner with private firms to increase enrollment: Bannon, L. (2022, July 6). That fancy university course? It might actually come from an education company. *Wall Street Journal.* https://www.wsj.com/articles/that-fancy-university-course-it-might-actually-come-from-an-education-company-11657126489
31. Barrow, C. W. (1990). *Universities and the capitalist state: Corporate liberalism and the reconstruction of American higher education, 1894–1928.* University of Wisconsin Press.
32. Stevens, M., & Kirst, M. W. (2015). *Remaking college: The changing ecology of higher education.* Stanford University Press; Posecznick, A. (2017). *Selling hope and college: Merit, markets, and recruitment in an unranked school.* Cornell University Press; Stiglitz, J. E. (2013, February 16). Equal opportunity, our national myth. *New York Times*, SR4.
33. Deming, D. J., Goldin, C., & Katz, L. F. (2012). The for-profit postsecondary school sector: Nimble critters or agile predators? *Journal of Economic Perspectives, 26*(1), 139–164.

34. The field of strategic management developed in response to "the limited help the study of economics was able to give managers in running their businesses" because of its resolute emphasis on a restrictive set of assumptions. In contrast, strategic management is applied in its focus, undergirded by economic principles. Examples of the restrictive assumptions include the following: Markets automatically move toward equilibrium, the decision-making of individuals is predominantly rational and information based, and economic decisions are understood in response to economic forces rather than the discretionary judgment of individuals. See Faulkner, D. O., & Campbell, A. (Eds.). (2006). *The Oxford handbook of strategy: A strategy overview and competitive strategy*. Oxford University Press, p. 2.
35. To maintain privacy, I have anonymized the names of the universities, individuals, other organizations, locations, and university documents to promote the confidentiality of the institutions and individuals who participated in this research.
36. Comparative endowment income data from the Integrated Postsecondary Education Data System.
37. Grawe, N. D. (2018). *Demographics and the demand for higher education*. Johns Hopkins University Press. The COVID-19 pandemic has exacerbated these enrollment projections.

1
The Traditional Strategy

"You Come . . . to a Tradition"

Introduction

For more than a century, Boxborough College and Havertown College embodied an ethos of prestige—a belief that tradition was experienced in person and in place, walking the same well-worn paths as generations of students who had come before. Over the years, the two colleges grew in a deliberate manner, remaining true to their roots while not losing sight of their educational mission, which one faculty described as "very noble" and "the driver of all that we do." But after a century's worth of growth, the leaders faced their greatest challenge yet. How would tuition-driven institutions like these grapple with neoliberal federal policy changes that incentivized colleges to pursue student enrollment growth while facing a demographic cataclysm once the baby boomers graduated? "When you're a tuition-driven school, keeping students coming is always a challenge, and there's considerable anxiety when the student count goes down," an academic official shared. The solution these schools arrived at can usefully be described as the *traditional strategy*.

At Boxborough and Havertown, it was assumed answers could be found by looking to the past—leaning on their tradition had been the solution many times before, and there was no reason to think that it would not hold the key for this next challenge, no matter how daunting. In adopting the strategy, they followed the established path of their prominent peers (commonly known as "aspiring Ivies"), who emphasized time-honored solutions rooted in customs of best practice, shared governance, and prestige.[1] Accordingly, the leaders of these two storied institutions reached back into their rich traditions in an attempt to formulate a strategy to navigate their schools beyond financial pressures the likes of which they had never experienced. Yet this time the crisis was truly unique, and the tried-and-true strategy of banking on tradition was inadequate to the task. Paradoxically, although the leaders strategically "doubled down on their heritage," the traditional strategy was their undoing—ultimately only deepening the intensity of the financial pressures they faced.

Influenced by Heritage

As the oldest institutions in *Capitalizing on College*, the heritage of Boxborough College and Havertown College had two dispositions that perennially influenced their institutional environment. From their founding, the two colleges maintained a cultural disposition that underscored *opportunity for the community*. Time and again, historical records offered images and accounts of serving the citizens of the local community by providing them with educational opportunities. This manifested in their determination to remain located within impoverished regions of the state despite many possibilities to relocate the institutions to more affluent areas. The universities remained beacons of hope in regions of the nation where citizens customarily had only meager economic prospects—distressed places that fought to overcome what one Havertown professor described as "the legacy of a plantation economy and sharecropping."

Boxborough and Havertown possessed a second and equally important organizational disposition focused on *raising their reputation*. Institutional leaders were devoted to advancing their collegiate prestige, grounded in their well-deserved reputations for providing a quality education to successive generations of students. Both schools maintained high academic standards and sought to ensure an elevated status among liberal arts institutions, underscoring academic excellence rooted in a residential model.

The president of Havertown captured the importance of heritage in retelling the development of the residential campus, from its days as a young academy established "in the aftermath of the Civil War" to one remaining "anchored in its founding purpose." He asserted in a stately tone that for schools like Havertown, "You come to a tradition." The president then paused, seemingly to consider the historical gravitas encapsulated in his concise phrase, before offering it a second time, in two distinct halves: "You come. To a tradition." Both dispositions of their heritage—opportunity for the community and raising their reputation—led to an underlying trait in their institutional environment best characterized as a "commitment to tradition" that supplied the elements that would lead to the traditional strategy.

Opportunity for the Community

Boxborough and Havertown have storied beginnings that reach back to an era in American history when a young nation was divided and at war with itself. One college survived the turmoil of the Civil War, while the other rose amid the reconstruction of the embattled republic. Among the earliest schools associated with each of their denominations, the founders of Boxborough and Havertown established institutions that have continued to embrace their focal cultural disposition—a duty to serve the local community by providing the opportunity for higher education.

Like many collegiate customs, the pledge of providing educational opportunity to the local community was rooted in the beginnings of each school, a promise that persisted into the present, as one vice president carefully explained:

> We're an opportunity school. A lot of students that go here didn't get into the first school they wanted to get into. So we provide opportunity . . . we take those students and help them make something of themselves . . . we help them to find a way to make a wonderful life for themselves in lots of different ways.

The early leaders of Havertown focused on providing a college education to local citizens in a rural region of the state, despite that commitment being challenged by man and nature alike. In one instance, a fire destroyed all but one building on campus, eradicating two generations of progress in establishing a toehold in a locale not known for prizing education. In other instances, wealthy benefactors repeatedly approached Havertown leaders with enticing proposals to relocate to more prosperous regions of the state. In a newspaper editorial, the president of that era discussed why he rejected their offers:

> At least three locations have offered to put up such buildings as would be necessary. . . . Plenty of people with wealth and brains will look after those places. If I leave here, the people are ruined. I cannot go.

But a commitment to service was not restricted to taking root and blooming into a tradition in the fertile soil of 19th-century rural America. With a similar pledge to provide educational opportunities to the local community, Catholic priests established Boxborough at the heart of a burgeoning metropolis whose intricate transportation hub of railroads and canals opened new corridors to the American frontier. The priests founded the urban college to provide educational access to waves of impoverished European immigrants who made their way west across the Atlantic in hopes of economic prosperity. The college annals repeatedly echo the sentiment that Boxborough was "closely tied to the local culture and responsive to the economic conditions of citizens." The financial state of the college remained precarious for decades because of fluctuating enrollments. When the school outgrew its original campus, rather than "abandon the college and leave the city," the priests relocated the institution to a larger property, where it remains in the third decade of the 21st century, carrying out the same emphasis on serving the local community.

This long-standing cultural disposition of providing educational opportunities to local citizens functioned as the backbone of the university culture leaders commonly referred to as "the pride of Havertown" or "the Boxborough way." In attempting to describe the spirit of the school, one distinguished Boxborough faculty member began by saying, "The culture of Boxborough is . . ." He abruptly stopped midsentence, then completed his thought:

> Let's do it "the Boxborough way," let's keep doing it this way because we've always done it this way. It's not necessarily a good thing, but it's also not necessarily a bad thing. There are some advantages to doing things the way that things have always been done.

A steadfast belief in creating educational opportunities for others provided leaders of Boxborough and Havertown with continuity, purpose, and a remarkably stable culture—all of which they leveraged to bolster their reputation.

A Reputation to Uphold

Throughout the 20th century, the two colleges developed a reputation within their surrounding regions as they educated successive generations in the liberal arts tradition. As the century progressed, both schools secured memberships in elite academic associations and national scholastic societies, increasing their stature. The historical publications for Boxborough and Havertown were replete with mentions that stressed this organizational disposition of raising their reputation. School histories "lauded" Havertown's standing within the "liberal arts, sciences, and professions" and championed Boxborough as holding a "distinguished and distinct place within the gallery of American colleges."

Boxborough and Havertown saw themselves as aspiring Ivies, a diverse group of colleges and universities whose storied traditions placed them within a prestige stratum just below elite American institutions. Within this sector are "hidden Ivies" (i.e., Skidmore College, Carleton University, Haverford College), "little Ivies" (i.e., Colby College, Trinity College, Lafayette College), and consortia like "The Five" (i.e., Amherst College, Hampshire College, Mount Holyoke College, Smith College, and the University of Massachusetts Amherst). Throughout the historical volumes and interviews, leaders commonly referred to the reputations and resources of other "aspiring" institutions: "Elon is an example of an institution that is reputable, an Ivy League school kind of reputation," a Havertown vice president noted, while a senior colleague observed that Richmond's reputation—"a wonderful endowment, a beautiful campus"—was something to aspire to: "We'd love to be like Richmond." Boxborough senior leaders similarly gazed toward their Ivy-aspiring peers, from the "affluence" of Boston College to Georgetown University's reputation of being "more scholarly based."

In many respects, the past remains readily tangible at Boxborough and Havertown in the present, feeding its modern-day reputation. A former Havertown administrator described that because of its past, the college is "a known quantity" with a strong "brand quality" and "positive reputation." As an organizational disposition, reputation hinges on differentiating the institution to improve its position or rank among a select group of peers.[2] In practice, reputation keeps one foot in the past and one foot in the present to advance among institutional rivals: "We put that Havertown brand out there and make sure that what we're delivering is of such quality that it surpasses others," one vice president stressed. In a similar manner, the historic reputation of Boxborough has become increasingly valuable over time; myriad professors and administrators referred to its "strong reputation," "elevated reputation," and "enhanced reputation" stemming from its past standing.

The historical emphasis on quality bolstered the reputation of Boxborough and Havertown, which was used to further strengthen their academic standing. A senior administrator at Boxborough remarked how the school "developed programs at the undergraduate and graduate levels that capitalized on the university's reputation, resources, and assets." The academic programs Boxborough established maintained its tradition of excellence that afforded the college the privileged status of continually being compared with elite Catholic institutions like the University of Notre Dame and Georgetown.[3] A senior administrator at Havertown similarly remarked that the institution was "a known quantity in our 500-mile radius." Its academic quality enabled Havertown to become one of the earliest institutions to secure an exemplary standing from its national accreditation agency. Both schools took strength from their history of academic excellence to sustain their standing as bastions of scholarship and learning.

The tradition of academic quality engendered a collective pride among students who became alumni and ambassadors of its reputation. "There's a lot of pride at Havertown for what it has been able to become from its roots as an academy proud of having graduates in the professional world," one vice president boasted. A professor at Boxborough echoed similar sentiments about the contributing role of alumni to its distinguished reputation: "The success of the organization very much is related to the fact that we have had successful graduates." If colleges and universities were ranked according to the influence alumni had garnered, Boxborough and Havertown would be among the most notable institutions, with graduates as sitting U.S. senators, chief executive officers of Fortune 500 firms, Pulitzer Prize winners, accomplished actors and actresses, countless professional sports all-stars and Olympians, and even a former Speaker of the House of Representatives.

Leadership carefully tended their school's reputation, recognizing that its preeminence had been deliberately crafted over time and exhibiting caution so as not to jeopardize their prestige. They knew that what one professor at Boxborough described as "the reputation we've been able to create for ourselves" was neither accidental nor fated, but rather the intentional product of successive generations of caretakers. Yet their organizational disposition of "raising their reputation" was no guarantee of long-term resilience. Reputation was recognized as a fragile quality whose state could quickly change and potentially alter the schools' financial trajectory and resources. As a Boxborough professor explained, "A reputation takes tens of years to build but only 5 minutes to lose." Any loss of standing could have effects that snowballed:

> If we don't educate students properly, if the output isn't what is expected, employers will not hire our students, word will get out, people will stop sending their children and donors will not give money.

For these two colleges, their established reputations and rootedness in their communities were integral components of their traditions—and therefore also served as guideposts for the economic model for how the institutions financially supported themselves.

Funding a Tradition

The cultural disposition (opportunity for community) and organizational disposition (raising their reputation) were dual pillars that supported an enduring trait of being "committed to tradition" that remained central to the Boxborough and Havertown heritage. "Tradition will *always* be alive and well at Havertown," its president preached, because it was what enabled the school "to thrive and carry out the mission." A senior administrator at Boxborough similarly exhorted, "We have a deep commitment to tradition ... the culture here is very much *rooted* in tradition." Boxborough and Havertown leaders spoke of tradition in a palpably binding manner, referring to a "strong sense of tradition," a "rich tradition," and a "deep connection to tradition." Whereas some schools have outgrown their origin story or do not have one to tell, an institution like Havertown, as the provost asserted, was "proud of its heritage, proud of its traditions."

The origin stories of how these two institutions funded their nascent schools were a direct product of their traditions having led them to put down roots in their communities and provide a quality education. The institutions emphasized academic excellence, and they were committed to educational opportunity and rarely turned a prospective patron away for lack of financial means. For example, historical records at Havertown indicate that as late as the 1930s, students were permitted to pay for their tuition through a system of bartering, with one student having submitted various amounts of "flour, potatoes, butter beans, string beans, shelled beans, cornmeal, and biddies [young chickens]." Boxborough leaders were similarly committed and established an institutional fund whereby any impoverished student could "borrow interest-free money for their education and delay repayment for 5 years." The unreliable flow of tuition dollars meant finances were often tight. When the institutions ran a deficit, the losses were commonly small enough that their religious denomination gifted the money or administrators secured a short-term loan.

Despite their precarious financial standing, in time, both schools were able to increase their facilities in a moderate manner through gifts. Boxborough relocated from "the factory district" to a larger campus in "the hillside" section of the city, while Havertown steadily increased the overall acreage of its rural campus. With more space, the institutions expanded the opportunities offered and grew their reputation by adding new buildings such as academic halls, student residences, and gymnasiums—funded through donations from prominent alumni and community benefactors. In an almanac, the Boxborough president of that era underscored the generosity of its benefactors as part of its tradition:

> I can tell you quite frankly that Boxborough could not operate in the black, that it would be out of business in a few short years if it were not for gifts. But I am proud to say that the institution was actually founded on the premise that gifts would always be forthcoming. All of our buildings have been built through gifts.

Contingent on the amount of funding received, some buildings were permanent additions, whereas others were temporary. When construction commenced, it was common for students and clergy alike to volunteer a significant portion of the labor to defray costs. Some of these timeworn facilities remain on the campuses today and bear testament to the commitment and craftsmanship of the era.

While both schools had endowments that began early in their histories, like their tuition revenue these funds were humble in their impact despite the fierce loyalty that drove their creation. The endowment for Boxborough began in the late 19th century with the death of a local wholesale grocer, whose modest gift "established a scholarship fund," and the creation of its alumni association, whose members "took an interest in the intellectual life of the campus." Havertown alumni were equally committed, with the inaugural benefactors of its endowment commonly emphasizing they felt compelled to financially support the vision of its leadership. An early donor asserted,

> I give to Havertown for two reasons. One, I do not give to institutions, I give to persons. I like [the Havertown president] and others who are affiliated with him at this school. Second, I am concerned about values and loyalties.

Like their campus, the traditions of both schools informed their endowments—their size reflected in their nascent reputations and leveraged to expand educational opportunities at both schools.

Unlike the large endowments of elite colleges and universities, the modest endowments of Boxborough and Havertown only generated modest returns at the time—returns that did little to address the shortfall in tuition dollars the schools regularly faced. In terms of funding the institution, both schools relied heavily on a "hidden" endowment in the form of denominational support for faculty and staff. For example, Boxborough relied on administrative and teaching services provided by 45 clergy whose salaries were paid by the denomination. One senior administrator described their "free labor" as "a matter of life and death" for the institution, saving it $300,000 in wages—an amount equivalent to "more than $6 million in invested capital." Similarly, Havertown was one of five schools in the region that received a large annual subsidy from its supporting denomination. Nevertheless, although neither institution had a formal fundraising office, by the middle of the 20th century the endowments of both schools had increased to approximately $1 million through donations provided by alumni, family, and friends of the colleges.

The Emerging Challenge

At the 20th century's midpoint, each school enrolled just shy of 1,500 residential students on unassuming campuses composed of a central administrative hall surrounded by a handful of academic buildings and a half-dozen single-sex residence halls situated adjacent to the sole athletic field and gymnasium. By early-21st-century standards, facilities were merely fair, a situation familiar to the many nonelite institutions of the era that embodied a tradition of academic excellence rooted in a residential model—one that was soon to be upended. Senior leaders themselves were equally modest, composed of devout clergy and parishioners rather than professionals. The Boxborough president summed up the spirit of the place while alluding to changes that were to come:

> It was very much provincial in all senses of the word, including the unkind senses—not ambitious, unsure of itself, lacking self-confidence, and so on. The single greatest contribution my predecessor made to the institution was convincing itself that it could dream big and succeed.

The 3 decades after World War II are commonly referred to as the golden age of American higher education, characterized by a rapid expansion in student enrollment and public support for postsecondary education.[4] During this era, it was commonplace for institutions, both private and public, to double in size within a matter of a few short years. Student enrollments ballooned with the stateside return of servicepersons from the war, and growth rates compounded further as greater numbers of women and minority students enrolled in colleges and universities during the Civil Rights Era. Campuses nationwide experienced a building boom. Science buildings quickly multiplied in a Sputnik-era sprint for knowledge, residence halls were erected in multistory form, and numerous fields and stadiums appeared to support the explosion in intercollegiate athletics.[5] But this kind of growth could not be funded with bartered tokens of chickens and cornmeal. During these years, federal funding mechanisms for all American colleges and universities came into place to funnel new types of support to schools like Boxborough and Havertown.

In the unprecedented era of public support for educational access, policy makers established neoliberal funding mechanisms to (in their eyes) more efficiently resource the nation's postsecondary system based on market principles.[6] Two highly influential shifts in public policy commenced during this time. First, federal tuition funding (known as indirect funding) was distributed to institutions on a "per-student" basis.[7] Prior to the change to this funding model, colleges and universities received monetary support from the federal government in lump sum form, where schools were entrusted to allocate the funds in the most effective manner. Now, schools were incentivized to grow enrollments if they wanted to increase their federal support. Second, loans were established to permit students and parents to use future monies to pay for present tuition costs.[8] Previously, only students who could pay could attend college, but the new student loan policies made it possible for students of lesser means to also receive a college education—if they were willing to assume the debt.

While these two monumental shifts in policy were intended to increase educational opportunity for individuals, who now could "shop" in search of the best educational quality, the mechanisms also incentivized institutions to increase student enrollment as an attractive option for pursuing additional financial resources. To step away from the edge of the financial cliff that Boxborough and Havertown always seemed to be toeing, they (and schools like them) dramatically grew during the golden age in order to secure reliable tuition revenue. As the Havertown provost explained, these federal policies served as the lifeblood for the institution: "We are dependent upon them as an institution. We could not make it without federal financial loans going to our students."

In the 3 decades that followed World War II, Boxborough and Havertown were transformed. A commemorative historical volume highlights how the Havertown president strategically "set out to make the institution bigger and better" with the addition of new residence halls, an expanded library, and hundreds of acres of land—all with an eye to strengthening an enrollment that doubled in size to 3,000 students. At Boxborough, enrollment demand exploded as well with the transition to coed education and the accommodation of hundreds of postwar veterans. As a result of the student population mushrooming to 5,000, administrators "had to turn away out-of-town students because of lack of housing on campus." By the close of the golden age, both colleges had found a firm financial footing, with Boxborough reporting it was consistently "ending the fiscal year with a modest surplus" and Havertown proudly proclaiming that it was "free of short-term capital indebtedness."

Yet with the end of the golden age in the final quarter of the 20th century, a series of factors converged that spurred both Boxborough and Havertown—as well as universities across America—to engage in a dramatically new phase of growth rooted in the effects of the federal financial policies sown during that first initial growth period. The change had its origins in the maturation of the baby boom generation into adulthood, resulting in a marked decrease in the population of college-going students, thereby reducing the supply of available high school graduates from which institutions could recruit. "The future is not very bright due to the decline in 18-year-olds," the Boxborough president observed, as he "feared future federal reductions in student loans." Unsurprisingly, competition among all institutions increased dramatically as many colleges and universities attempted to preserve their federal loan revenue stream by maintaining levels of student enrollment.

In the words of one Havertown vice president, the challenge that confronted institutions was how to remain competitive when "everybody is going after the same kid." The competition was further intensified by the cadre of public institutions that were also increasingly aiming to grow their tuition revenue levels in response to steady but persistent declines in state appropriations.[9] Beginning with the economic downturn in the 1970s, state lawmakers had large deficits to resolve, and to balance their budgets they made consistent reductions in funding for public institutions of higher education in the name of "privatization," shifting the burden of paying for college to the individual consumer.[10] As they gradually decreased or eliminated subsidies altogether, public institutions responded by increasing the price of tuition and expanding student enrollments to make up for the financial shortfall.[11] In short, the transformative changes to higher education financing incentivized *all* institutions to behave in highly competitive ways to obtain the necessary financial resources.

Compounding these factors was the fact that despite the successful enrollment gains during the golden age, the endowment income for Boxborough and Havertown had lost its purchasing power and thereby declined in its effectiveness, with the same amount of charitable money now having to support more students. Havertown administrators were facing a similar conundrum: the "noble army of upholders . . . without whom Havertown could not stand" could not give enough money fast enough to cover the shortfall caused by the growth in the number of students. Leaders at both institutions lamented that the small size of their endowments rendered them ineffective at subsidizing the growing gap between tuition and the true cost of college. It was clear to the leaders of these tuition-driven institutions that they needed to identify and pursue new financial resources within their limited means.

Sidebar: A Revolution in Student Loans

Confronted with challenging circumstances, the leaders of Boxborough and Havertown had to locate additional sources of revenue—students to replace and replenish the shrinking pool of typical applicants to their schools. Historically, institutional enrollments were predominantly supported by White men of means, with a limited number of schools having been established as women's colleges and/or historically Black colleges and universities. Those of lesser means looked elsewhere within society in pursuit of opportunity. During the golden age, the available population of students swelled to include veterans and then greater numbers of women and minority students as a result of the civil rights era. But with the neoliberal transformation of student loans, now previously disenfranchised students without the economic means to pay for college could apply and enroll—albeit at the cost of financially leveraging their futures. The changes in higher education dictated by market logic created entirely new pools of applicants these schools could go fishing in—if they could catch the students within them.

To secure federal funding in the form of student loans, institutions had to attract students for whom college was previously not on their horizon to come to their schools. An enrollment executive at Havertown vividly described the changes they made with the end of the golden age to increase their applicant cadre:

> [Now] you go out and buy 50,000 names from the College Board or the ACT group, you mail out your brochures and catalogs.... We tried to ramp up as many applications as we could get, and we went from an average of say, 3,000 to 4,000 applications in a year to 12,000 applications, and it about killed our staff... [enrolling] 800 students would be a typical year, [but] now we're more like 1,000 to 1,200 new students a year.

But regardless of the federal loans they received, many of these students were financially ill-prepared to pay for a private college education. A Boxborough administrator framed the challenge in stark financial terms:

> People are just questioning whether they want to spend $30,000 at a private school.... I could spend a fraction of that at a public school, or I could spend my first 2 years at a community school and get all the core stuff out of the way, the required courses, and then come here for the last couple years. I think it is going to be a challenge for us.

To meet the challenge posed by more affordable public institutions, private colleges and universities competed against one another using customized financial aid packages composed of grants, loans, and work–study options to target these previously untapped student enrollment markets. As products of economic reasoning, financial aid packages were market-based tools that permitted a college to strategically respond to the emerging challenge in market-based ways—seemingly the only option available to schools like Boxborough and Havertown. As one professor at Boxborough observed, the growth in tuition cost made customized financial aid packages necessary to offset the cost of attendance: "As a private institution, tuition can be expensive . . . the financial aid packages have been very competitive to help attract students to come." The Havertown enrollment executive summed up the situation pithily: "We have responded to the market with what the marketplace needs."

Yet over time, the composition of the customized financial aid packages that institutions used to attract students evolved in response to changes in student loans. With the end of the golden age and the spread of neoliberalism, student loans gradually became more market-oriented in their scope as lawmakers established new policies. One example was the changes made to "guaranteed loans" between students and private lenders when lawmakers created "unsubsidized loans," where the federal government raised loan limits but no longer subsidized the interest rate.[12] The shift resulted in expanded borrowing possibilities and greater numbers of students maximizing their loan amounts (all while accumulating interest). In another development, lawmakers created "parent loans" to help finance the shortfall in estimated family contribution.[13] Keen to eliminate all traces of a public subsidy, these loans were the riskiest option offered by the federal government because they enabled borrowers to take out even larger loans with higher interest rates while offering the fewest protections. The student loan seed planted in the golden age thus sprouted a variety of increasingly individualistic neoliberal loan policies that shifted greater amounts of financial debt onto the student and their family.

Responding to these policy changes, institutional financial aid packages underwent a similar transformation characterized by a change in institutional scholarships from need based to merit based. A Boxborough enrollment executive recalled how the impact was felt across the field of higher education in the *type* of student who received institutional scholarships—and those who did not:

> More and more parents of means have invested funds to make sure that their students score well on standardized tests . . . they are taking as many AP classes as they can, anything that you can possibly think of to give them a leg up, and they want

the highest [merit] scholarships. Here are the highest-income people demanding the highest scholarships. But folks coming from rural schools or lower economic situations that do not have the means to have an SAT tutor or be able to pay the fees to take the ACTs six times . . . are at a real disadvantage. . . . I think we are increasingly closing that door to the lower income and the lower middle class.

The shift in the emphasis of institutional aid to students with better academic records—which research shows is closely correlated to their socioeconomic status—meant that students with lesser academic success and lesser financial means had to increasingly rely on student loans to pay their tuition balance, while wealthier students acquired scholarships and thereby lessened their debt burden with comparatively fewer student loans.[14] The transformation generated a double bind for some students who in the past would have received those need-based scholarships, creating a greater need for loans to gain access to higher education coupled with larger loan amounts.

Driving the revolution in student loans was the market-oriented belief that providing individuals with choice brings about increased competition among institutions and thereby improves both the efficient distribution of resources and product quality. Yet quality is difficult for students and their families to determine or assess in higher education, and recognizing the increased loan burden students were carrying, institutions predominantly responded by modifying price rather than quality to attract students. At one end of the spectrum were struggling institutions that merely threw "unfunded" money at the problem, offering steep tuition discounts in hopes of garnering the students they needed to survive. As one Boxborough senior administrator noted,

A [nearby university] is "buying" their classes. . . . Instead of trying to increase your quality, you allocate more financial aid. . . . [Their] brand is not strong enough, so they are couponing more, discounting [price] more.

The Boxborough leader saw this financial sleight of hand as admissions roulette, whereby the school was pinning all their hopes on their competition perishing before they did. "You never know how long they can last, but usually it is 3–6 years, and then they run out of money. They are hoping somebody *else* goes out of business or gets hurt before *they* run out of money." He offered this telling observation:

Our discount rate has risen over the last 20-some years, but we are still significantly under those that are our local competitors. We are about 45%, which is high—higher than it's ever been—but we're going up against local competitors that are 60% and 65%. I do not know how you stay open.

At the other end of the spectrum were the highly endowed elite schools. These institutions had the luxury of taking a "funded" approach to competition using scholarships financially underwritten by the university endowment to attract students. Elite institutions with massive endowments could recruit the students they wanted with packages that proved highly attractive to students who otherwise would have to leverage their futures with student loans to go to college.

But a solution rooted in altering their financial aid practices to attract students was not an option, either economically or philosophically, for prestige schools like Boxborough and Havertown. Getting into a discount battle was viewed as a losing strategy, yet neither of these schools nor the schools like them had the endowment resources to go the elite route. A senior administrator at Havertown framed the dilemma facing her school this way:

> There are so many really good schools in the state that to be one of [nearly 40] privates you have to have a niche. And if you don't have a niche . . . you're going to be struggling to make ends meet.

To find their niche, Boxborough and Havertown adopted a new strategy—one that responded to the pressures caused by demographic trends and neoliberal policies—by "doubling down" on the heritage philosophy undergirding these prestigious institutions. This traditional strategy was the logical outcome of the underlying trait common to both schools—a deep-seated commitment to tradition—but it meant that they would be slow to react to the rapidly evolving tectonic changes in how higher education was financed.

Pursuing the Traditional Strategy

Dependent on tuition yet determined to survive, the leaders of Boxborough and Havertown adopted what could be described as the traditional strategy toward sustaining the institution, relying on expanding residential enrollments while simultaneously growing the university endowment. At the root of the traditional strategy's aim of generating the necessary financial resources was a heightened emphasis on conventional, prestige-focused methods to expand the college's core residential enrollment as well as its endowment. While a constellation of alumni, friends, and foundations offered generous financial donations to bolster the endowment, the administrations of both schools sought to expand their residential enrollments to generate revenue from student tuition and federal financial aid. In considering the recent decades of change at Havertown, its provost underscored that the institution collectively focused much of its effort on these two fundamentals: "in program building, establishing new programs, *and* trying to lift up the endowment—all at the same time" (Figure 1).

The decision to face the challenge by adopting the traditional strategy was driven in no small part by these schools' conception of their resources. Although they lacked the national name recognition of elite institutions and the financial security they enjoyed by virtue of their endowment, both schools saw their heritage as the key to their future. They made the logical decision to double down on their belief in their traditions and grow the residential core and endowment simultaneously. The dual emphasis inherent in the traditional strategy was vital given the financial shortcomings that would result if only one approach was pursued. The stakes were made earnestly clear by a Havertown senior administrator:

> You have to grow to survive. You hear what I am saying? You have to grow to survive in higher education. It's not that you're the aggressive entrepreneur, [but] you recognize that old statement, "You either move ahead or you've fallen back."

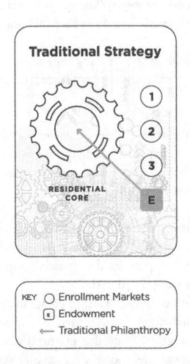

Figure 1 The Traditional Strategy for Sustaining the Core

Growing the Residential Core

The words of Havertown's president succinctly expressed the philosophy behind the traditional strategy regarding how heritage would be transferred: in person. "You come . . ." embodied the standard model of higher education whereby the process of going to college presumed the individual must actually come to the institution to receive an education. The second portion of his stately phrase—"to a tradition"—emphasized the centrality of the prestige Boxborough and Havertown had established. This was dual traditionalism in the sense that coming to the schools had been the tradition throughout their history, and only through coming to them could tradition be inculcated.

Beholden to this philosophy of place, Boxborough and Havertown responded to the challenge by expanding their residential enrollments at both the undergraduate and the graduate levels. Recognizing that the university was heavily tuition driven, the presidents of Boxborough and Havertown recommended their schools pursue a larger, more stable and select group of full-time day students. As a Boxborough senior administrator put it,

> The fact that we're so tuition dependent becomes very much a numbers game. We've had our largest-ever freshman class last year, and hopefully we'll have a similar class this coming year . . . how do we keep the business going forward?

According to the traditional strategy, the only answer available was growth into new residential markets. An enrollment executive at Boxborough observed,

> The demographics of the state . . . show a declining high school graduation population over the next several years . . . and so we have to look outside of our primary market . . . in order to achieve our enrollment goals and net revenue goals. A successful institution has to be driven by demography.

In addition to maintaining the traditional undergraduate liberal arts experience, the institutions developed night classes, weekend classes, and graduate professional programs that permitted alternative opportunities for students to experience what the campus offered.

Both institutions bent over backward to create multiple avenues whereby if students wanted the education afforded by these prestigious schools, they could come and get it. But the unquestioned axis around which all residential enrollment decisions were made was encapsulated in a remark offered by a senior administrator at Boxborough. In considering other educational possibilities the university might offer to local students, she asked, "How can we help students continue to get their education if they want to *come here*?" Their unwavering educational philosophy stressed the physicality of their in-person and in-place approach. This was central to the traditional strategy and would ultimately prove to be its undoing.

Aware that too much growth too fast might lead to a dilution of the traditional experience, leaders of the two institutions endeavored, in the words of a senior leader at Boxborough, to maintain their "historical reputation" and "pervasive quality" by pursuing what they saw as targeted student enrollment growth. Havertown leaders underscored that the graduate emphasis was imperative for economic reasons: "New professional programs draw in a different student population that we can draw from given economic trends," one dean stated. The upmarket emphasis was where enrollment opportunities lay. "Professional more than the traditional liberal arts degrees are where the growth is occurring," a Boxborough senior leader asserted.

Indeed, the emphasis on bolstering their academic prestige focused their attention upmarket as the colleges added various graduate and professional programs in law, healthcare, and business. After listing a dozen new graduate programs, a Havertown vice president boasted, "We've brought a lot of professional programs in the last 10 years, particularly in the last 5 or 6 years." One executive at Boxborough pointed to the reputation of the business program as an example of how prestige drove residential enrollments: "I would say our historical reputation, other schools were afraid of our reputation, at some point in time we had two thirds of the [regional] market. We could not be touched . . . we were really fucking good!"

But just as important as what the schools did do is what they did not do. The dictates of the traditional strategy specifically prohibited both schools from pursuing enrollment growth in nonresidential markets. The leaders of the two institutions endeavored to maintain reputation and quality, and their fundamental belief in what it took to transfer the heritage of the school—"bodies in the seats"—meant that alternative nonresidential routes for generating revenue were ruled out. For example, one senior administrator from Havertown looked back to the nascent era of online education in the early 2000s and described the deliberate approach the university took to eschew the online enrollment market:

> [Online education] was meant to supplement a traditional educational experience, not supplant. We're aware that there was great profitability in it over the last decade. But sometimes a cautious approach [is necessary] to ensure quality integrity of the program rather than risking a low-quality inferior experience in trade for money, for revenue.

The emphasis on academic quality and its association with institutional reputation remained the focus. In the words of one academic official at Boxborough, the reason the school did not offer online classes was because they could not separate quality from place: "how to offer good quality online courses that have the Boxborough academic rigor associated with them." Leaders who embraced the traditional strategy were unmistakably clear about their emphasis: "It's about more than just the money. It's a matter of quality integrity of degrees and programs," the Havertown provost asserted. "It would've been easy 5 or 10 years ago to jump into this and to make it just a strictly margin-based profit operation . . . but I think we've done it the right way. We've been deliberate about it." The steadfast emphasis on tradition and prestige informed which enrollment markets the institutions would expand into—as well as those they strategically opted not to pursue.

At Boxborough and Havertown, quality came through the community fostered between teacher and student, mentor and mentee. Generations of students had experienced this in-person communal approach, which one Boxborough professor elucidated was at the core of the educational experience: "It's a very collegial environment, very caring environment. You really get the feeling that everybody on campus cares about the welfare of others on campus." A Havertown vice president echoed how central the "sense of community" was:

> You can walk across the bricks at Havertown and you're going to see someone that you know, and you're going encounter someone that will call you by name. . . . This is a place where people care about you, a place where people are working to help you prepare yourself for your future. Community is what the culture is all about.

But while the courtyard bricks may have facilitated countless opportunities, the in-person approach they fostered was expensive—and sustaining those paths required not insubstantial financial subsidies.

Expanding the University Endowment

At the turn of the century, the two schools generated approximately $6 to $10 million annually in endowment income that their leaders used to subsidize the core residential model, which, as with all colleges, fell short of being fully funded with tuition revenue. The administrations of both schools therefore sought to significantly grow their endowments to support the influx of new students—an influx that required offering increasingly generous tuition discounts subsidized by the endowment.

Interest from endowment accounts provides institutions with the annual revenue they use to offset operating expenses. Many colleges and universities direct their interest revenues toward discounting their tuition price in the form of student scholarships. In explaining the role of endowments in subsidizing tuition revenues, one Boxborough executive noted how elite schools—which Boxborough sought to emulate—used their endowment interest the same way (albeit at a very different scale):

> There are schools like Princeton, Harvard, Yale, Boston College, Northwestern, University of Chicago, that have endowed scholarships. I mean, Harvard's endowment is huge . . . so just the revenue off of that was their scholarship money.

The substantial endowment revenues of elite institutions stood in stark contrast to the revenue picture for schools at the opposite end of the spectrum: "Most of the schools that are going to close in the next 20 years don't have that kind of endowment," he continued. "They basically have to take the sticker price [of tuition], discount it, and then operate off of the net revenue. It's effectively . . . a coupon of sorts." Endowment revenue was vital for schools like Boxborough and Havertown, "because that improves your operating budget—not having to pull money out of the operating budget to cover financial aid that is used for students."

The method of bolstering the endowment in the traditional strategy was achieved through *traditional philanthropy*—gifts and donations solicited from a constellation of alumni, friends, and foundations. Although both schools had sought to grow their endowments in the past, the aim now was different. In the words of Boxborough's president, "Boxborough must proceed with a capital campaign, and the endowment must grow in real terms . . . [the school must] change the use of its endowment from a source of income to real growth." The same attitude was heard at Havertown: "We're building an endowment!" one of its vice presidents advertised. "We're close to $200 million right now in money under investment, and that's where we *need* to be." Like the growth seen in the residential student body, the development office would seek to grow new avenues of traditional philanthropy to meet the challenges posed by neoliberal fiscal policies and the transformation in student demographics.

When asked about the sources that supported the university endowment, a Havertown fundraising executive described its cultivated philanthropic constellation as,

> Predominantly alumni that graduated in the '50s and '60s, people who have reached an age they can do that, and private foundations. Some friends of the university, and I would be remiss in not saying predominantly people out of the university Board of Trustees.

The same was true at Boxborough. "We've been able to reach out and embrace difference constituencies in a period where money is tight, finding those new deep pockets . . . foundations, legislators, corporations," one Boxborough senior leader explained.

A leader at Havertown summed up the traditional philanthropy approach, asserting that "it gets back to loyalty" because people give where they have a meaningful connection. At each institution, the sole person responsible for maintaining the perpetual velocity of the philanthropic constellation was the president. One Boxborough professor noted the unenviable fundraising efforts of the prior president in a tone of understated admiration: "He put a lot of time and energy into fundraising and capital campaigns."

But instead of just hoping that these groups would donate to the endowment, a Boxborough trustee observed that endowment growth of the kind aimed for in the traditional strategy was a result of periodic fundraising initiatives: "The president is doing some groundwork for another capital campaign . . . he said it was going to be basically for the endowment." In a departure from past fundraising efforts that relied on a narrow band of donors, leaders of the two institutions leveraged their tradition and prestige to grow a diverse constellation of financial contributors.

Members of the development office deliberately included multiple university constituents, taking a "leave no stone unturned" approach to fundraising not seen before at the institutions. They included opportunities for giving through expansive alumni associations that were tended to like never before. The development office targeted events on the university's calendar to ensure fundraising was always a part of the planning. Boxborough's president highlighted this by pointing to a nationally known athletic event with a rival university where they "combined alumni, development, admissions, and athletics" to meet multiple institutional goals—including fundraising for the endowment. The schools even reached out to employees in giving campaigns. One academic chair at Havertown enthusiastically replied, "I'm trying to push my department. We're at 92%; I want to have 100%." Fundraising processes became more sophisticated for both institutions, yet they relied on their traditions and institutional standing.

Despite the seemingly relentless fundraising efforts, administrators of the two tuition-driven colleges often expressed that the size of their endowment was never truly sufficient. At Boxborough, a senior administrator lamented, "If you look at our endowment compared to other schools, it's not that big *and* we are tuition dependent." Similar sentiments were commonplace at Havertown, with a senior leader observing, "We don't have a huge endowment. You know, we have a long way to go in comparison with a lot of institutions." Leaders routinely contrasted the size of their endowment with those of elite institutions. In speaking of Havertown's endowment, a fundraising administrator highlighted the fact that "Duke has a $5 billion endowment."

A faculty member at Boxborough voiced similar sentiments about the recent campaign, which, although it "made a huge difference in the endowment base," still lagged behind the size of endowments of other schools: "It's not a Harvard, it's not a Georgetown, it's not a Holy Cross." Both schools enviously eyed the endowments of elites and even the aspiring Ivies because the endowments granted those institutions financial freedoms Havertown and Boxborough did not enjoy. Whereas 90% of Boxborough and Havertown's revenue was tuition dependent, the excessive endowments of elites meant tuition comprised only 20% of their overall revenue stream. Growing the endowment was imperative if Boxborough and Havertown were ever going to free themselves from the enrollment "numbers game."

Yet something curious happened on the way to the bank for these schools in their attempts to increase the size of their endowments in order to attract students. The challenge of increased competition along with a shrinking pool of available students meant they had to work even harder to attract those all-important tuition dollars. And in the new competitive environment, attracting those students was expensive—very expensive.

"If You Build It, They Will Come"

As the 21st century commenced, the clash over enrollment intensified between institutions of higher education. An important facet of the struggle was that university leaders had come to believe that their physical facilities and student enrollments were correlated.[15] The Havertown provost put it succinctly: "We were *very* lackluster in our facilities." In fact, Havertown leaders regularly made comparisons to the building boom of the golden age. "We were not competitive when we looked around at what families were seeing at other schools. This was 2003, not 1975 anymore, when everybody probably had okay facilities," mentioned one vice president. A colleague shared his assessment: "Our infrastructure was very problematic. We'd been living under 40 years of deferred maintenance." With the shrinking pool of applicants, converting interested students to enrollees took increasing priority. It became an article of faith that the appeal of tradition alone could not stand up to the offerings of other schools, leading, in the words of one Havertown professor, to a "system-wide arms race":

> If the students aren't comfortable, and they think they're going to a place that's not up to date, they're not going to come. They're going to go somewhere else... that's one of the challenges of any school the last 15 years. If you're not updated, you better get that way.

And the clearest route to comfort was to construct it. A Boxborough leader candidly summed up the response of everyone: "Other places are building. We have to build too."

In short order, tuition-driven institutions like Boxborough and Havertown began a relentless building campaign to attract prospective students using modernized facilities. A Boxborough faculty member revealed that senior leaders were continually "thinking of ways to make us more attractive to students." To appeal to the next generation of students, administrators intentionally catered the design of their physical infrastructure to preferences sought by this population. "When a student comes, they look for several things," a vice president at Havertown observed:

> They want to know where do I eat, where do I sleep, and where do I work out or where do I play?... Those three things are what we focused on and said we're going to have the best we can have.

Accordingly, the two colleges prioritized spending for athletic facilities, erecting state-of-the-art arenas and multisport complexes whose stadium lighting kept campuses aglow late into the night, along with highly attractive intramural and club sport facilities.

Residence halls were no longer the spartan rooms of lore, replaced with amenities more in line with contemporary student expectations.[16] As one professor at Havertown put it, "The 'modern student' expects a dorm room that looks something like a Hilton Hotel and must have [their] own bathroom... I think we've made a big effort to cater to that." Drafty dining halls were a thing of the past: "They have an awesome cafeteria area now," one Boxborough leader enthused, his voice reflecting how important this was to meeting their enrollment goals. According to one Havertown vice president, forthcoming construction projects prioritized amenities that would have seemed absurd in another era:

We're going to build us another nice residence hall [and] put a nice saltwater pool over there between the halls. We're [a couple hundred] miles from the coast. Kids come here and they like to get a tan before they go to the beach. Let's give them a place to get a tan.

But the changes to schools employing the traditional strategy were not limited to the spaces most frequently traveled by students. To generate residential enrollments, these colleges undertook a comprehensive transformation of their entire residential campus. As a senior administrator observed, Havertown leadership "saw very quickly the need to catch up." They marshaled the support of the trustees "to bring on board contractors and architects that would ... not just throw up one building but think through a 25-year plan." Within a decade, the Boxborough and Havertown campuses would become radically different physical spaces that astonished guests, particularly alumni returning after many years. Havertown's administrative manager noted, "When they come back, they're just amazed at how this university has developed." But what mattered most was how prospective students felt. "They walk onto the campus and just see it fits, it feels right," a Havertown vice president acknowledged. "They cannot explain it or define it in a term, but they say that."

The strategy underlying the physical transformation of the residential campus not only appealed to contemporary student preferences but also functioned as a proxy for educational quality. Leaders understood that in the absence of information about educational outcomes, prospective parents and students looked to buildings and facilities as a sign of the possible return on their tuition investment. According to one Boxborough leader, in the decades before the traditional strategy was adopted,

> There was not a strategic master plan for building and renewal of the plant and the facilities on the campus. From a student enrollment perspective, that sends a message that if you're not taking care of your buildings, you're not going to take care of your students.

The changes taking place on Boxborough's campus were designed to send a clear signal to students and parents alike: in the words of one professor, "An education from Boxborough is a marketable degree ... it's a high-quality institution."

But the changes went beyond simply uprooting the campus infrastructure to seemingly affecting the very soil these schools were built on. In describing how the overhaul registered at his school, one Boxborough senior administrator confessed that "it impacted not just physically—[it] impacted the culture here." The remark captured something fundamental about the traditional strategy—a strategy where schools steeped in over a century of tradition could be transformed by market forces to such a degree that a distinguished faculty member at Boxborough would unselfconsciously claim about a new high rise that "this building is very, very important." Instead of bringing students to experience a tradition, the schools were reconfigured to elicit a feeling. As one senior administrator at Havertown admitted, "What you see today, this nice green campus with nice sidewalks . . . you *feel* like you are at a special place." The appeal of prestige had been replaced with a material appeal to place.

The primary purpose of investing in the physical transformation of the two campuses was to attract students in what had become an increasingly competitive resource environment. By that measure, both schools were quite successful, with a Havertown vice president acknowledging that his college "just does not look like any kind of school in our area." But what happened was something deeper: a reinterpretation of the belief that "you come to a tradition." There was the creeping sensation among some community members that the ground was shifting under their feet—that the very culture of their school was undergoing an overhaul even more significant than the physical transformation seen on campus. A Boxborough College professor spoke for many when he summed up the change he saw the traditional strategy was having on the culture of these institutions: "If you build it, they will come. That seems to be the marketing philosophy."

Overhauling the Offerings

While administrators at both schools asserted buildings and student recruitment were correlated, they also described the extensive programs developed to widen the pool of potential college applicants from which they might draw. One professor framed the dilemma facing schools like Boxborough and Havertown this way:

> A public institution roughly 70 miles from here is our number one competitor, hands down. We hear that every day from families and young people coming here. And why do we compete against the public sector? Price and programs. Price and programs.

By the logic of the traditional strategy, to effectively compete with other institutions, Boxborough and Havertown leaders had to establish new program offerings to expand the reputation of the institution beyond the state into farther corners of the country. In turn, these well-resourced athletic and academic programs would provide the colleges with a distinctive marketing niche their leaders could leverage to expand the reach of their schools nationwide and thereby increase the pool of potential tuition-paying students.

Most avid sports enthusiasts across America are now familiar with the athletics dynasty Boxborough developed during this period. This familiarity was by design. As one senior administrator put it, "If we're going to grow, we need to attract more of a national student. There was a strategic decision made years ago to use athletics as a vehicle to promote the university, which has served us extremely well." Of course, Boxborough was not the first school to invest in athletics to raise their national visibility. As one senior leader remarked, "The same thing has worked for Notre Dame, and it's worked for Georgetown, and it's worked for Boston College." Echoing the president, who was focused on "enhancing the brand of the university so as to drive positive revenue growth," the vice president was unambiguous about why Boxborough adopted this approach: "It had a good impact financially for the university and allowed us to do other things."

Boxborough leaders focused on the sport most likely to offer the biggest return on investment—men's basketball. A professor at the college commended the president for focusing his attention on the team and the thought process driving the decision: "If we got a national reputation from the team, then it would attract students. It's paid off... it helped the profile of the university." As a vice president observed, "Prior to Boxborough's basketball program taking off 10–15 years ago, I don't know if people on the West Coast would have really known who Boxborough is." As part of a regional athletic conference, the basketball program provided Boxborough with "free" advertising across many nearby states, while each March, Boxborough was rewarded with a coast-to-coast marketing system that was expansive and illustrious. "The exposure that we get through our games on television, through our participation in the NCAA tournament," one senior administrator gushed, "that is publicity that Boxborough cannot buy!"

Leaders emphasized that the school's athletic program was integral to maintaining the college's admissions and endowment. "Athletics is central to the university in a variety of ways, whether it is enrollment management [or] development," observed a vice president. "Our vice president for enrollment realized we can leverage our national reputation that basketball gives us by [placing] enrollment personnel in all marketplaces," an executive acknowledged, while noting that the endowment benefited as well, allowing for "an increased focus on the academic side to look at new programs, future programs, to what I would call investing in ourselves." Nor did all this happen by accident: "Because it is such a visibly strategic piece ... the president and the senior leadership ensure that how athletics is represented ... is consistent with the overall university," observed one vice president. In the competitive college recruitment race, leaders deemed that if they were to successfully maintain enrollment, prospective students and their families had to know the prestigious Boxborough reputation. Its men's basketball program was arguably the key element in the expanded marketing strategy.

Like Boxborough, Havertown College also implemented extensive efforts to strengthen its reputation beyond its own state. To increase its prominence, Havertown leaders opted for the steady expansion of academic programs rather than athletics, systematically launching a diverse array to grow the school's reputation. A Havertown finance executive framed their decision to expand their academic offerings in stark terms:

> We realized ... that growth is through programs. And you don't have to grow a program every year, but if you don't do one every 2 to 3 years ... you're going to start dying. You've got to keep moving on the tracks. You've got to keep moving. If you stop, you go backward.

Since the late 1980s, Havertown leaders continually looked upmarket to develop graduate and professional programs to create new pools of student applicants they might draw on. Their new academic programs emphasized quality from inception to implementation. Executives built top-of-the-line academic facilities and hired renowned experts in each field to quickly establish program notoriety, academic excellence, and superior graduate placement. University publications prominently mentioned the national rankings of its programs among peer institutions while frequently identifying the accomplishments of former students (including their nearly perfect pass rates on professional exams). The reputation for quality Havertown established quickly extended beyond the state and region to rival that of peer institutions in distant regions of the country.

The progressive upmarket focus enabled Havertown to capitalize on a social phenomenon known as *credentialism*, whereby advanced graduate credentials are increasingly necessary to secure higher paying jobs.[17] With the traditional in-person undergraduate market tapped out in their eyes, Havertown leaders recognized that the graduate market offered many opportunities to widen the pool of potential college applicants from which they might draw. The upmarket emphasis on graduate and professional programs provided Havertown with not only larger student enrollments, but also a specific type of student. A professor remarked that an influential factor for the changes that swept through the health sciences at Havertown was that "not only do you enroll more students, but you also enroll a higher caliber student."

True to their prestige philosophy, these programmatic changes at Boxborough and Havertown remained focused on the in-person and in-place residential model that expected students "to come to a tradition." Yet as with the overhaul of the physical infrastructure of these schools, there were inklings that these changes were a departure from tradition versus a continuation of it—and not just because of their exorbitant cost. As a leader at Havertown remarked, "There is a market for certain programs that we are looking at in our business school. Those [programs] are not religiously or ideologically driven; they are vocationally driven." Another Havertown leader fatalistically confessed that times had simply changed:

> Twenty years ago you went to college to be educated and get a degree. That beautiful time of just . . . wanting to study and be self-actualized is not the case anymore. They are coming to get a job.

Good Stewards of Opportunity

How did Boxborough and Havertown pay for the new infrastructure and programs? A senior administrator at Havertown did not exaggerate when she said that "millions and millions of dollars" had been spent to improve their facilities and programs to increase enrollment, and the same was true at Boxborough. But where did the money come from? The schools that implemented the traditional strategy initially financed their growth through fundraising. The presidents of both institutions retained oversight of the fundraising process to ensure its success. According to one senior leader at Boxborough, "If the university needed something, [the president] could go out and ask for it, and they would give him the building." An executive at Havertown was equally quick to note that "our president worked very hard, had very effective fundraising, and [generated] a huge influx of support for the institution."

But the physical transformation told only part of the story—in the words of one Havertown professor, the newly instituted programs also needed "maintaining and feeding." At Boxborough, alumni were delighted to support the school, especially with its men's basketball enjoying deep runs in the NCAA tournament, and its president was not shy about asking for donations to support new programs. As a senior administrator at Boxborough observed, "Investing in our men's basketball program was an opportunity. . . . And it's been extremely successful. And I don't think you would be here today if we didn't make that commitment." But that program itself required a considerable level of investment as well: "I don't think that anybody feels great about saying that their basketball coach is their most 'valued' employee . . . they're compensated the most because you've got to compete in the marketplace."

A similar narrative emerged at Havertown. According to a vice president, with the financial backing of the board, its president threw his full weight behind programmatic initiatives, leaving a legacy that has "really driven the student population." The provost underscored how program growth was also instrumental in generating additional revenue in the form of federal grants: "We are becoming more effective at securing federal funds and federal grants and things, but to be honest, that's because of the establishment of a medical school and some of our professional degree programs." Nevertheless, program expansion required significant financial outlays to come to fruition as well.

A closer look at Boxborough and Havertown's fundraising strategies reveals their heavy reliance on traditional philanthropy to literally pave the way. As a finance official at Havertown proudly crowed,

> [The] board was supportive beyond belief, from their time, from their energy, from their money. We had a board member give us $4.5 million so we could build a convocation center. We built a $36 million convocation center with zero borrowing and zero debt. We built a $13 million pharmacy addition with zero debt. We built a $7 million chapel with zero debt. That is where they're giving you the money up front. It's just beyond belief!

Both Boxborough and Havertown leaders described their approach to fundraising as being "good stewards" of the donated monies, a view that was closely informed by the schools' traditions. In the words of one, the growth initiated by the traditional strategy "was deliberate, supported from a stewardship perspective, [and] a good use of limited resources." If there was an element of entrepreneurialism to their stewardship of the funds they raised, it was in the willingness of the leadership of both schools to pin their hopes for a sustainable future on the traditional strategy. The Havertown president drew the connection explicitly: "If you are a good steward of your opportunity and the need around you . . . you have got to take risks."

One obvious risk was that their approach was in direct conflict with the goal of growing their endowment to cover the additional shortfall in tuition revenue caused by increased enrollments. Both schools therefore embarked on an additional funding strategy at odds with the traditions of both schools: borrowing. Given the extensive scope of the campus transformation, there were instances where campus executives opted for loans or bonds. Although these only comprised a small part of the overall strategy both schools took toward fundraising, this option permitted leaders to pursue blended forms of funding to continually initiate new projects. One senior leader at Havertown described how the process worked:

> In the last 10 years we have invested about $150 million in the infrastructure of the university. We raised $120 million, which is by far the most prolific fundraising period we've ever had, and then covered the rest in institutional loans. . . . A lot of schools really leverage themselves, and Havertown has been blessed that we've not had to leverage ourselves.

Leaders at Boxborough also pursued blended forms of fundraising and loans to keep pace with the extensive renovation plan for the campus. One professor explained that "buildings came from restricted funds [where] people would donate money, and our chief financial officer issued bonds to finance the growth."

But while loans are a time-honored way for colleges and universities to fund construction, there were disincentives in taking such a route. As one vice president at Boxborough noted, lending institutions made their borrowing rates conditional on the rate that colleges discounted their student tuition. "Once your discount rate jumps above 50%, then your bond ratings go down. So it's going to cost you more to borrow money to build buildings." Discounting tuition and building infrastructure were key elements of the traditional strategy designed to attract the students needed to pay tuition, but taking out construction loans pitted them against one another. The administrator pointed out that with their tuition discount, Boxborough's $30,000 tuition was closer to $16,000. In walking the knife's edge on loans and tuition discounts, both schools exemplify just how slim the margin of error was should the traditional strategy fail.

For many years, the traditional strategy appeared to be a success, with both schools being successful at raising endowment funds through traditional philanthropy. By 2000, the Havertown endowment had grown "from less than $1 million to nearly $100 million," and in the same year the Boxborough endowment also surpassed the $100 million threshold. But by 2015, it was becoming apparent that no matter how much energy was channeled toward traditional philanthropy, there would never be enough money to fund everything called for by the traditional strategy. The matter of limited endowment resources unsettled one Boxborough trustee at the time, who foreshadowed the soon-to-arrive financial crisis for schools that adopted the traditional strategy:

> We are still under-endowed. Our endowment is over $125 million now, but it should be at least double that. . . . One of the downsides of this place is that we never have enough money to do what we really should be doing.

In short, neither school had escaped becoming the very thing the traditional strategy was designed to avoid: a small, private, struggling university that did not have a huge endowment.

The Wages of Prestige

An ardent effort to expand both the endowment and the residential enrollment provided Boxborough and Havertown with vital monetary resources the two colleges needed to implement the traditional strategy. Leaders frequently pointed to peer institutions that had adopted a similar prestige-focused resource approach, including Furman University, Emory University, Villanova University, Santa Clara University, Wake Forest University, Davidson College, and the many aspiring Ivies previously mentioned. Yet despite their relentless work and commitment to fostering the twin demands of the traditional strategy, that approach was ultimately unable to offer a sustainable fiscal return for the residential model both schools were committed to. The two colleges entered a crisis of survival wherein leaders eventually concluded there was an urgent need to identify a new financial solution.

The crisis Boxborough and Havertown leaders experienced by implementing the traditional strategy was the result of several factors. The fundraising approach supported by traditional philanthropy became notably strained in its ability to simultaneously sustain two monumental objectives—expand the endowment to support competitive admission offers that included significant tuition discounts *and* comprehensively transform the residential campus and programmatic offerings. Compounding the problem, because of the tradition-minded cultures of these institutions, they were not quick to respond to the rapidly changing external circumstances and seek alternative financial practices to sustain their residential core. One Boxborough vice president did not mince words regarding the costs of focusing on the past:

> We had a historian as a president, a historian as a provost, and no one who was keeping an eye on how higher ed was changing, and as a result, we weren't changing. Therefore, we've gone through a period of budget and operational challenges that needed to be dealt with *very* quickly.

The inability to successfully compete in attracting students to their campus combined with their inability to quickly pivot led both schools into a downward revenue spiral. "The biggest challenge the university faced this decade has been declining enrollment," a Havertown vice president bemoaned, while a Boxborough academic dean pointedly echoed, "When we did not meet our numbers, it really put the university into this financial shock." Institutional leaders were left expressing an incessant need to catch up to the level of competition and expectations brought about by other institutions that had suddenly entered their once-dominant regional enrollment market.

The Limits of Fundraising

The biggest obstacle to maintaining the dual-focused fundraising approach of the traditional strategy was a series of changes to the external resources both schools had come to rely on. Both schools felt the loss of institutional support they received from their denominations, and the global economic recession brought on by the financial crisis of 2008 had an even bigger impact. In the case of Havertown, the supporting denomination decided to terminate its decades-long subsidies, while at Boxborough the financial and human resource contributions withered with the numerical decline of its clergy— the backbone of its "hidden endowment." During the recession, not only did the leadership at both schools face monumental challenges in soliciting donations, but also their endowment did not produce the expected annual financial yields most institutions of higher education had come to rely on.

In fact, according to one financial administrator, Havertown had to make withdrawals ("4%, give or take") from its endowment capital. The recession eliminated the endowment revenue Boxborough and Havertown were using to fund student scholarships, significantly impacting their ability to offer competitive financial aid packages to prospective students.

But the financial crisis both schools faced was ultimately the product of a self-inflicted wound—the adoption of the traditional strategy itself. Experts had cultivated a constellation of family, friends, and foundations to provide both colleges with funds to theoretically expand the endowment while simultaneously transforming the infrastructure of its residential campus. Boxborough and Havertown leaders had described their approach to fundraising as sophisticated, but traditional philanthropy could not approach the scale needed to pay for physical and programmatic growth *and* fund the aggressive student admission packages needed to attract students. Leaders had strategically secured between $100 and $200 million to update their physical campus and programmatic offerings to remain competitive, but did so using conventional fundraising approaches they had previously leveraged to increase the endowment. As a result, the large philanthropic sums used for campus upgrades came at an opportunity cost to the endowment itself, a point one Havertown vice president highlighted with great alarm:

> The president is smart enough to figure that out and put all the resources into those things [facilities] . . . but there is only so much money. And if you are spending in one place you are not spending in the other.

In the end, the traditional strategy "ate" the endowment growth both schools relied on to subsidize bringing students—and their tuition loan revenue—to their schools to enjoy the new buildings and programs designed to entice them.

Although Boxborough and Havertown could both boast of having a healthy endowment at the turn of the century, when revenues from the endowment as well as support from the wider community began to decline, the traditional strategy had to be put on hold—quite literally in the case of renovations to Smith Hall at Boxborough: "We are facing financial issues like any other university is . . . our main classroom facility was taken offline a few years ago," one faculty member shared, while a vice president explained the stoppage in a broader market-influenced context:

> How do we decide to make a good financial decision on when to build, how to fund, and can we get private donations? Without solid information that's a tough decision

to make. The academic hall . . . we've gone a year and we'll go next year without our main classroom building! [In the end] it became a business decision [based] on funding.

Leaders at both institutions were sent scrambling in search of a new approach. Ironically, instead of providing the critical revenues Boxborough and Havertown required to subsidize their residential core, the endowments merely delayed the crisis of survival that left administrators grappling to cut costs, develop new products, and establish new enrollment markets.[18]

Changes in external resources forced leaders to look for alternative fundraising approaches to offset the reductions in their endowment revenue. Visibly distressed, the Boxborough vice president did not hesitate to suggest what was previously an avenue of last resort: "Do we issue bonds?" he wondered out loud. An executive at Havertown observed that while their fundraising model still relied on "a lot of individual donors and foundations . . . we are becoming more effective at securing federal funds and federal grants." Boxborough leaders sought auxiliary revenues, with a college trustee explaining how "we rent things out . . . we're doing anything we can to use the property to make money." The school even turned to life insurance. The trustee went on to explain how the president "kept asking trustees and benefactors if they would take out multimillion-dollar life insurance policies and name the university the beneficiary . . . when they die, we will get a couple hundred million." But as the trustee noted, the problem with this approach was practically Monty Python-esque: "They're not dead yet." The promise of future payouts did not offer a workable solution to the crisis.

In the end, there was a persistent degree of uncertainty as to whether the alternative fundraising decisions could sustain the traditional strategy. As a Boxborough administrator forewarned and foreshadowed, the auxiliary approach put at risk:

> Schools our size . . . because they cannot afford to make too many bad decisions, right? I mean you make one or two of those and it impacts you. If we have a $5 million miss because we have invested in the wrong area, that is jobs for us. That is not, "Oh our endowment is going to absorb it."

Senior leaders at both institutions arduously fundraised for over a decade in a zealous attempt to overhaul their campus infrastructure while expanding their endowment. Despite the progress both administrations made "pushing the campus into the 21st century" (in the words of a Boxborough trustee), the demands for additional financing and more construction seemed endless. One Havertown vice president admitted as much in a tone of sheer exhaustion: "A lot of schools really leverage themselves. We've not had to leverage ourselves. We've paid for one program along [at a time], but it's been kind of nonending. There has been a new significant facility every year on this campus since 2005." Leaders conceded that in the absence of an enormous endowment, in the billions of dollars, major changes with a focus on achieving financial sustainability appeared inevitable. But correcting course and making those changes proved difficult.

In the Absence of Speed

In many ways, Boxborough and Havertown embodied long-standing professional norms foundational to American higher education. In postsecondary education, it is customary for faculty to share in the governance process, alumni to help financially sustain the school, administrators to strategize via committees, and the institution to continually invest in its people.[19] The academy has been organized around myriad smaller communities within itself that contribute to sustaining the institutional mission—communal norms that extend its communal values. These professional norms have provided American institutions of higher education with an internal stability that has contributed to their enduring nature for hundreds of years as an integral part of society.[20]

The enduring professional norms at Boxborough and Havertown influenced the pace of their organizational culture. One senior administrator contrasted the culture of Boxborough with his prior employment in a marketing firm and lamented, "Things move slower, because so many people have to be involved, and everything has a committee." Despite the tremendous change the traditional strategy had wrought to the grounds of both schools, from a business perspective those changes had occurred at a stately or even snail's pace. In large part, this was by design; for example, the Boxborough culture was one that historically made tremendous investments in its people and was predominantly understood in relational terms. Administrators at Boxborough fondly described "a family-oriented culture," one centered on "a culture of consensus." Faculty described Havertown as "a very welcoming, laid-back culture" and administrators as enjoying "a culture of comfort and longevity." At both schools a relational emphasis was part of their DNA; in the words of a professor at Havertown, "It's a positive, affirming kind of culture very much impacted by its heritage."

Institutional leaders conceded that these long-standing professional norms influenced the pace of decision-making. Once they embarked on the traditional strategy, administrators found it difficult to alter or reverse course. At Havertown, one faculty member pointed out that slow-moving deliberation was a vital part of decision-making processes:

> Deliberation is necessary to make sure everything is clear.... So there isn't a whole lot of "by the seat of your pants" kind of moments, if you will. And when things need to be done, you just need to be patient because that is the culture here.

At Boxborough, their commitment to people shaped decisions. "There's definitely a care and concern for individuals—for students, for employees, for everybody," one vice president surmised.

> It gets in the way of making difficult business decisions, that particularly in this day and age is more important than ever before.... There's a family culture [that] creates some level of comfort that may hurt the productivity or the performance that is necessary.

The rationale for adopting the traditional strategy was plain at the time: to boost enrollment and avoid the drastic measures other surrounding schools had to resort to. An enrollment executive at Boxborough made the case bluntly:

> The common characteristic among them was low endowment, and they'd made one last hurrah. So they built a new athletic facility, they built a new science building, they built a new student union, they built a new dorm, they did something gambling that the one thing would be enough to turn the institution around. And they did not. And so they ended up with no endowment and a campus they couldn't afford to maintain. And they had to lay people off.

With more than 150 colleges and universities in the state, Havertown leaders faced a daunting competitive context: "It was very much about catching up with the institutions in our state that had already done that work [of building] and we were so far behind," a vice president asserted. "And I think today we can say that we are in a much better place. You can see our facilities and see they are much more appealing than they were in 2000, but there are *still* very critical needs," he emphasized while mentioning a series of successive shortcomings. His administrative colleague was equally adamant: "We have to reach out, we have to cast a wider net... there are *so* many things we can do that would be competitive and draw students here!" she emphasized. Unfortunately, the adoption of the traditional strategy and the prevailing mindset to engage in prolonged decision-making processes in the face of immediate crises only delayed the measures Boxborough and Haverford ultimately had to take in response to the loss of revenue.

Yet while the leaders of Boxborough and Havertown were engaged in deliberative internal discourse and decision-making, their external environment rapidly changed. One executive at Boxborough highlighted the resulting mismatch: "The commitment and the personal care were beautiful things, but higher ed has changed really rapidly, and we had a provost who moved at a glacial pace." Nowhere was that more vividly illustrated than in how unforeseen competition upended the regional enrollment landscape for both Boxborough and Havertown.

The Enrollment Cliff

In the early 2000s, one wave of unexpected competition came from institutions that provided online education. These institutions often lacked a local campus and could not easily be identified as competition, like nearby regional schools. A Havertown leader explained how online institutions significantly impacted the regional dominance the college once possessed.

> Students in our state now have access to programs that could be cheaper, presumably more fitting to their lifestyle, and potentially easier for them to achieve. It's changed things in terms of competition—in particular, the resident population, which is our bread and butter.

An anxious faculty member at Boxborough was even more blunt: "Online schools are popping up everywhere! I mean there is every kind of online program ... now we have got competitors everywhere!"

The second wave of unexpected competition for Boxborough and Havertown emerged with respect to student loans. Other institutions within their geographic region began to undercut Boxborough and Havertown's financial aid packages, resulting in schools engaging in a bidding war for student tuition dollars. A Havertown enrollment executive explained how prospective students began to bargain, saying, "This is what I am getting from this school. What more can you do for me?" While lawmakers had strategically designed market-oriented policies so individual students could shop across schools in search of high quality and low cost, haggling in the admissions marketplace was an utterly unexpected development. Apparently, the buildings and programs at the core of the traditional strategy were not enough to meet the emerging challenge.

The circumstances were particularly acute at Boxborough. "Two years ago, the revenue expense lines crossed ... it was a shock to the system," explained an executive. "The plan was to increase the number of undergraduate students and use the extra revenue to pay down all of the unfunded mandates." But instead of increasing revenue, the traditional strategy resulted in a financial chasm: "The growth of $8 million instead came out like $10 million in the hole. It was actually worse with 1,000 more kids. People started asking, 'Who is going to save us?'"

The traditional approach of increasing residential enrollments had previously worked because there had always been a donative body of alumni continually "saving" (i.e., subsidizing) the overall cost. But the "solution" began to falter in the context of increased competition and the shrinkage the endowment experienced as a result of the recession and its failure to grow—because of having to pay for the new facilities and programs. A vice president at Havertown noted that leaders had specifically refrained from establishing certain academic programs despite there being a market for them. "Do we go for every program or policy the market wants? No, not necessarily. We still have to be true to ourselves and who we are." These commitments also explained why leaders initially eschewed novel enrollment markets—an approach the strategies described in subsequent chapters explicitly embraced. "We really don't have any online [courses]," one professor at Boxborough explained, "because we are high touch." Institutional leaders had strategically pursued only residential markets that aligned with the in-person and in-place emphases integral to their "commitment to tradition."

Yet growing residential enrollments proved to be cost heavy and complicated to forecast. "Everybody has gone local to regional to national, even international recruiting," one senior administrator at Boxborough confessed. To maintain their prestige-focused niche amid escalating competition, the two colleges spent even greater sums of money to attract students to their schools. Yet in their attempt to maintain prestige, the Boxborough senior administrator explained that leaders had "grossly overestimated their market cache" and significantly misjudged enrollment outcomes, which fell by 15% at each college between 2000 and 2015.

Leaders were thus forced to make considerable alterations to their enrollment strategies merely to secure enough annual funding—alterations that challenged previously inviolable stances that reflected cultural commitments at both schools. In the words of an enrollment executive at Havertown,

> The University of Virginia doesn't have to nurture anybody ... "Look to your left, look to your right," and all that nonsense. At Havertown we cannot afford that. But we still want to recruit the right students and we want them to be successful.[21]

Hidden in the remark is the acknowledgment that Havertown needed the tuition dollars every single student brought. As the enrollment executive later confessed, "We're not trying to weed anybody out, are you kidding? That is $30,000 a year in tuition!" But when the financial crisis hit, even public universities nominally funded by state revenues began admitting students who were academically unprepared for the rigors of college. This had particular consequences for prestigious schools like Boxborough, as an enrollment executive there revealingly admitted:

> [We] are not prepared for the students who will be enrolling over the course of the next 10 years. Because they are probably not going to be White, English will probably not be their first language, and they are going to need more and more specialized services to help them adapt to a faculty that has been used to teaching Caucasian White males and females that come well-prepared.... The uniqueness of the student is not going to match the services the traditional university is used to providing. The university has been used to having white bread. Now they are going to have wheat, and they are not going to understand how to do that.

A Havertown leader also lamented how unprepared his school was for the change: "We're bringing in students who are probably not prepared for college. We don't offer developmental coursework ... we're setting them up for failure!" he emphasized.

> When we accept them, when their SAT scores are in the hole, high school GPA is minimal, when they're not even sure they want to come here or get a job or go in the military—that means a lot of tutoring, a lot of babysitting, a lot of making sure they're going to class.

Predictably, along with the overall enrollment decline came an increased drop-out rate, which in turn put even more pressure on the admissions process at both schools.

With the decline in enrollment and the arrival of the financial crisis, leaders at both schools were ultimately forced to cut labor costs to save money. The staff at Havertown were asked to take salary cuts, and at Boxborough the cuts were even more severe and resulted in terminations. The reduction caused community members to question the prioritization of resources, resulting in obtuse defenses of the traditional strategy like this one by an administrator at Boxborough:

> I'm not sure people are recognizing to get enrollment we need to have beautiful grounds; we need to have safety. We've been putting up more lights and signage. Some people might say why did we lose five positions and put signs up?

Attempts to defend both layoffs and lights as creating a more sustainable business model could mean only one thing: the writing was on the wall for the traditional strategy.

Challenged to Catch Up

By no means were Boxborough and Havertown leaders unproductive or apathetic. On the contrary, leaders were dedicated to the traditions of service and opportunity, having worked hard to sustain them while adhering to conventional higher education norms. Despite their hard work and effort, their persistent reality was that they still trailed the competition. Boxborough was described by a senior administrator as "[an] institution where people worked really hard, were really committed, *but* we were behind the times." At Havertown, a senior leader bemoaned that their greatest challenge was "very much about catching up . . . with the institutions in our state . . . with everybody else." The sentiment was the same at Boxborough. "We needed [to do] some catching up," admitted a senior administrator. "We have been forced to do that by leaps and bounds—so we are. But there are growing pains." Yet after all the labor the leaders expended to transform the residential campus and program offerings, what more could be done?

As both schools discovered, catching up with the competition turned out to be not about working harder at transforming or improving the residential core. Rather, catching up was about competing with other colleges and universities in an entirely different manner—in other words, abandoning the traditional strategy altogether.

At Boxborough, the president and trustees hired a "business-savvy" executive to help the institution gain lost ground in the area of academic competition. Her immediate assessment of the college was that the school had "tremendous excess capacity"; in other words, the college's academic units were producing at a considerably lower output than they were capable of.

How was that possible in light of the tremendous growth the university had seen over the past several decades? As she explained, the institution had,

> No online degree programs, no training system, no external vendors, a handful of courses, [and] no international programs other than a couple of faculty who do tremendous programs—but they are 'his Rome trip' [and] 'her Paris trip.'

She fervently continued the list: "Financially, they did no travel, no international partnerships, couple million in research grants, huge cache in community service but not integrated, and no experiential learning to speak of. And I am looking at this place going, 'Holy shit!'"

Many of the areas the Boxborough executive ticked were markets the college had overlooked in its devout residential focus. Boxborough and Havertown had worked hard to offer different conventional options for students to come to their residential campuses. In contrast, the peripheral enrollment markets the competition established—online, international, satellite, and more—took education *to* new groups of students in new ways that were not constrained by a residential campus. By establishing versatile models of educational delivery, the peripheral enrollment markets of other institutions permitted them to compete directly with the exclusive residential model Boxborough and Havertown maintained. Thus, catching up to the competition did not mean leaders needed to work harder at further transforming their residential core; rather, they needed to abandon their exclusive residential model and quickly develop adaptable forms of educational delivery to attract prospective students and their tuition revenues.

At Havertown, leaders similarly insisted they needed to catch up to academic competition from other schools that seemingly caught them off guard. A senior academic official expressed particular concern that "in the realm of online programs . . . we're kind of a fledgling. We've been very cautious and very careful. We're responding and we're going to grow to help meet that and remain more competitive and more relevant." Despite having established myriad reputable graduate and professional programs across 2 decades, Havertown leaders were forced to admit that competition from the online enrollment markets of other schools was a significant threat to their residential strategy.

And so, both schools found themselves back where they started before they adopted the traditional strategy—debating how to thread the needle between their need for tuition revenue to survive and their desire to remain true to their roots. The tension was palpable: one senior administrator at Boxborough acknowledged that solely focusing on tradition would result in "things spiraling out of control pretty rapidly, and we'd be out of business." But to let financial considerations dominate would mean sacrificing the tradition-based experience "that has been our hallmark for generations" and lead to an even worse outcome: "We'd lose our soul."

According to an enrollment executive at Havertown, the same sort of worries permeated discussions there: How could the school "balance between trying to appreciate our heritage and the values from whence we came ... but be a relevant institution for the 21st century?" Yet having pursued the traditional strategy in hopes of leveraging tradition to increase revenues, the time had come to confront the immovable object that a purely residential model had become. Only one question remained for a vice president at Boxborough: "How do you compromise without losing your soul?"

By 2015, faculty and staff at both institutions appeared either poised or resigned to abandon their belief about the incomparable value placed on the residential experience. The Havertown provost observed that the increased pressure to change their culture and catch up was something confronting not only his school, but also "all institutions" of higher education, while a Boxborough administrator summed up the new entrepreneurial mindset that was becoming the norm:

> We've changed our culture to be more innovative rather than conservative. I think that we've learned to be more agile in adapting to change—change in demographics and change in market. It gives me a lot of hope for the future, because we've learned to be innovators. Even faculty have learned to be more innovative in our thinking.

One professor at Boxborough spoke for many as he zigzagged through the options available to prestige schools—not unlike what Robert Frost did when contemplating the choice facing the narrator in "The Road Not Taken":

> One path is to really emphasize the bottom line—make decisions based on what is going to bring in financially the most students, the most tuition, revenue.... That would be one road where the prize at the end of the road is revenue generation. And the prize at the end of the other road is realizing the mission of the university. It's not an either/or choice. You have to be financially solvent. You cannot [embrace tradition] and just totally ignore the fact that you've got to pay your bills.

A faculty colleague at Boxborough was even blunter: "You should be able to see the mission in the balance sheet." Were Boxborough and Havertown reluctant to take the road less traveled, or in pursuing the traditional strategy had they already—only to return to Frost's forest to take the path to financial security instead? In either case, it amounted to the same: an implicit admission that the residential philosophy of these schools was truly a thing of the past. The Boxborough professor perhaps did not realize how prescient he was when he accidentally referred to the next wave of Boxborough students as the "revenue generation."

Conclusion

What was the lesson that Boxborough and Havertown leadership took from their experience? It is not an exaggeration to say they concluded that tradition cannot compete in the market. Although both institutions developed sophisticated fundraising systems, donations were not enough to simultaneously fund millions of dollars in construction projects, subsidize rising operating costs, and bolster the university endowment. The regional recruiting dominance that took Boxborough and Havertown decades to establish withered within a matter of years as competing institutions grew their enrollments to secure more tuition revenue. In the face of stiff competition, Boxborough and Havertown enrollment fell, forcing leaders to eliminate programs, cut budgets, and shed personnel. Adherence to tradition and attempts to leverage it through the traditional strategy left these institutions struggling to survive. And yet the traditional strategy is the dominant strategy for those institutions of higher education (many of them aspiring Ivies) that model their approach after elite colleges and universities.

By industry standards, Boxborough and Havertown leaders did everything right. They emphasized traditional education norms throughout the institution—decision-making was an inclusive and deliberative process, learning outcomes adhered to professional standards, and there was an equal commitment of care for faculty, staff, and students alike. Leaders endlessly fought to sustain the institution in the right way. "We want all the revenue we can possibly get at Havertown, but we don't want to do anything that's going to compromise the Havertown brand," one vice president remarked. Yet in the end, Boxborough and Havertown were forced to abandon the traditional strategy because it failed to offer a viable, long-term, financially sustainable model.

Boxborough and Havertown leaders were forced to scramble and look for a more sustainable approach: "We're having to grow to be able to become what we need to be sustainable with the new higher ed model," a Boxborough vice president confessed. This time, however, selecting a strategy would be based on "the university that you have, not the university you *want* to have." In response, Boxborough and Havertown executives worked to establish new academic products to tap enrollment markets (and the accompanying tuition loans) they had previously eschewed. "Resources can no longer be assumed!" exclaimed a Boxborough vice president, while her senior colleague urgently concluded, "We've got to look outside of our primary market and look to secondary and tertiary markets in order to achieve our enrollment goals and net revenue goals." A senior academic official exulted that Havertown had recently secured approval from its regional accreditor to develop multiple online degree programs. For more than one professor, there was no concealing that with these changes came changes in the college experience. "More and more of what we do is providing a product," he uttered, shaking his head as he spoke. These market-informed responses to the shifting demand for higher education were a stark contrast to what had previously been a prestige focus for Boxborough and Havertown. Whether or not online education really is the same as the in-person residential model was ultimately immaterial in the face of financial ruin.

Some senior administrators cautioned that the new market-focused trajectory had already begun to impact the institution in disconcerting ways. A Havertown leader warned of "losing sight of who we are," while the Boxborough provost fretted that "the fact is that we do not know who we are. We've lost our way." A Boxborough official framed the matter tellingly: "The need to navigate a middle ground between our mission and context in which we reside ... is a messy business of compromise in many cases. And how do you compromise without losing?" He paused for moment, then finished voicing his concern: "You need to do that in a way to hang on to your soul."

The change in attitude was reflected not only in the actions of these institutions but also in the many colleges and universities attempting to navigate the market-focused environment brought about by neoliberal funding policies. As one Boxborough vice president contended, the competition fostered by such policies was likely to persist and even intensify well into the future: "It's fine if you have got a $10 billion endowment and you are not tuition dependent, but for those that are tuition dependent, we're going to have to put our business hats on." It was a shift that was hard to swallow for many within the Boxborough community. "People are having difficulty marrying the business side with the mission side," an administrator observed. But for others, the future was clear. A Havertown professor shared, "You can see how private education, if it is going to survive, has to be innovative," and a different vice president at Boxborough was even blunter: "If you're not willing to adapt, close your doors now, just get it over with, seriously." Ironically, these two tradition-bound institutions could no longer look to the past to sustain their future; instead, they would have to break with the past to innovate and survive.

Notes

1. Striving to achieve the elitism of the Ivy League colleges, the aspiring Ivy institutions model their processes based on the pursuit of prestige. Greene, H., & Greene, M. W. (2010). *The hidden Ivies: 50 top colleges—from Amherst to Williams—that rival the Ivy League.* Harper Collins.
2. Reputation differs from legitimacy and status: "Legitimacy is political, status is honorific, [and] reputation is fundamentally *economic*." Deephouse, D. L., & Suchman, M. (2008). Legitimacy in organizational institutionalism. In R. Greenwood, C. Oliver, K. Sahlin, & R. Suddaby (Eds.), *The Sage handbook of organizational institutionalism* (pp. 49–77). Sage Publications. .
3. Reputation is a continuous measure that orders institutions on a continuum from best to worst and is referred to as a comparative "social judgment." Bitektine, A. (2011). Toward a theory of social judgments of organizations: The case of legitimacy, reputation, and status. *Academy of Management Review, 36*(1), 151–179; Deephouse, D. L., & Carter, S. M. (2005). An examination of differences between organizational legitimacy and organizational reputation. *Journal of Management Studies, 42*(2), 329–360.
4. The term specifically refers to the 3 decades from 1945 to 1975 that have been covered extensively in volumes by education historians. Geiger, R. L. (2019). *American higher education since World War II.* Princeton University Press; Thelin, J. R. (2004). *A history of American higher education.* Johns Hopkins University Press.
5. Freeland, R. M. (1992). *Academia's golden age: Universities in Massachusetts, 1945–1970.* Oxford University Press; Kindel, A. T., & Stevens, M. L. (2021). What is educational entrepreneurship? Strategic action, temporality, and the expansion of US higher education. *Theory and Society, 50*(4), 577–605.
6. Neoliberalism refers to the process of replacing values commonly associated with the public social sector—liberty, justice, fairness, and the public good—with market values. Harvey defined neoliberalism as a constellation of practices based on the idea that "human wellbeing can best be advanced by liberating individual entrepreneurial freedoms and skills within an institutional framework characterized by strong private property rights, free markets, and free trade"; in Harvey, D. (2007). *A brief history of neoliberalism.* Oxford University Press, p. 2.
7. While per-student funding commenced with the implementation of the GI Bill in 1944, the funding only applied to veterans. The Higher Education Act in 1965 expanded these educational benefits to all citizens. See Loss, C. P. (2012). *Between citizens and the state: The politics of American higher education in the 20th century.* Princeton University Press, p. 212.

8. Similarly, the National Defense Education Act in 1958 introduced the notion of federal subsidized loans and loan forgiveness to students enrolled in fields of study related to national defense, such as foreign languages, math, and science. The passage of the Higher Education Act in 1965 created a package of financial aid options that expanded these educational benefits from students in defense-related fields to all citizens. See Loss, C. P. (2012). *Between citizens and the state: The politics of American higher education in the 20th century*. Princeton University Press, p. 212.
9. Archibald, R. B., & Feldman, D. H. (2006). State higher education spending and the tax revolt. *The Journal of Higher Education, 77*(4), 618–644; Cheslock, J. J., & Gianneschi, M. (2008). Replacing state appropriations with alternative revenue sources: The case of voluntary support. *The Journal of Higher Education, 79*(2), 208–229; Jaquette, O., & Curs, B. R. (2015). Creating the out-of-state university: Do public universities increase nonresident freshman enrollment in response to declining state appropriations? *Research in Higher Education, 56*(6), 535–565; Rizzo, M., & Ehrenberg, R. G. (2004). Resident and nonresident tuition and enrollment at flagship state universities. In Caroline M. Hoxby (Ed.), *College choices: The economics of where to go, when to go, and how to pay for it* (pp. 303–354). University of Chicago Press.
10. Privatization literature applies to public and private institutions: McClure, K. R., Barringer, S. N., & Brown, J. T. (2020). Privatization as the new normal in higher education: Synthesizing literature and reinvigorating research through a multilevel framework. *Higher Education: Handbook of Theory and Research, 35*, 589–666.
11. Delaney, J. A., & Doyle, W. R. (2011). State spending on higher education: Testing the balance wheel over time. *Journal of Education Finance, 36*, 343–368; Tandberg, D. A. (2010). Politics, interest groups and state funding of public higher education. *Research in Higher Education, 51*(5), 416–450; Webber, D. A. (2017). State divestment and tuition at public institutions. *Economics of Education Review, 60*, 1–4.
12. Fuller, M. B. (2014). A history of financial aid to students. *Journal of Student Financial Aid, 44*(1), 42–68.
13. Zaloom, C. (2019). *Indebted: Student loans, fragile families, and the future of the middle class*. Princeton University Press.
14. Goldrick-Rab, S. (2021). *Paying the price: College costs, financial aid, and the betrayal of the American dream*. University of Chicago Press.
15. Brown, J. T., Volk, F., & Kush, J. M. (2023). Racial and economic stratification on campus: The relationship between luxury residence halls, race, and academic outcomes. *Journal of College Student Development, 64*(1), 108–113; Brown, J. T., Volk, F., & Spratto, E. (2019). The hidden structure: The influence of residence hall design on academic outcomes. *Journal of Student Affairs Research & Practice, 56*(3), 267–283.
16. Brown, J. T. (2023). The ethical poverty of dorms for the rich. *The Chronicle of Higher Education*. May 2.
17. Collins, R. (2019). *The credential society: A historical sociology of education and stratification*. Columbia University Press.
18. The institutions examined in subsequent chapters lacked an endowment and therefore encountered a crisis of survival much earlier, which compelled their leadership to adopt alternative strategies focused on peripheral (nonresidential) enrollment markets to generate the necessary revenues to survive the twin crises of demography and neoliberalism—the very markets Boxborough and Havertown ultimately found themselves turning to.

19. Gerber, L. G. (2014). *The rise and decline of faculty governance: Professionalization and the modern American university.* Johns Hopkins University Press; Gasman, M., & Bowman, N., III. (2013). *Engaging diverse college alumni: The essential guide to fundraising.* Routledge.
20. Abbott, A. (2014). *The system of professions: An essay on the division of expert labor.* University of Chicago Press.
21. A phrase traditionally used during first-year orientation to explain retention and persistence, where university leaders would customarily say, "Look to your left, look to your right. By graduation, one of you will not be here."

2
The Pioneer Strategy

"We Build With Adult Money"

Introduction

Located in disparate regions of the country, the University of Malvern, Lansdale University, and Stoneham University were a triad of schools that embraced a spirit of innovation coupled with a steadfast commitment to the value of relationships over the course of their history. For more than a century, these institutions were accustomed to modifying their organizational form in enterprising ways through mergers, relocations, and acquisitions in an effort to sustain their mission and serve the overlooked: "Lansdale sees itself as a genuinely welcoming and hospitable place, reaching out to the marginalized," one professor offered, while a contemporary echoed with sincerity, "I believe in Stoneham's mission of giving those who would not have a chance a chance." But when the end of the baby boom coincided with the shift toward neoliberal policies for funding higher education, these schools faced their stiffest headwinds to institutional survival. Rather than fold, these schools embraced their "value entrepreneurism"[1] roots and developed what can usefully be referred to as a *pioneer strategy*, adopting a heretofore unimaginable model for higher education that innovatively took "place" to populations of students previously excluded from the exclusive residential model.

Lansdale, Malvern, and Stoneham had overcome repeated threats of closure by turning to their spirit of innovation to fulfill their mission, and this time was no different. But unlike those schools that adopted the traditional strategy and invested in the heritage of place, these schools developed a model where higher education would meet students where they were. In a brief time, these schools transformed themselves from struggling residential campuses on the brink of closure to "flagship" institutions that steered a fleet of periphery locations whose surplus revenues sustained and grew the infrastructure of the core residential campus. "He had a vision to be a flagship university," a seasoned Lansdale professor said of its prior president, "and that really created a process that moved this place from thinking about themselves as a small place to a place that was going to compete on the national scene in every way."[2] Yet despite initially staving off closure, over time, the pioneer strategy began to undermine their relational values, and leaders found themselves in the same place they began, frantically in search of another "first-mover" opportunity that would provide new enrollments and new sources of revenues to sustain what had become complex multisite institutions.

Inspired to Evolve

Although each university community was distinct in its own right, Lansdale, Malvern, and Stoneham possessed similar environments composed of two persistent dispositions. First, the universities possessed a mission-oriented focus underscored by a *steadfast commitment to values*. More specifically, administration, faculty, and students were committed to fostering meaningful human relationships within and beyond the classroom that propelled the day-to-day functioning of the university and its mission. Second, university leaders maintained a state of *continuous organizational change* to escape the persistent threat of closure. For more than a century, Lansdale, Malvern, and Stoneham administrators repeatedly adapted the organizational form of the schools, from physically relocating their core residential campus or merging with a nearby institution to establishing affiliated high school programs to enroll additional students. Together, the two dispositions—the premium placed on relationships and reinventing organizational arrangements to ensure those relationships remained central—engendered an institutional environment centered on the trait of *value entrepreneurialism* whereby their core outlooks allowed for a spirit of innovation that paved the way for the implementation of the pioneer strategy.

The Malvern provost captured the essence of the disposition toward enduring values within a model of continuous change as he retold the school's historical trajectory. In conveying the two questions that plagued the present administration, he revealed the culture of a school with a steadfast commitment to values in the context of organizational change: "What's the next frontier? How does that fit into our mission?" Tellingly, he pivoted to the past to describe the kind of school that embraces these questions, conveying their perennial quality: an institution with "a fearless entrepreneurial spirit, where we don't just say, 'No.'" For these schools, the unpardonable sin would be to reject the entrepreneurial spirit and not try. Contrary to the senior administrator at Havertown in Chapter 1 who foreswore being an "aggressive entrepreneur," the Malvern provost heartily embraced the description, explaining that schools like his are "willing to experiment, do new things, to reach out to minister to students that are not being well-served by other modalities or deliveries." These two ideas conjoined to form a value entrepreneurialism that lay at the heart of the pioneer strategy.

The Importance of Connection

The cultural disposition of these universities is characterized by a commitment to meaningful human relationships, a value that permeated the historical record and the present-day in-person interviews. This deep-seated pledge to fostering relationships was often the primary characteristic members used to describe the university culture. "The best way I can describe the culture is community," explained one Stoneham senior leader, who then emphasized his point: "[It's a] family, you're-not-a-number-here, we-know-you, relationship." The Malvern University president expressed similar sentiments about its cultural emphasis on connecting: "I think in this culture that translates to an interest in care for relationships." In a similar vein, the most vital feature of working at Lansdale, according to an administrator, was understanding that "the culture is *very* relational."

Since their earliest years, Lansdale, Malvern, and Stoneham have been mission-oriented institutions that valued relationships. Not only did institutional leaders commonly reference the values in present-day university publications, but also, equally as important, they emphasized "the steadfast adherence to the founding vision through 100 years of growth" and how this enduring value was manifested across historical eras. At times, leaders grounded the value put on relationships in the founding of the institution: "What changed very little over these 120 years are Stoneham's mission and values." In other instances, they grounded the values in earlier historical eras, such as the nascent years of the specific religious denomination—the "monks and nuns" who "established a blueprint over 1,500 years ago for successful life and leadership in a challenging world." And sometimes it was just the principle of the thing: "We enrolled our first Black student when it was illegal in this state to have a Black student at a university," a Stoneham vice president shared. Values permeated these schools.

But regardless of its source, what truly matters to the cultures of these institutions is how the value placed on relationships endured over time. As if tracing a biblical lineage, leaders were keen to highlight the continuity of the relational values. For example, the Lansdale centennial volume stressed the importance of its relationship with a particular family: "Since the school's founding, the family has played a significant role in the institution's growth and development. Nearly 100 years later, a [family member] still sits on the Board of Trustees, offering business expertise, financial support, and wise counsel." The historical record describes the relational values the initial chairman of the board—who was also a member of this family—held: "He believed in personal contact with prospective students and alumni," whereby "his efforts, coupled with intense public relations campaigns, began to bear preliminary fruit [as] enrollments improved." At these schools, the relational values inherent in their mission yielded important implications for both the product (i.e., student experience) and the performance (i.e., student enrollment) of the institutions.

This commitment to relational values was a comprehensive feature of the universities, infusing not just the leadership but also faculty, staff, and students. "*Everything* is done by relationship at Lansdale," asserted one professor, while a Malvern vice president underscored that the most important aspect about the institution was that "relationships run deep." Faculty shouldered the responsibility of infusing the curriculum with the customary knowledge of their academic discipline as well as the communal values the universities publicized to prospective students. These were central, according to one Lansdale professor: "You have to have a heart for students. Without that, you don't last very long." Another colleague conveyed that "not caring about relationships is the death knell of a person working here." The commitment to meaningful relationships was a vital part of the extracurricular aspect of the universities as well. In describing the "warm rapport" she developed with students across multiple decades of service, one of the few remaining nuns at Stoneham emphasized that relationships are "not just in the college classroom." Even staff who held positions with minimal student contact referenced relationships. The chief financial officer of Landsdale who oversaw the bottom line repeatedly emphasized the school's commitment to students: "We are *big* on mentoring," he stressed.

The emphasis on relational values provided faculty and staff at these universities with a collective vision of an interpersonal culture that created meaning and purpose for the overall educational experience—as well as for those who produced it. Whether in the historical record or in executive interviews, leaders of the schools perennially referenced how the value placed on relationships was their institution's enduring raison d'être: "The element that endured with little change at all is our values . . . Stoneham's values were always present throughout our history." But perhaps the most obvious (yet unstated) reason why so much emphasis was placed on community remaining steadfast across generations of students and faculty was that another key aspect—their organizational form—was regularly transformed over that same history.

A Culture of Change

Universities rarely relocate. They are typically immobile institutions that remain physically situated in the same location for generations. When an institution does move, such a monumental undertaking is often made possible because of the involvement of exceedingly wealthy philanthropists, as was the case with the R. J. Reynolds heirs who financed the relocation of Wake Forest University.[3] Yet for every university that moved, there are a dozen that proudly declare that although they were tempted to pull up stakes at some point, they chose to stay put. In contrast to the value put on place at Boxborough and Havertown, the leaders of Lansdale, Malvern, and Stoneham seized opportunities to move and transform their institutions, repeatedly changing their organizational form to sustain the enduring value put on relationships for future generations of students.

Lansdale, Malvern, and Stoneham were all established near the turn of the 20th century in the disparate southern, western, and midwestern regions of the United States, but came of age during a trifecta of global and economic crises in the early 20th century—World War I, the 1918 influenza pandemic, and the Great Depression. These crises, in the words of a Lansdale historical volume, "brought problems ... to schools everywhere," whereby changes to organizations seemed commonplace, particularly among senior leadership. During these years, Lansdale cycled through 10 presidents, Stoneham rotated through 8, and Malvern endured 5 leadership overhauls.

In the uncertain environment, finances seemed tenuous and setbacks were commonplace. As one Lansdale historical volume recounted, adding to the frequent changes in administration during these years were "small enrollments usually running between 50–100 ... the buildings were described as 'decrepit' and in 'disrepair' ... [and] finances were critically low." Things took a turn for the worse at Stoneham when many of its buildings were destroyed by a fire. Truly telling was an incident at Malvern. Lacking the funds to build a much-needed gymnasium, the student body oversaw the fundraising and construction of the building themselves because they did not want to "be an imposition"—as if providing facilities was simply too much to expect from a school.

Responding to the scarce availability of financial resources, these institutions adapted their organizational forms, most notably their features and boundaries.[4] This was achieved through relocations, mergers, acquisitions, and, in some instances, establishing entirely new educational markets that provided the schools with greater numbers of tuition-paying students. When enrollments slipped precariously, these schools modified their "boundaries" by adding a preparatory school or military academy component. Lansdale established elementary and high school programs that functioned as "feeders" for the university, while Stoneham added a 2-year military academy for boys. During times of financial scarcity, it was also common for the boundaries between the university and its affiliated denominational organizations to become more porous. At Malvern, financial resources were shared between the university and the church, while Stoneham increasingly relied on shared labor resources between the school and the adjacent monastery and priory. The institutions also adapted "features" such as their physical location to improve enrollment options. Malvern relocated to a new campus vacated by a state college, while Lansdale moved five times in the first 4 decades of its existence.

The patterns of altering the organizational form continued for these schools well into the middle of the 20th century, which permitted Lansdale, Malvern, and Stoneham to locate the financial resources necessary to continue their value-focused mission. Malvern acquired one institution and briefly merged with another. Lansdale likewise acquired another college and successfully merged with a third to bring about a name change that remains to this day. These efforts highlight that the institutional culture was predisposed to organizational change as a method of pursuing vital resources—nowhere more evident than in name changes.[5] Taking Shakespeare's dictum from *Romeo and Juliet* to heart—"A rose by any other name would smell as sweet"—the institutions changed their names to reflect the adaptations in organizational form: Malvern experienced 4 name changes, Lansdale underwent 5, and Stoneham cycled through no fewer than 11 different names.

A Spirit of Innovation

Uniting the twin dispositions of a steadfast commitment to relational values and continuous organizational change was an underlying spirit of innovation that flowed through these schools. That spirit of innovation, seen clearly in the dedication to organizational change to preserve the mission, was also crucially informed by the schools' hardscrabble pasts. Yet the spirit of innovation transcended reduction to "necessity being the mother of invention." In attempting to explain how innovation was at the core of the Landsdale experience, a vice president drew an informative comparison between their school and Stanford University.

> I think they [Stanford] are a lot more resourced on all levels. And I'm not just talking about the billions in endowments and buildings... they get to draw the best minds of the world. And then they get to come up and incubate them. And they're set up like "the land of anything is possible."

The senior administrator then pivoted to the conditions that inform the meaning of innovation at Landsdale:

> I think the students and the faculty have that sense of higher calling also, to make a difference and have an impact like creating the common good, but they're not resourced in the same way in terms of the smartest and the richest. I think resourcing makes a huge difference because I think people are a product of their culture and their environment.

While resource disparities between the two schools were certainly notable, what was striking about the administrator's comparison were the differences in what innovation was for. The different values both schools embrace emerge clearly in Landsdale's approach to innovation, which is not Stanford's "innovation for the sake of innovation itself," but rather is intended to serve the critically important relational component manifested in "making a difference" and the "common good."

Nor was this attitude confined to Landsdale: the Malvern president was at pains to distinguish between championing innovation in a setting where "relationships are at the center of your culture" versus one where "the patterns of relationships are routinized and codified... based on structures, patterns, and policies and so forth." The relational emphases were a fundamental component of the trait of *value entrepreneurism* found at these schools, whereby leaders sought to establish innovative value-based approaches toward developing their "object of focus" or "product"—the students.[6]

Across these schools, leaders repeatedly described entrepreneurialism as a pervasive "spirit" or "culture" whose essence was a fundamental characteristic of these relational institutions. Stoneham was said to be "spinning in an entrepreneurial spirit," Malvern possessed a "fearless entrepreneurial spirit," and Landsdale (according to its president) was "chronically entrepreneurial." A Stoneham professor described the culture as one that "builds innovation ... builds the interest and intrigue for new ideas," while another at Malvern explained that over the years, innovative members of the community were honored and praised: "The culture has been one that has rewarded and encouraged people to think outside the box ... to see what might be on the horizon of higher education, and to figure that out ahead of other people."

Innovation was praised not as an end in itself, but for how it allowed the school to meet its entrepreneurial vision of fostering relationships: "The culture for us has always been innovation—to keep looking at where we need to be *and* how to serve our students," a Malvern professor dually emphasized. At Stoneham, priests were routinely charged with establishing relationships with community leaders in new regions as the foundation for opening up new enrollment opportunities. "I care about the growth and the future of the university. Because we are tuition driven, we need students who can come to Stoneham, and our university ministry worked in partnership with the school to open up new markets," one of its clergy explained. An encounter with a Lansdale vice president typifies this value entrepreneurism mentality. Her primary role within the university was to "create community synergy around ideas of innovation." She then explained what that meant: "creating internships and alumni networks" with the sole aim of "better serving the students." Leaning forward from behind her desk, she delivered her coup de grâce with a wry grin: "We *are* innovative. It's an *entrepreneurial* thing." Like the air she breathed, the spirit of innovation was practically tangible to the community at all three schools.

Unsurprisingly, the most important feature of the spirit of innovation for Lansdale, Malvern, and Stoneham was that it had remained embedded within the organizational culture across successive generations. One Malvern provost, speaking of the school's past, praised those who came before them for their "commitment to innovation, commitment to service, to creativity, a commitment to entrepreneurism," noting that those values have "persisted" and are "an important part of the culture." Another provost—this time at Lansdale—was similarly moved by how the school's history is not in the past, but lives on in the present:

> You hear all the stories from the past of an institution that struggled for its existence and so it had to constantly reinvent itself, went through a series of mergers over time, which is part of being creative to sustain itself over time ... it just shows innovation is one of those things that kind of outlives people because the people can change, but the openness to innovation remains.

At these schools, relational values and changing organizational forms repeatedly came together in novel ways to bring about new financial resources. Institutional leaders were accustomed to pursuing innovative rather than traditional forms of funding to sustain their people-centered mission, from selling vegetables to recruiting students from afar. It then comes as no surprise to hear a Malvern vice president champion that attitude as they looked ahead to innovating in the market to meet the next challenge:

> It has been the innovation and the flexibility and the willingness to change and adjust . . . we continue to retool and re-engineer. . . . We don't want to be market driven, but it is great when the marketplace and our mission come together.

Supporting the Mission

The latter decades of the 20th century presented Lansdale, Malvern, and Stoneham with new sustainability challenges as each approached their centennial on the heels of the golden age of higher education. In these years, the schools (like many tuition-driven institutions) were confronted with a retreating economy, aging facilities, and enrollment declines that placed them in a precarious financial situation—a situation the Malvern president described as "teetering on the edge of viability." The "birth dearth" that followed the post–World War II "baby boom" brought about a marked decline in the number of high school graduates, which catapulted competition in higher education as institutions jostled for students to maintain the federal loan revenue they possessed, brought about by market-informed education policies. As enrollments deteriorated, so did the revenues needed to maintain campus infrastructure. "Campus was run down . . . walls were yellow and dingy pipes were leaking. It was not a beautiful campus at all, and enrollment was a struggle," a Malvern vice president admitted, and they remembered thinking, "We may not even survive." A university almanac specified the severity of the situation at Lansdale:

> Declining enrollments came as a financial shock [and] rapidly rising interest rates provided another complication. . . . Little wonder that in 1979, the school ended the year with a deficit in the operating fund of [approximately $1 million], its first deficit in more than 15 years. The president reported a serious cash-flow problem. . . . All of these factors, plus a weak national economy, made a simple solution impossible.

Stoneham experienced a particularly acute enrollment strain. One long-serving senior administrator recalled, "We were literally dying. Campus enrollments had fallen below [1,000]. We weren't even being told anymore how many students we didn't have." One professor recalled the era with embarrassment, noting how a friend of the president described the campus as "a third world country. The buildings were in shambles, we'd lost so many students. It was just unbelievable, the sad state of affairs."

With many private and public institutions chasing the same traditional-aged students to meet residential enrollments, school leaders grappled to find resources. A senior Malvern leader recalled, "We were borrowing money to make payroll. It wasn't far from shutting down . . . the trajectory wasn't good." Stoneham leaders took an equally desperate tack, trying to scale back: "The mentality was to cut, cut, cut, cut, cut and just hunker down and wait for it to go away," one senior sister explained. "People were pretty much kind of waiting for the other shoe to drop."

These schools persisted through their lean early years by continually altering their organizational form, but they lacked the ability to pivot to a fundraising structure like the traditional schools developed to subsidize the costly residential core. The absence of a substantial endowment vexed senior administrators, who were unable to generate revenues to augment the large sums of money required to operate residential campuses. In the mid- to late 1980s, the total size of each endowment for these institutions ranged between only $3 million and $5 million.[7] Unsurprisingly, the annual revenue generated from endowment interest was paltry at best, necessitating that leaders focus their attention elsewhere to establish a resource solution.

Looking back on the era, a director explained that institutions like Lansdale had two options they could pursue: "One, you can go out and build your endowment and get more donors; or two, you can change the model of how you're doing things and actually create alternative pathways." The first option was a nonstarter, because these schools lacked a tradition of fundraising and deep-pocketed alumni. "Our alums are social workers, nurses, clergy, lots of bleeding-heart type people . . . people that aren't going to cut you big checks," a Lansdale vice president bemoaned. The thinking among leaders at these schools was that the survival of the organization hinged on strategic enrollment growth. A long-serving Malvern administrator recalled the attitude among its board members:

> We needed to grow, we needed to draw students, so let's build really nice dorms, let's offer a ton of programs and make this a really different place . . . something that no one else similar to us is offering . . . we have to grow or we are going to die!

For schools with limited financial means, acquiring resources through student enrollment growth was inevitable. As a result of educational policies aligning with market logic philosophies, the belief that growth was essential for colleges and universities became a widely held view. At a minimum, enrollments had to be maintained year after year if an institution was to remain viable, but growth was essential if a school wanted to stop scraping by. The pervasive mindset that developed during this era was neatly summed up by one of the nuns at Stoneham: "Growth and increase in [the] student body are absolutely paramount, [because] you have to have money to do stuff." Nor was this need covertly expressed; the Stoneham president once told the group of nuns, "You see all this nice stuff here? It takes money to build it, to make it, to create it, and in order to have the money you have to have the students." The sister calmly concluded, "That was his way of telling us indirectly, 'Don't get so freaked out about academic standards because we need the bodies in the chairs.'" But rather than complain about the reductionist mindset that turned students into dollar signs, the nun backed the analysis put forth by school leadership: "I do understand where the president is coming from. You've got to have the money!"

Many institutions of higher education focused on enrollment solutions to generate additional tuition revenues in the final quarter of the 20th century. The Stoneham provost explained that for most, the options were constrained to "grow the student body or increase the tuition—or do both." These two enrollment solutions became so widespread among colleges and universities that they even became the prevailing approach adopted by leaders at public institutions.[8]

However, an emphasis on enrollment growth came with a latent challenge that policy makers appear not to have considered. The Stoneham provost explained that expanding residential enrollment came with a serious dilemma: "Of course you grow more students, but then we've got to have [more] faculty teach them. We have to have buildings to teach them in. They cost money, right? More overhead." The provost laughed at what was seemingly obvious: "And it's not just simple *arithmetic* growth; it is *geometric* growth [we need]." The difference between the "arithmetic" growth laden with fixed costs and the more profitable "geometric" growth was in the varying surplus revenues, or profit, between the two. While revenues increased with enrollment growth, at certain intervals the revenues decreased when leaders added fixed costs by hiring faculty or building facilities. The residential core remains an expensive model to deliver because the expectations associated with it require costly buildings and facilities on a physical campus to provide in-person educational experiences. Residential enrollment growth is rarely profitable because of the high arithmetic costs associated with it.

With many public and private colleges alike increasing their growth and raising tuition to secure financial resources, locating surplus revenues became an opportunistic focal point for leaders like the Stoneham vice president, who viewed a college or university as an educational business, one that operated with both purpose and profit:

> If you don't keep the appropriate business focus, you'll not be around to do the educational piece. It's not that it is any less of an institution because of that. There's a lot of emphasis put on educational quality, but ultimately if you don't look at it in a sense of profit and loss, if you don't have enough profit, you're ... going out of business.

Because of their history of embracing the trait of value entrepreneurism, the leaders of the schools felt no conflict in being passionate educators devoted to their missions yet clearly innovating ways to bolster the bottom line. They made no bones about understanding that their universities required money to sustain their missions. The challenge was rather in figuring out how to grow. They quickly realized that not just any enrollment growth would do: that only the elusive geometric enrollment would work in the end.

"There is no getting blood from a turnip" is a centuries-old adage that describes the futile effort in trying to get money from sources that simply have none. Yet, as it turns out, squeezing surplus revenues from tuition is not impossible: you just need to convince enough people to enroll and sign on the dotted line for a student loan.

Sidebar: Margin Capitalization

Although many colleges and universities began to expand their residential enrollments in the latter part of the 20th century to secure funding resources, the pursuit of financial margins predominantly remained an uncharted fiscal frontier. Thus, when the leaders of these schools encountered a crisis of survival during these same years, consistent with the value entrepreneurism they espoused, they ventured into the financial hinterland in search of the one remaining resource opportunity unclaimed by other institutions—margins.

Margin refers to the monetary surplus that an organization produces on its product. It is the financial profit that remains once all the costs to produce a good or service have been paid. Some industries, like tax preparation, and products such as children's toys are understood as *high margin*, with yields of between 20% and 40%, whereas grocery stores are understood as *low margin* and yield only 2%–3%.[9] Higher education, with its traditional emphasis on delivering education via the residential core, has historically been a low- or no-margin industry. And yet behind closed doors, in offices and boardrooms, university administrators are just as concerned with the financial margins of the institution as the leadership of any other business.

The pursuit of financial margins in charitable sectors like healthcare and adoption services has been traditionally scorned. Although margins can be found throughout the field of higher education in all types of institutions, they are commonly explained as the differentiating factor between the for-profit and nonprofit sectors. Nonprofit colleges and universities have been characterized broadly as mission-focused institutions that eschew margins in favor of providing an affordable service for "the public good."[10] In contrast, for-profit institutions have been characterized by their predatory admissions practices and pursuit of maximizing margins.[11] Neoliberal policies that provide the opportunity for many for-profit institutions to use federal financial aid to maximize their margins were viewed as anathema by nonprofit institutions—that is, until recently. As it turns out, market-oriented education policies provided similar opportunities for both sides of the higher education coin and have slowly shaped behavior across all institutions of higher education. The earlier dichotomies that created a chasm between institutional types no longer accurately capture the social world neoliberalism produces.

The financial surpluses nonprofit organizations generate through margins cannot be paid to persons, like they can be paid to the shareholders or executives of for-profit organizations. At the same time, federal policies limit how nonprofit institutions spend surplus revenues. In the words of one senior administrator at Lansdale, at the fore of leaders' minds was how to "stay disciplined on our strategy of delivering bottom-line profit without just spending the money." When a nonprofit does yield a financial surplus, it must "reinvest" the money in the company in one of two capacities—subsidizing the operating costs to offset the losses or investing in tangible (i.e., buildings) or intangible (i.e., endowment) assets. Looking across the newly erected buildings of the transformed Malvern campus, its vice president acknowledged how leaders generated financial margins from student tuition and where they reinvested the surplus:

> We didn't borrow money to get where we are. We used the growth, and we turned that money that we were making off of our adult program, which was a tremendous amount, and reinvested it in our programs . . . and hard assets.

Higher education has been traditionally characterized as not only low margin, but also asset heavy. It is customary for institutions to own substantial amounts of capital assets, including land, buildings, laboratories, computers, libraries, machinery, and vehicles. Physical assets like athletic complexes, residence halls, and dining facilities are vital enrollment components for institutions during the admissions process.[12] A Malvern official explained how the architecture and uniform aesthetic across their capital assets were necessary to "attract" prospective students:

> We realized that the campus at that time was so old and beginning to run down that we had to come along and [build]. You hate to have buildings be an attraction. But it does become an attraction for this generation that we're working with. . . . Architecture tells people, "Are you up-to-date or are you still living in the past?" Buildings become a real key, it gives you kind of the theme of what you believe in . . . that we really are starting to seek the future: "This is who we are as a university, this is the priority of who we are."

And yet physical assets posed a challenge for places like Lansdale, Malvern, and Stoneham. Like their traditional strategy counterparts, the schools that would adopt the pioneer strategy needed modern facilities to attract students, but these institutions lacked the extensive fundraising resources the traditional schools leveraged to achieve their multimillion-dollar campus transformations.

In business, the process or action of funding capital assets of an organization to ensure its successful continuance is known as *capitalization*.[13] To achieve this, an organization often turns to entities that are willing to finance or invest in its mission. Many organizations turn to banks to secure the credit necessary to pay for start-up or production costs, or they pursue investors who "buy in" to the firm with venture capital or private equity funding, holding shares of its stock in return. When the six entrepreneurially oriented schools discussed in this and the next two chapters were confronted with closure and urgently needed to fund their capitalization efforts, they did not primarily turn to banks that held credit or investors who held shares. Instead, they innovated, developing entrepreneurial strategies involving *margin capitalization* that relied on students with federal financial aid.

Margin capitalization—a term coined to explain the monetary patterns these schools engaged in—is the process of generating a financial surplus in a periphery market that is then used to fund the infrastructure of the core. To achieve this, leaders of the pioneer, network, and accelerated schools developed periphery enrollment markets for groups of students who previously did not have access to educational opportunities provided through the core residential model. By expanding educational opportunities beyond the residential core for adult, military, distance, international, online, vocational, and other marginalized students, leaders in turn expanded their institution's opportunities to secure funding through federal financial aid.

Periphery enrollment markets provided these institutions with new students and therefore new money. Yet educational opportunities for students in the periphery enrollment markets looked considerably different than those for students in the residential core. These previously untapped student pools attended classes in hotel conference centers, shopping malls, high schools, churches, military bases, regional centers, and eventually online. These periphery options lacked (from one point of view) or did not require (from another) the expensive capital assets associated with the residential campus, therefore presenting the institutions with the opportunity to generate a financial surplus: "We have tied [our periphery] to a third of the cost of a residential Lansdale experience," its president highlighted. With the realization of a newfound convert, one of the deans at Stoneham emphasized how critical the peripheral-market students became to the financial health of the institution: "The president pointed it out numerous times until we finally realized that it was true," she exclaimed, "that the *real* place where we were making money was *out there*." The key point of departure for pioneer schools from their traditional brethren was in abandoning enrollment growth in the residential core as the route toward revenue generation. While the residential core was needed for legitimacy (in particular, its physical infrastructure), these schools were pioneers in discovering how to leverage margin capitalization to find the necessary revenues to survive and even (for a season) to thrive.

The six entrepreneurial schools in the remainder of this book implemented strategies of margin capitalization and provided new modes of education to students beyond their residential core. As a result, pioneer, network, and accelerated schools experienced dramatic growth in their periphery markets. As the trailblazers in this group, the pioneer schools did not foresee the dramatic enrollment increases on the horizon. A Malvern leader recalled in a tone of awe,

> It really unfolded faster and larger than anyone could have ever predicted.... The board or the president could have never planned what happened. It was double-digit growth for years, every year. They just never could have predicted that.

As a result of their explosive growth, for the schools that implemented the margin capitalization strategies, the periphery enrollment markets became their financial engine. But the pioneer schools were also aware of a fundamental difference in the operation of peripheral markets. While they were willing to share their institutional cachet with programs in the margins, they were keen to keep the periphery as its own organizational entity that would grow on its own terms—albeit one that could be used to feed the core that produced the cachet needed to attract students to peripheral markets in the first place. As a vice president perceptively articulated, Malvern's president "created a structure that it could operate as its own ecosystem. It generated revenue, it could reinvest, it brought money back onto this campus, which we could continue to grow and benefit from, but [also one] that was transformational toward growth."

Instead of tapping nonexistent endowments or taking out loans, the marginal revenues generated by periphery enrollment markets were used to fund the capitalization efforts of the pioneer schools, essentially financing construction their residential campuses needed to remain competitive. "We quickly got out of debt early on in the late '80s, then started using that money to reinvest, to start transforming this campus into something pretty special," a Malvern vice president explained. "People were excited because there was a new building going up literally every year." Gesturing to two herculean cranes outside his office window, a Stoneham finance official explained how university leaders relied on the efficiency of the margin capitalization approach to strategically fund construction projects:

> You notice a new building going up over there? . . . Most of it is being funded by internally generated cash. You lay out the strategic plan, here's what we would like to do over the next 5 years, and here's how we are going to afford it. . . . The numbers are good, we have the enrollments, we've got the cash. Start!

In its race for survival, Lansdale similarly used its initial money from the periphery to build a state-of-the-art event center and athletic complex that one faculty member asserted "put them in a different class" because "building was definitely a big deal." He reaffirmed that the efforts were simply a necessity given the many competing institutions throughout the metropolitan area.

The margin capitalization approach using federal student aid provided the pioneer schools with hundreds of millions of dollars to fund their campus transformations. For schools like Malvern, the innovation that margin capitalization represented became "part of their DNA" for a generation. "We have invested probably $300 or $400 million over the last 30 years," a seasoned administrator recalled. Malvern's president could not emphasize enough just how instrumental the financial approach was to moving them off organizational life support, describing margin capitalization as "a lifeline." But it was how they spent the money that set pioneer institutions apart from their peers:

> The old president . . . said to the board, "You have to make a rule that we cannot use the excess revenue produced by the adult [education] programs to operate the campus. The only thing you can allow us to do with that excess revenue is to do capital improvements, investment in the buildings, renovations and that sort of thing."

Malvern's president explained that other institutions used tuition margins from periphery programs to fund the operating expenses in the residential core rather than solely capitalize on their physical infrastructure. "Most presidents start those [periphery] programs to get money to operate the campus—to prop it up. The old Malvern president saw that if you did that, you would only cripple the campus. The fundamental systemic problems of the campus had to get fixed on their own for it to be healthy long term." The president hailed the decision-making of his predecessor, applauding that "it was absolutely a genius decision because it set in motion the process whereby the campus organically could begin to be better."

As was the case for traditional schools, the strategy pioneer schools adopted was the logical outcome of their deep commitment to innovatively pursuing their relational values through value entrepreneurism. At the same time, just as they were unprepared for the influx of enrollees on the peripheries, the pioneer strategy also meant they were unprepared for how their strategy would impact their commitment to relational values—the very thing that made the school attractive to students in peripheral markets in the first place.

Pursuing the Pioneer Strategy

Confronted with closure but resolved to persist, the leaders of the three institutions—Lansdale, Malvern, and Stoneham—employed the pioneer strategy, an approach that relied on early opportunities as first movers in new enrollment markets to build a fleet of periphery locations that generated financial surpluses (i.e., margins), which they used to subsidize the core residential campus. At the core of the pioneer strategy was a persistent spirit of innovation that emboldened leaders to reject the taken-for-granted assumption that going to college historically focused on young adults aged

18–23 who moved to experience the benefits of place on a residential campus. Holding fast to their value entrepreneurism, pioneer leaders jettisoned this widespread assumption and took place to marginalized populations of students previously excluded from the exclusive residential model. They did not seek to replicate the status of the aspiring Ivies or even religious schools like the University of Notre Dame, which had become in the eyes of some "a Catholic Yale," as a Stoneham professor offered. "The president's vision for this place is what Notre Dame *used* to be—the great hope of the Catholic working-class." This meant establishing an array of satellite locations in "education deserts" near the students themselves to allow for in-person learning in unconventional classrooms that included shopping malls, high schools, hotel conference rooms, and military bases. "We follow where the students are," the Malvern president succinctly stated. Despite pioneer schools having expanded educational opportunities to marginalized communities, established institutions of higher education scorned their approach and berated the pioneer schools as illegitimate "degree mills" (Figure 2).

The decision to adopt the pioneer strategy and overcome the social stigma inherent with innovation was driven by the likelihood of closure and the availability of tuition as a financial resource. But the multisite organizational form that Lansdale, Malvern, and Stoneham developed required a new

Figure 2   The Pioneer Strategy for Sustaining the Core

level of understanding to maintain a value-entrepreneurial emphasis across multiple locations. Operating as a supportive fleet to the flagship, these programs were innovative not just in bringing place to students, but also in how they transformed the perception of these universities into widely admired private versions of public flagship institutions (i.e., the premier public school in a state).[14] That language permeated discussions at the schools, with a Malvern academic official proclaiming, "Our school is the flagship school for the whole denomination. People look to us to see how we do things." The Lansdale transformation was characterized similarly. "Lansdale is the largest in the [professional association], the proverbial flagship of about 150 institutions," one professor proclaimed. Stoneham administrators repeatedly boasted they had been hailed as "the model of the university for the 21st century."

Enrollment growth at the various outposts initially came with ease as the periphery fleet of regional locations yielded generous marginal revenues and ironically became the financial "epicenter." Without mincing words, one Malvern professor simply referred to their periphery as "the gravy train bringing in good revenue." Even the nuns at Stoneham believed the innovation of the pioneer strategy would sustain them into the future: "People are looking at the way this place is structured and how people go about things here, and they said, 'This is it! *This* is how a school will be able to survive.' You cannot just count on the 18- to 23-year-olds anymore [or] you will go out of business," proclaimed a sister. Little did she know that although university leaders had innovatively taken place to new student populations, the novel approach created "space" between the many campuses that challenged leaders to foster their relational values across distances in new ways at the periphery. As events would bear out, faith alone would not be sufficient to withstand the oncoming market competition.

Opportunities to Reconceive Place

For centuries, elite institutions like Harvard, Princeton, Yale, and other Ivies shaped the traditional understanding of what it means to participate in higher education—that a group of young adults "goes away" to a particular place (a residential campus). This societal understanding of what it means to go away to college has informed how institutions look and the best practice norms by which they operate. But as greater numbers of jobs required a college degree in the latter decades of the 20th century, it became increasingly important for individuals of all ages, not just traditional-aged college students, to obtain a degree—a phenomenon known as *credentialism*.[15] With the educational needs of the national adult population escalating, the financially strapped pioneer institutions found themselves presented with a series of unexpected opportunities. The Stoneham provost clarified,

> It was purely coincidental that we were invited to go to the military bases . . . they wanted to expand and go into different areas . . . they had tried to reach out to the state school, [who] didn't have time for that! So, we went, and from there word got out.

A senior leader at Landsdale openly admitted their approach was "more opportunistic": "An idea comes along, and we don't necessarily do all the research and all the planning—we just kind of jump."

The broad outlines of how these opportunities emerged were largely the same. Notable gaps in educational access existed in the states where the pioneer schools resided because elite and traditional institutions had yet to deviate from the core residential model. Additionally, their state legislatures historically allocated most financial resources for education to public research universities and had yet to establish alternative educational pathways in the form of a community college system. According to leaders, these two factors created education deserts, or geographic regions that lacked proper in-person higher education support for local communities.[16] As a result, the leaders of Lansdale, Malvern, and Stoneham were approached by various agencies—the military, primary/secondary school systems, vocational centers, and social services—whose employees required training and credentialing that were not available through elite and research institutions. For example, when the U.S. Department of Defense sought to establish formal educational avenues for its servicepersons, Stoneham was among a handful of institutions the agency contacted. "It started with Hansboro Air Force Base down in Erwin," a Stoneham senior administrator recalled. "[They] invited a number of colleges in the area to come and teach classes to their military personnel." A Lansdale historical almanac explained that school systems and social service agencies throughout the region needed additional educational credentials for teachers and family programming professionals. Meanwhile, Malvern was approached by an institute that "developed adult education for firemen and policemen," the president explained. "And it was the institute that came to Malvern and said, 'We're looking for a partner; would you be interested?'" The leaders of the pioneer schools emphasized that these unexpected opportunities were enticing—but they came with a catch.

Agencies that approached Lansdale, Malvern, and Stoneham conveyed that these educational services were needed by people who were not traditional young adults able to go away to a residential college. Instead, the agencies asked the pioneer schools to seize an opportunity to make higher education available to persons who were unable to come to college in the traditional sense because they were restricted to their own place as a result of professional and/or personal responsibilities. They were enmeshed in their families and communities and not able to pull up stakes and make the traditional move to a residential setting. Thus, if education was to happen for these populations, it was not the prospective students who were going to have to move; rather, the universities had to figure out how to relocate and reconceive place. Of course, innovating through moving was something the pioneer schools had been accustomed to since their founding.

To seize the opportunities, the leaders of Lansdale, Malvern, and Stoneham tapped into their value-entrepreneurial cultures of innovation and developed unconventional methods of delivering in-person education in new places. Initially, each pioneer school emphasized a different place based on the contextual needs of the student population. "The conference room. That is the model we started with," explained a Malvern professor, who was preparing to teach her in-person class in a hotel that evening. "I am teaching it in a Comfort Suites. . . . The students are from the Artas area. . . . I'll leave today at 3:30. Drive to Artas, teach from 6 to 10 p.m., and drive back." Landsdale's "opportunistic" outlook and its "strong commitment to new ideas and new approaches" meant that its administration seized on the opportunity to offer in-person academic programs in unorthodox settings like shopping malls and high schools. Stoneham opted to reconceive the military base as a place of learning. One senior administrator recalled the informal details of early efforts to establish the in-person program:

> They [the Department of Defense] wanted us to open a center. We put up shingles, set up shop, and just waited for them to come through the door and signed them up for classes. And if they wanted to major in whatever, we'd say, "Okay, sure!"

He noted the early efforts were rudimentary. "We sent someone to go up there and he recruited students and sold books out of the trunk of his car and established a presence." Yet despite these unconventional settings, the money was good ("It was a good gig, a steady source of income," the provost imparted), and all three schools soon found themselves in the midst of a growth boom the likes of which they had never experienced—a boom so bewitching that the lessons history teaches about what follows such a boom were somehow forgotten.

Managing the Multisite Form

Seemingly overnight, Lansdale, Malvern, and Stoneham transformed from small liberal arts colleges in a single location to a fleet of "periphery" sites that supported the flagship residential campus. The many satellite locations for each college provided students with in-person learning opportunities across an expansive geographic region, some within a single state and others across multiple adjoining states. Successfully managing the new multisite organizational form required leaders to focus on two enrollment fronts: "building" new locations within the periphery fleet while physically transforming the core residential campus to competitively maintain in-person enrollment at "the anchor of the university" (in the words of a Malvern senior leader). The historical mergers and relocations previously required these universities to continually innovate their organizational form, and the new multisite form necessitated the same to ensure its viability and legitimacy.

Leaders set to work implementing their new periphery model into a supportive constellation of locations, with the periphery soon outpacing the core in enrollment: "You know, the bricks and mortar at this campus, what you see here is the smallest portion of the university," a senior Stoneham leader pointed out. The historical record at Lansdale highlights the "surprising growth" that occurred, with satellite campus enrollment equaling residential enrollment 2 years after inception. Stoneham's provost said their enrollment explosion was a result of their military ties:

> We were approached by the Educational Service Officer from Whiting Air Force Base ... and from there we were invited to another air force base ... word got out, so then the army started inviting us ... and then the navy started inviting us.

At Stoneham, a senior academic official noted admissions personnel just had to wait. "They've not had to recruit, they've not had to market. They simply wait for the educational service officer to send the [military] student to their door and they sign them up." To develop its periphery locations, Malvern simultaneously leveraged the recruiting capacity of the institute for police and firepersons while tapping the physical assets of one of its board members who ran a chain of hotels. The university expanded to "sixty-some locations in the state," a professor proclaimed. "We didn't have to pay for buildings, we just rented conference space in hotels." By reducing the costs at their periphery sites, pioneer university leaders generated notable margins from each student they enrolled and found themselves with a financial surplus.

Tuition margins soon became the financial engine of the pioneer schools. In the absence of a robust endowment, senior leaders relied on the revenues at the periphery as the one viable funding source to sustain the organization. As a member of the president's inner core at Stoneham bluntly shared, "We were using them as a cash cow. I don't know how many people are going to admit that. But that's what we were doing." The peripheral expansion at Malvern was equally dramatic: "I think we approached 20% growth in one year [and] 8%–15% growth during our biggest years," its senior-most leader explained. The enrollment growth provided Malvern with an intense interval where finances seemed unlimited; one cabinet official exulted about the "8-year period where there was no shortage of money." At Lansdale, one of its senior leaders recalled the boom-era mentality that began to pervade the school: "Very, very, heavy, really, really steep growth. And that became kind of the norm."

But rather than use the margins from the periphery to grow the periphery further—which admittedly did not need much in the way of investment in infrastructure or recruiting—leaders focused on a second enrollment frontier in developing the new multisite form: a flagship at the center of the fleet. Although the pioneer schools lacked the vast fundraising structure of traditional schools, they still had to compete with them (and with other institutions) for the limited supply of residential students.

The marginal revenue generated from the periphery provided the leaders with financial resources to transform the grounds of the core residential campus to recruit this in-person population. A Malvern senior leader candidly admitted as much as he motioned toward the new construction dotting the campus: "Every building you see was built debt-free, most of that on revenue over expense from the adult education program." One Stoneham senior administrator with oversight over the periphery specified with numerical certainty how reassignment of their revenues was a vital component of the financial model: "Most of my time was focused on *mining* a $56 million cash cow," he noted, with the administration saying, "Just send us the check," because his program was "the stepchild" of the residential core. Malvern leaders also adopted a margin capitalization approach whereby they used surplus tuition margins from the periphery to overhaul the physical assets of the core. A Malvern senior administrator summed up the philosophy pithily: "We build buildings with adult money here."

To attract residential students, leaders prioritized the construction of essential supplementary facilities (i.e., residence halls, student unions, and athletic complexes) viewed as critical for recruitment, and only then shifted to academic facilities. In emphasizing residence halls (and even the outright purchase and conversion of nearby buildings) to meet the needs of enrollment growth that even the core was experiencing, a vice president contrasted Landsdale's approach with the endowment focus of the traditional strategy:

> Most schools have had time to grow their endowment, and out of that, they have had time to build an infrastructure and housing.... But we cannot. We're like, "We have 700 students coming, so we need to buy this housing [complex] across the street."

The order in which buildings were erected at Stoneham during the construction streak was determined by the president and left no illusions as to what his priorities were. As one senior leader observed,

> He grew the campus, but it took until this year [year 17 of his presidency] to build a new academic building.... Before that we had no new classrooms. So where are we going to put these people to teach? To take classes? We can build the residence halls and house them there, but what are they going to do during the day? ... We finally got him convinced we had to build another classroom building!

By then, the marginal tuition revenues from the periphery had fully funded a dozen new residential campus structures. A vice president approvingly quipped, "We've got it here, the glitz and the glam of the residence halls and *all* that."

However, the margin capitalization approach was not without its critics—most notably faculty in (and therefore on) the periphery. One Malvern professor who taught at the hotel locations recounted an administrative confrontation regarding the specific uses of the tuition margins. "We asked the question, 'What's going to happen to the excess?' Because we were $20 million above and the residential side was $3 million under." After being told by the chief financial officer that the excess would be applied to the core, the professor cynically remarked, "We're working so you can build more dorms."

Maintaining the new multisite form required a level of organizational innovation by the pioneer schools that was similar to what they had previously shown during their multiple mergers, acquisitions, and relocations. The administrative operations were truly intricate, as one academic dean explained:

> Take a person who has been at a regular university, one that just has the residential campus with no adult, no [periphery]. For that person it's like learning how to fly a Cessna 150. Then you come to Malvern, and it's like getting into the cockpit of a 747 . . . all these gauges and knobs and all these things have to be adjusted and tuned, and this thing has to fly.

But this two-front approach proved difficult to keep aloft, and leadership began to notice cracks in the airframe of the multiplace model. As a Stoneham vice president remarked, "We were crying in the wilderness, saying, 'We're running surpluses, stash that money aside,' but they kept building things and they kept adding programs, and we're like, 'This isn't going to last!'"

The First Movers

Inspired by their value-entrepreneurial roots, Lansdale, Malvern, and Stoneham were early adopters of innovative approaches to educational delivery whereby learning occurred not only on a traditional residential campus, but also in such nontraditional venues as hotel conference rooms, military bases, and shopping malls. Pioneer leader narratives were replete with self-described terms like "early adopter," "first mover," and "early engager." In a value-entrepreneurial approach, new markets provide an opportunity not only for expanded revenues, but also for new relationships that yield opportunities to expand their values. It is a proselytizing entrepreneurship of sorts that seeks new frontiers in the people it reaches for both purpose and profit. These innovative notions were important components of their institutional identity: "We're an entrepreneurial place. We looked early on in terms of nontraditional programs like adult ed," the Lansdale president asserted. A faculty member at Malvern underscored this point: "We were the first movers, or to use some of the business terminology, we were the ones that had a niche market because nobody else was doing it," while a Stoneham vice president echoed, "They saw the opportunity [and] decided to jump on it before a lot of other schools did."

First mover is a key management term that describes the timing of an organization's entry into a specific market.[17] In this instance, first mover refers to the entry of the pioneer schools into nontraditional student enrollment markets, providing the institutions with a competitive leg up that allowed them to establish a known brand and gain privileged financial resources with ease. "We were flying under the radar for sure," touted one Stoneham dean. In the case of the pioneer schools, the early-adopter status provided them with a competitive recruitment advantage in enrolling nontraditional adult, working, and military students, which resulted in significant enrollment growth and expansion of their satellite campuses.

But being a first mover does not ensure that an organization will maintain its privileged advantage as the market evolves and competition intensifies. Once ahead, first movers must work to remain ahead of entering competition. The early lead of the first-mover advantage can be swiftly curtailed if there are considerable incentives for other organizations to enter the same market space—such as the market-oriented "per-student" federal education policies that award funding to institutions based on student enrollment. Such neoliberal funding mechanisms meant that to find a new enrollment market was to dig up a pot of gold—so long as you found it faster than your neighbor who was shoveling next to you and could hold onto it once unearthed.

By choosing to reconceive place and develop a fleet of periphery locations for previously marginalized groups of students, the pioneer schools became subject to an intense social stigma associated with deviating from traditional enrollment norms and best practices asserted by elite institutions. Legitimacy is a powerful force in American higher education, one whose standards are maintained by isomorphism: the idea that, over time, organizations begin to look the same to become more legitimate.[18] Guarded and maintained by elites, within higher education the isomorphism of a residential core proves one is legitimate, whereas innovation on the periphery raises questions.

While first-mover status provided pioneer schools with opportunities for quick growth, it left them with tensions because they did not look institutionally normal. "We were early engagers of adult learners, even when the rigor and legitimacy of that was questioned in the academy," explained one Malvern leader. The Lansdale president suggested that the criticism that pioneer schools were only interested in the bottom line was near-constant: "There will always be people who say we chased growth." Some elites took their criticisms further and chastised the schools for eroding the quality of higher education more broadly. "Everybody was basically calling us a degree mill and all different kinds of names about what we were doing to higher education," mentioned a Malvern faculty member. The ostracism administrators were subject to was intense. Thirty years after these events had transpired, I watched the Malvern president grimace as he thought back to when his predecessor launched the innovative "hotel classrooms" idea:

> He paid a huge personal price . . . for defending and protecting the adult programs at a time when that was so strange and new that everybody didn't think it was

legitimate. And because it was growing, he would never go to professional meetings... because he got hammered.... Presidents would say, "What are you doing in my community? Why are you here? Are you trying to put me out of business?"

Like the marginalized populations of students they strived to serve, pioneer institutions and their leaders became marginalized actors within the higher education milieu.

With such profound levels of social stigma associated with pursuing innovative educational delivery methods, it seems unimaginable that a school leader would deliberately guide an institution into a perennial state of being publicly ostracized. At the same time, pioneer leaders were confronted with an even worse scenario—the real likelihood of closure. "Either you adapt or die off," a Lansdale vice president stated while pantomiming a guillotine motion. In the face of leading either a stigmatized or a shuttered institution, leaders opted for the former. A faculty member recounted the life-saving role of the periphery in the near-death era for Stoneham: "The Board of Trustees were ready to close this university." What saved the school was "all the initiatives that he [the president] started... the satellite campuses and all." Her colleague recollected how the severity of the situation created the conditions where the stigma was more easily sloughed off by faculty:

> They've been here through everything: when there was no money, when they didn't know if they were going to get paid, and they thought the institution was going to close each semester. I think what a lot of people don't recognize is that a lot of the culture that we see here comes from a place where so many people have been here for so many years through all of that turbulence.

For the pioneer schools, the weight of financial uncertainty eclipsed concerns about social stigma that came with the innovative pursuit of resources needed to save its existence. A senior administrator recalled for Malvern what it was like being taken to the edge of the resource cliff only to discover a bridge across the chasm: "A small struggling school . . . getting to that edge, that precipice where maybe the school goes away—and then it went through this renaissance!" As another leader clarified, the "renaissance" came because the school's DNA was such that it embraced the stigma associated with innovation and change: "A lot of institutions cannot do that . . . for some of them it's so painful that they would just as soon die than really change." Yet while pioneer schools might be willing to bring education to new venues, it remained an open question whether their values could be transferred to such spaces.

Mission-Centered Growth

The impetus of their value entrepreneurialism—the innovative pursuit to develop a periphery enrollment market—was an opportunity to save the values of the institution by saving the school itself. Key to understanding that rescue is recognizing the role relational values played in propelling and governing growth in the transition from a singular campus to a multisite organizational form—the fleet that kept the flagship afloat. On the one hand, the mission of the pioneer schools motivated the enrollment growth. Values were leveraged to attract students, as one senior leader at Stoneham explained:

> Every single course has a core value embedded in it . . . and when you talk to our students, they will say that that's one of the reasons they selected us, you know, the fact that we're a mission-driven institution.

The values also propelled the development of entire models of educational delivery, such as this description by a Malvern senior finance official:

> That decision to start adult education was mission driven; it wasn't money driven . . . when they started it, I don't think anybody knew how profitable it would or would not be. . . . I see the things that we are going after. What we're going to make off them is not what drives it. The mission has really driven it.

The role values played in developing the peripheral models of education was a recurring theme across all schools.

On the other hand, the university values governed—and therefore limited—enrollment growth of the schools. The Malvern president made this explicitly clear, "If we don't do something as an expression of our mission, then we really shouldn't be doing it . . . even if it causes us to have to limit our growth." Leaders across the three universities described their approach using terms that conveyed a sense of intentional limitation, like "managed growth," "measured growth," "managed affordability," "steady growth," "controlled growth," "useful growth process," and "smart growth process." As one senior Lansdale administrator conveyed, the values were the guiding ethical frames of the university community.

> I describe Lansdale as a mosaic . . . you've got lots of beautiful parts of this puzzle, but there's a frame around it, and the frame is kind of like what our university values are . . . and these are the things that are important in this community.

University leaders understood that navigating the competing tensions between the desire to expand enrollments and the frame of their value system necessitated a negotiation between the two components of their value entrepreneurism. The Stoneham vice president framed matters this way:

> What I need now are business-minded educators. I still need them to be the advisors and the mentors for students, I still need them to continue to educate students, but they've got to do that with an understanding of the business and what we need to do. And the business does not mean that we cut corners; the business means that we focus on the recruitment, enrollment, and retention of students, because each of those students will help us to continue to bring in more institutional money to continue to grow.

Such a mentality was aimed at preventing the worst fear of university leaders. They repeatedly conveyed concern that their institution might be broadly perceived as a factory that emphasized academic mass production. "The threat is this pressure to grow, grow, grow, grow . . . to become a diploma mill where students have gotten a Lansdale education, but it means almost nothing," a senior administrator mentioned. Pioneer leaders learned that if left uncontrolled, growth challenged the institutional values. "When we grew quickly, we had a hard time accommodating that growth and having the quality and the ethos that we wanted," the Malvern president noted in describing the one year the school experienced a 20% growth rate.

As enrollments and periphery locations expanded, pioneer leaders found themselves challenged to foster the communal and relational values in faculty and staff across their many periphery locations. To address the challenge, administrators not only governed growth, but also implemented practices and processes to specify the content of their relational values, which took the form of crafting a mission statement and core values. Interviews were replete with phrases emphasizing that the schools were "mission driven" and dedicated to their "six core values," "three core principles," or "four cornerstones."[19]

University leaders generated involvement and buy-in by articulating and promulgating these values across the university community and its multiple locations. At Lansdale, the president said of his predecessor, "The president comes in . . . and the first thing he does is he pulls the faculty in and staff and board committee," seeking input from all constituencies in crafting the mission. As one cabinet official recollected, the Stoneham president similarly established a university-wide group to unify the campuses: "There was a representative group of people from all parts of the university who worked on this. Now we have got our student-centered mission, our values, and then to have the vision." The process at Malvern was similarly intended to "reaffirm identity, vision, and purpose," explained an administrator. The approach was a "collaborative effort of pulling the gifts and talents [to] help support the vision and the mission." Moreover, in their collaborations, group members turned to their institutional history to codify relational values in written form through mission statements and lists of core values.

Once established in written form, pioneer leaders used the codified values as a benchmark for decision-making. One of the Stoneham nuns asserted their centrality: "The core values [and] mission statement, all of these things are very much embedded in the way the university is run." The value emphasis embedded in decision-making was stressed by one senior administrator:

> The core values are what drive the university ... when we make decisions, how we operate, whether it's building a new school for arts and sciences, to serving in ministry, to how we perform on the athletic field, to a professor in the classroom, everything—the way we make decisions and impact students' lives is rooted in those six core values.

While the values impacted organizational decision-making, one of the most important effects they had was guiding how much to grow the fleet of periphery locations. One executive at Stoneham succinctly asserted when asked about peripheral growth, "I mean, when it comes down to making difficult decisions, you go back to the values." Just as the relational values informed their commitment to an in-person model of education, the values shaped the "managed growth" of the institution. The development of peripheral markets was yet another instance of how the pioneer institutions were "guided by their mission," illustrating how in value entrepreneurism the values are equally vital as entrepreneurial innovation.

The collective efforts of developing mission statements were attempts to unify the value content across the core campus and periphery locations. When the pioneer schools established enrollment markets to develop an in-person model of education for new student populations, their institutions experienced enrollment gains and expansion. But savvy administrators understood that relational values were an essential component of their product that could be damaged with too much growth. Thus, to expand the periphery, leaders also had to be mindful to foster values that were part of their market niche. The tension was a delicate balance between what one

Malvern professor described as "trying to be ambition-driven but market-sensitive." In short, the pioneer strategy was innovation within limits—limits that in the end proved to be the strategy's undoing.

Values Across Space

In their effort to rethink place for marginalized adult, working, and military student populations, the unconventional approach Lansdale, Malvern, and Stoneham took to providing in-person educational opportunities created distance—space—between the core residential campus and the periphery locations across the region. For the traditional schools, it was understood that values were transferred by coming to the core residential campus and experiencing the traditions embedded there. But when the pioneer schools reconceived the notion of place, the significant space that developed between the core and the periphery locations raised concerns as to how values—a vital part of their market niche—would transfer to students.

Central to their value entrepreneurism, pioneer universities promoted a values-oriented experience for students, which distinguished them in a crowded higher education marketplace. In addition to "graduating with a marketable degree," students would also "graduate with [the] values and ethos that we all consider to be important. Those essentials are not compromised," a Lansdale vice president asserted. A Stoneham faculty member opined that the school's values were a vital part of the curriculum: "Everything is the core values ... all the way down to the classroom and the students." In other words, values were not just a component of the broader organizational *culture*, but also a fundamental element of the school's intended *product*.

When leaders implemented the pioneer strategy and established multiple campuses for previously marginalized students, they worked to develop values as a fundamental component of the educational experience across the space between the periphery and the core. One vice president emphasized that Malvern had always had a "history of figuring out how to deliver education to new populations in ways that were accessible to students who otherwise might not be served." Leaders therefore sought to create the strong cultural dispositions in the periphery markets that previously existed in their residential core—an effort a Lansdale academic official referred to as establishing "communiversity." A Stoneham vice president emphasized the value approach leaders adopted, explaining the extensive institutional reach to maintain touch with the periphery locations: "*All* of our students—not just our traditional students—have exposure to the core values." Another vice president observed, "It was really kind of starting from ground zero, and kind of developing all of that, but then developing in a way that worked at [the] locations."

To achieve these ends, pioneer leaders focused on people and positions. Hiring processes at Lansdale, Malvern, and Stoneham were foundational to ensure values spanned space. Administrators were explicit in their expectations that faculty "live the values," be "servant educators," and "integrate faith and learning." The provost at Lansdale called attention to this notion when he asserted, "How you hire becomes critical to maintaining your identity, your values, your ethos as an institution." An executive at Malvern similarly emphasized,

> What I want someone to know—a new employee—whether they have a direct touch with the students or not, is that we're ... a community that has to work together for the goals of the institution, for our mission statement.

The values were "not just signs on a wall. People really are expected to do things like build community, care about integrity, and all the other ones," a Stoneham professor noted as he recited the core values. The purpose of strategic hiring was to locate persons who possessed values that aligned with the mission. "We have hiring practices ... based on mission, what we consider mission fit," explained the Malvern vice president.

The interviewing executives approached the process in different ways. Some leaders identified values in candidates in somewhat transcendental language. One vice president at Lansdale went so far as describing "searching your heart in terms of your soul," while a fellow administrator described the process in less lofty but equally value-driven terms:

> Core values [are] truly who you are ... when I'm doing the interviewing, I'm looking for [our three core values] in some form coming out in the interview process, and if the candidate doesn't express at least two of those, I don't really consider them as a candidate, because those are so core [to] who we are. That's not something you can teach.

The intent behind the process, a Stoneham vice president asserted, was to locate persons who would "not only be able to talk those values but to be able to walk those values in everything"—including their interactions with students in the residential and peripheral markets. The educational component of the institution's values was frequently conveyed by administrators and faculty alike: "We teach our core values," "The values are integrated into every class," "Faculty incorporate those values," "We expect them to teach as well as live by our values," and "We tailor our courses to the values."

In addition to recruiting value-oriented candidates, pioneer leaders established specific positions within the institution to ensure they would foster relationships wherever students might be in the periphery. A senior Lansdale administrator underscored how these positions were a vital component of their business model and embodiment of their value entrepreneurism:

> We have people who are not faculty, they're not the recruiters, they actually are in relationship with these students, it's built into the business model. It's a profitable place for us because it increases retention. But we have people who are in relationship with these students, and they care about what they're learning and how they're going to complete their program. As you may know, the business models [of] the for-profit online programs racked up tremendous debt, students dropped out, [and] there was not completion. We saw that and so our model is really different in that area.

Pioneer schools recognized that they had to establish processes that would maintain the value-oriented educational experience for students across the periphery. The emphasis on values and mission in university hiring processes was viewed as essential to the development of core values in the students who enrolled in different campuses. But as time would tell, teaching calculus in a hotel conference room proved to be much easier than transferring values to that same space.

Confronted With Consequences

For more than a decade, the first-mover advantage inherent in the pioneer strategy afforded Lansdale, Malvern, and Stoneham effortless enrollment growth and supplied leaders with generous financial surpluses that enabled institutions to expand from a single campus into an array of regional locations that catered to nontraditional students. Despite the early competitive edge the strategy provided the schools, over time the approach could not sustain the necessary revenues to simultaneously support the residential core and the vast number of satellite locations. Other universities like St. John's University, Brigham Young University, Drexel University, Ohio University, the University of Connecticut, and the University of Kentucky also adopted the branch campus model, adding to the ever-increasing competition to secure financial resources through enrollment growth.[20] With competition having burgeoned, leaders were forced to curtail institutional spending and hiring, and executives underscored an urgent need to identify the next educational innovation that could offer a new first-mover advantage in untapped enrollment markets.

The crisis Lansdale, Malvern, and Stoneham underwent as a result of implementing the pioneer strategy was the result of multiple factors. The innovative approach the schools took with respect to place also meant that, in the face of increased competition, leaders were forced to defend against enrollment losses to both the flagship and the fleet. "The competition quickly heated up within our segment," a Lansdale professor said with astonishment. Those losses were compounded when administrators prioritized values over speed, allowing competing schools to encroach on enrollment markets they once dominated. At the same time, the pioneer strategy undermined relational values the schools espoused, as substantial increases in workload and cutbacks in resources undermined the ability of faculty to foster relationships with the students the schools relied on for their educational cachet. Student enrollments cratered, and the excess revenues used to transform the residential campus evaporated. In the end, the marginal tuition revenue the pioneer strategy generated merely postponed the crisis of survival for Lansdale, Malvern, and Stoneham—just as the endowment revenue generated by the traditional strategy postponed the same for Boxborough and Havertown. The additional revenues both strategies differentially generated were insufficient to stabilize the residential core in the face of rising competition.

A Two-Front Defense

University leaders explained that when they initially implemented the pioneer strategy, recruiting nontraditional students to the satellite and branch campuses came with such ease for more than a decade that it allowed them "to think of themselves as educators rather than as businesspeople." But even as students clamored for the new approach to place, the enrollment tide began to change. As one Malvern executive acknowledged, "When we got into the business . . . we were a very early adopter. And we were riding the wave of easy street basically. . . . Obviously within the last decade competition has just exploded." The change in the competitive landscape surprised Lansdale, Malvern, and Stoneham leaders who had become accustomed to years of effortless enrollment growth. "We have really had to rework how we do our business in order to stay competitive," the Malvern executive conceded.

Leaders at the three institutions commonly retold the same narrative, noting that early competition came from for-profit institutions. As a senior executive at Lansdale observed,

> The for-profits have taught us a lot in terms of how quickly they've adapted to the needs of society, and I think the traditional higher education institutions have been somewhat in the ivory tower saying, "Don't touch us, we'll survive."

But increased competition also came from nonprofit colleges and universities in need of new sources of revenue. A Stoneham administrator commented that his school initially remained a leader in this sector, "keeping ourselves differentiated from the hundreds of other people going into this quickly as a revenue-generating kind of savior for their university." But the pioneer strategy could not withstand the pressures of the declining national economy, increased reliance on student financial aid to secure per-student federal funding, and the widespread impact of privatization in higher education—another impact of market logic.

Indeed, an intended outcome of economic reasoning directly impacted the student mentality around enrolling. One vice president at Lansdale admitted,

> There is a lot more mobility of students and we don't know how to account for that. There's not a lot of loyalty to an institution right now. It is, "I'll go where I can get in, and once I'm in if I can move to a better college for a lower cost, I'll probably do that."

As a result, enrollment growth stalled. "We plateaued," explained the Malvern president. "Between the recession and those regulatory changes, our institution could not shift gears fast enough to find a way to keep the growth going." As the first decade in the 2000s drew to a close, Lansdale, Malvern, and Stoneham found themselves defending their enrollment markets from the encroaching competition to maintain the same annual level of revenue: "Every student that walks across the graduation stage has got to be replaced for us to stay in business," a Malvern vice president candidly acknowledged.

The schools soon felt the impact of peer institutions entering their periphery markets. As one professor at Malvern explained, "You are used to being the leader, not paying really close enough attention, and then suddenly you realize, 'Holy cow! There are 16 competitors . . . where did all the 18- to 22-year-olds go?'" With branch campuses across the tristate region, Malvern leaders understood all too well they had to guard against losing a specific type of student who was providing profitable revenues for the university: adults.

As one leader confided, "Let's be honest. There are a lot of us competing for the same set of students.... I think on the adult [education] side, the challenge is the fact that we're not the only ones doing this anymore."

When probed further about the competition, school executives mentioned how competition undercut the pioneer strategy and "the work done to make a high-quality product," as one Stoneham administrator put it. Competitors found it was easy to lure students away by offering less rigorous or more condensed academic programs. An exasperated Stoneham official described how a competitor's curriculum influenced student enrollments at one of their satellite locations at Overley Air Force Base:

> One of the other schools decided to offer courses toward an associate's degree with the community college that are 5 weeks long. How can you learn English in 5 weeks? And math, or some of those other courses? I don't know what they're going to cut out of the book to be able to do that! The whole thing is ... it's going to affect enrollments, we're going to have problems because we're already having students ... go over to the other school to take the 5-week course rather than the 8-week course with us.

If leaders wanted to maintain their first-mover advantage in periphery education markets, defending them from competing institutions on this enrollment front was imperative. But with the pioneer schools having opened the door to a compressed educational timeline at some of their remote locations, it did not require a leap of the imagination to see that students would pursue even shorter courses of study. As a Stoneham vice president aptly framed the conundrum, "I think one of our challenges is differentiating our box of corn flakes from the other."

Although taking the classroom to the nontraditional student was an innovative approach to place, it meant the institutions that implemented the pioneer strategy were forced to keep a watchful eye on *two* enrollment markets—the periphery and the residential core—rather than being able to exclusively focus on one, like the traditional schools could. The Stoneham director of admissions explained that competition for enrollments at the residential core left the school with little choice but to respond in ways that echoed the response of the traditional strategy. Attracting students meant maintaining an almost exclusive focus on facilities to remain competitive. "One of the biggest challenges is how do you respond to this great demand and keep up your facilities and your classrooms and everything so that they are cutting edge and current, because that's what keeps you competitive," a senior administrator at Stoneham confessed. "You could never continue with the old rundown facilities" and even hope to maintain pace with the competition. Facilities were an essential feature in the recruitment process that created a modern yet pastoral feel about the flagship campus, one that conveyed that Stoneham offered a quality educational experience to current and prospective students. Yet despite a relentless building campaign, schools that embraced the pioneer strategy soon found themselves in much the same boat as traditional strategy schools with respect to residential enrollments.

A senior Lansdale administrator explained how pioneer strategy institutions quickly modified their residential recruiting: "How can we accelerate and push even harder and soften the blow?" The answer, he conceded, was to turn to transfer students. "Usually, we'll get a couple hundred transfer students and maybe a handful of freshmen, first-time freshmen, and just push hard and recruit in the spring and see if we can backfill some of that." He disclosed that the school had to recruit greater numbers of minority students to meet residential enrollments. "Our demographics have changed dramatically, too.... This year's incoming class is 55% non-White." The competition forced Malvern to re-examine its residential admissions approach as well, with an executive confiding, "There are a lot of us competing for the same set of students, and because we're not good at reaching out to minority students, we're competing for the same set of White students."

Institutional leaders at Lansdale, Malvern, and Stoneham grappled to address enrollment losses in both their periphery and their residential markets. One Malvern professor described the administrative mindset as a "frenzy," where "we've got to get going on this thing or we're going to be left behind." With tuition dollars at stake, she characterized her own sense of urgency as feeling the necessity of "keeping up with the Joneses." While divulging that they all might be headed for a cliff, she alluded to a safety-in-numbers mindset: "When the competition says, 'Oh my gosh, if we don't do this, we are idiots!' Well, let's follow suit." It appeared leaders at pioneer schools were in the grip of an idea: if they were going to retain their first-mover advantage, there seemingly was no other option they could pursue than their frenzied two-front defense.

The Challenge to Values

As Lansdale, Malvern, and Stoneham continued their attempts to dually defend the first-mover advantage the pioneer strategy provided, administrators explained that the intensified recruiting tactics from competing institutions challenged the values at the core of their value entrepreneurship.

Competitors attempted to increase their market share by creating academic and admissions "shortcuts" to bolster student enrollment. These shortcuts put Lansdale, Malvern, and Stoneham leaders in ethical dilemmas where they felt forced into choosing between money and mission. Administrators and the broader university community required time to deliberatively process how they would respond to the profit-versus-purpose puzzle in light of their values. However, the deliberations were so methodical that the institutions did not react swiftly and lost their competitive advantage to institutions that decided to prioritize revenues above everything else—and were more than willing to undercut the lead that pioneer strategy schools initially enjoyed by using compressed production timelines, persuasive recruiting, comparative marketing, and a minimized curriculum.[21] Snapshots of how the values at the institutions came into conflict with the competitive pressures of the enrollment marketplace create a portrait of the value entrepreneurship that undergirded their decision-making—and why the emphasized values were ill-suited for adapting to the quickly evolving enrollment landscape.

As the competition for students was ramping up in the early 2000s, Stoneham bolstered its admissions efforts by hiring an outside agency to assist with recruiting prospective students. The company provided admissions services to hundreds of colleges and universities on a graduated fee scale. The more a school paid, the greater the level of admissions attention and recruitment services. Although the company provided Stoneham with consistent enrollment yields, in time "things came to light" about the nature of the contracted services. As one administrator explained, "There were definitely issues surrounding integrity with the kinds of things they were doing behind the scenes on our account." He suggested the tensions were rooted in the divergent missions and values between the two organizations. "They were in it for profit. And that does not jibe with our student-centered mission. We're in it to educate people who want an education."

The Stoneham president established a confidential committee reporting directly to him composed of "members from different parts of the university that can possibly have a need to know and an impact on how [enrollment] comes out." A committee member confided they worked secretly for 2 years to terminate the company's contract and to recruit students themselves in a manner that emphasized integrity over high volumes of applicants. Values were the line in the sand between purpose and profit that motivated leaders to limit the ungoverned and accelerated pursuit of scaled enrollment growth. But once the partnership ended, Stoneham discovered that they were ill-suited for the recruiting tactics needed to attract this generation of students.

When the Malvern president was asked why the school did not maximize peripheral enrollments, he highlighted that the years of expansion were driven by the relational values of service and identity:

> [The year] we grew quickly, we had a hard time accommodating the growth and having the quality and ethos we wanted. We liked steady patterns of growth. I think part of it is our Midwestern mindset . . . we're not Silicon Valley where we're trying to quadruple it year after year. . . . The [question] was how do we continue to feed the growth so that we serve the population and do it consistently with who we are, what our identity is? That was the ethos here . . . more than we want to use all that money and triple that enrollment.

In the years that followed, Malvern administrators rejected offers to partner with a prominent investor renowned for having brokered multimillion-dollar university buyouts that would have propelled the school's student enrollment and its marginal revenues. Despite their first-mover advantage eroding and competitors surpassing the school in enrollment, Malvern's president proclaimed that the institution remained steadfast in its focus of adhering to values. He likened the development of the school to a maturing young adult: "It's like an adolescent who [is asked], 'What do you want to do with your life?'" His tone deepened as he mimicked the voice of a teen: "'Well, I got big. I want to get big.'" He reverted to his natural tone, concluding, "That's not a way to define an institution. That may be a characteristic of you, but it isn't who you are."

Leaders at Lansdale faced similar challenges as competitors employed assertive admissions practices that emphasized "comparative marketing" whereby they "talked about other schools . . . pushing them down to build themselves up." This "negative" admissions approach tested Lansdale, whose admissions director pridefully insisted,

> We don't compete on financial aid. . . . We don't want to overstep our bounds to just compete with [other schools], just to try and undercut each other on financial aid. That's an ethical parameter . . . that should be widely embraced.

Although college admissions have always been a competitive landscape, the admissions director explained the field has traditionally been guided by a commitment to "principles of good practice, ethical boundaries . . . and limited competitive standards" developed by professional postsecondary associations.[22] The commitment to these principles was "not just an ethical bond but a relational bond with those schools." Most important, the admissions experience was fundamentally about the students: "We want it to be about the best information for the students and to help them find the best fit as far as an institutional match, not to be wooed by some of the accessories that come along with being recruited."

Yet while Lansdale leaders remained devoted to their principled approach, they also developed considerable envy for the growth rate of their primary competitor, Grand Canyon University, which adopted the accelerated strategy (see Chapter 4) and used comparative marketing techniques to quickly surpass Lansdale in enrollment. When the Lansdale president was asked why his school did not go the route of Grand Canyon, he leaned back and let out a notable laugh of regret, then allowed a long period of silence to hang in the air: "We missed it," he finally averred. "We were dumb. I wish we had."

In the end, the value entrepreneurship Lansdale, Malvern, and Stoneham espoused cut both ways—it was a benefit and a burden. On the one hand, the relational values predisposed pioneer strategy institutions to embrace the first-mover opportunity to reconceive place and develop novel educational models for nontraditional and marginalized students. But on the other hand, the values of these pioneer strategy institutions limited the ability of leaders to retain their first-mover advantage when competitors employed academic and admissions shortcuts. By the time university administrators realized their revenues had been impacted, it was too late.

Taxing Relationships

Again and again throughout the interviews, leaders at Lansdale, Malvern, and Stoneham made it clear that within their academic communities, employees were to embody and foster the institutional values. A senior spokesperson for Stoneham made the connection explicit:

> We only hire people who are willing to do the values. . . . And living by the values means a lot. . . . We have people who really want to live by the values, and we want our students to have the best experience.

An astute Lansdale administrator underscored the fact that employees were essential to fulfilling their value entrepreneurship focus: "It's interesting to me that you don't put human capital on a balance sheet," she remarked. "Because you take away faculty and it doesn't matter what you have on your balance sheet . . . you cannot sustain the mission." Their mission statements conveyed that the institutional aim was to impart the knowledge of values. And despite the hundreds of millions of dollars leaders of the three universities spent transforming capital assets on their residential campuses to attract students while pursuing the pioneer strategy, the people who comprised their human capital were equally vital given that many students enrolled because they wanted a value-based educational experience.

Yet the emphasis on values generated a latent tension between educational quality and community. A Lansdale senior administrator described the emphasis associated with both:

> There's a high expectation of excellence with an almost sacred value of community and relationships. And so, the tension is to do things well, to do it with excellence; at the same time, relationships and community are very high values.

This natural tension between quality and community intensified when university leaders responded to increased competition by decreasing resources for employees to reduce organizational costs. Yet altering the resources for one correspondingly influenced the other. As a Malvern faculty member explained with a quickening tone of exasperation,

> We're afraid we're going to have fewer students and we will have even less money. We're going to cut health benefits, we're going to freeze faculty hires, we're going to keep costs low for students no matter what. But what are we offering them? You know, I don't know.

The faculty member shrugged her shoulders as if to enunciate her deep uncertainty and feelings of discouragement about the enrollment crisis and its consequences:

> I think they [administrators] are going to squeeze us a little more . . . I'm more concerned that we cannot hire faculty when we need to than . . . cutting my health benefits at this point in my life, or . . . not getting a big raise or whatever. I really am concerned about us being a kind of place where students can really thrive as whole persons, can really flourish, and that we help them. And you cannot do that if money is always the priority.

Yet for schools who embraced the pioneer strategy, the reality was that competition had increased substantially—as hoped for when neoliberal policies came into effect—and therefore money *had* become a greater priority—as also hoped for when neoliberal policies took hold.

In an attempt to contain costs while remaining competitive, the leaders of the pioneer strategy institutions made a series of further cuts in resources. Malvern executives endeavored to quietly reduce their workforce through "staffing adjustments... in the form of attrition," the chief information officer related. "As people left, we just didn't backfill the positions." The labor reductions adversely impacted employee morale. "There were struggles within, there were people leaving, there was a negative vibe going on. I mean you're cutting budgets, you're cutting people, that's going to be there," a faculty member explained. Substantial staffing adjustments were also made across Stoneham's regional locations to save money. Administrators distributed directives from the core campus that the regional centers must hire part-time adjunct faculty. A tenured professor described how the cost-saving directives had negative implications for Stoneham students:

> We're hiring more adjuncts. How does that concern everybody? Well, most adjuncts are not going to deliver the same education.... I hear from my students that this is the perception—they [adjuncts] are not going to deliver the same education that a full-time person who is dedicated, this is all they do, this is what their job is.

The continued reductions in resources and personnel had a downward spiraling effect on morale at all three institutions. And it also rubbed members of the community the wrong way with respect to their values: "There's an economic logic there that of course defies Catholic social teaching across the board," a Stoneham professor pointedly observed.

Amid the severe cutbacks in resources and substantial increases in workload, employees struggled to foster relationships with students, which was the educational calling card of all three pioneer strategy schools. A diminished faculty was called on to shoulder the responsibility of having to impart knowledge of their respective disciplines as well as foster the relational connections with students that the schools publicized, which necessitated they work extraordinarily long hours to meet high teaching, advising, mentoring, and counseling loads for an increasing number of students. To compound the matter further, many faculty and student support professionals took reductions in pay to sacrifice for the greater good of the students and the mission. One Malvern faculty member quipped, "We've got these narratives that are, 'Austerity is next to godliness,'" while another ruefully observed, "For the folks who have been here longer they've made sacrifices because they believe in what was going on here. My pay is [such that] I could probably double my salary at a state school." While the dictum "less is more" was embraced by modernist architects like Mies van der Rohe, its applicability to values-laden institutions of higher education was suspect.

The specifics of trying to produce and foster relational values in a context of reduced resources taxed faculty members professionally and financially. "The entrepreneurial spirit can sacrifice anything to make the university successful. A lot of us have sacrificed health, family, and spiritual life for the sake of the organization," opined a Lansdale administrator-turned-professor. Despite the sacrifices employees made to sustain their institution, its values, and the pioneer strategy, uncertainty remained, particularly regarding future enrollments. A Malvern senior administrator expressed with trepidation,

> We don't know if we're going to hit our goal for next year or not. We've just gone through cuts. We may have to make more cuts in the fall when the enrollment numbers are in. And we know if we don't hit the goal, we're going to have to do it.

What the executive may not have fully realized is that not only had the first-mover advantage already been relinquished, but also a broader enrollment pullback was on the horizon.

The Perils of Pullback

Similar to a growth stock that experiences an initial period of rapid expansion followed by a correction in price, the three universities that implemented the pioneer strategy were subjected to a pullback in their enrollment growth. Recall that Boxborough and Havertown, having implemented the traditional strategy, maintained their enrollment plateau before eventually experiencing a precipitous drop. In contrast to the enrollment plateau, Lansdale, Malvern, and Stoneham experienced an enrollment peak, a period of notable growth followed by a corrective pullback when their first-mover advantage quickly eroded. While both strategies ultimately resulted in a decline in enrollment, the periods preceding the drop differed. The decline in student enrollment brought a host of additional complex stressors, including budget reductions, increased debt, residence hall closures, and, at one institution, the removal of its president. "The last 2 years really feel like precipice years," a Lansdale academic official nervously mentioned. While the pullback at each of the three pioneer schools materialized in different ways, senior leaders at all three institutions disclosed the daily fear and uncertainty they experienced. At the close of an emotional recounting of the Lansdale pullback, one leader firmly reiterated, "It was stressful. Those are *not* trivial events."

The Stoneham provost dolefully recited a litany of losses:

> Enrollments are down in our continuing education centers. A couple of small centers have low enrollments . . . but some of the larger centers are in trouble. Whiting, they have more students than we do on campus. . . . But their enrollments are way down. Springbrook is way down.

The intensity of the Lansdale pullback was the product of "2 bad years of extremely low enrollment," where annual totals were off by hundreds of students. But the impact of those 2 bad years was felt for many more. A senior administrator explained that the lingering effect of the enrollment loss was a "huge challenge" because "it's like the snake bit the mouse and it's going on for 4 years." The absence of those missing students (and their tuition dollars) was felt for a long time.

The challenges caused by the enrollment pullback created a major revenue dilemma for all three pioneer schools. At Stoneham, one vice president revealingly admitted,

> The surpluses from military education dropped precipitously. That was the cash cow that allowed them to sort of just coast and do nothing for a long period of time. And all of a sudden, the cash cow was not giving any cash!

The provost made a point to articulate that part of the financial dilemma they faced involved the costs associated with satellite centers: "That's going to be a major challenge: what to do with these centers that are declining in numbers, but we still have personnel there, we still have students there, we still have overhead." They confessed that some in the administration had not come to grips with the new reality. "We talk about adding centers. We've got to start talking about eliminating centers." The pullback brought about tense conditions that left both Stoneham and Landsdale administrators grappling for a solution.

At Malvern, the pullback did not just leave its leaders grappling for a solution—it caught them so off guard that it cost the president his job. Of the three institutions that implemented the pioneer strategy, the enrollment pullback hit Malvern the hardest, blindsiding the administration. "I mean, we lost students. We *never* lost students. That was just so different!" a vice president relayed with astonishment. "All of a sudden, 'BOOM! We have a decrease in enrollment! What was that? We have empty beds?'" a Malvern senior leader recalled in disbelief. But competition had changed the landscape, and "reality caught up with us"—leading to the dramatic closure of residence halls in the heart of the campus that previously had been bursting at the seams.

Many in the Malvern community saw the overbuilding as a failure of leadership that warranted immediate correction. "The president says publicly in the first town hall meeting I attended, 'You know, I really didn't see this coming,'" laughed one academic official before she added, "I thought, first of all, you just admitted that publicly. The leader of the institution and you were clueless. You didn't see this coming?" Shaking her head in disbelief, she pointed out the assumptions that blinded the president:

> We're Malvern, we're big, and blessings come in the form of more, right? So more, more, more. Then suddenly the numbers are harder, and it caught the leader completely off guard . . . he was out at the end of the year.

The leaders who employed the pioneer strategy expressed regret at losing their first-mover advantage to the competition and not using a decade of student tuition surpluses more frugally. "We created a lot of fat in what we were doing here," a senior administrator at Malvern admitted, "and we were not efficient with our money." With many lean years ahead, the schools had already abandoned the pioneer strategy at the time they were interviewed and turned their attention to finding new enrollment markets to establish a more sustainable solution that met their financial need. "The organization is stressed and anxious. The business model has to change if the school is going to remain viable," confessed one Lansdale vice president. A vexed colleague of hers emphasized that the acute challenge that confronted the pioneer leaders was how to move beyond the ideal and establish a mix of additional enrollment markets:

> It runs in the face of the old stereotype that college means going somewhere hundreds of miles away from your home and living in the dormitory, which I think everyone is saying, "That is a *model*, that is a small percentage now for all college students." And yet we continue to kind of cling to that idealized image. For us, we have to say, "Well, what is the reality for us?" We cannot cling to an image that is likely to be fading, so let's consider what *the right mix* would be for us.

In searching for the right mix, the schools were conceding that the pioneer strategy was no longer viable in the higher education landscape—a resource landscape that was increasingly looking like the same educational desert the marginalized students these schools served had wandered in for decades.

Conclusion

The leaders of the pioneer schools experienced the tenuous reality that came with being the first mover in a new market—in their attempt to innovatively take place to marginalized student populations, they became marginalized institutions themselves, with administrators incessantly stigmatized by their professional colleagues. Although the pioneer strategy provided Lansdale, Malvern, and Stoneham with an infusion of students in an array of periphery locations and the prized tuition margins, leaders painfully discovered that being first in one regard meant being last in others. Leaders also discovered being first was an impossible lead to maintain. The value entrepreneurialism of pioneer institutions prohibited the schools from the pure pursuit of growth and profit come what may. Their commitment to relational values tempered their enterprising approach while competing institutions overtook their early-adopter advantage.

Executives at the schools remained committed to their belief in innovation and were continually on the lookout for the next thing that would give the institution a leg up on the competition by providing them with an altogether new first-mover advantage. "We've got to find what the next innovative, entrepreneurial, new, and not faddish thing is in order for us to continue the upward trajectory in the next few years," a Malvern academic dean urgently avowed. But lightning did not strike twice, and having relinquished their competitive advantage, new tuition margins were desperately needed to replace those that evaporated with the first-mover advantage, a loss that challenged their identity. "Where Malvern is in these days is a little bit like going through puberty. Nobody wants to show their middle school pictures. But it's a part of growing up and figuring out who you are," one vice president revealed.

Ultimately, Lansdale, Malvern, and Stoneham leaders were forced to abandon the pioneer strategy to pursue new forms of financial sustainability. In fact, the strategy itself was not exempt from the schools' commitment to innovation: "What you find out with innovation is, when you move fast, some things you do don't work.... Well, it didn't work; let's scrap it and move onto the next thing," explained a Malvern administrator. Pioneer leaders understood their present context warranted a new approach. "It's more realistic to think that we've got to be in a constant state of change," the Lansdale provost acknowledged.

Compelled by broader neoliberal market forces, pioneer leaders shifted their gaze away from the innovation approach to one that did not rely on a dominant periphery market, but rather leveraged many different types of enrollment markets to sustain the residential core. At the time of the interviews, executives at all three pioneer schools were fervently considering new types of periphery markets that included international campuses, transfer programs, hybrid pathways, military education, dual enrollment, vocational training, and even online education. The vision one senior leader put forth was that Lansdale quickly needed to become "this kind of multifaceted but integrated university that provides a variety of *types* of education for a variety of types of needs." Their new pursuit of developing a diversified array of periphery markets to sustain the residential core was a more advanced form of margin capitalization, one that looked to the approach seen in the next chapter—the network strategy.

To make sense of the future, the pioneer leaders repeatedly juxtaposed their past approaches with the rapid developments unfolding in their present environment. One executive summed up the situation aptly:

> Malvern has to in a sense regain the entrepreneurial spirit that it had, but it has got to be a new neo-entrepreneurialism ... you cannot go back and recreate the things from those days. But what are the new entrepreneurial things that we should be doing now? ... We have got to start thinking far more globally than we do as a university right now ... I think you have got to think new educational technologies ... I think you are going to see a real strong period of hyperbolic change in the way education occurs.

Leaders were certain that navigating the uncharted higher education frontier would require not only new techniques of innovation, but also a new type of innovation itself—an emergent "neo-entrepreneurialism" with the foresight and vision to act in a manner to sustain the institutions amid the oncoming "hyperbolic change." As for traversing such a frontier, the pioneer strategy would no longer be sufficient.

Notes

1. Value entrepreneurism refers to the innovative approaches that actors take toward value work or practice. By adopting values as its object of focus, it remains a distinct form of enterprising apart from social and cultural entrepreneurism.
2. Flagship refers to the centrality of the residential campus among its fleet of periphery locations and the status of the institution among a specific group of institutions (professional, denominational, geographic, etc.). Douglass, J. (2016). *The new flagship university: Changing the paradigm from global ranking to national relevancy.* Springer.
3. Wilson, E. H. (1988). *For the people of North Carolina: The Z. Smith Reynolds Foundation at half-century, 1936–1986.* University of North Carolina Press.

4. Hsu, G., & Hannan, M. T. (2005). Identities, genres, and organizational forms. *Organization Science*, *16*(5), 474–490; Santos, F. M., & Eisenhardt, K. M. (2009). Constructing markets and shaping boundaries: Entrepreneurial power in nascent fields. *Academy of Management Journal*, *52*(4), 643–671.
5. Morphew, C. C. (2002). "A rose by any other name": Which colleges became universities. *The Review of Higher Education*, *25*(2), 207–223.
6. Value entrepreneurism differs from other forms that take their object of focus as social problems (i.e., social entrepreneurism) and broader culture and the institutions that reproduce it (i.e., cultural entrepreneurism), both of which were embraced by schools discussed in Chapters 3 and 4, respectively.
7. Integrated Postsecondary Education Data System.
8. Since the 1970s, state policy makers reduced funding for public institutions, wherein university leaders responded by increasing student tuition and enrollment to make up for the reduction in funding, a process commonly known as privatization. Fryar, A. H. (2012). What do we mean by privatization in higher education? In J. C. Smart & M. B. Paulsen (Eds.), *Higher education: Handbook of theory and research* (pp. 521–547). Springer.
9. Levinthal, D. A., & Wu, B. (2010). Opportunity costs and non-scale free capabilities: Profit maximization, corporate scope, and profit margins. *Strategic Management Journal*, *31*(7), 780–801; Burt, S., & Sparks, L. (1997). Performance in food retailing: A cross-national consideration and comparison of retail margins. *British Journal of Management*, *8*(2), 133–150.
10. Labaree, D. F. (1997). Public goods, private goods: The American struggle over educational goals. *American Educational Research Journal*, *34*(1), 39–81; Marginson, S. (2011). Higher education and public good. *Higher Education Quarterly*, *65*(4), 411–433.
11. Breneman, D. W., Pusser, B., & Turner, S. E. (2012). The contemporary provision of for-profit higher education. In D. W. Breneman, B. Pusser, & S. E. Turner (Eds.), *Earnings from learning: The rise of for-profit universities* (pp. 3–22). State University of New York Press.; Iloh, C. (2016). Exploring the for-profit experience: An ethnography of a for-profit college. *American Educational Research Journal*, *53*(3), 427–455.
12. Brown, J. T., Volk, F., & Kush, J. M. (2023) *Equality and a built environment of differences: Towards more equitable residential life experiences.* Columbus, OH: Association of College and University Housing Officers – International (ACUHO-I); Volk, F., Brown, J. T., Gibson, D. J. & Kush, J. (2023). The anatomy of roommate change: Residence hall design, academic performance, and differences in race and socioeconomic status. *Journal of College and University Student Housing*, *49*(2), 48–65.
13. Muniesa, F., Doganova, L., Ortiz, H., Pina-Stranger, Á., Paterson, F., Bourgoin, A., Ehrenstein, V., Juven, P. A., Pontille, D., Saraç-Lesavre, B., & Yon, G. (2017). *Capitalization: A cultural guide* (No. halshs-01426044). Presses de Mines. https://doi.org/10.4000/books.pressesmines.3463; Leyshon, A., & Thrift, N. (2007). The capitalization of almost everything: The future of finance and capitalism. *Theory, Culture & Society*, *24*(7–8), 97–115.
14. Turner, J. K., & Pusser, B. (2004). Place matters: The distribution of access to a state flagship university. *Policy Futures in Education*, *2*(2), 388–421.
15. Brown, D. K. (2001). The social sources of educational credentialism: Status cultures, labor markets, and organizations. *Sociology of Education*, *74*(extra issue), 19–34.

16. Hillman, N. W. (2016). Geography of college opportunity: The case of education deserts. *American Educational Research Journal, 53*(4), 987–1021.
17. Suarez, F. F., & Lanzolla, G. (2007). The role of environmental dynamics in building a first mover advantage theory. *Academy of Management Review, 32*(2), 377–392.; Lieberman, M. B., & Montgomery, D. B. (1988). First-mover advantages. *Strategic Management Journal, 9*(S1), 41–58.
18. Deephouse, D. L. (1996). Does isomorphism legitimate? *Academy of Management Journal, 39*(4), 1024–1039; Stensaker, B., & Norgård, J. D. (2001). Innovation and isomorphism: A case-study of university identity struggle 1969–1999. *Higher Education, 42*(4), 473–492.
19. Gehman, J., Grimes, M. G., & Cao, K. (2019). Why we care about certified B corporations: From valuing growth to certifying values practices. *Academy of Management Discoveries, 5*(1), 97–101; Gehman, J. (2021). Searching for values in practice-driven institutionalism: Practice theory, institutional logics, and values work. In M. Lounsbury, D. A. Anderson, & P. Spee (Eds.), *On practice and institution: Theorizing the interface: Vol. 70. Research in the Sociology of Organizations* (pp. 139–159). Emerald Publishing Limited. https://doi.org/10.1108/S0733-558X20200000070004.
20. Other institutions that employed this model can be found in the National Association of Branch Campus Administrators membership.
21. See Chapter 1, "In the Absence of Speed," for a discussion of deliberative processes in higher education.
22. National Association for College Admission Counseling.

3
The Network Strategy

"In Growth We Trust"

Introduction

Situated in two of the largest metropolitan areas in the United States, Pepperell University and the University of Winchendon were two Catholic institutions founded with an emphasis on including others and the benefits of stable leadership. The institutions were part of an amalgamation of social services to address inequality that clergy established within impoverished 19th-century immigrant communities—in the midst of a cholera outbreak and the 1918 influenza pandemic. For more than a century, these institutions remained a critical part of a local social safety net that aspired to provide "access for all" while embedded in communities of need. However, in the latter decades of the 20th century, the pipeline for Catholic workers collapsed, baby boom enrollments plummeted, and the neoliberal shift in education policy resulted in rising costs, leaving one source of hope for the two institutions—tuition revenue from student enrollment. Confronted with closure, these schools held fast to their "social entrepreneurial"[1] origins and developed the *network strategy*—a hybrid model of higher education that established diversified sources of funding while providing opportunities for educational access.

The network institutions did not have anything resembling the endowments elite and traditional institutions possessed—these schools had nothing, yet boldly resolved to continue providing educational opportunities within immigrant communities that were similarly empty-handed. Nor did they wager their future, as pioneer schools did on being "first movers" into a new periphery market. To stave off closure, the university governing boards hired entrepreneurial leaders who established dozens of new periphery enrollment markets that in time spanned the region, state, nation, and even globe. Their efforts transformed the institutional form of the schools from small colleges into "multiversities," or what the business sector refers to as "multi-divisional organizations."[2] The structural form of these multiversities was a network

Capitalizing on College. Joshua Travis Brown, Oxford University Press. © Joshua Travis Brown (2025).
DOI: 10.1093/oso/9780197780701.003.0004

of specialized divisions that delivered multiple types of educational products in multiple enrollment markets. The approach provided leaders with an agile advantage: "With that network, we build tailor-made programs, adapt, and have the flexibility to deliver what other countries want," a Winchendon senior leader stressed. Growth became the singular focus, because through growth you could offer opportunity. "Growth for us isn't about size. Growth for us equals access," the Winchendon president explained:

> Access to underrepresented minority groups that wouldn't have the opportunity to be a lawyer or a doctor or whatever if it weren't for Winchendon.... We want to grow because we want to give more students access to the entrepreneurial spirit here.

The network of periphery campuses provided the once-ailing schools with millions of dollars in surplus tuition revenues, which leaders used to transform their residential campuses and regain local competitiveness. Yet over time, the network strategy became a victim of its own success, as the dozens of periphery markets stretched the capacity of leaders to balance a complex system and incentivized them to pursue revenue over relationships to increase margins generated from each student.

Commissioned to Care

The bold histories of Pepperell and Winchendon are characterized by two abiding dispositions that actively inform their passion for education. Since their earliest years, the universities possessed a welcoming culture that *prioritized inclusion*, an emphasis that readily focused on "the other." In their continual pursuit of welcoming others, Pepperell and Winchendon maintained extraordinarily diverse multiethnic and multireligious student populations. Through their enduring commitment to serve underprivileged students of a particular locale, the founders also displayed *stability of leadership*. Their devotion to their schools and the immigrant population modeled a continuity of service so profound that university employees followed their example. Together, the two dispositions of prioritizing inclusion and stable leadership fostered a long-lasting institutional environment of *social entrepreneurialism* that embraced an access-for-all mentality. This trait laid the groundwork for the implementation of an inclusive network strategy to rescue these schools from the financial chasm they found themselves perched over after the demographic collapse and increased competition for students fostered by market logic "reforms."

Founded as "immigrant schools" in the 19th century to support people with few means and even fewer opportunities to receive an education, Pepperell and Winchendon continued to draw on their deep-rooted access-for-all culture a century later. One of Winchendon's storied professors shared how the emphasis of inclusion was carried forward by stable leadership of the sisters from the institution's impoverished founding: "In the mid-1800s, they came answering a call . . . a lot of orphan children were left because their parents died of cholera. They set up orphanages, educational resources [via] the school, and also medical facilities." The sisters persisted, and in time their meager goodwill operations transformed into enduring institutions: "Their medical facilities eventually became the hospital system . . . [while the] school is now the university." The professor emphasized that each era was interwoven with a broad-based access mandate:

> Their whole focus was on serving through education and medical assistance. It's still the underpinning of everything that we do here. . . . [It's in] the DNA of the place.

Prioritizing Inclusion

One central cultural disposition of Pepperell and Winchendon can be understood through a succinct phrase members of both universities' communities used repeatedly to describe their commitment to inclusion: "a welcoming culture." This emphasis on inclusion was a relational commitment held by Pepperell and Winchendon that resembled the relational value of the pioneer institutions, underscoring the priority placed on human connection. However, there was an important difference between the two, one embodied in the words of the Pepperell president: "It's a culture that respects *the other*." For the pioneer schools, the human connection they sought to make emphasized a "we," whereas at these institutions the focus was squarely on "you." This focus had profound implications for Pepperell and Winchendon in terms of their historical trajectories and how they responded to both crises and opportunities.

The priority placed on inclusion had its origins in the early history of both schools. In a manner that notably differed from that of traditional and pioneer institutions, their historical narratives were part of the common knowledge among members of the university communities. Sometimes leaders explained how the institutional culture was rooted in the centuries-old denominational tenets that predated the schools, like the Pepperell provost who said, "We get our engrained culture from those hallmarks of St. Ignatius." But it was more common for leaders to retell narratives drawn from the institutional founding. The words of one Winchendon vice president were representative of this: "There was no distinguishing between race, color, creed, or anything. Everyone was welcome." Similarly, the Pepperell chancellor explained that its founders emphasized service: "Costs were kept down . . . [in] trying to serve the immigrants and help them kind of get into a well-educated place in society."

Though their founders had been dead for many generations, the values they espoused at both schools seemed very much alive in the institutions' day-to-day operations. The continuing influence of the founders was experienced and felt throughout the community. People commonly told founding stories in the same breath as they described the present culture of inclusion: "The culture here is a very welcoming culture, a very open culture, and a very giving culture. . . . A major part of that has to do with the founding clergy," a senior Winchendon administrator explained. The provost at Winchendon was clear in connecting the present-day mission of the school to its past: "We have always, throughout our history, been focused on the needs of the population of the region." An administrator at Pepperell made it explicit that the priority of inclusion was continually reborn: "People have a friendliness and openness about them, and it's been passed on from generations of faculty and staff."[3] A Pepperell director described the culture of inclusion as "tangible": "It's something that I feel that you can experience when you're here, and the students tell us that year after year." Similar remarks permeated discussions at Winchendon, where one of its vice presidents commented,

> The footprint that they left here is, "You need to help others to become better citizens, better persons, better people." And if you walk on this campus, you will feel it, this feeling of the sisters is that footprint. . . . That's the legacy here on campus.

University leaders conveyed that the natural outflow of this cultural disposition to prioritize inclusion was their commitment to diversity. Senior administrators continually invited people to become part of the institution whose commonality was their differences: "We're welcoming beyond just people like ourselves. We have a very diverse student body, and people are comfortable with that . . . hospitality for me means welcoming the stranger," the Pepperell president relayed. His counterpart at Winchendon asserted that even religious differences were not a barrier to inclusion: "It doesn't matter what faith you are. But grow in your faith. . . . We welcome Muslim students here, and we want them to become better Muslims through the Winchendon experience. [And similarly] better Jews through the experience." Leaders were committed to supporting diverse groups of individuals welcomed into their institutions. As one Pepperell vice president asserted, inclusion and support went hand in hand to create a culture of "hospitality and concern for the individual ... we try to take care of each student, take care of their needs." For these two institutions, there is an inherent simplicity to the legacy and ramifications of their inclusion, captured in the insightful remark of a Winchendon professor: "The human being is the common denominator."

Stable Leadership

The storied pasts of Pepperell and Winchendon include detailed descriptions of the literal journey founders made, arriving by foot and stagecoach. But the hardships the founding clergy encountered in their mission to welcome others highlight a second disposition: a leadership that endured. While it was and remains common for many denominations to continually rotate their clergy from place to place, the individuals who founded Pepperell and Winchendon resolved to remain at their posts during their lifetime of service. Their commitment indicated they would not abandon their communities, creating a second focal organizational disposition that emphasized stable leadership.

The dedication of the founders to the success of Pepperell and Winchendon provided enduring stability during those tumultuous early years. Leaders' perseverance during this era enabled them to develop a long-term vision to meet the social and educational needs of the immigrant communities they served. When the founding clergy arrived, they established educational outposts with clergy committed to communities of place on residential campuses that later became the "core" of their growth strategy. And the constancy of this vision—"the footprint that they left," in the words of a Winchendon vice president—has lasted for generations.

The two institutions flourished throughout the early and mid-1900s under the steadfast leadership of the clergy who served as the faculty and administrators for the colleges. "They were all nuns," the Winchendon chancellor conveyed: "There was no such thing as 'It is 3:00 and I have to go home.' These people worked from 7:00 in the morning until 10:00 at night. They made this thing run." The provost at Pepperell recounted a similar historical narrative:

> The forefathers of this institution . . . their whole mantra was to provide an affordable, accessible, [denominational] liberal arts education to every student

who desired one. The monks built this place with their blood and sweat . . . just think about everything that they went through.

With each passing decade, these schools—under the steady hand of long-serving leaders committed to the founding vision—remained quiet but stalwart forces in their communities, providing educational opportunities for those who needed them.

As the years passed, the same steadfast commitment of the school leadership to serving the educational needs of the local population was adopted by many employees who worked at Pepperell and Winchendon, reflected in their long-standing service to the schools at all levels. "We have very energetic people; they love to work here. We have an attrition rate of less than 3% . . . most people leave by retirement or death," the Winchendon president asserted. He pointed out that employees possessed a "sincere belief in the leadership of the university," characterizing "strength of leadership" as a key reason for the low employee turnover. Conversations with other administrators illustrated this was not mere self-congratulation on his part.

Nor was the characteristic of stable leadership limited to just the office of the president; an assistant observed that Winchendon had "steady leadership among our executive team. Most of them have been here [an] average of 15 years." The same level of commitment was found at Pepperell, where its provost noted that "a core group of [senior] people have provided stability." The long view of leadership at these institutions ran counter to the pervasive administrative norm in higher education, where senior leaders serve on average for only 4 or 5 years.[4] But for the leaders of Pepperell and Winchendon, employment was more than just a job—it was first and foremost about service and meeting the needs of "the other." As one Winchendon academic official noted, that ideal of welcoming the other had been modeled by long-serving faculty and administrators since the founding: "Their whole focus was on serving through education . . . and that's still the underpinning of everything that we do here."

Broad Access for All

The two enduring dispositions—prioritizing inclusion and stable leadership—functioned as dual pillars supporting a broad access-for-all atmosphere permeating Pepperell and Winchendon. When the monks and nuns embarked on their journey toward different burgeoning immigrant communities, they carried ambitions greater than just creating educational opportunities. At the time, the national systems that provide present-day individuals with a social safety net spanning healthcare, welfare, and education had yet to be created, which left individuals vulnerable to natural disasters, pandemics, economic fluctuations, and even war. "Not only did you have cholera and yellow fever, but also the consequences of the Civil War," a Winchendon professor grimly remarked. The founding clergy took it on themselves to establish multiple socially focused organizations that offered services to address the seemingly insurmountable social problems that plagued the local communities. These individuals embodied the modern trait of *social entrepreneurism*: they innovatively built institutions, organizations, and programs to advance solutions to social problems.

In the case of Winchendon, upon arriving in an ox-drawn stagecoach, the sisters found themselves surrounded by death and the anguish of an ongoing cholera pandemic. They had some training as nurses and "were able to find a way to work with the physicians so that they could actually build the beginning of a healthcare system," as one Winchendon vice president explained. The pandemic subsequently brought a complex nexus of social ills to the immigrant community: extreme poverty, child abandonment, illiteracy, and death. In an attempt to address these concerns, the sisters established multiple organizations that provided social services to the community. As one professor related, "A lot of orphan children were left because their parents died of cholera. So they set up orphanages." But a roof over one's head was not enough for parentless children, so they also started a local school they called Winchendon.

In the same era, a group of brothers journeyed by foot to arrive at an immigrant community burdened with a similar set of social ills: economic hardship, malnutrition, illiteracy, and child abandonment were some of the problems that plagued their new home. When severe illness ravaged the community, the historical record notes that countless were "left widowed, without a parent, or orphaned." In an attempt to alleviate these intertwined calamities, the brothers established multiple organizations that provided social services to the community. In describing the founding brethren, one Pepperell senior administrator conveyed how they "started a school [and at] the same time started a press." The archives divulge that the founders created an orphanage and extensive agricultural system to provide the community with a reliable supply of meat, produce, and grain. As the nation sank into the Great Depression, the monks of Pepperell—like the sisters of Winchendon—had already established multiple organizations that provided the immigrant community with a safety net of access-for-all social services, with educational opportunities numbering among them.

For the founders of these schools, addressing social problems like poverty and illiteracy meant acting as social entrepreneurs rather than lobbying others or the government to act. Improving access to education simply meant they should open their own school. One of the present-day nuns offered a succinct phrase from the founding era to illustrate how they understood the cost of improving access would be borne: "The utility for others, the trouble for ourselves." She noted that as the composition of the immigrant communities changed over time, the leadership adapted to meet the changing educational needs of the population: "The mission is dynamic, it's not static. And while those sisters did what they did back then ... they were constantly moving." In time, the labels changed along with the population in the community, but the commitment to broad access for all endured. Leaders broadened their social entrepreneurial scope to include other marginalized populations in the area: one might note, "We're about access to underrepresented minority groups," while another observed, "Part of the mission is to serve ... a large number of Pell-eligible students," and a third claimed, "We're for access to all those first-generation students that are out there." One of Winchendon's many ethnic minority professors spoke about how access and support were intertwined:

> Most of our students could go to the state university down the street. But they would get lost because they're coming out of weak schools. They're coming from families where they don't have a lot of experience in the college world—how to negotiate through college. What I see is a place that gives an academic opportunity to a lot of people who otherwise wouldn't have it.

She asserted that Winchendon's personal support made all the difference for marginalized students:

> You can ship them off to an institution with 50,000 people and there's no advisor, no one looking out for them, no one to help them transition from high school to college ... Winchendon *can* provide that support. That personal support makes a *big* difference.

Amid the changes from their founding eras to the present, the sense of increasing access remained central to the mission of both schools. "At the end of the day, you ask, 'Is it consistent with the mission? Is it in the best interest of the students? Will it help us be able to provide affordable access to [a] Pepperell education?'" the provost elaborated. At Winchendon, access and mission were equally intertwined: "Our mission is about access and support ... that's what we do. Our students are afforded every opportunity to be successful because of access," urged one professor. Social entrepreneurialism was woven into the fabric of their history. As one faculty member offered, "We have a noble mission":

> We expect our students to understand and contribute to society, and most of our students do understand poverty and vulnerability because they come from those backgrounds. We have a lot of students who struggle. We have a lot of students who are needy, and we are committed to their success, and we are committed to what they can become and how their lives will be changed and how their families' lives will be changed through education.

Another professor reiterated the same point succinctly: "We're dedicated to providing access and to moving individuals from thinking, 'I cannot do something' to 'Yes, you can, *and* you can transform the world!'"

Passing the Torch

The middle decades of the 20th century were truly a golden age for Pepperell and Winchendon as their role in providing educational access to the local population expanded. By the 1970s, both schools, like many colleges of the era, had transitioned to a coed residential model and maintained levels of enrollment between 1,500 and 2,000 students drawn primarily from their respective metropolitan areas. Each school secured postsecondary accreditation from a reputable accreditor, and the successive generations of sacrifice by the clergy seemed to have positioned the two schools on a permanent upward trajectory. However, as they approached their centennials, the final decades of the 20th century resulted in an organizational about-face as both schools entered a season of persistent enrollment decline coupled with substantial cost increases.

A sharp drop-off in the supply of clergy resulted in a substantial increase in labor costs for both universities. Senior administrators at Winchendon noted that in prior eras the sisters "populated the whole school, from the president to the registrar's office down to the recruiters, the teachers and the custodians." A similar situation prevailed at Pepperell, where "the costs were kept down" through the voluntary labor of the brothers. However, because of factors related to Vatican II, the leadership pipeline for institutions run by the Catholic Church all but collapsed within a few brief years.[5] A former nun-turned-professor recalled the "Great Exodus": "More than half of the order that I was in left. It wasn't just the young sisters.... There were people who had been there for 30, 40 years." At the same time, changes came to higher education. The organizational culture previously maintained by clergy dedicated to religious service had to become more professional in focus if these schools were to remain legitimate educational institutions. To keep the university running, leaders replaced the voluntary clergy with credentialed experts, which caused an explosion in payroll costs that were offset by dramatic increases in student tuition or selling university assets like the agricultural land Pepperell owned.

The physical and social environments on the two residential campuses slowly fell into neglect, placing further downward pressure on student enrollment. At Winchendon, the historical record describes a deteriorating core campus during this period. The badly outdated fleet of university vehicles traversed campus roads pockmarked by potholes. A grove of ancient oak trees had overgrown many of the buildings, while the historic mansion at the center of campus had been gutted by fire and remained unrestored because the school did not have the funds. Circumstances on the Pepperell campus were arguably worse as pervasive racial tensions in society found their way to campus, further compounding the critical enrollment situation. "Kids [were] being shot on campus ... you had riots in the dorm, kids coming from other cities and destroying the place," the president recalled. Another individual painfully described the state of fear that permeated the campus: "When I got here, Pepperell was like walking into 1954," referring to the social tensions resulting from *Brown v. Board of Education*. "I mean, it was scary! We had several really ugly racial incidents." The physical and social collapse of the residential campus environment made it extremely challenging to recruit prospective students and thereby maintain student enrollment. "No one was sending us their students."

The rising costs and falling enrollment led to a financial crisis. A long-serving Pepperell professor explained, "Our enrollment was going down; our facilities weren't very good, [and] none of us really understood what was going on in terms of the money hole." Neither school had endowment reserves they could draw on. Winchendon's endowment was valued at $2 million, with few methods of adding to it, given most of the 8,000 alumni were "nuns, nurses and educators, [and] they ain't got any money," as one administrator griped. With only tuition dollars as revenue, a senior leader described just how bleak the financial outlook was for Pepperell:

> We didn't even have a system to be able to track our financial situation. We were having difficulty collecting our receivables because we didn't know what the right balances were.... Our line of credit was maxed out. We couldn't borrow any money. We couldn't pay the bills. And we couldn't collect from the students, because we didn't know what they owed us.

A Winchendon senior leader bluntly recalled that the school "was on the verge of failing."

Toward the close of the 20th century, the Pepperell and Winchendon governing boards were confronted with the likelihood of closure. The financial situation was desperate, and repairing the core residential enrollment pipeline amid tumultuous racial circumstances and physically deteriorating campuses seemed insurmountable. In fact, Winchendon leaders had already prepared for the school's demise. "We had a closing plan here," a senior administrator shared. A Pepperell executive similarly recalled, "It was 'going out of business' time." Desperate to avoid the ignominy of closing, the governing boards of each school sought salvation in hiring a new type of president for the schools—laypersons with entrepreneurial vigor who would secure the financial resources necessary to sustain the century-old organizations and lead them out of the financial wilderness. Everything was on the line, and in many senses these unconventional hires were a last-gasp attempt to save the schools.

These were not, however, flash-in-the-pan hires. Although they were entrepreneurial laypersons, the presidents hired to address the crisis were deeply committed to preserving the welcoming ethos and broad access that were hallmarks of the schools. Both presidents were also staunchly committed to staying at the institutions to see their rescue plans through (one remarked that he was so committed to the institution he would be buried next to the sisters). These presidents earned the respect and trust of the boards and faculty they led, making the switch to being led by lay leaders less a revolution than a passing of the torch to a new generation.

Each president put forth aggressive plans designed to resuscitate their dying institutions. The plans were similar and simple and offered only two alternatives. As the Pepperell president related, the governing board had to make an either/or resource decision: "I said, 'You have two choices. Either you want me to raise and develop income sources or go out and get money for an endowment.'" The president of Winchendon similarly insisted the board must choose between generating income or creating an endowment. But both also made it clear there was only one answer they wanted to hear. The president of Winchendon put it this way: "I gave the board two options... Option A is an aggressive option. It could put us into debt, but it will protect our future. Option B is how we'll close this place in 5 years." He continued with a wry smile: "You pick B, I leave. You pick A, I stay. They picked A."

This way of thinking established the fundamental financial paradigm for both organizations moving forward—revenue generation rooted in margin capitalization—as well as the bold style of leadership required to carry it out.

The new Pepperell and Winchendon presidents immediately set to work looking for new revenue sources to stop the financial hemorrhaging caused by the residential core. Rather than rely on the largesse of philanthropists to establish an endowment, as Boxborough and Havertown had done, the new presidents looked back to the founders of their institutions and drew inspiration from the broad network of social services the clergy established for the local immigrant community. In doing so, they would come to establish their own network of educational services that would provide not only access to higher education, but also vital enrollment revenues needed to revive their campus cores.

But the exclusive focus on enrollment growth came with its own liabilities. Relying solely on student enrollment required both schools to rapidly respond to any shifts in the various markets they established. As the Winchendon president cautioned, "We need to be on top of our game all the time!" But that was not the only liability: the exclusive focus on margin capitalization meant that every problem had the same enrollment-focused solution. A Pepperell professor explained how this "business approach to responding to challenges" impacted the school's enrollment philosophy:

> Double enrollments, triple enrollments—get any student from anywhere, anyone who will pay, from any country. It doesn't matter who they are, what their background is, or what they want to do. If they want to study something, we'll create a major, pretend we have it, take their money, and see you later!

Winchendon leaders found themselves entrenched in the same single-solution dilemma: "You want a raise this year? Well, where are we going to get that raise? We've got to either increase the tuition or get more students. In fact, we're probably going to end up having to do both," the chancellor bemoaned. Although leaders at both schools labored in entrepreneurial ways to extend their revenue canopy as far as they possibly could, the stark reality was that all the resources driven by margin capitalization stemmed from the same source—enrollment growth. This transformed small schools dependent on student tuition into large, networked schools still dependent on student tuition.

Sidebar: Paid Partners

While the financial circumstances for most institutions may not have been as acute as the imminent closure that confronted Pepperell and Winchendon, many schools in the late 20th century experienced constraints associated with contending for scarce financial resources coupled with deferred maintenance catching up to their physical plant just as the demographic bottom fell out of the baby boom. With limited resources available to them, their leaders encountered the formidable challenge of reviving and sustaining ailing and financially enfeebled organizations. A senior Pepperell leader offered an apt metaphor to describe the challenge: "All of a sudden you are looking in the medicine cabinet at what can I actually grab onto that can help me meet the business objectives of enrollment?" For many schools situated toward the bottom of the highly stratified system of American higher education, their institutional medicine cabinet appeared bare. But this prompted some leaders to turn to "paid partners" for assistance in providing services and solutions to the resource challenges they faced.

Looking to organizations outside the university for service solutions has been a customary practice in higher education for decades. For example, since the 1940s, most institutions have relied on the Educational Testing Service to provide academic assessment services by administering exams such as the GRE, SAT, Praxis, and TOEFL.[6] But since the early 1990s, institutions have increasingly turned to paid partnerships for assistance in four areas: auxiliary services (printing, athletic concessions, vending, travel agencies, and retail), student services (residential dining, student housing, bookstores, counseling, and child care), enrollment services (admissions, retention, and marketing), and even academic services (course design, course delivery, and advising).[7] Sometimes institutions simply hired the services of consultants to help them make sense of their enrollment strategy and identify new markets to pursue new students and their associated financial aid. Other times—because they either lacked the resources or wanted to quickly establish a presence in a specific market that would have cost millions to do themselves—they outsourced an entire function, such as marketing.

By tapping the market-oriented innovation of using a paid partner, a university could pursue their goals for a fraction of the cost to develop these areas on their own. In exchange for services and expertise, the paid partner required remuneration in the form of billing a fee for service (e.g., consulting), invoicing based on volume (e.g., admissions software), or charging a percentage of student tuition (e.g., enrollment revenue sharing). The latter approach gave paid partners "skin in the game" by rewarding them with a percentage of tuition margins, committing them to an unrelenting focus on growth. While each of these four types of paid partnerships enabled universities to deliver services more efficiently, some offered opportunities for institutions to rapidly generate financial resources. If an institution found itself in a dire moment of survival (as both Pepperell and Winchendon did), its leaders could quickly establish new sources of tuition revenue by pursuing paid partnerships in enrollment services and course design—sources that in their commitment to diversity could be made to appear consistent with their enduring broad access mission.

What the new presidents at both schools proposed—and university administrators across the nation would also embrace—was to rely on outside organizations to assist with services traditionally considered *internal* to the institution. This solution opened the doors to neoliberal entities—"third-party vendors," "external business partners," "edu-businesses," and "embedded for-profits"—to provide an array of services under the market logic of outsourcing, privatization, independent contracting, and subcontracting to effectively achieve student enrollment growth.[8] With most financial resources concentrated in elite institutions at the top of the stratified higher education system, paid partnerships offered an enticing opportunity for low-resourced institutions to have access to services, information, and technology that were customarily beyond their financial reach. They seemed to equalize entrepreneurial opportunities in a competitive environment for institutions like Pepperell and Winchendon, who were committed to providing higher education to impoverished communities but were constrained by resources.

Consistent with their social entrepreneurial spirit, the Pepperell and Winchendon presidents pursued relationships with paid partners as part of their response to the fiscal calamity facing their schools. In the words of one senior administrator, Winchendon employed the services of Alpha Consulting to assist with "generating higher net revenue through retention," while a Pepperell executive explained that the school secured a relationship with Omega Services to "help us create, market, and recruit for nontraditional accelerated students." Both paid partners drew extensively on their business expertise to help university leaders strategize about making enrollment operations more efficient, as well as how to improve operations to maximize tuition revenue. These paid partner relationships rooted in market logics had, according to one Winchendon senior leader, a "tremendous influence" on how leaders came to understand student markets:

> I had an a-ha moment 15 years ago. The president hired a consultant to come get our business office in order. After working with the procedures and trying to find

out exactly where the institution was going with financial aid and the business office, she made the statement, "This is an enrollment-driven institution, not a net revenue-driven institution." What that means is that what we want are as many bodies as possible.

The distinction the consultant pointed out helped the Winchendon administrator understand there were differences in enrollment growth that had implications for the overall revenue model.[9] Traditional schools pursued revenue generation through increasing enrollments in the residential core. But both pioneer and network schools jettisoned that approach in favor of leveraging margin capitalization strategies to generate revenues needed to overhaul the residential campuses and retain legitimacy, and paid partners played a pivotal role in shaping those strategies.

For example, paid partners shaped how university leaders thought about not only the number of students they enrolled, but also the *type* of students they enrolled. One senior Winchendon administrator carefully explained the input Alpha offered: "The admissions office ranks students in tiers one through five, a schema that Alpha introduced [for] leveraging financial aid." The categories were part of a broader framework the consulting firm established for Winchendon to strategically leverage resources from student tuition. "The tier one students are your most academically prepared and maybe they have even the most financial resources. The tier five [students] are your least academically prepared and the most needy." Each category in the hierarchy differentiated between combinations of student academic and financial attributes and could be examined across the 4 years a student paid tuition to determine the enrollment efficacy of an individual:

> We started looking at the populations most at risk, and they are those tier four or five students. The graduation rate drops off dramatically after tier three. Tier one students in this region, if you're Hispanic and [high] SAT—they want you at Harvard. We don't keep the tier one students. Tier two and three are really our "bread and butter."

Alpha Consulting's admissions tiers highlight the tremendous influence paid partners possess in shaping how institutional leaders make sense not only of prospective student markets but also of the different financial "types" of students within those markets.[10]

While paid partners have shaped how institutions pursue prospective students, it might come as a surprise to learn they also play a considerable role in which courses institutions offer. When an institution needs to recruit students to garner additional financial resources, it must have the relevant courses to "sell" to prospective students. In the early 1990s, colleges and universities began to turn to paid partners for course design and distribution (with the expansion of digital learning, this sector has become known by the term *online program managers*).[11] With the rise of paid partners and third-party vendors, institutions that previously lacked resources to develop timely and relevant courses could draw on the assistance of external organizations. This was the case at Pepperell: "As a small private institution, we didn't have the technology, so we worked in partnership with a firm that did," a senior leader admitted.

In partnering with an external organization, a university could quickly secure a foothold in an emerging market, while other institutions that relied on internal processes trailed behind because of resource limitations. The provost of Pepperell reflected on multiple instances where the speed of the paid partnership was advantageous for them: "We were the first one in the marketplace on a variety of different things that then hit ahead of the competitors." He explained that "sometimes it was nothing more than an education endorsement or a new certification that we tapped into, and then we'd saturate the market." In outsourcing course development and delivery, leaders could rapidly broaden their product line without having to invest the necessary funds to expand the infrastructure related to delivering new educational products. By the time competing universities concluded their lengthy internal development processes, Pepperell had secured a foothold in the market and was drawing handsomely on tuition revenues.

The agreement to share revenues—a percentage of the margins from student tuition—meant that universities like Pepperell and Winchendon were required to first distribute a percentage of the surplus tuition revenues to their paid partners before they could use the tuition margins themselves (i.e., margin capitalization). This neoliberal revenue-sharing agreement also meant the external organization could earn greater sums of money by successfully marketing more courses on behalf of the university. Just as the federal government distributed tuition funding to universities on a per-student basis, thus incentivizing enrollment growth, universities paid their external partners on a per-student basis, further incentivizing enrollment growth throughout the system.

Two decades into the 21st century, paid partnerships have become an entrenched practice throughout higher education, becoming a lifeline for university leaders in search of additional financial resources.[12] In the online program manager sector alone, an estimated 525 colleges and universities have partnered up to meet their course design and delivery needs.[13] In many senses, paid partners have become a fundamental component of the financial engine for any institution attempting to pursue greater tuition revenues in a highly competitive landscape.

That certainly was the case at Pepperell and Winchendon, because these schools transitioned from organizations run by the goodwill of clergy to highly nimble institutions that were competent and competitive to keep pace and survive. The newly appointed leaders needed well-resourced and entrepreneurial experts to help them acquire revenues quickly through market logic means. Similar to what happened at the traditional and pioneer schools, the strategy the network schools adopted was the logical outgrowth of their long-standing social entrepreneurialism and their deep commitment to open access to all. Yet network leaders were unprepared for the organizational complexity brought about by the relentless addition of periphery markets—and how the pursuit of growth would impact the value of inclusion that made educational opportunity available to countless students at the network institutions.

Pursuing the Network Strategy

After the two troubled universities hired turnaround presidents[14] to save them from closure, the new leaders of Pepperell and Winchendon immediately set to work implementing the network strategy, a margin capitalization approach that relied on maximizing the frequency of multiple types of revenue-producing enrollment "legs" for the purpose of using their surplus margins to support the "tabletop"—the core residential campus. For the network schools, their residential campus was the central feature of their organizational saga—tangible evidence of the unique accomplishment of the founders to bring educational opportunity to communities of need.[15] Their century-old founding narratives were embedded in these institutions and offered a compelling portrait of purpose and mission. "One of the things that I think is very much within the bricks of this institution is the service to the need . . . always adjusting to the needs of the community," explained a Pepperell board member. The core residential campus served as the "legitimating" mortar that united the vast network of periphery enrollment markets leaders constructed—mortar that was in desperate need of refurbishing and upkeep (Figure 3).

At the heart of the network strategy was a social entrepreneurial vision of access for all, which motivated leaders to continually establish educational opportunities in need-based markets. Leaders at both schools were keenly

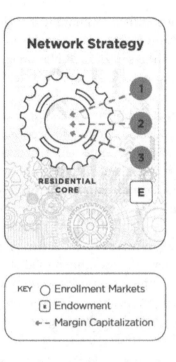

Figure 3 The Network Strategy for Sustaining the Core

attuned to the needs of others because an unmet educational need was an opportunity to provide access and establish new enrollment markets. Network leaders were social entrepreneurs who understood that opportunities in markets presented themselves through the needs of the people the institution serves: "We're very cognizant of a business approach, but we also know it's not just a business: it's a hybrid." On the one hand, their social entrepreneurism galvanized leaders to meet educational needs in innovative ways, but on the other hand, the social focus prohibited the schools from engaging in the unadulterated pursuit of growth and profit—something leaders explicitly emphasized: "We don't answer to shareholders. There's more at the end of the day than the bottom line," the Pepperell provost asserted. The hybrid emphasis was an equal focus on mission and money, each keeping the other in check and creating an unmistakable element of their culture—one a Pepperell professor plainly laid bare while laughing: "The pope wears Prada, man!"

The decision to implement the network strategy to sustain the entrepreneurial approach to access was motivated by the impending closure of the institution, as well as the availability of student tuition as a financial resource. The multiversity and multidivisional organizational form that Pepperell and Winchendon developed drew on the example of their founders and strengthened their commitment to first-generation students and U.S. citizens—but now reached far and wide to meet educational needs from across the state to the soil of multiple foreign nations. Once leaders identified an educational need, they rapidly developed new programs and forms of delivery to saturate markets others had previously overlooked: "I want to do the things that just disrupt the industry," the Pepperell president asserted. Like a diversified portfolio of investment stocks, the network strategy spread the work of revenue generation across multiple types of periphery enrollment markets and reduced exposure to sharp fluctuations in a single market the pioneer schools ultimately experienced. As one Winchendon executive noted, the efforts required incessant creativity: "A lot of schools could be successful if they just had a really large bank account. We do not. The fact that other schools are suffering while we're growing and finding new markets, new sources of interested students, is a testament to creative thinking." The emphasis on inclusion ultimately enabled Pepperell to become one of the largest "producers" of Muslim graduates in the United States and Winchendon to be similarly recognized for the number of degrees it conferred to Hispanic students.

The Tabletop Model

For nearly a century, leaders of Pepperell and Winchendon focused on providing impoverished populations with access to education, but their charitable efforts of inclusion failed to develop a prestigious alumni network that would provide the underpinning for an endowment that could financially shore up their residential core. The absence of a strong endowment made the financial situation for the network institutions particularly acute, in that leaders needed immediate access to revenues rather than relying on the steady flow of interest from savings.

Both presidents explicitly rejected the traditional strategy and its endowment emphasis in favor of a different approach focused on revenue generation. And both ardently proclaimed the institutions needed to focus on "going after income sources, running the place like a business, rather than a traditional college," as the Pepperell president put it. He bluntly described his perspective as captain at the helm of a tuition-driven institution while shaking his head:

> I think that endowments are fool's gold! It doesn't mean I don't want a big endowment, but no institution is endowment driven. You take the University of Virginia,

your total endowment, and divide that by your operating costs, and you see how long you will exist. Not very long.

The Winchendon president offered an identical analogy: "We're not endowment driven; we are enrollment driven." He went on to observe the crux of the matter that led to the network strategy: "We're in a local market, so anything that happens locally affects us immediately."

With the competition for residential students in their local market having intensified considerably, the leaders of the network schools focused on generating tuition revenues in periphery enrollment markets, not unlike the pioneer strategy approach. But there was a key difference between the two approaches. The president of Winchendon likened the network strategy to a jigsaw puzzle: "I have all the pieces of the puzzle . . . I've got adult continuing education, adult evening, all the professional schools, the graduate school, all growth programs." At Pepperell, a tabletop analogy was frequently heard "of adding legs to the table—a revenue diversification strategy," the Pepperell provost articulated. Whereas the pioneer strategy focused on establishing multiple *sites* for a select type of periphery enrollment market—a single leg—the network leaders created multiversities, focused on maximizing the multiple *types* of periphery enrollment markets—a many-legs approach. In the network strategy, the aim was to maximize the number of periphery enrollment markets, constantly focusing on filling in gaps in the puzzle.

While the network strategy emphasized maximizing the legs of the table, the core residential campus—the tabletop itself—also held a vital role in the margin capitalization imagery. The Winchendon provost shared the unapologetic viewpoint of the president: "'We have to preserve the main campus. That's our main reason for being . . . it's what provides access.'" While the many legs functioned to provide a diverse supply of enrollment revenues, the tabletop served as the institutional "face," the vital welcoming characteristic of the school that undergirded its mission. Prospective students, particularly those in the periphery enrollment markets (i.e., international, adult, online, vocational, dual enrollment, military, transfer), associated the bricks and mortar of the residential campus with the permanence and quality of a "real" college education. Although the core residential campus was ailing financially, it remained the central component that grounded the various features of the strategy into a coherent vision—one that inverted the traditional strategy's "you come to a tradition" to a strategy where broad access meant "the tradition comes to you."

The president of Pepperell went on to explain not only that "the more legs I have, the sturdier the top," but also how "each leg is a separate income source."

The tabletop model was not just about establishing additional legs, but also about strategically accounting for the fact that each leg was dynamic and varied from year to year. "We started with undergraduate, graduate, adult, online, Farmington, Hartly. I keep adding different sources, so when certain numbers are down, other numbers tend to be up." Each new periphery enrollment market generated varying degrees of marginal revenues from year to year: "Our students pay what I think the market will bear. So I have a different price in Farmington, I have a different price in Hartly, a different price online," he clarified. "I've got over 50 sites in the northern part of the state, most of them at different prices, because the market bears different things." Declines in one student enrollment market were offset by gains in others. Taken as a whole, the aggregate approach resulted in annual increases in both student enrollments and revenues for Pepperell and Winchendon. This approach provided the institutions with a financial buffer against the fluctuations inherent to market systems, allowing them to "shim" different legs in different years given prevailing market conditions. As a Pepperell business professor observed,

> You may take a hit in any given year in one program, but it's not going to be the death of what you're doing, because you've got a lot of other things that are going on ... [that's why] you've *got* to have multiple legs on the stool!

The bold plans proposed by the executives brought on by the governing boards gained momentum, and the network strategy accordingly came to look like the natural evolution of the schools' broad access philosophy. The decision to ensure that multiple revenue types were established ultimately reinforced the idea the university should be run like a business where revenues equal or exceed expenditures. A Winchendon financial official explained, "Being able to tie the enrollment piece with the budget piece, knowing the critical nature of what we need ... [means] being able to read the tea leaves ahead of time." A colleague offered a more judicious explanation of the underlying strategy that redeployed resources from student tuition:

> We are not-for-profit, but we substitute the word profit with surplus. And you need surplus revenue for a nonprofit to survive. You have to be able to invest back into your organization ... those revenues are fed back into the organization for growth.... It's a question of how do we use our surplus for growth?

But not everyone was so nuanced. A Winchendon vice president with oversight of a periphery enrollment market bluntly explained, "We're truly a cash cow for Winchendon. And I don't care, that's fine; I love making money."

Network leaders continually identified communities in need and established dozens of periphery programs—adult learning, international branch campuses, online programs, transfer partnerships, graduate medical programs, military education, and dual enrollment—that enabled them to use tuition surpluses to reinvest in the residential campus using a margin capitalization approach. Absent this approach, both schools would have shuttered within the decade, but by embracing the network strategy, the schools grew in ways aligned with their core mission that allowed them to survive. "The university was growing at a frenetic pace," a Winchendon nun recollected of the implementation era. Yet each new leg added a degree of complexity to the table that over time began to resemble an unwieldy structure—one that counterintuitively added weight to the tabletop, which ultimately began to crack under the pressures of servicing numerous legs.

Buildings and Bodies

Despite their relentless focus on establishing multiple periphery enrollment markets, network leaders never lost sight of the necessity of transforming their residential core. They recognized that without the tabletop to anchor the legs, all they were doing was delaying their inevitable demise. "If you don't pay attention to your main core, you can make *big* mistakes there," a Winchendon senior leader intoned. Their deliberate transformation of the core using the peripheral revenues was directed at two primary areas—buildings and bodies. Network leaders spent hundreds of millions of dollars erecting new academic buildings, state-of-the-art sports complexes, dozens of modern residence halls, and multiple dining facilities, recreation centers, and student unions. "Climbing walls, football programs, luxury dorms, and swimming pools, we've gone right down that road," the Winchendon chancellor confessed. Perhaps revealing changes to the culture as a whole, the physical element of the residential campus and not the welcoming character of the school was what left the most notable impression on prospective students. "When people walk on this campus, they're impressed with the buildings," a Pepperell coach candidly said of his recruits, before remembering to add what used to come first: "and the people."

Because they lacked the extensive fundraising resources available to the traditional institutions, network leaders funded the substantial overhaul of their physical infrastructure using the same margin capitalization approach the pioneer institutions used—surplus marginal revenues from periphery enrollment markets were reallocated to fund the residential core. "A lot of these buildings are paid for by having issued bonds and paying those bonds off through the continuing revenue stream that is generated from enrollments," a Pepperell finance official explained. Winchendon's president offered the most telling remark: "We need to make money so that we can pump it into . . ." He paused, appearing to recall the dire straits of just a few years ago, and its meaning was unmistakable: there but for the grace of peripheral markets goes Winchendon.

Time and again, administrators referred to the margin capitalization reallocation processes as the solution to their financial dilemma. "Since you are growing, you grab the resources from the new students coming in," a Winchendon senior leader said. And the neoliberal loan policies (discussed in Chapter 1) were central to the strategy. As the Winchendon president stated, "We couldn't furnish [the education] if it wasn't for the feds. If we didn't have Pell Grant and guaranteed student loans, half of our kids couldn't come to school." The Pepperell chancellor was equally blunt: "You become dependent on federal money."

But what was truly telling was the interaction between the peripheral market and the paid partners. A newly established leg might yield little surplus revenue the first few years if the institution bore the start-up costs itself, whereas another enrollment market established at the same time might yield substantial revenue margins right away if a paid partner was hired. A vice president explained that when Pepperell established its online periphery enrollment market with the assistance of a paid partner, the revenues improved their transformation possibilities considerably: "We were making so much more money because of the [partnership], so then all of a sudden, we're having all this money coming in . . . a pervasive positive started happening."

Year after year, network leaders focused on establishing additional legs to fund new buildings they erected as part of the transformation of their residential campus. "We've built about 26 buildings on campus in the last 15 years," Pepperell's president relayed. The Winchendon provost similarly reckoned, "We've been building constantly for 30 years. There's always construction going on." The new buildings in turn strengthened the enrollment momentum of the residential core. "When you build a new facility and you have all the accompaniments related to programming and bells and whistles, you get about a 50% enrollment spike," the Pepperell provost explained. Total student enrollments for both universities increased three- and fivefold during the boom years.

Like many institutions of higher learning, during the 1970s the student body at Pepperell and Winchendon experienced a cultural transformation as the schools shifted from single-sex to co-educational campuses.[16] Two decades later, the student bodies of the network schools underwent a second and equally profound cultural transformation. One Winchendon executive explained that network schools lacked the generational enrollment stability of traditional institutions: "At my former university [there] was a many-generations-deep alumni base. There were people whose parents went there, and they went there." Rather than legacy admissions, the network schools recruited heavily from their own metropolitan areas, which subjected their core residential campus to demographic shifts in local markets. Ethnic demographic changes in the 1990s and 2000s within the communities of the network universities meant a new generation of students began knocking at their doors. Consistent with their welcoming philosophy and staunch commitment to providing local educational opportunities, both schools pivoted to meet the needs of their new student communities. Winchendon embraced the opportunity to teach Spanish-speaking Hispanic students from low socioeconomic neighborhoods, while Pepperell's ecumenical outlook led them to seek out nearby Muslim students.[17]

Network institutions expanded their residential enrollments by recruiting marginalized communities other institutions neglected. "In the U.S., demographics are changing, and many universities didn't want to see that or didn't want to gear towards that. But we did," explained one Winchendon vice president. The Pepperell president insisted it was a matter of inclusion: "People say to me, 'How much money do you spend on the Muslim students for marketing? What countries do your Muslim students come from?'" After listing three or four nearby towns rather than foreign countries, the president continued, "They are third, fourth, fifth generation. It was our ignorance not knowing they're part of the community." And although operating a residential core was still a "loss leader" for network schools, there were financial incentives for pursuing students in overlooked communities. In welcoming Hispanic students, Winchendon became eligible for federal minority student funding when enrollments surpassed the 25% threshold.[18] And for Pepperell, recruiting the local Muslim population had spillover effects in attracting students of color from other predominantly Muslim cultures as well.[19] These schools' mission of offering broad access thus aligned with their economic interests—a true social entrepreneurial blend.

In the process of transforming the lives of a new population of students, the culture of the residential core was transformed. Walking about campus, multiple languages could be heard, traditional attire was commonly seen, and dozens of international flags were showcased atop poles. The network leaders worked to establish academic support and advising services for these populations that previously did not have higher education on their radar: "You've got to have all the safety nets, bridge programs, student support services to be able to support these students from a retention standpoint," the Pepperell provost asserted. But senior leaders believed that including new groups of students would ensure the future of the institution. The Winchendon president proudly contrasted his school with others in the region:

> They're what I call the schools of yesterday, because they look like the state of yesterday. They have less than 20% minorities. We're 50% Hispanic, almost 20% international, 6% African American, 2% American Indian. We're the school of today and tomorrow. Their markets are shrinking, my market is growing. They may have a big dollar endowment, but they don't have a future. I got a future.

Taking "Place" Abroad

In their endeavor to add as many legs to the tabletop revenue model as possible, the leaders of the network institutions looked for enrollment opportunities abroad in ways other institutions did not. While most colleges and universities commonly recruit foreign students to the United States or send American students to study abroad, the network institutions boldly chose to educate foreign students in their own country, on their own soil. Pepperell and Winchendon established new international markets by taking in-person learning to foreign nations in a manner similar to how the pioneer institutions' took place to marginalized populations in the United States through unconventional classroom settings. The effort to take place abroad was both social and entrepreneurial—it aligned with their mission to provide education to communities in need, but it was also an opportunity to establish an educational market with few competitors. The network leaders built a global network of branch campuses across Asia, Europe, and Latin America such that a Pepperell professor declared, "When the sun rises and the sun sets, it's rising and setting on a [Pepperell] course somewhere in the world."

In the 1990s and 2000s, Pepperell and Winchendon began to establish the beginning of an important leg in their tabletop model—international branch campuses. This was a unique characteristic of the schools that adopted the network strategy and highlighted the extent of their interest to act on their social entrepreneurialism to create periphery enrollment markets. Leaders were selective with the nations they chose to work with: "There's no university in the world that can be good at every country," the Pepperell president cautioned. He elaborated how selecting a nation provided them with the confidence to build a network of in-person campuses across Asia:

> I wanted Pepperell to focus on a single country, [to] get extremely good at it so we become the portal to that country, [and move] from this country to that country.... The country I picked was China, and it has just blossomed for us.... We have 1,000 graduates from our programs just in China, a huge network of Chinese students coming to this university, and many, many, many Pepperell students going to China on Chinese government scholarships.

The deliberate approach in selecting a focal nation to concentrate on proved to be invaluable for Pepperell and Winchendon because the initial relationship set a precedent for continued enrollment success. "The market that we're serving, we're approaching in a very supportive way, in a very strategic way, seeing them as our customers. We understand them very well," offered a Winchendon senior leader. The Pepperell president was decidedly more blunt: "I wish I had picked the lottery like I picked China," he quipped.

In establishing their first international branch campus, network leaders discovered what worked and what did not in the new context. Leaders drew on these experiences to create a template to establish additional branches and condense the time frame in which they were able to deliver new courses and programs. A professor working in the program asserted once the template was established, "It isn't a challenge if you want to grow internationally." The template contributed mightily to the ease of implementation, with faculty confessing to the remarkable agility when it came to "setting up shop": "It really takes us just 2 weeks to set up a system to get ready to offer a bachelor's degree in [lists countries]. We have the structure for it." The professor reiterated his point with a quickened cadence: "Other than the physical infrastructure, we just need 2 weeks to set up our system over there with the instructors and the curriculum ... we have the infrastructure from here to just go mobile." The international template the network institutions established was comprehensive in scope and merely required leadership to execute. The school's prior involvement with paid partners to establish other enrollment markets afforded them a refined knowledge of the components needed for "templates" that could be transferred across markets—templates Winchendon leaders further innovated across foreign contexts and cultures.

Using their template approach, the Pepperell and Winchendon presidents provided the decisive leadership needed to establish additional international campuses. The vice president at Winchendon with oversight of teams exploring different countries explained,

> Once we find that opportunity . . . I just walk to the president and say this is the opportunity, this is what we need, this is the risk, the disadvantages, the advantages, and the outcome, and he's going to say yes or no.

He clarified that once the president received the information, the decision could take less than a week depending on the circumstances. He was quick to point out how the overall process stressed efficiency:

> We can move really quick and that gives you the ability to create initiatives that in the long term are going to bring you students. The model works really well because it isn't bureaucratic and it isn't long. And the key is the president of this university allows you to create. If it is a good idea and is going to be beneficial for the students, for the university, he's going to say yes.

The template approach and decisive leadership were two key factors that enabled network institutions to draw on their social entrepreneurial roots to establish a network of branch campuses across broad reaches of the globe. "We have a lot of students in East Asia," the Winchendon chancellor pointed out, wryly adding, "The president likes to say, 'You cannot throw a stick in East Asia without running into our graduates.'" Although they were quick to establish international programs, the leaders of network schools were in it for the long game. One Winchendon vice president noted,

> The difference is many universities are working or are going out there in the world and they recruit students for the next semester, and it isn't worth it. We go and we plant the seed, we work, we keep going. We keep going until we know that those results are going to be seen later.

The approach paid off, and both schools were repeatedly invited by foreign governments to establish additional branch campuses.

The international legs the network institutions created were remarkably successful with regard to generating new campuses and new enrollments that took into account a complex array of nations and cultures, one that few colleges and universities in the United States accomplished. They were successful early adopters of the international brick-and-mortar model. As one Winchendon professor boasted, "Harvard couldn't do it, Yale couldn't do it. A small

Catholic institution did it. I mean, that's a huge deal!" While the addition of each international campus broadened the expansive reach of the revenue canopy, the cultural challenges and administrative burden of managing a widespread network began to tax the abilities of even the most skilled executives. Over time, the demands of many programs spread over a wide array of countries meant that cracks in the educational edifice these schools were building would inevitably appear.

The Two Academic Towers

University leaders traditionally solicit the collaborative involvement of faculty to establish a new academic program or initiative, a practice known as *shared governance*. But when asked how he developed a new periphery revenue source for the tabletop, the president of Pepperell quipped without hesitation: "Didn't ask the faculty. I just started it." Instead of the deliberate approach the traditional schools embraced—one that contributed to their undoing—turnaround presidents jettisoned the collective approach for a top-down method of execution. Pepperell's president confidently continued, "Twenty years ago, faculty would have railed, 'You need our permission!' No, I don't, I just did it." Encapsulated in his words was an intimate knowledge of a tension between the academic tradition of collective shared governance and the unencumbered decision-making of the corporate sector that senior leaders desperately desired.

According to the presidents of network institutions, to repeatedly establish new periphery enrollment markets in a timely manner, they needed an unobstructed path of production and approval within the organization. When navigating the creation of innovations like overseas branches, it is common for organizations to "decouple" the espoused channels of authority one expects to see—like processes of shared governance—from the new practices and actions that aim to enhance the prospects of survival.[20] Rather than decoupling organizational practice from organizational structure, the presidents of the network institutions innovatively established entirely separate structures through which select production functions and approvals might flow more readily in a multidivisional form.

Despite being well versed in the culture of collective governance, the network presidents made two carefully planned structural changes. First, the presidents modified or removed authoritative aspects of the existing faculty governance structure—"bottom-up" channels within the university that slowly moved vital information through formal committees and multiple processes as a class or academic program was developed. Debate and deliberation at each stage are not only common, but also expected, as faculty governance—like peer review—aims to emphasize collective knowledge production within the academy. The Winchendon president attempted to dilute the collective authority of the faculty senate by establishing three unique faculty councils that reported to three separate university executives. Senior leaders also made changes to the Pepperell Faculty Senate to hasten its processes. An academic administrator at Pepperell asserted these changes were vital to eliminate existing bottlenecks in its decision-making channel:

> We knew we needed to diversify, and we knew that we needed to have a governance structure that required you to go through your processes, but we knew we needed to streamline a governance process. We knew that we needed to give a lot of autonomy to people and that we could not have every single constituency involved in decision-making. So we did an academic reorganization.

The network leaders made a second structural change regarding faculty governance, one that established a separate "top-down" channel to guide production and approval from upper administrative levels directly to their intended areas within the university without any obstruction resulting from bureaucratic processes. In short, the network presidents desired the periphery revenue-generating parts of the organization to report directly to them. To be sure, the idea of having a revenue-generating area of the university report directly to a president is by no means a foreign practice in higher education. The most common occurrence of this practice has been maintained for decades with the elite institutions in Power Four conferences,[21] whose athletics departments report directly to the university president for scrupulous oversight of their revenue production and branding. Yet while it has become commonplace in higher education for athletics to have this top-down channel, it is unusual to have an academic revenue structure report directly to the university president as Winchendon and Pepperell did—that is, until the network strategy came into vogue.

A vice president asserted the independent structure enabled the division to function more efficiently outside the traditional academic division:

> I have my own marketing and recruitment director, I have my own accreditation director, I have my own director of strategic initiatives. We have our own advising. We do our own admissions. So really, we're very stand-alone. And that's made it really easy to get this done ... because the president is a forward thinker.

As the vice president explained, academic courses, programs, and strategic plans for the periphery could be established without involving a single faculty member in the Winchendon residential core. The multidivisional form enabled bypassing the "bottleneck." Although the changes left the faculty governance structure intact, it possessed considerably less authority moving forward, as one professor lamented:

> We have a faculty assembly, but we do not have a senate. It doesn't have any real power. We have a university planning council, but they don't have any real power. At a lot of levels, he [the president] can just think up shit and do it.

These top-down channels to the presidents facilitated rapid decision-making and improved speed for product implementation (courses and programs) that in many cases resulted in the schools successfully saturating the market.

Indeed, as a result of circumventing the bottom-up collective decision-making path driven by faculty, dozens of revenue-producing legs were rapidly added to the tabletop because senior administrators had achieved the necessary authority to establish new periphery enrollment markets. "Let's take Farmington and Hartly," one Pepperell administrator conveyed with a furrowed look of dismay. "He didn't ask anybody's permission, he didn't come to the faculty and say, 'Will you help me?' I mean, psh, he just went out one day and did it." A Winchendon vice president explained the advantages a top-down model offered and how it set network schools apart from competitors, enabling them to quickly establish periphery enrollment sources. "When there's a new program out there, it doesn't take us years of hand wringing and getting consensus on committees to go after something. The president [just] says, "We're going after this.'" In the top-down channel, revenue-generating programs could seemingly be created ex nihilo—through the spoken word of the one in charge. While multiple channels made it easier for leaders to repeatedly establish new enrollment sources, they made the ongoing task of managing the many periphery sources complex—a phenomenon that led to an overload of the strategy itself.

Speed and Saturation

If the network institutions were to survive, leaders needed to act unmistakably fast. Not only were the two universities in need of immediate revenue, but also they were ailing in an era one Pepperell administrator recalled as "intense and incredible competition" among institutions. There was a prevailing mindset of urgency: "If we cannot offer the format and the courses that the students need in a timely manner, we're going to lose our share." Realizing they could not keep pace with the intensifying competition for residential students, the network leaders focused on implementing quick decision-making to dominate periphery enrollment markets before competing universities could enter the same space. A Winchendon professor described the rapid recruitment resolve in blunt terms: "This is a place where we say 'Yes' first and 'How?' second."

According to the network leaders, the competition to enroll students became particularly acute as many nearby colleges and universities also pursued enrollment growth, thereby intensifying pressure to secure residential students. And if there was one essential facet of the market to which network leaders were resolutely attuned, it was toward those institutions they deemed direct competitors. Following the adage of keeping your adversaries close, one Pepperell senior leader disclosed details regarding a recent engagement with a university president: "I had dinner with him. He welcomes us in with one hand, but he is competing," the leader remarked. He then smiled and said, "We're going to compete back!"

Senior administrators found it more challenging to grow their core residential population to secure revenues and conveyed that circumstances required an immediate change.

> For-profits [were] starting to explode, online education starting too, all these kinds of things. We realized that we had to really get busy. And it could not be business as usual in taking 2 or 3 years to make a decision . . . from then on, we realized what needed to happen.

A Winchendon executive asserted that withstanding sharp competition through adaptation was essential. "The customer is changing. The economy is always changing. So you have to adapt to that situation." With physical campuses in need of repair, leaders understood they could not solely pursue measured growth in residential markets; rather, the network institutions needed to quickly adapt to the competition, as a Pepperell administrator poignantly clarified: "[We] didn't run from the competition. We realized that we had to have a sense of urgency without creating panic." The approach became a key part of the Pepperell administrative culture and decision-making where they quickly confronted competitors head-on by focusing on speed and saturation.

To create new enrollment markets that could withstand competition, the network leaders worked to anticipate market demand for new educational programs whose revenues could then be used to support the residential campus through margin capitalization. One Pepperell vice president explained,

> You have to be able to invest in understanding your industries and your markets in advance, because you have to be able to get new program development and program revisions done now for things that you're going to be delivering in 9 months, 12 months. Completely done.

The Pepperell president repeatedly described this approach as anticipating what may be coming.

> Bill Gates has a book out called *The Road Ahead*. [In it] he goes to Atari. What was the earliest computer? It was a Commodore. And he said that the problem with those [two] companies was they did not look around the corner. We need to look around the corner.

Pepperell and Winchendon leaders always had an eye out for their own opportunity to create new periphery enrollment markets, but they also—as if engaged in a game of chess—always took into account how the competition might respond. "That's the biggest challenge," shared one Winchendon professor. "Are we seeing the right future and are we preparing for it correctly?"

Network leaders executed quick decision-making to saturate a new periphery enrollment market before competing institutions could do the same. It was here that the market-oriented paid partnerships truly reaped dividends for network institutions. They contracted with paid partners to help develop online programs, establish a template to mobilize international branch campuses, and create administrative "channels" within the university to guide the development of new courses and programs. The aim of these approaches focused on condensing the "speed to market" of the innovation in question with the aim of inundating the market: "It's pretty entrepreneurial and innovative, we don't discuss things to death. You go through your processes in 60–90 days and 'BOOM!' make a decision," the Pepperell provost proclaimed.

But unlike the pioneer schools, which concentrated their efforts on a single periphery market, the "first-one-in" approach of network leaders was composed of many *types* of concentrated revenue legs of all different "lengths" added to support their tabletop. A senior official shared the diverse offerings Pepperell created during these years and the lengths to which the school's leadership would go to gain an advantage in a particular market:

> We did all kinds of strategic innovative things. We were one of the first comprehensives to partner and do degree completion on community colleges' campuses. [We]

used differential tuition rates. [We] did wrap-around gen ed stuff. [We did] 3 + 1 kind of partnerships,[22] just all kinds of different things that we were willing to do.... We were willing to explore anything.

While both network and pioneer leaders sought to be first, pioneer institutions were the first in a given enrollment market and created multiple *sites*, whereas the network institutions repeatedly aspired to be first in many different *types* of enrollment markets. The entrepreneurial approach taken by the network leaders highlights that in the marketplace of innovation and ideas, speed to market influences the extent to which an organization can capitalize on maximizing the possibilities for growth. It also highlights how leaders created new arenas of competition by pursuing new periphery enrollment markets when the competition for residential students substantially increased among local institutions. Administrators readily understood that their survival rested on surplus tuition revenues generated from enrollment growth. "Everything in those last dozen years have been intentionally strategic decisions," the Pepperell provost pointed out. "We have a growth-driven board, growth-driven abbey, growth-driven president, put a growth-driven senior team together, we [even] have the saying: 'In growth we trust.'"

Like their pioneer counterparts, network leaders pursued economic reasoning through a margin capitalization strategy where growth alone was supposed to prevail. With a dual focus on both mission and money, leaders labored relentlessly with paid partners to expand their network by adding new revenue legs. Yet in their pursuit of developing a diversified portfolio of resources whose balance could withstand the fluctuating whims of the market, the network strategy overloaded the tabletop, which forewarned of an oncoming collapse.

The Dilemma of Diversity

For more than 2 decades, the Pepperell and Winchendon presidents provided network institutions with stable leadership committed to welcoming others wherever they were located and whatever they wanted to learn. Lacking substantive endowments, leaders worked quickly and relentlessly to establish many different types of periphery enrollment legs that provided the institutions with marginal tuition revenues and momentum to develop a network of regional, national, and international campuses within communities of need. The two schools transformed into multiversities not unlike their more famous research-focused brethren, the University of

Washington and New York University, both known for "doing many different things simultaneously" and whose "defining characteristic was its reliance on many different forms of revenue to fund diverse activities."[23] The network schools differed slightly in that they were multiversities with multiple enrollment interests. "We are bigger than Notre Dame . . . but we're different. They have mostly residential students; my kids are all over the world," the Pepperell president asserted. Their approach as social entrepreneurs offered countless opportunities to identify need-based markets where network leaders could pursue both educational access and neoliberal tuition resources, but the ever-broadening scope of their enrollment success became burdensome. University leaders were forced to shutter select periphery campuses, abandon building projects, and reduce spending in an acutely challenging resource environment. As one senior administrator from Pepperell observed, "The tectonic plates are shifting beneath higher education," and the tsunami generated eventually reached the shores of the network schools.

The tidal wave Pepperell and Winchendon faced when the network strategy was rocked by the higher education earthquake was the product of external events and internal tensions. To stay ahead of others competing for the same students, leaders embraced greater levels of risk that "pushed the envelope" of their inclusionary values. In addition to the external competition with peer institutions, leaders were unexpectedly confronted by an internal competition where siloed divisions within the university competed with each other as a result of the added organizational complexity. In their incessant efforts to add new revenue-generating legs, network leaders created what amounted to a second tabletop in the form of satellite campuses that siphoned off the financial support existing legs were offering the residential core. The complexity of the vast network became overwhelming for individual leaders to monitor and the system developed significant financial imbalances along with cultural tensions. Ultimately, a few critical decisions by leaders cost the network schools substantially—millions in lost revenues and negative national media coverage—and their university communities were left grasping for a sense of stability and wondering what strategy to turn to next to support their residential cores.

Living on the Edge

As network leaders established new satellite campuses, new professional schools, new international locations, and new construction in the residential core, they did so in ways that challenged existing norms. Like their pioneer brethren, which had been labeled degree mills for being first, network institutions were socially stigmatized. One Winchendon administrator explained how in the eyes of the higher education world, endlessly adding revenue legs was seemingly a mark of madness:

> Nobody else was doing this then, but [the president] said we need to be doing this, so we created the adult degree completion program. It was the only face-to-face, accelerated, 8-week term [program] around.... People thought he was crazy.

Senior leaders acknowledged the "insanity" in their leadership approach. "Adding our professional schools.... A lot of people thought we were crazy," a Winchendon senior leader confessed. The China programs and satellite campuses were so against the grain at the time that everyone outside the network schools (and not a few inside their walls as well) thought the school leadership was driving the institution into the ground. One professor contrasted Pepperell's approach with his prior experiences at elite institutions: "When I look at the organization of the institution, I see a lot wrong and a lot of risk . . . this one is crazy in a lot of ways."

To stay one step ahead of institutions competing for the same students, university leaders embraced greater levels of risk associated with the neverending admissions efforts needed to recruit students. Senior administrators were expected to "be a risk taker without jeopardizing . . . the reputation of the university," a Winchendon director confided. An administrative colleague similarly observed they had become an institution that lived on the edge: "We're risking a lot. The [new professional] school, as the president says, is like a fire hydrant that somebody opened up and it's just running water, and we don't have a student in there yet!" Further diversification demanded further risk, opening up the possibility that multiple enrollment markets might move in concert—positively or negatively. Instead of the risk traditional schools faced in concentrating their efforts on the endowment or facing "two fronts" as the pioneer schools did, network leaders were simultaneously buffeted on all sides by the need to keep stabilizing the table using many legs.

At its core, the network strategy was supposed to mitigate the risk of enrollment decline by spreading the burden across multiple types of fluctuating enrollment markets. However, the process of establishing multiple enrollment legs engendered a mindset of going beyond acceptable limits, whereby leaders risked violating their values. In a tone of regret, one senior Winchendon leader candidly confided,

> Years ago, one of our former general counsels [said], "You do realize you just crossed this line in the sand?" I thought to myself, "Gosh, he may be right here" . . . we had pushed it right to the edge, but it took him pointing it out to me that maybe we went over the line this time.

The tension between increasing enrollment and undercutting values became particularly palpable in their relationships with paid partners—the external organizations that provided outsourced services to establish new periphery enrollment markets.

Winchendon leaders pivoted away from their relationship with Alpha Consulting, the paid partner who helped them improve admissions strategies in multiple enrollment markets. But the impact of the Alpha framework lingered among administrators who continued to frame admissions and financial aid using the student ranking schema. With most of the local tier one students bound for elite institutions, the enrollment challenge that vexed Winchendon leaders was where to locate more bread-and-butter tier two and three students who could secure federal financial aid and graduate, rather than the many local underprepared students (tiers four and five) the university had been admitting to sustain enrollment growth, but who customarily dropped out. "Where am I going to get more threes?" an admissions director exclaimed.

> We've really saturated our geographic area, so to get more threes and twos, we have to go outside of our market area. Do we want to creep more widely outside of the state? We cannot seem to get fours and fives graduated—is that a moral and ethical issue for us?

Neoliberal policies essentially incentivized a "students-as-resources" mentality at these schools, leading to a "devil made me do it" attitude at odds with their mission. As a Winchendon faculty member put it,

> I have concerns about their debt load, the students that we attract. Many of them borrow as much money in a year as their parents make in a year . . . to end their university career with $40,000 or $50,000 in student debt with an undergraduate degree in art?

The Alpha admissions framework set Winchendon leaders not only on an upward trajectory of enrollment growth, but also on a path to make decisions they described as going over "to the dark side." One vice president explained a worrisome practice involving finances and maximizing enrollment that posed a value risk:

> I guess to use an ugly phrase, it's kind of like the bait-and-switch. You come to our school, we give you a good financial aid package up front for year 1 . . . they aren't necessarily going to be successful students, but they can borrow.

The administrator continued in a lower voice:

> Year 2 rolls around. Because they're not [the] top tier students . . . they don't get those academic scholarships, and so now they need loans. Students who are borrowing money to go to school, and not necessarily going to be successful—that's another way to really boost your net revenue.

The senior leader concluded with a postscript about how the mission can become twisted on the path to growth. "This is just not what we're about . . . I don't think people sat around in a smoke-filled room and hatched this plot. I think it's just our penchant for growth that resulted in this."

Pepperell similarly jettisoned its relationship with a paid partner. "Are you sure this is confidential?" a senior official cautiously inquired. Competition had recently increased and made it challenging to maintain the rate of growth that had been providing the margin capitalization revenues. The solution arrived at was that Pepperell should pursue the tuition margins being distributed to the paid partner (typically 25%–50% for most schools) rather than just enrollment growth alone. "If you're taking all this off the top [for the paid partner], and yet we're still making all this money, why don't we do it ourselves, so then we can make all of it?" The proposal carried significant risk to secure the additional margins and was a stark shift in thinking—from "More students provide more money" to "We can get more money from each student." For this administrator, the decision blatantly crossed the line: "To me, it's kind of a gluttony question. It's so not Catholic. It's like, so sinful."

Pepperell leadership ended the contract with its outsourced provider and worked to create its own digital infrastructure to offer online courses themselves. However, the effort to recapture surplus tuition margins backfired, causing enrollment to plummet:

> So they cut the contract, which of course said, "You cannot use this, this, this, and this for so many years," which was the base of the income. Then we didn't replace them with knowledgeable people, so it's as if you traded in the Bentley for the old Chevette.

Leaders were left with limited courses to develop and restricted intellectual property, and they no longer possessed the technology and admissions resources the paid partner previously provided. Despite countless attempts to resuscitate their online enrollment market, the senior leader described the damage to the leg as irreparable: "All of a sudden we went from getting millions of dollars to virtually nothing."

Competition Within and Without

Like most colleges and universities in this era, Pepperell and Winchendon leaders were confronted with intense enrollment competition from nearby institutions of all types. The admissions environment was understood as stiff competition for students who had plenty of options: "This is a competition, and the market is really hard," an exasperated Winchendon admissions leader vented. The two metropolitan markets in which the network institutions were located remained a focus of for-profit institutions that relied heavily on marketing. The Pepperell provost did not mince words in describing their competitive presence: "The constant threat of for-profits, they are beasts! They're not going away, and they continue to explode like crazy! And not only that, but the amount of money they have behind them for marketing!" he exclaimed in a tone of envy and disbelief. More important, leaders asserted that local institutions were competing for all student types:

> It's just so much more competitive and so much more market driven, traditional [enrollments] even. Nontraditional has always been market driven, but traditional for the first time in the last 5 years or so has also become far more market driven.

While most institutions experienced competition from one another, network institutions were unexpectedly confronted by a second level of competition—one that strangely came from within.

With their focus on serving many different types of student markets, Pepperell and Winchendon (from the inside) appeared as complex as the higher education landscape itself. With their multiple types of enrollment markets spread nationally and internationally, the network institutions possessed an organizational complexity that mirrored multidivisional-form corporations. According to leaders, such complexity created conditions whereby parts of the institution competed with other parts for students and resources in the same way they competed with peer institutions. At Winchendon, the internal competition for resources between the professional programs and the residential undergraduate programs was palpable. As one senior academic official explained, by choosing to grow in different enrollment markets, Winchendon leaders subjected themselves to competing accreditation policies[24] that governed the flow of resources within the institution—some of which were the opposite of the streamlined operational model they sought:

> If you have a [professional] school, the [professional accreditors] are going to come and tell you, [that] you need a dean and four assistant deans. And every one of those assistant deans needs a secretary. And if you have this many students, you're going to hire this many faculty and they're going to have this many secretaries. And you're going to have this many counselors. And anything less we're not going to approve.

The same internal tensions were present at Pepperell, with different areas of the organization competing for resources. As one senior leader explained, "Marketing and I have had the conversation, 'How do we find the time, and what do we put first?' I mean, there are financial resources that are being fought for and pulled when you look at the competing priorities."

The organizational complexity also created recruitment competition in areas where multiple enrollment markets overlapped, particularly in the local metropolitan area. A Pepperell executive shared her frustration with the self-inflicted dilemma: "We have a Woodside campus and adult accelerated programs versus main campus—adult to graduate programs—those are same dollars competing for [the] same market... we're recruiting the same student market!" A colleague corroborated that the challenge was institutionally produced: "I'd say that sometimes we have competing priorities... that, to me, is an institutional problem, not an industry problem."

In some instances, the internal competition caused the tabletop model to backfire. Resources that were supposed to flow from peripheral legs to residential core were actually reversed. A Pepperell vice president tasked with launching a new in-person branch campus in another state described the dilemma.

> The start-up and the creation of our Farmington campus [is] pulling on the time and availability of existing staff resources that are *here* to support the main campus enrollment and growth and success. We're doing it, [but] it's just really hard.

A senior colleague of hers reiterated that the reversal of resources was not unique to the particular branch campus and had spread to other legs: "The problem is, all the things that we were supposed to, that should have been used to constantly work *here*, were being sent all these other places, and then Asia."

The reversed flow of resources from the tabletop to the leg negatively impacted employees who were expected to cover duties in multiple locations.

A senior Pepperell leader who had just concluded his long-serving administrative tenure cautioned, "I think that we can get ourselves spread too thin. That we can find ourselves committing resources to sustain programs or activities that may not reach critical mass." As he continued, he shifted his concern to one that focused on the broader impact multiple underperforming periphery markets would have on the institution: "And so, you get into a situation of how much can you invest in making this work before it becomes something which is going to drag down the institution in more general ways?" In theory, each of the various periphery enrollment legs was intended to generate surplus revenues to prop up and subsidize the core residential campus, but the resource competition between legs that developed with the never-ending addition of new enrollment markets began to undercut individual legs and the overall stability of the tabletop model.

The Leg That Wasn't

Pepperell and Winchendon leaders worked year after year to add enrollment legs that would generate financial surpluses to support their core residential campus. They innovatively added different types of periphery enrollment markets throughout their geographic region, online, and abroad. The highest levels of leadership displayed a willingness to support nearly any idea. At Winchendon, the president asserted that the openness to new ideas stemmed from the university governing board:

> The sisters are very open in all ways. I mean open to new ideas, open to new projects, new investments, open to other religions. They let you work, and they are completely different than any other [board]. They're extremely open.

And at Pepperell, the provost described the mindset of the senior cabinet:

> We didn't say, "That's the craziest thing I have ever heard!" or "That cannot be done," [or] "We cannot do that." We were willing to explore anything! At the end of the day, [we] asked, "Is it consistent with the mission? Is it in the best interest of the students? Will it help us be able to provide affordable access?"

For the leaders of network institutions, welcoming new enrollment ideas was simply the natural outgrowth of their inclusionary priorities.

There were few opportunities network leaders would not pursue. And yet, in their frenzied attempts to establish new periphery markets, leaders added what ultimately amounted to a second tabletop—a second campus—rather than a revenue-generating leg. This particular addition for each university was predominantly a value-driven decision to provide residential learning opportunities to marginalized students in another part of the state (Pepperell) and in another country (Winchendon). Leaders were forced to divert resources from revenue-producing legs—as well as their main campus—to support the inadvertent second tabletops.

Prior to adding the second campuses, network leaders only established periphery enrollment markets that could support the core residential campus. According to network leaders, periphery enrollment markets possessed two fundamental features. First, there were no residence halls in periphery enrollment markets, which avoided fixed costs that were expected when a student lived on campus as part of the educational approach—housing, dining, entertainment, transportation, and others. Periphery markets provided an education without the amenities, and sites could be easily accessed by the targeted student population. As a senior administrator from Pepperell pointed out, "We're actually 3 miles away [from main campus] right off an exit from the expressway. . . . For the adult students, if they can exit off of an exit ramp and go to class right there—that's where they need to be."

Second, periphery enrollment markets were addendums or add-ons. They were designed to provide as-needed educational opportunities and possessed a quality of contingency unlike the main campus. Such sites were appendages that, if necessary, could be dismantled. According to Winchendon's provost, before adding a periphery market, the president was thinking about contingency: "His thinking is, 'I could sell off these professional schools. They're not located on the main campus. They're out in these other buildings. If I had to raise money, I could sell them off.'" A senior colleague corroborated the president's approach, noting his attitude was,

> We own those buildings. One is a strip mall [and] one is an old office building. He could sell those buildings. . . . He is always thinking: "How can I ensure the integrity of this main campus?" Because you cannot go sell one of those buildings [on the main campus].

However, when Pepperell and Winchendon were presented with an opportunity to add campuses located hundreds of miles from their main campuses, they mistook distance versus a pared-down infrastructure as the defining feature of a periphery market.

Winchendon leaders were invited to provide an American education on Chinese soil—a seemingly ideal opportunity to further include international students. They established a new campus that boarded primary, secondary, and postsecondary students, as well as faculty. Leaders labored for nearly a decade to overcome many cross-cultural differences and financial tensions the program encountered, which required additional resources from the main campus, including investors, technology, and personnel. One leader who devoted an arduous amount of effort toward saving the program defended it in terms that revealed how burdensome it had become. "The president is very, very strict that it has to be cost-effective. It doesn't have to be profitable, but it has to be cost-effective. We wouldn't be in China if we were losing money," he asserted, not willing to concede that the point of peripheral markets is to support the residential core. Tellingly, shortly after the administrator offered these comments, the university severed its China program.

Pepperell leaders were also approached with an educational opportunity that was difficult to refuse. A group of nuns who maintained a college in a rural region of the state for nearly a century suggested Pepperell leaders acquire the school amid its financial difficulties. The offer was given consideration and accepted as a measure of inclusion and goodwill. An administrator conveyed,

> We went to the campus in Hartly, an existing institution. [It] was run by an order of nuns that our monks felt was something that we might be able to do in terms of helping there. Eventually we absorbed that institution.

He continued, his tone darkening: "There have been some challenges. That growth has been challenging," he offered as a foreboding understatement. Pepperell leaders rerouted resources from the main campus to the new campus—including faculty, finances, and aggressive marketing efforts—to bolster student enrollment. Despite nearly a decade of relentless administrative effort, the labors of goodwill seemed to perennially falter. "It takes a long time for a college to die financially," the provost regrettably surmised. "We saw that with the one that we partnered with down in Hartly. It had been part of the community forever," he continued with a moment of profound realization. He then drew a comparison of having to close the Hartly campus in light of the broader college-closing phenomenon:

> [The] recession took a hard hit on them.... A lot of them are dying slow deaths right now. And those are the ones I worry about because they've been part of college towns or they are just middle America.... Those places have been part of their local communities for so long. Then one day they are going to be gone.

Balancing the Portfolio

The hidden irony embedded within the network strategy is that while in principle the additional revenue legs strengthen the core, each new revenue leg increases the administrative instability of the overall model, which was governed at the main campus by senior leaders in a "central command" manner. Each leg demands attention from a main campus administrator, leading to coordination challenges because the addition of enrollment legs oftentimes impacts others through competition or diverted resources. What went unsaid in the pursuit of the network strategy was the unavoidable outcome of its complexity—a continually expanding system at risk of collapsing under its own weight if not carefully tended to every step of the way.

Having to continually monitor and evaluate a complex enrollment network took an immense toll on leaders. Not only did they convey that they were "spread too thin" and "pulled in competing directions," but also the complexity of the system demanded an equally complex skill set to manage it. A Pepperell leader equated it to the cognitive demands required of her prior experiences in an elite national symphony:

> As a musician, we learn to think on multiplanes. We have to learn how to produce a sound, we are looking at mathematical descriptions on a page . . . I'm doing that in my brain in this *horizontal* plane. Then when I play in an ensemble, I'm doing it on another plane, because now not only do I have to calculate the equations and symbols, [but also] produce the sound . . . rhythmic-wise stack [it] *vertically*. And then you add the acoustics of the space, when you're adding all those other pieces together. So that's it—the same thing here—I do my job, but my job is fitting into fifty thousand million other things that are going on . . . I don't see that happening in how the university runs itself. It doesn't see how all those pieces fit. . . . I think it's so overwhelming to most people to think and feel on all those levels simultaneously, that you cannot.

With their many enrollment legs distributed across the state, region, and world, the complexity of the two institutions seemed to surpass leaders' capacity to reasonably monitor their many facets.

In overseeing the expansive interconnectedness of the network model, leaders noted problems that emerged in both the core residential and the periphery markets. Notable effects in the periphery were readily seen where enrollment quickly changed. When Pepperell terminated its paid partner contract, a domino effect on enrollment was unleashed. Their resources were immediately used to support the tabletop and the ailing leg that required technological resources to replace those lost through the termination of the paid partnership. A member of the president's cabinet explained the impact:

> It went from making millions—how much we got out of that was substantial—to completely shutting down. Yet we still have Hartly to cover, we still have Farmington

to cover, and we still have all the stuff there to do in Asia . . . [we] are so busy trying to calculate all these other places!

When enrollment changes occurred in the Winchendon periphery, similar effects in the core occurred. The relentless expansion of professional programs across the metropolitan region impacted resources at the residential core. As one academic official noted, "The faculty who are unhappy, they're not unhappy with having a [professional] school. What they're unhappy with is that the undergraduate thing is wobbling while these really good programs are thriving."

University leaders were keenly aware the network model was sensitive to substantial fluctuations in expenditures in the residential core. At Winchendon, the decision to pursue Division I athletics and fund it through market capitalization created a spending drain that proved taxing to maintain. Senior leaders erected a state-of-the-art athletics complex and established new sport programs despite objections by the few remaining sisters, a topic interviewees described in discomforting detail. A senior leader at Winchendon spoke for many when they observed,

> The faculty members know we were not ready for that. Maybe I am just not a businessperson, and I don't take those kinds of risks. But to me, putting money into Division I is a huge risk, and we need money for the [academic] buildings. We need money for labs.

At Pepperell, similar tensions emerged as the pressure to fund campus construction amid enrollment declines in periphery markets caused leaders to overextend. With widened eyes and an emphatic tone, one university leader recounted the explicit warning she conveyed to the vice president of finance regarding the new wave of spending amid periphery enrollment declines:

> I said, "If you over-extend, and you don't invest in your core, your core will eventually implode, because it cannot self-sustain. And it's because you have taken the resources that would've normally supported it, and you've extended it all out there [in the periphery]. But those other sources are not reaping."

She was not the only one concerned whether the stalled construction project would resume. A Winchendon senior academic official distilled the dilemma down to student need versus organizational need: "That cash cow—wherever it is in a school—these are students, and you ought to be giving them the very best you can, not thinking about how they can give us the very most we need."

For over 2 decades, leaders at both institutions worked to improve the survival chances of their schools by employing a network strategy of margin capitalization—one in which they added revenue sources from multiple student enrollment markets that spanned the city, region, and globe. Even though 20 years of exceptional growth had brought the universities to student enrollments that were five times larger than they were in the 1990s, they had returned to a moment of eerie familiarity—an organizational déjà vu where they faced the same challenge of limited financial resources that they faced 2 decades prior. Solutions based on growth appeared to have reached their limits, and wobbly legs could no longer be shimmed to balance the tabletop.

Conclusion

Although the leaders of the network institutions embraced an "in growth we trust" philosophy, the reality university administrators encountered was that growth alone could not save their organizations. While Winchendon had become one of the largest private universities in the state and Pepperell one of the fastest-growing universities in the country, the superlatives did not last. Despite the considerable revenue gains both schools experienced that pulled them back from the brink of closure, the growth Pepperell and Winchendon experienced had costs as well as limitations that over time inched them closer to the cliff again. Leaders acknowledged the success of their network strategy was temporary at best. "We were the fastest growing yesterday, not necessarily today," the Pepperell president revealed. Nor was the approach rationally sustainable in the long term. "As someone who has overseen a large amount of growth in this institution," a senior Winchendon leader began to concede, "to personally hold onto that image that we are going to be number one, I find it unsupportable to tell you the truth ... I've seen Notre Dame for God's sake!" As other institutions pursued enrollment growth as a form of generating new revenue, the highly competitive environment made it impossible for network institutions to sustain the kind of growth that hinged on a proliferation of periphery markets.

In due time, the network strategy buckled under the weight of its success. The dozens of periphery enrollment legs stretched the capacity of university leaders to manage the complexity of the system across its internally competing divisions and countless fluctuating markets, requiring it to accept greater risk to remain competitive. True to their belief that periphery markets were an add-on or appendage to the core residential campus, executives began cutting underperforming enrollment markets. Campuses that were developed and nurtured through years of tending to relationships that bridged cultural and ethnic divides were severed to ensure the core residential campus stayed afloat. "I told the head of finance, 'You've got to be careful, because if this campus implodes, all of that falls into the hole!'" one Pepperell leader cautioned.

Like the leaders of the traditional and pioneer institutions, network leaders understood their rapidly changing context warranted a new approach. Everything seemed unstable: "Higher ed is changing, the market is changing, what the public wants is changing. To put it simply, we have [to be] more able to change and adapt quickly," urged one Winchendon vice president. In the competitive and dynamic environment, the Pepperell president cautioned that continuing to look back to prior options and strategies had become a liability. "If there's a message out there, it's, 'Know all the data [and] all the statistics are looking through the *rearview* mirror.'" He pressed home the point with the slap of his hand on the conference room table at which we sat:

> That's a world that no longer exists. Presidents and the leadership have got to look out the front of the window and look around that corner. Because if they don't, they're going to die. They're going to take their institutions down the wrong path.

The future has no data and no well-worn paths forward: the only thing certain to these leaders was that the network strategy was a thing of the past.

At the same time, leaders had difficulty imagining a future where peripheral markets were not just multiplied but also brought to scale. The paid partnership with the online program management provided enrollment growth, but not the elusive scaled enrollment growth. When asked why the school had not wagered everything simply on scaled online education, the Winchendon president removed the smoldering cigar from his mouth and, waving it in the air, loudly declaimed, "Because we aren't a *diploma mill*!" Tapping his cigar vigorously as if seemingly insulted by the question, he went on: "Education has to be quality . . . if you're going to do it cheaply, then you're not going to have the quality, and you're going to ruin your brand." In a competitive environment where scarce financial resources have been strategically designed for distribution using market-based policies, it would require a new kind of university leader to forge a new vision in search of greater tuition margins to sustain their institutions—one that foresaw economic reasoning leading to an entrepreneurial form of margin capitalization more accelerated than the trailblazing pioneer leaders or the inclusive network leaders had been willing to previously implement.

Notes

1. Problems social entrepreneurs attempt to ameliorate include inequality, healthcare, poverty, climate change, and social injustice. These problems often have no determinable stopping point and lack a definitive solution, usually because of the number of people involved or because knowledge of the problem is incomplete, economic burden is substantial, or it possesses an interconnectedness with other problems. Bornstein, D., & Davis, S. (2010). *Social entrepreneurship: What everyone needs to know*. Oxford University Press.
2. "Multiversity" describes the complex form institutions that balance multiple interests take: "a whole series of communities and activities held together by a common name, common governing board, and related purposes." See Kerr, C. (1982). *The uses of the university* (p. 1). Harvard University Press.
3. For a further explanation of the "ongoing founding" phenomenon, see Brown, J. T. (2021). The language of leaders: Executive sensegiving strategies in higher education. *American Journal of Education, 127*(2), 265–302.
4. The 2017–2018 Administrators Survey in Higher Education conducted by the College and University Professional Association for Human Resources.
5. Wilde, M. J. (2018). *Vatican II: A sociological analysis of religious change*. Princeton University Press.
6. Lemann, N. (2000). *The big test: The secret history of the American meritocracy*. Macmillan.
7. Bea, D. W. (2004). *Modernizing higher education administration: How market and economic factors are changing small college and university business operations* [Doctoral dissertation]. Claremont Graduate University.
8. Wekullo, C. S. (2017). Outsourcing in higher education: The known and unknown about the practice. *Journal of Higher Education Policy and Management, 39*(4), 453–468; Williamson, B. (2021). Making markets through digital platforms: Pearson, edu-business, and the (e)valuation of higher education. *Critical Studies in Education, 62*(1), 50–66; Blumenstyk, G. (2018). One way to set up liberal-arts majors for success: Focus on skills. *The Chronicle of Higher Education, 5*(1), 1–14.
9. See "arithmetic" versus "geometric" enrollment growth in Chapter 2.
10. The latest development is the use of artificial intelligence to identify prospective students and allocate scholarships to boost enrollment. See https://www.brookings.edu/research/enrollment-algorithms-are-contributing-to-the-crises-of-higher-education/.
11. Acosta, A., McCann, C., & Palmer, I. (2020). Considering an online program management (OPM) contract: A guide for colleges. *New America*. https://www.newamerica.org/education-policy/reports/considering-online-program-management-opm-contract/; Carey, K. (2019, April 1). The creeping capitalist takeover of higher education. *The Huffington Post*.
12. Ryan, H., & Hamilton, M. (2019, June 6). Online degrees made USC the world's biggest social work school. Then things went terribly wrong. *Los Angeles Times*, https://www.latimes.com/local/lanow/la-me-usc-social-work-20190606-story.html
13. Busta, H. (2019, February 28). As traditional colleges grow online, OPM relationships shift. *Education Dive*. https://www.educationdive.com/news/astraditional-colleges-grow-online-opm-relationships-shift/549414/

14. "Turnaround" refers to a management process whereby a leader focuses on saving a failing company by restoring its financial solvency. Boyne, G. A., & Meier, K. (2009). Environmental change, human resources and organizational turnaround. *Journal of Management Studies*, 46(5), 835–863; Walshe, K., Harvey, G., Hyde, P., & Pandit, N. (2004). Organizational failure and turnaround: Lessons for public services from the for-profit sector. *Public Money & Management*, 24(4), 201–208.
15. Clark, B. R. (2017). *The distinctive college: Antioch, Reed, and Swarthmore*. Routledge.
16. This pattern reflected enrollment trends in single-sex colleges during the 1960s and 1970s. All-male institutions began to admit women, including Princeton University (1969), Johns Hopkins University (1970), Brown University (1971), Duke University (1972), and Harvard University (1977). Similarly, all-female institutions began to admit men, including Sarah Lawrence College (1968), Vassar College (1969), and the University of Mary Washington (1970). Miller-Bernal, L., & Poulson, S. L. (2004). *Going coed: Women's experiences in formerly men's colleges and universities, 1950–2000*. Vanderbilt University Press.
17. Multiple administrators referred to a commitment to *Nostra Aetate*. The commitment stems from the Second Vatican Council (1962–1965) in the *Declaration on the Relation of the Church to Non-Christian Religions* that presents a charge for Catholics to engage in dialogue and charity with Muslims and other religious faiths.
18. Between 1992 and 2007, the U.S. federal government created additional funding policies and institutional designations for colleges and universities whose student enrollments surpass specific demographic thresholds for minority students. When a college or university surpasses the following thresholds, they are eligible for additional funding and institutional designation: 40% Black American enrollment to become a predominantly Black institution, 25% Hispanic enrollment to become a Hispanic-serving institution, 10% Asian American or Native American Pacific Islander to become an Asian American Native American Pacific Islander–serving institution, 10% Native American to become a Native American–serving non-Tribal institution, and 20% Alaska Native or 10% Hawaiian Native to become an Alaskan Native–serving institution or Native Hawaiian–serving institution. The historically Black college and university and Tribal college designations and funding are dependent not on enrollments, but rather on institutional founding and historical mission. Thus, it is possible for some historically Black colleges and universities to be composed of mostly White students because of demographic changes in the local population, such as Bluefield State (West Virginia) and West Virginia State Universities. Brown, J. T. (2021). The evolving missions and functions of accessible colleges and universities. In G. Crisp, K. R. McClure, & C. M. Orphan (Eds.), *Unlocking opportunity: Broadly accessible four-year colleges and universities*, 65–81. Routledge/Taylor & Francis Group.
19. The Muslim population at Pepperell was commonly stated as being slightly over 30%.
20. Bromley, P., & Powell, W. W. (2012). From smoke and mirrors to walking the talk: Decoupling in the contemporary world. *Academy of Management Annals*, 6(1), 483–530.
21. The four most prestigious athletic conferences in the United States are commonly referred to as the Power Four conferences. The elite institutions that comprise the Power Four rely heavily on traditional forms of philanthropy whereby presidents have established direct administrative channels between themselves and the valuable financial resources the athletics divisions generate for the organization.

22. A 3 + 1 program aims to create alternate pathways of educational access by establishing partnerships between a university and community colleges where students can complete an associate's degree in 1 year at the community college and then transfer to the university to earn a bachelor's degree during a subsequent 3-year period.
23. Excerpts and sample institutions are taken from the typology of multiversities in Taylor, B. J., & Cantwell, B. (2019). *Unequal higher education: Wealth, status, and student opportunity*. Rutgers University Press. The term *multiversity* has predominantly been used to refer to institutions with multiple interests—research, teaching, athletics, and service. It is used here to describe the multiple enrollment interests of the network universities.
24. Regional accrediting bodies such as the Middle States Commission on Higher Education, the Higher Learning Commission, and others provide oversight of an institution. In contrast, a professional accreditor such as the Accreditation Board for Engineering and Technology (engineering), the American Medical Association (medicine), or the American Bar Association (law) provides oversight of a specific academic program. An institution typically maintains accreditation with one regional accreditor and many professional accreditors.

4
The Accelerated Strategy

"More Money Than God"

Introduction

The youngest of the eight universities discussed in *Capitalizing on College*, Ardmore University is a Protestant institution whose close-knit leaders embraced a family firm management approach en route to implementing a transformational model of education reflected in their motto: "For God." The university—and the church that founded it—held fast to an ambition of cultural reformation focused on "changing the world." Everything was done to scale because time was nigh. But as their efforts to achieve their vision seemed to gain momentum in the final decades of the 20th century, it collapsed under the combined weight of nationwide religious scandals and institutional probation from an accreditor that all but revoked the university's eligibility to receive federal loan dollars. Rather than shutter the institution, Ardmore leaders firmly focused on their "cultural entrepreneurism"[1] and developed the *accelerated strategy*—a model of higher education that scaled up a periphery market by developing replicable systems of growth that simultaneously held costs flat.

In adopting the strategy, Ardmore became part of a select group of accelerated institutions in American higher education that achieved rapid enrollment growth—and enormous financial returns—by scaling their online divisions.[2] Commonly heard during interviews with university officials were remarks like this one from a college dean: "The online model is very, very lucrative, very, very profitable. It's just unbelievable." Central to this strategy was the innovative use of surplus tuition margins that displaced traditional philanthropic fundraising with a new form I term *margin philanthropy*, which funded university investment accounts using money from current students rather than wealthy benefactors. Not only did Ardmore adopt business practices that rivaled those of Fortune 500 companies, but also implementing the accelerated strategy yielded marginal revenues from tuition that rivaled the profits of such companies. Senior leaders had every reason to be confident of their dramatic turnaround: "Nobody does business outcomes like we do.... We know how to make money. We know how to run it as a business," a vice president boasted. Ardmore differentiated itself among accelerated institutions by emphasizing its religious outlook. To maintain its competitive advantage, it adopted a business model that emphasized being (in the words of one faculty member) "quick on your feet." Its leadership developed innovative approaches to financialization that generated "superprofits," partnered with Silicon Valley tech firms to scale the workforce of tomorrow, and labored to lure students from competing institutions using what one senior leader called "guerilla competitive research." In the end, Ardmore administrators successfully modeled a strategy to escape the throes of organizational death; the question for higher education is at what cost?

Called to Change

The history of American higher education is rooted in institutional exceptionalism—one where each college and university emphasizes a unique characteristic that sets it apart from hundreds of others. For centuries, Harvard, Yale, and Princeton Universities have epitomized prestige and reinforced their uniqueness through selectivity. The modern founding of Ardmore arose from within this pervasive exceptionalism as its leaders sought to establish an unparalleled Protestant institution with global impact. From its founding, the Ardmore community held to a unique disposition, understanding itself to be *guided by God*. There was an assumed supernatural involvement that portrayed God to be an active participant in the day-to-day events as well as the university trajectory—both its founding and its future. But a second and different disposition was equally as important to the decision-making structure that Ardmore's entrepreneurial founder developed—a management model known as the *family firm*. Common to many organizations, the family firm approach channeled the charisma of the founder, permitting rapid resolution of major decisions. Together, these dual dispositions of being guided by God and the family firm fostered an institutional environment centered on a *cultural entrepreneurialism* that advanced a belief in changing the world. This trait would catalyze the rapid implementation of the accelerated strategy when leaders were confronted with financial collapse and regulatory probation, saving the institution and paving the way for others to emulate the strategy.

Ardmore founders sought to establish an unprecedented university whose aim focused on changing the world "for God." One of its leaders explained,

"Ardmore was founded with the intention of making a *global* difference—not just a local or state or even national or regional difference." A senior vice president summarized how the influence of the supernatural and the impact of the family on the institutional mission remained central in the past and the present. "God and the mission of the institution have coincided in an inherent meaning behind everything we do . . . a clear mission and broad vision that came in the very beginning [from] Ardmore's founder." He observed that people were highly motivated toward action and sacrifice to achieve a grand narrative that would not only impact this world but also stand the test of time:

> There are lots of really talented people at Ardmore that could be doing lots of other things with their lives, but they've made a choice to invest their lives at Ardmore. . . . They believe in the vision of young, educated, changed lives.

Guided by God

A focal cultural disposition of Ardmore can be found in the opening line of its commemorative volume, which showcases the involvement of a supernatural other: "God has blessed Ardmore University." Like the traditional, pioneer, and network institutions, the cultural disposition of Ardmore reverberated throughout interviews with university leaders and its historical publications, one that commonly referred to an explicit engagement with a transcendental guide: "The grace of God sustained the dream and the wisdom of God guided it," one publication purported, while another put forth, "Ardmore University is truly God's school . . . from its inception, it has been molded, shaped, and fashioned by the hand of God." While the pioneer schools examined in the earlier chapters pursued a human connection that emphasized a "we" and the network institutions a focus on "you," Ardmore underscored a sacred connection "with God." This transcendent focus had profound implications for Ardmore's historical trajectory as well as how its executives framed what ultimately became explosive growth.

During the mid-20th century, when the traditional, pioneer, and network institutions were expanding their enrollments amid the golden age of higher education, the Ardmore commemorative volume chronicles how a bold pastor felt a holy obligation to found a world-class university. The Protestant leader drew inspiration from the religious founding of many U.S. colleges, which had since jettisoned their commitment to religion, thereby creating an opportunistic need in contemporary higher education.[3] More than just a curio from a bygone era, this was an institutional distinctive Ardmore leaders worked hard to popularize. "We hear from the senior administration that we don't want to become like Princeton and Harvard that have gone away from their theological and ethical moorings. I *know* we do *not* want to do that," one senior academic official dutifully emphasized. To protect against this ideological drift, the founder embedded the religious distinctive within the university motto: "For God." "Talk about brilliance in marketing! How do you really improve on that statement for a university?" a senior vice president guffawed. "The founder cornered the market with just two words."

Drawn to this transcendent vision, one August an inaugural group of young adults found themselves taking classes in facilities that could charitably be described as rudimentary at best. As the commemorative volume chronicled,

> 154 students arrived for their first day at the new college, which they soon discovered had no campus. Little four-room houses had been purchased across the street from [the church] to serve as dormitories for 20 students each. . . . The entire staff of the college consisted of four full-time faculty members. . . . Classes were held in the church and its educational buildings. Gym classes were held in the parking lot!

The church and its larger-than-life pastor soon purchased additional properties to educate students bused between an eclectic patchwork of buildings they referred to with names like "the hotel" or "the island." The president reminisced how many present-day employees still fondly recollect memories of Ardmore's first decade: "It gave our people sort of a desire to achieve and a school spirit that you might not find at an institution that's been there for 150 years."[4] Like the traditional, pioneer, and network founders from a century prior, early Ardmore faculty and students made sacrifices to establish the fledgling institution, believing they were doing so with supernatural support.

Leaders wasted little time acquiring land to develop a residential campus whose facilities were needed to attract greater numbers of students than hotels and youth camps. Although the pastor's church (with its national media network) functioned as the resource conduit through which financial support flowed to the university, leaders expressed that the nascent school was supernaturally tended to during its early years when its financial needs seemed insurmountable. A senior vice president recalled one such occasion: "There was a building at Ardmore, [that] had been built, but inside was nothing. And we didn't have any money."

The founder said [to the student body], "We're going to leave this convocation today, and I want you to walk with me over to this new building, and we circled it, and we're going to pray God will give us $5 million so we can have a cafeteria" . . . we went out there and we prayed, and he put it on TV and [the] money came in.

The Family Firm

One of the persistent paradoxes of Ardmore is that while it was purported to be God's school, it was unquestionably managed as a family firm. Leaders throughout the institution repeatedly used the phrase "family business" to describe the distinct ethos that persisted from the founding to the present. Although unusual in higher education, the family business model is a common approach to managing an organization, with nearly one third of all S&P 500 companies organized in that fashion, as are many notable companies like Walmart, Ford, Porsche, Dell, and Berkshire Hathaway, whose leadership and governance structures are sustained from one generation to the next through familial ties.[5]

Most leaders described this organizational disposition of Ardmore in a matter-of-fact manner. One academic dean plainly explained that nepotism was at work: "People that are close to the family really are the ones that run the school." But another senior leader offered a positive characterization of the benefits that accrue from the family firm model, namely, being "fairly open to risk [with] quite an appetite for innovation."[6]

The family business model concentrated authority with the charismatic founder and trusted family members. As the senior-most leader, the founder strategically appointed family members in instrumental areas throughout the university, including human resources, finance, alumni, athletics, student programs, and construction. This created a high degree of trust among the administration that is unique to family firms. "The founder very much relied on [one of] the senior vice presidents from a human resources perspective to kind of be that central hub who helped control things," an administrator said of a pivotal family appointee. According to an academic dean, even the board possessed limited governing authority in contrast to the web of family members involved in day-to-day operations: "It is like any business that is owned by a person—it's ultimately their business and so what they want to do really flies . . . the board was not as involved as it should have been."

The family firm approach is also an essential lens to more accurately understand decision-making, power, and resource acquisition in American Protestantism, which has relied on the family firm approach to perpetuate universities (e.g., Bob Jones, Liberty, and Oral Roberts), megachurches (e.g., John/Joel Osteen, Robert/Robert Schuller, Jerry/Jonathan Falwell), ministries (e.g., Billy/Franklin Graham, John/Mark MacArthur, Kenneth/John Copeland), philanthropy (e.g., Arthur/Mark DeMoss, Richard/Dick DeVos, Howard/Howard Ahmanson), media (e.g., Mike/Sarah Huckabee, Jay/Jordan Sekulow, James/Ryan Dobson), and businesses (e.g., Chick-fil-A, Hobby Lobby, Tyson Foods). Within these (typically patriarchal) organizations,[7] privilege and authority are maintained across generations, with power passing from father to son (with some notable exceptions).[8] At Ardmore, the family surname was a powerful credential both inside and outside the organization.

The interconnected web of family provided leaders with an organizational disposition they relied on, in ways similar to how pioneer leaders looked to institutional mergers and network leaders turned to enduring leadership. As a member of the board explained, it offered Ardmore's leaders an opportunity for focused decision-making in times of abundance or scarcity: "Decisions from conception to action are done much more quickly and involve fewer levels of decision-makers . . . not a democracy by any stretch of the imagination!" Decision-making authority was reinforced by the widespread belief that the founder had received "a vision from God" to found and manage the university—sentiments echoed in a more elaborate form in a commemorative volume:

> When God chooses to accomplish His purposes in a generation, He looks for a servant . . . one to whom He can impart His vision and trust. . . . The miracle of Ardmore University required an extremely unusual servant—one whom God found in [the founder].

The notion that the Ardmore founder possessed a connection to God provided him with an unparalleled decision-making authority, particularly in the areas of enrollment growth, real estate development, and employee salaries. "Ardmore is run by a very strong personality, who firmly believes *he* should make all the major decisions," a board member candidly confided.

The founder and his family took part in an ongoing dramaturgy[9] where they showcased themselves before the university community. Ardmore publications were replete with pictures of the founder and family members standing among powerful people in powerful places. At public gatherings like academic convocations and graduation, the founder commonly discussed intimate family details, including their accomplishments, births, marriages, and international travels. The university magazine recorded how the graduation stage proved to be a fitting setting for the engagement proposal of one key family member as thousands of Ardmore graduates patiently waited to receive their degrees while their families looked on. The reoccurring dramaturgy was essential to maintain an understanding among the Ardmore community that God selected members of a specific family to manage the institution and its ambitious mission to produce graduates who would change the world.

The Grand Narrative

The two abiding dispositions—guided by God and the family firm—functioned as the foundation that undergirds a pervasive changing-the-world narrative embedded throughout the environment of Ardmore. When the pastor-founder established Ardmore, he put forth a far-reaching vision of education, one that was arguably even more expansive than the "access-for-all" vision of network leaders. At Ardmore, education was part of a grand narrative of cultural change. According to a senior vice president,

> It's something much bigger than the student. It's about impacting the world the student is living in. Not just about training students to be successful, [but] at every turn a vision of what could happen in a world of students trained by Ardmore University.

This "bigger than the student" outlook, the senior leader elaborated, was woven throughout its mission. "Everybody in the institution, at certainly the highest levels of the institution, believes they're part of something that is changing the world one individual student's life at a time." If students were the end at other schools, they were the means to the end at Ardmore: the goal was nothing less than using them as conduits for social reformation and change. Ardmore was thus founded on a trait of *cultural entrepreneurialism*, led by persons who strategically used symbols to create organizational forms, generate support, attract resources, and shape the future of broader social institutions.[10]

Leaders at Ardmore believed changing the world required an emphasis on sheer volume rather than the limited elitism of the Ivy League. It was a prominent element of campus culture whose scope seemed limitless, as a senior administrator underscored:

> It's very much an institution that envisions being for the everyday regular person [and] getting them a quality education that will allow them to change the world. We want to make it affordable and available to masses what has often only been available to a select few.

He went on to observe that "in higher education you measure academic credibility by how many people you turn away. Well, we absolutely accept students that other institutions would turn away." The president adamantly proclaimed Ardmore would never jettison its own founding ideals, as Harvard, Princeton and Yale had:

> Private schools have gotten fat and lazy over the years, become focused on things other than their original mission of teaching and educating students . . . their loyalties were to research, to donors, to state subsidies, and you see across-the-board tuition hikes because of those financial pressures. I think the pressure is on all those schools to get back to their core mission of teaching. We never moved away from that.

In talking about the founder, an administrator and church member elaborated how talk of quantity hung in the air at Ardmore:

> His vision was always for the numbers, getting as many Christian kids educated as possible, because that was what would change America. That was his dream. Why did he want 50,000 people at Ardmore? Because in numbers, you'd be able to change America. . . . That was his motivation, very much a marketing mindset.

An academic dean similarly described how the founder "thought almost in statistical terms . . . everything was always framed in numbers." Marketing materials emphasized scale and invited everyone to attend. "You reach every available person by every available means at every available time," a vice president proclaimed. "That's the heart of the institution. We just believe every student in America ought to come to Ardmore and they ought to have the opportunity to." Leaders cast a metaphorically wide net to generate student enrollment; in the words of one dean, "many schools approach recruiting like sport fishing; we approach it like trawling."

As cultural entrepreneurs, leaders were keenly aware numbers helped quantify progress toward the vision of cultural change the founder supernaturally received. To attract greater numbers of faculty and students, Ardmore's executives acted as cultural entrepreneurs framing efforts to change the world within a transcendent grand narrative for God. One administrator described the community as "a bunch of people working for the university [who] have a strong commitment towards God and [whose] leaders frame the things they do in terms of biblical moral issues." Through these lenses, persons could be part of the grand narrative by enrolling in classes, teaching, playing a sport, or working as staff. University members readily voiced they wanted to play their part in the proposed supernatural storyline. "I really did believe in the stated mission statement of training people to go and impact the world for God, and I wanted to be a part of that," one administrator professed. Similarly, a vice president shared his belief that "everybody feels a part of something of meaning and significance."

The entrepreneurial framing by Ardmore's leaders left powerful impressions on former students and alumni who emphasized their experience was "more than" about education alone. In their tribute to Ardmore, an impassioned group of alumni collectively asserted,

> We were given far more than just the tools to compete successfully in this world. We were shown that erudition alone is not enough, that many brilliant scholars have shipwrecked on the shores of blind ambition, materialistic greed, and consuming selfishness.

A senior vice president shared similar sentiments: "It's more than a university, more than my alma mater," he underscored. The impact of the entrepreneurial framing on his own life was profound:

> It's not that I was a part of Ardmore as it was that Ardmore was a part of me. It's still inside me. . . . It was effective in forming me as a person and has influenced every aspect of my life . . . it's just so much more than a university.

Overcoming the Double Hundreds

The early growth of the university was extraordinarily rapid as the school's cultural entrepreneurialism attracted hundreds of students and necessitated the equally rapid development of campus facilities. During Ardmore's nascent years, the financial model relied on reallocating donation revenues from the church to the university.[11] The president explained how the church subsidized the university through its scaled approach to donative fundraising.

> My father had the [church]. He was one of the pioneers of broadcasting and he actually paid for the school buildings and the operations with money from masses of people over the television . . . gifts that averaged maybe $15.

Guided by the vision he received, the founder drove the growth focus that was the preeminent characteristic of the church and the university. Growth meant a greater possibility for changing the world, but it also meant a greater opportunity for fundraising by taking $15 donations to scale. Enrollment growth at the university was so explosive that the subsidies were spent on constructing the campus. "Because there were the millions of dollars that were being raised going into building a campus," one leader recalled of the founding era, "there was no money to help the people develop, the leaders develop, the administration develop, or the faculty develop." A seasoned leader summed up the financial focus: "It all went into buildings."

The financial engine for the church was a large "call center" that facilitated the scaled-up donations processes through telephone and mail. It was a finely tuned fundraising machine whose replicable systems meant hundreds of employees annually interacted with millions of supporters to process tens of millions of dollars. After describing its operational intricacies, one senior leader proclaimed, "Did we make money back in those days? We were printing money! It was pouring in."

Despite the waterfall of cash streaming in daily, the school struggled to make ends meet. Construction timelines funded solely by donations restricted the founder's urgent vision to change the world, and university executives pursued funding to expedite the vision via loans. "The school was financed with just sort of a haphazard loan from this donor, a loan from that bank. It was all short-term," the president explained. "The founder was always a day late and a dollar short. He was paying off last year's debts and fighting to stay alive." At the peak of the subsidizing efforts, the church allocated tens of millions annually toward expanding Ardmore's residential campus. But the peak unexpectedly turned out to be a precipice as leaders were hit with "the double hundreds," a pair of devastating setbacks in the form of more than $100 million in debt and more than 100 noncompliant policy infractions reported by accreditors.

In the 1980s, a series of national religious scandals damaged the public perception of organizations like Ardmore.[12] According to its president, "After the scandals, people stopped giving" and revenues "all dried up." The financial impact that confronted school leadership was profound: "Contributions for the year following the [Bakker] debacle were diminished by $25 million. This 'bleeding' continued for the next 4 years," the founder stated in his autobiography. The subsidies ceased, and Ardmore "had to completely change the business model," the president grimly stated. "The school had to become self-sustaining. It had to not only pay all its bills to operate but also had to assume all the debt that had been incurred"—to the tune of $110 million. To overcome this financial hurdle, leaders established a hybrid model that combined financing and fundraising. "I could go on all day about the different types of creative financing that was done with bond issues and short-term loans from insurance companies and banks and individuals," the president shared. The complexity of the circumstances lacked any identifiable textbook solution or template response.

The extreme financial circumstances took a toll on employees, many of whom were shocked by the turn the grand narrative had taken. As one senior vice president admonished, "How do you change the world as a scrappy young institution when you don't know where the next dollar is coming from?" An administrator pointedly recalled, "That summer I missed two paychecks," while a faculty colleague shared the uncertainty her family experienced: "I was 9 months pregnant . . . I remember where we were living and thinking we're not going to make it this month, we cannot pay our house payment." To compound matters, executives asked employees to consider additional financial sacrifices, as one vice president recalled:

> Ardmore ran out of money and did some crazy things, to the point where they challenged employees to mortgage their homes . . . anything they could do to help the university. People really believed in the university and did it.

Leaders were aware that although the circumstances were dire, many employees remained committed to the grand narrative and offering their contribution for God.

The president offered a glimpse into the financial asperity of the situation from the vantage point of those attempting to salvage the family firm. "[There were] a lot of sleepless nights and weekends where paychecks went out on Friday and dad and I would spend all weekend calling donors and anybody we could think of to borrow money to cover them." His father laid off a quarter of his church employees. One senior leader expressed that he knew the situation had become grave when "we did not have enough money to run our call centers." An academic dean recounted shuttering the call center under the darkness of night. "The [founder] had a big mahogany-lined office over there. In the middle of the night, he had to move to the [university] mansion." In grasping for finances from all conceivable places to cover the $25 million annual shortfall, one academic official recalled being pressed by the founder to report particular enrollment figures to ensure government financial aid was not similarly impacted:

> I was asked to lie about the enrollment, assuming that we'd have a number the founder wanted by the end of drop/add. I would not. I know that we were in serious financial [trouble], but it was only a week. Why couldn't the founder trust God for another week? I told the founder to his face we may not get caught today, but we will get caught and have to pay the money back.

As the financial decline intensified, it weighed on the academic performance of the university. Adequate resources for academic programs were scaled back and, in some cases, understaffed. The reoccurring 10-year visit by the accrediting agency came due as leaders were laboring vigorously with lawyers to restructure the debt. In their review of both the financial status and the performance pertaining to academic policies, accreditation officials cited Ardmore with over 100 noncompliant "recommendations." Colleges and universities customarily received a handful of recommendations during a 10-year accreditation review, but to have so many was a clear signal that management of the institution was falling notably short. An Ardmore administrator tasked with accreditation oversight explained, "When you think about 100, that many recommendations from [the accreditor] at one time, I mean holy jumping, you know what I mean? The fact that we were not shut down is truly . . ." His voiced cracked. "I really do believe that God spared us from ourselves."

The $100 million-plus debt or the 100-plus noncompliant recommendations alone would have been enough of a hurdle for any one institution to overcome. But to simultaneously tackle both seemed insurmountable. The upstart university and the grand narrative Ardmore purported were in unmistakable peril. One university historical volume succinctly summed up the mood of the moment: "Failure seemed imminent."

Sidebar: Margin Philanthropy

For years, Ardmore's founder focused on scaling donative fundraising that provided the church with millions of dollars. Its donative emphasis resembled the traditional strategy, which also focused on the generous contributions of others, but for an endowment whose revenues subsidized the residential core. In these early years, Ardmore did not have an endowment, but it did have a national church community the founder could literally call on. An Ardmore professor described the administrative mindset of that era as "just keep building things" because "it's fairly easy to raise money to build things." But while the masses were motivated to give toward tangible expansion efforts, they were not as keen to bail out a school whose leadership had overextended themselves.

When Ardmore's financial circumstances became perilous, executives turned to the largesse of traditional philanthropy for a possible solution. But the philanthropy challenge Ardmore leaders faced was illustrative of the same fundraising dilemma that confronted the leaders of other tuition-driven institutions when faced with a financial crisis—to locate a donor of magnitude equal to the crisis itself. With much of the large philanthropic giving in the United States concentrated among elite institutions, the possibility of securing a sizable financial gift from a philanthropist for most tuition-driven schools is rare. Nevertheless, after years of searching for a benefactor, Ardmore leaders located a large-gift philanthropist to pay off a major portion of the debt the school had incurred. "[Ardmore] was really just on the edge of survival," the president recalled, "but then we got some big contributions that paid our debt down to $20 million by [the late 1990s]."

Despite the acquisition of the multimillion-dollar donation, the institution was unable to overcome its orientation toward indebtedness. Their spending habits were a perpetual financial albatross of sorts—a fundraising dilemma that, as one senior vice president explained, seemed an inherent characteristic of being a nonprofit institution. "Like every other nonprofit, you raise money. But there was never enough money in the world to achieve the vision of what Ardmore was founded to do." Rather than adapt the scope of its changing-the-world mission, Ardmore leaders remained devoted to their cultural entrepreneurism and innovatively chose to adapt the financial model to develop a new scalable approach to fundraising and philanthropy.

For most nonprofits, a traditional approach to philanthropy focuses on the acquisition of donations from a network of supporters and wealthy benefactors to fund construction and grow the endowment—an approach showcased in the traditional strategy. Yet the nonprofit classification of an organization means that at the end of the year it must reinvest any profits back into the company rather than distributing them to shareholders or investors (as is the case with for-profits). To reinvest the profits (or margins) into the institution, leaders have two options—use them to build the infrastructure (the margin capitalization prominently figured in the pioneer and network strategies) or use them to philanthropically build the endowment (an innovation in the accelerated strategy).

Like the pioneer and network institutions, Ardmore did not have an endowment it could turn to. But unlike these institutions, an important understanding lay "hidden" within the family firm about how to take business processes to scale. The Ardmore founder and his close-knit group of family executives drew on their prior knowledge of scaling and turned to an altogether new solution—*margin philanthropy*. A term coined through this research, margin philanthropy is an entrepreneurial form of endowment growth that supplants the traditional fundraising supported by donations of alumni, employees, and philanthropists and instead leverages scaled marginal revenues from *student tuition and financial aid* to fund university investment accounts.

Traditional philanthropy relies on individuals sufficiently advanced in life who possess financial means from which they might donate. One group that is automatically excluded from that form of philanthropic support are current students, who have little earning power and instead predominantly rely on student loans for their tuition. Yet that was precisely where Ardmore executives turned to scale up their endowment. With most tuition-paying students backed by guaranteed federal financial aid and student loans, the institution could increase their tuition margins and thereby create a new and heretofore undiscovered kind of philanthropist—current students. If the tuition margins and the student body were large enough, the institution could fund its endowment with the margins of today's students rather than through nonexistent gifts from graduates of yesteryear.

Margin philanthropy is a scalable form of neoliberal fundraising that relies on reoccurring revenues from countless "customers" who generate small amounts of money. In contrast to a wealthy benefactor with millions of dollars at their disposal, students have much smaller amounts of financial aid and loans for tuition, room, board, and books. By shifting the focus from individual megadonors to thousands of tuition-paying students who provide reoccurring marginal revenues, leaders employing the accelerated strategy would establish a fundraising system resting on economic reasoning nearly identical to the scaled donative fundraising systems used by American politicians and religious leaders that leverage limitless small contributions from the masses.

Imagine a scenario in which the tuition margins for each student range on average from $1,500 to $2,500 at a university that scales enrollment to 100,000 students. The excess profits the institution garners beyond its expenses range from $150 million to $250 million annually. By repeating the process, the tuition excesses accumulate to $1 billion within 5 years and $2 billion within 10. These billion-dollar totals resemble traditional fundraising campaigns for elite and research institutions, but such substantial sums can also be achieved through margin philanthropy—and in compliance with federal financial aid and nonprofit policies. When the marginal tuition revenues are invested in the endowment, an institution earns additional profits (i.e., endowment revenues) on its prior profits (i.e., tuition margins), in what is described later as "superprofits."

But how does an institution scale its student enrollment to six figures? The entrepreneurial executives of Ardmore found a way to maximize tuition margins by establishing a periphery enrollment market in online education that they scaled at an unprecedented rate. One board member explained,

> We just were bumping along with no real upside. Somebody kept telling the founder that there was an upside, and that upside was in online education, *if* it were operated *other than* in a very carefully measured, controlled, safe manner.

Shaking his head at the recollection, he went on: "The founder decided to embrace the more radical, more aggressive, less safe method, and it worked.... We actually got traction. We actually got cash flow." With their "aggressive" embrace of online education, Ardmore leaders created replicable systems that permitted them to scale their online product and revenue model. One senior vice president described the change as nothing short of revolutionary:

> Ardmore now has a different model than it had for its first 30 years. The model now is not a fundraising model. The model now is producing revenue ... forcing the institution to make the financial decisions it needs to make so that it's not just run at a profit, but run at a profit with a future in mind.

The senior leader took care to assert that the purpose of the revenue emphasis was about the future—having enough money to sustain the mission of changing the world for generations to come. The new cost-conscious margin philanthropy approach shifted the fundraising burden from an individual soliciting donations to every individual in the Ardmore community doing their part—employees containing costs (which maximized margins) and students paying tuition (from which the margins were derived).

Margin philanthropy not only permitted leaders to sufficiently resource the mission, but also, once established, offered administrators important newfound financial freedoms, including pursuing the mission with an eye on the long game. A senior vice president explained how a margin philanthropy approach strengthened the integrity of the mission:

> One of the reasons why we are really committed to having a business model that works for the institution that is profitable is so that a generation from now we're not in a position where we have to rely on major donors in order to keep the institution afloat, and major donors in turn [can] influence and change the [religious] integrity of the institution.

The new approach of building up a financial reserve using resources from current students was strategically intended to preserve the institutional mission from the erosion or decay of its founding religious focus by the unwanted influence of philanthropists.

Ardmore executives also explained that margin philanthropy provided them with remarkable opportunities for unrestricted spending, which contrasted with the designated or "earmarked" giving in traditional fundraising. One senior administrator explained, "The reason why we're in such a better place than other universities like us is because those funds are not earmarked, and so we can do whatever we want with them." Funding received from wealthy benefactors came with greater spending restrictions than marginal tuition revenues culled from unencumbered financial aid and student loans. In the event of another crisis, Ardmore administrators had a cash reserve that could be used anywhere in the university "to weather storms, financial and otherwise," the president contended, rather than solely for a designated purpose.

Last, by pursuing margin philanthropy, leaders happened upon increased freedom from the public accountability inherent in the traditional approach. An academic dean highlighted this fact: "Back in the day, if you were depending on major donors or donors reached through television, if a decision was made that was unpopular with the constituency, that would have an impact on money." There was an element of checks and balances inherent with donors that senior leaders had previously been conscious of and tended to. But now the situation was different: "You have tens of thousands [of] online students all paying tuition." Once enrolled, the thousands of paying students were less likely to stop (and therefore less likely to stop "giving") if they did not like a particular policy decision—quite unlike donors who did not "need" the institution in ways students did. The academic dean reflected on the legacy the "tens of thousands" of students have had on the institution: "I truly believe they're the reason why we're blessed, because if you look at the numbers 15 years ago, we shouldn't be around."

In the end, Ardmore leaders resolutely embraced the trait of cultural entrepreneurialism and touted the necessity of having to outright reject the traditional philanthropic approach to fundraising that fed a philosophy that nearly resulted in their demise. The provost brazenly contrasted the traditional philanthropic approach of a nearby elite institution with Ardmore's "nouveau" approach leveraging neoliberal funding policies:

> They look down on Ardmore as this populist institution for the unwashed. But the truth is Ardmore matches or exceeds their standards, but they've convinced themselves they are elite and we are not. What they are is a Sorbonne of education in their own minds, but they have less than 6,000 students after years and years and years of operating with a huge endowment. Now they've burned their way through the endowment and they're about 3 years from hitting the wall.

In contrast, the "unwashed" margin philanthropy approach provided Ardmore with greater freedom and ample funding to sustain its changing-the-world mission. Somewhere along the arduous journey to survive, the circumstances for Ardmore and its leaders seemed to radically reverse themselves. As one professor candidly proclaimed, "The school was just frantically trying to survive. But now it's got more money than God."

Pursuing the Accelerated Strategy

With the imminent closure of Ardmore having jeopardized the possibility of changing the world, university executives wasted no time implementing the accelerated strategy, an approach that utilized margin capitalization and rapid scaling up. Leaders developed scalable systems that enabled explosive enrollment in their online market while simultaneously holding costs flat. Scaling up allowed Ardmore's leaders to break free from the linear revenue–cost relationship and pursue enrollment growth that curved upward, yielding greater rates of surplus with each additional student admitted. The unlocked secret of scaling incentivized speed: "Everything that we do is related around student enrollment [through] business outcomes and speed. The reason why we care about speed is we want to get things done quickly so we can get more students here," a senior leader averred. The way forward was unmistakably clear: maximize the margins quickly to maintain the mission (Figure 4).

At the center of Ardmore's accelerated strategy was a cultural entrepreneurial vision that motivated its leaders to swell enrollment in an expedited manner to produce "students of character who would change the world around them." Leaders moved in entrepreneurial ways between cultural spheres: "When it suited the university to be a ministry [or] an academic non-profit, that is what they were, but when it suited them to be a business, that is what they were," a vice president explained. In their moment of crisis, the family firm organizational form Ardmore maintained provided the founder and his close-knit leaders with latent entrepreneurial knowledge they gained a decade earlier when scaling the call center that provided the church with tens of millions in donative revenue. Thus, Ardmore leaders quickly established replicable systems and scaled characteristics of the university at an accelerated pace: online courses, programs, admissions, marketing, physical infrastructure, and even a new form of fundraising—margin philanthropy—that relied on tuition surpluses from thousands of current students as the new philanthropists. An academic dean highlighted that the growth-focused approach stemmed from the highest

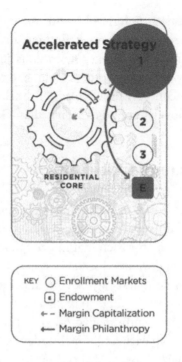

Figure 4 The Accelerated Strategy for Sustaining the Core

level of leadership: "The president brought with him the legal aspects, the business aspects, the entrepreneurial aspects to make [scaling] happen in a very straightforward kind of hardcore way." This cultural entrepreneurial approach enabled Ardmore's leaders to pursue unconventional educational innovations and rapidly expand their online offerings, which resulted in explosive growth and placed the school back on course for changing the world.

Scaling Up

In developing the accelerated strategy, Ardmore leaders understood there was a distinction between the linear "arithmetic" growth described by the Stoneham provost and the parabolic "geometric" expansion in scaling up. An Ardmore administrator highlighted this difference when she directed my attention to a framed graph that hung on the wall in her office. "It's just pretty *linear*," she nonchalantly remarked as she traced her finger across 20 years' worth of gradually inclining enrollment bars. Once her finger hit the "elbow" in the chart, she briskly traced the line of exponential enrollment growth, gleefully declaring, "And then the stars line up!" The stars lining up was the transformative moment Ardmore leaders successfully implemented the scalability component inherent to the accelerated strategy—Ardmore's leap into online education.

With arithmetic growth—or expansion—an institution increases its costs at the same rate it increases its revenues when expanding enrollment. An institution must also sustain larger losses from adding facilities, personnel, technology, and other costly resources to gain the increased revenues that come with additional enrollment growth. In contrast, the "geometric" nature of scaling up allows a college or university to exponentially increase revenue through expanded enrollment while constraining costs that maximize its margins. The critical feature in scaling up is establishing a replicable system to deliver a product or service that permits an institution to increase enrollment without increasing overhead at the same rate. The more efficient the replicable system becomes through automation, the more scalable the university becomes.

Since the 1920s, higher education scholars have focused on examining the aspects of expanding the academy, including administration, research, teaching, and enrollment.[13] One of the most notable periods of growth occurred following World War II when the entire American system more than doubled in size to accommodate those taking advantage of federal funding made available through the GI Bill (leading to scaling in large lecture halls for introductory courses). More recently, elite and research institutions have focused on opportunities presented by the scalability in free, massive open online courses, where thousands of non-degree-seeking students enroll in a single course.

Ardmore executives concluded that if they were going to impact society as cultural entrepreneurs and achieve their changing-the-world mission, they needed to scale their efforts without accumulating substantial costs. An academic dean who oversaw Ardmore's online expansion pointedly recalled, "I believed that we would hit an enormous number of students because that is what the founder wanted to do. So to me, then, we needed to prepare for that." He also explained that an important element of scaling enrollment was the replicable system his team established that was embedded with "trigger points." These alerted administrators when new components of the administrative structure needed to be added: "At what other point do you hire another instructional mentor or an online chair? Those metrics... a lot of it was based on the 20–25 [student] system." The trigger points promoted the efficiency of scaling processes, which emphasized the reproduction of key areas and the containment of operating costs for personnel, technology, facilities, and other expensive resources. At their most basic level, trigger points ensured wider margins generated from student tuition.

Scaling up with speed was the blueprint for everything in the years that followed the elbow in the graph. Administrators developed replicable systems to scale major areas of the university. Leaders expanded the call center—the financial engine of the university—using automation processes to expedite services and educational products to hundreds of thousands of persons. Information technology (IT) experts engineered course templates (known as "shells") to quickly reproduce online courses and programs. This focus on replication even permeated Ardmore's approach to capital expansion; the template approach facilitated the hurried construction of dozens of new residence halls, funded using a margin capitalization approach. As one senior leader explained, the speed of scaling was rooted in their cultural entrepreneurial beginnings:

> It all comes from the founder; he'd have an idea and they'd strike immediately because they didn't have the money, but what they did have was the desire to push. He put out this culture where a little bit less quality could be accepted—although that's not something we state—but *not* delivering quickly is *never* accepted in anything.... Our president said in October, "We're opening new dorms by September," and everybody said, "Are you kidding me? That's impossible, that is 11 months!" And he said, "It's going to happen, or you're not going to get the contract." That's just how we roll.

The scaling-up blueprint was unmistakably successful on the financial plane, but there were ominous forewarnings of its impact in other realms. For instance, rather than just "growth," senior administrators and faculty routinely described the decade and a half of astounding enrollment increases in sensational ways, referring to it as a period of "phenomenal growth," "exponential growth," "growth curve," and "rapid growth." But there was one particular word that hinted at challenges inherent in the accelerated strategy: *explosive*. The word echoed throughout descriptions of the university. "Not long after I got here, specifically the online [went] from a manageable number of students and faculty to what felt like overnight being an explosion," an academic dean recalled, while another leader exclaimed, "That is a big, big challenge, just managing the explosion!" The unforeseen consequences of the explosion slowly manifested themselves—but first came the innovations that fleshed out the accelerated strategy.

A Store With Two Products

While multiple stars converged to bring about the explosive elbow moment for Ardmore, two fundamental pillars—technological infrastructure and product innovation—supported the scaled enrollment engine on which the accelerated strategy ran full throttle. The expansive scope of each pillar was successively developed by two separate "architects."

In an attempt to generate self-sustaining revenues that did not rely on subsidies from the church, Ardmore leaders first established a "distance-learning" periphery market that focused on offering courses to students through VHS videos. One administrator recalled that to sustain the distance-learning division, some in leadership wanted to upgrade from videos to DVDs, while others advocated for an entire new market.

> I remember the chief information officer (CIO) having major arguments with the administration back in the early 2000s when they championed getting rid of VHS in favor of DVDs. And [the CIO] said, "No, we're not going to change media—we are going to change platforms. We *need* to do this online thing."

Instead of pursuing the more acceptable "upgrade" many in leadership and higher education more broadly were accustomed to, the founder boldly supported his digital architect and pursued the online option. While a family firm model might be assumed to limit innovation, in Ardmore's case they were on the cutting edge. Rather than add a new periphery market or leg, like the network leaders had, Ardmore opted to entirely jettison the old leg in favor of pursuing an entirely new periphery market. But what was truly unique about this particular leg was how it could scale. Instead of needing multiple legs to balance the tabletop and ensure stability, this solitary online enrollment leg swelled in size, offering remarkable financial stability through volume instead of diversity.

Ardmore leaders developed the university's technological infrastructure that enabled the rapid scaling of their online enrollment leg by emphasizing mobility and standardization. As one director observed,

> When you look at the IT infrastructure the CIO put in place . . . we standardized a lot of our operations. For instance, we decided that we would equip all faculty with laptops. . . . The CIO saw that mobility was going to change the way the university functioned.

The scope of the technology infrastructure influenced every aspect of the institution as it added a student information system, data storage capacity, wireless network, web integration, course design, learning management system, automation, and digital product delivery. The cumulative efforts brought about a new way of educating students in a new market. "When all those pieces started coming together—a way to build courses fast with consistent and repeatable shells—we had a way to deliver from the IT perspective," one leader noted. Ardmore leaders successfully launched their online division and began to offer new courses to students. But the enrollment elbow did not materialize through technological infrastructure; it required the support of a second pillar—product innovation.

Academic leaders and faculty at Ardmore began methodically expanding the new online periphery market. In the first 4 years, they achieved an 8% annual growth rate in enrollment. But the growth provided neither the enrollment nor the revenue the founder envisioned with the decision to switch to online. The founder intervened with the intent to accelerate his cultural entrepreneurial vision and appointed a new executive with oversight of the online division who possessed a singular directive—achieve exponential enrollment growth:

> When he brought me into the direct administration of the university, there was an adamant resistance to anything but carefully measured, responsible growth of the online division. They had several theme words they used to justify very slow, methodical, careful growth. The founder's orders to me were, "I want a train wreck." And I said, "Give me 3 months to figure it out, and I'll come back to you with the recipe for a train wreck." And I did.

In analyzing the countless online courses the university had developed, the new executive came across a startling discovery: "We only had two degree programs available." What was needed for scaled growth were students taking a series of multiple classes, something only a program could ensure. But the current programmatic offerings were insufficient to the task. One was a standard master's degree in business administration and the other "was this tramp stew thing that they sold to military people as being an all-purpose, accept everything you can accept, shortest direction to an undergraduate degree." The executive then shared the insight that drove Ardmore's explosive growth in the online space:

> I had the nearest thing to a vision I've ever had. It's a simple thing. You're standing on a street looking at a store, standing on the sidewalk, and it's a typical mom-and-pop store. It's got two little display windows and a front door. You open the front door and shelves going all the way down both walls and across the back. *Two products* are all that is in there—in the entire store. I kept having this view of that [store] and said, "What could we do? ... What would we do if we had something to sell?"

In his search for additional storefront products, he identified dozens of existing Ardmore courses that could be wrapped anew: "I looked at 85 courses that we offer *residentially* ... if we were to take those 85 and convert them to online offerings, we could offer 30 programs of study to sell." If the senior leader could successfully bundle the same strings of individual courses together that were already available in person into a brand-new format, he could innovatively create a myriad of new products for the online Ardmore storefront.

Of course, this approach to product innovation is not new.[14] The transformation of a good or service by leveraging existing materials or redesigning its established elements is a critical component of product innovation. In the case of Ardmore, product innovation transpired through redesigning the 85 existing residential courses for an online format. Similarly, product bundling[15] is a low-cost approach to innovation used to transform entire industries, such as cable companies (who bundled television channels), computer firms (who bundled laptops with software), travel agencies (who bundled all-inclusive vacations), and even fast-food chains (who bundled "combo" meals). In many instances, product bundling creates an entirely new product, as was the case at Ardmore. Its bundling of individual courses to create 30 fully online programs transformed the school's entire online market emphasis from selling courses to selling degrees.

To manage the shift, the executive leveraged Ardmore's existing technological infrastructure, particularly an obscure academic support department to work with course development. He bluntly shared what happened: "I hijacked them. Turned them into an assembly line." As one employee recalled, "When I worked there . . . we ended up creating 88 courses . . . all in one summer." At the same time new courses were being moved from residential to online, the senior leader challenged admissions to begin selling the new programs: "While they were building them, we came up with our new marketing copy . . . and went from 8% growth to 42% overnight!"

For Ardmore and other accelerated schools, the enrollment elbow did not come about by establishing a first-mover foothold, as the pioneer schools had done. Rather, it was the result of having erected two important pillars—a technological infrastructure that enabled innovation and product bundling—an important point made by one professor. "The idea of putting whole programs online was financially huge," she said. Her next remark inadvertently hinted at the tremendous growth to come, as well as the impact of the unexpected outcomes of embracing the accelerated strategy: "Once they did that, it was just breathtaking what happened."

The Salt Mines of Academia

The enrollment explosion at Ardmore's pivot point brought about the need to provide services at scale. Providing course bundles and degrees online was innovative, but ensuring Ardmore was remunerated in the form of tuition and student loans was the crucial step. Services like course registration, academic advising, and counseling, in addition to those concerning financial matters, have customarily been provided to students in the residential campus setting by professional experts. The online setting challenged these in-person approaches and posed a real conundrum for administrators. "How do we service everything that you could normally walk into someone's office and do virtually?" one leader inquired. Critically important to the success of the enrollment elbow was developing the financial services needed at scale if Ardmore was to maintain its accelerated growth en route to changing the world.

Ardmore leaders discovered the services-at-scale solution for the university in what was once the financial engine for the church—a call center. Although the founder was forced to shutter it in the wake of national religious scandals, the specialized knowledge of having previously coordinated a massive ensemble of employees remained embedded within its organizational form as a family firm. A vice president described the early fundraising by the founder as "coming up with crazy ways to market the church and get the elderly to basically call in and give money over the phone." The founder and other senior executives drew on this prior knowledge to offer services at scale and cultivate what became the indisputable financial engine for the university—essentially shifting their focus from processing donations from thousands of elderly supporters to processing loans and financial aid from thousands of students. One leader recalled the growth and scope of the facility:

> They have gone from probably a couple hundred people in the early days of my tenure to well over 1,000. . . . I don't know of other higher education institutions that I've ever heard of that have that size of a call center—that services not only the recruiting of students, but the advising and the customer complaint and the billing and the financial aid assistance and all those other pieces.

The call center for the church had previously been housed in a state-of-the-art business park, but Ardmore leaders opted for a less opulent option in a vacated shopping mall. "Its parking lot is full every day of the year," the president acknowledged, pointing out the corner window of his executive suite at the sprawling off-campus facility before concluding: "Ardmore's recruitment department has always been very aggressive and it's always been innovative."

Ardmore leaders relied on the technological infrastructure to maximize the productivity of "callers" to sustain its accelerated enrollment growth. The call center provided the service support necessary to remain competitive in attracting prospective students with speed. "If you go to Ardmore's website and express an interest in one of our programs, chances are you will get a call within a few hours," the president confidently proclaimed. In fact, according to another leader, the time was significantly less:

> You're going to get a phone call in under 10 minutes because we roll it into a blended dialer. Certain admissions people, if they're not taking a phone call (inbound), they are automatically placed onto a phone call, and we dial (outbound).

He explained that the technological automation even governed the time between calls:

> You'll have 90 seconds to write up your phone call when your phone call is done. At 70 seconds in they are already dialing the next person. And then, BAM!, you have your headset on, and your screen pops and you are talking to do your pitch.

At the end of the day, executives assessed the compliance of call center employees through productivity reports. One vice president explained,

> We call it a utilization report. With it, we metric out how many touches you had a day, how often you went over your time to go ... we want to make sure that they're getting from call to call. *Speed is everything*. We use utilization reports to squeeze as much time out of you as we can. We metric how much time you're away from the phone in the bathroom.... We metric everything. We listen to your phone calls. And because of that, it's not an environment where somebody is going to work and have a career there for 20 years.... We *need* those people, it serves a great thing, but the call center is a hard place to work.

Employees were essentially cogs in the reborn call center, strategically designed as a workplace panopticon—a technology-supported environment that continually monitored employee performance with an all-seeing eye aimed at maximizing productivity to sustain accelerated growth.[16] As one employee succinctly stated, "I'm always conscious of what I'm saying and how I'm saying it.... Our lives are monitored. We live in a box."

Most colleges and universities maintain call centers, but the scale and scope of Ardmore's put it in a class of its own. Senior leadership worked to expand its scope, which brought about an organizational complexity that relied on the technological infrastructure for coordination across multiple divisions to sustain the enrollment growth the founder sought. One administrator attempted to convey just how complex the technological coordination had become:

> It's not just a call center meaning telephones, but you've got your CRM,[17] you've got screen pops, you've got your dialing that goes out, you've got recordings, you've got all the integration with all the mailings and all the emails and all the reports. There's a lot of stuff that all ties in together that most people do not realize.

Investments in the call center yielded high financial returns throughout the university. As one administrator remarked, "We've continued to grow that machine!" But what senior leaders made explicitly clear is that the call center employees—like the students they were compelled to enroll—were merely means-to-an-end commodities needed to bring about the vision of changing the world through sheer size. One of the senior-most administrators described it unsparingly:

> The culture—I had heard from the call center workers—is really the salt mines. It's an environment where—I'm not saying this is negative—but we try to get the most that we can out of employees, and really people are phone-hour, phone-minute commodities.

He concluded with a shrug, "After all, it's not like they have a lot of institutional knowledge."

Containing the Costs

A critical element of taking a product or service to scale is holding the cost of production flat, which enables margins to widen as additional units are produced. As seen in the pioneer and network strategies, without holding costs flat, growth remains linear when costs accumulate as quickly as revenues and eventually "eats" the margins. Ardmore administrators deliberately kept education costs cheap: "We operate more like a business, and the reason we do that is because we spent so many years barely surviving. We learned how to operate frugally and the importance of fiscal responsibility," the president contended. While the call center provided Ardmore leaders with an engine to accelerate enrollment growth, replicable systems offered the opportunity to contain costs that weigh down the scalable efficiency of colleges and universities. Giving equal attention to both components—growth and cost—is essential to scaling up, and Ardmore leaders relied on three replicable systems that perpetually held their production costs flat: centralization, wage containment, and standardization.

Centralization was a one-way expressway moving expeditiously from top to bottom: "It's pretty much a top-down, 'This is what we want you to do' kind of thing, which is reflected in the curriculum and organizational structures," a professor commented. Another leader adeptly identified the centralized approach as one that not only permitted quick decisions but also controlled them: "It all comes through one pipe." The single "pipe" was an uncommon characteristic for a college or university, but one Ardmore leaders embraced to control costs. "One of our strongest reasons why we've been able to scale quickly and cheaply is because we have centralized IT," one senior leader noted. An administrator contrasted how it worked at a nearby elite school compared to Ardmore:

> If you're in the biology department and you want to buy a computer, you can go to Dell, you can go to Apple, HP, you can go to the university bookstore and buy it. Or you can go to IT—and not only go to IT, but your biology department IT, executive and administrative IT, or law school IT. So you actually have multiple departments at the university bidding against each other and outside companies. Instead of that, at Ardmore we go to Lenovo and say, "You're buying from me. I don't care who comes through you. Nobody can buy a computer at Ardmore but me. You're going to give me the best price possible." That's why the [elite schools] of the world cannot even touch our *per-student spent*.

Centralization permitted top-down executives to contain the per-student costs in ways competitors seemingly could not. "Other people have *de*centralized IT. You're idiots! You're losing so much money!" the vice president declared.

Ardmore leaders also focused on wage containment to keep their per-student educational costs lower than that of their competitors. For many tuition-driven universities, the cost of labor accounts for two thirds to three quarters of their total expenditures. Ardmore leaders understood the ebb and flow of online course enrollment. This meant that the school "could not put everybody in contract," a director explained, "because we may not need that many in the spring or summer . . . so we moved to the adjunct model." According to an academic dean, the university hired its initial cadre of online adjuncts as independent contractors, a decision that saved the school millions in payroll taxes. There were further cost-containing measures because the adjuncts were paid a specified stipend per course and lacked any employment perks: "They can find adjuncts to teach it for $2,100 [with] no office, no 'bennies,' no salary, no insurance, no retirement. Holy cow. What a deal!" Ardmore's administration remained committed to multiplying the bare-bones employment approach to the point where one professor remarked, "In our department now there are probably 150 adjuncts." Without having to pay the cost of employment perks for its online workforce, the per-student expenditures remained remarkably low, further sustaining the generous rate of margins from student tuition. Ardmore leaders maximized margins further by refusing to increase compensation for thousands of online faculty for more than a decade.

Wage containment efforts at Ardmore were not confined to the army of adjuncts. Senior leaders also strategically controlled labor costs for faculty and staff in the residential core—what one professor described as "getting the most out of little." He attributed that mindset to a carry-over from the ailing era when Ardmore nearly closed:

> The people who worked back then thought of that as a ministry. The problem is when that environment went away . . . they kept the machine going and pushing that "Let's not compensate, let's just get as much out of people as we can [mentality]."

Another professor observed that "there was only one institution in the state that paid less than we did." While many employees felt caught between inadequate compensation and their commitment to the changing-the-world mission, the professor observed that Ardmore leadership leveraged this tension to achieve increased financial gains:

> You have a whole lot of people that are really committed to what they believe the mission of the university should be. Because of their commitment, they're willing to work for less pay; however, their salaries aren't enough to actually get them what they need, and they work even extra hours doing the online stuff . . . the university is really able to capitalize off that.

Even efforts at wage parity possessed inherent cost-containment elements that enabled administrators to curb their overall per-student expenses. One senior leader described how she and other executives established the university-wide salary scale:

> We were matching jobs to industry . . . there was a percent below center we were comfortable with. We would say, "Let's put a range of minus 10% and plus 10% around that, and that is your job category. You can move around in there. If you're awesome, you can be plus 10%. If you suck, you can be minus 10%."

Even under the modified structure, many interviewees commented that their salaries remained a fraction of what colleagues in similar positions at peer institutions earned. "I was making a third of what I could make elsewhere," a director lamented, while a dean similarly disclosed that the salary structure possessed "a lot of giant inequities. The people who created it did not seem to understand the disparity. But [for] anybody in the ranks, the hardship was real."

Finally, Ardmore leaders created replicable systems based on standardization to contain costs. The school was among the first to standardize courses and course development processes to curtail per-student expenditures. "Our kind of 'factory model' was at the time innovative," explained an academic dean. "We spend very little on developing the online courses. We do it on the cheap," a professor added. "The typical model they're pushing is an 8-week module," another faculty explained.

> There will be a short video introduction of 5–10 minutes, then read the following chapters and take assessments [made] using test banks from textbook companies.... There might be some discussion boards or activities, but there isn't a lot of customization of the instruction from the faculty.

The standardized template approach saved the university considerable amounts of money in labor and production costs. Furthermore, once a course was developed, it could be mass-produced to sell multiple sections of the very same course every 8 weeks for multiple years simply with a click. An academic dean explained that Ardmore administrators could save even more money if they replaced the residential faculty member entirely once the online course had been developed. "Let's say I create a course online. Pretty soon, if that course takes off, they will say, 'We can find some adjuncts to teach it, we don't need you to teach it anymore.' You created a baby that grew up to eat you."

The Superprofits of Financialization

Like the other institutions examined in *Capitalizing on College*, the attractiveness of Ardmore's campus was an essential feature in generating the levels of student interest necessary to increase residential enrollment. "We used to almost have to beg students to come here because we did not have facilities," the president said of their early patchwork campus. But the success and size of the online enrollment gains provided the financial backing Ardmore leaders previously sought to develop for decades through donors. "The explosion of the online program has really been the financial machine that has given the resources to build these buildings," remarked one senior leader. He pointed through his floor-to-ceiling windows at the half-dozen tower cranes that dotted the horizon: "It's dorms, it's dining halls, it's libraries, it's educational buildings, we're building up the stadium . . . this is amazing to see!"

Margin capitalization funds generated from the enrollment engine in the call center were used to transform the physical campus, and within a few short years, enrollment growth in the residential core was also characterized as explosive. The deliberate combination of the core residential campus and the periphery online market generated a symbiotic relationship, with the president emphasizing why the physical campus transformation was vital for both:

> The online program would never have been successful if it weren't for the residential program . . . because the only thing that gives the online program credibility is the fact that it's anchored by the residential campus. . . . I credit the success of that program to the fact that there's a *real* bricks-and-mortar college . . . I also credit the online program with giving us the resources to rebuild the residential campus.

It appeared the accelerated strategy was the solution that made good on the *Field of Dreams* promise of capitalizing the core: "If you build it, they *will* come."

But rather than expanding the residential core in the service of the mission, now the core was seen as serving the profit imperative. As one senior leader explained, construction had one justification: "We're only going to do it if it's going to be profitable, right? If we build a library, how's it going to make us more money?" In fact, while Ardmore leaders transformed their residential campus using the same margin capitalization approach as pioneer and network leaders, the accelerated method generated such enormous returns (combined with the linear arithmetic limits on how fast a physical campus can grow) that leadership literally "could not spend money fast enough." But rather than deposit those dollars in an endowment with modest returns, Ardmore's executives decided to invest the remaining margins, aiming to generate additional profits in a scheme some called superprofits.[18]

In the 1980s and 1990s, the American financial sector composed of banks, investment companies, insurance companies, and real estate firms—with its emphasis on making money from money rather than making products—assumed a greater role in the national economy. This phenomenon (known as financialization) is where "profits accrue primarily through financial channels rather than through trade and commodity production."[19] A product of neoliberal financial reforms, financialization encourages organizations to become market players themselves who seek returns from financial assets by using select forms of capital and debt leverage.[20] Since the Great Recession, elite and research universities have turned to forms of financialization to generate new sources of revenue by leveraging the wealth of their existing financial assets.[21] By incorporating tools of financialization as part of their campus transformation, Ardmore leaders discovered they could do more than just build their residential campus anew—they could build *and* make more money.

In the midst of the 2008 financial crisis, Ardmore administrators commenced with an aggressive plan to spend their burgeoning online revenues to overhaul the residential campus. As one vice president explained, the decision took advantage of opportunities brought about by the economic collapse: "In 2008, something became very apparent: Money became cheap, and building became cheap. . . . The supplies for construction are cheap, the labor for construction is cheap, and the money for construction is cheap." Ardmore leaders modified their strategy to take advantage of the "cheap money" available through low interest rates. A senior vice president explained how it happened: "We went to [an investment firm] and said, 'We want to invest so we can build,' and they said, 'No, no, no! We can issue a bond!'" Public bond offerings presented Ardmore leaders with an opportunity to create their very own initial public offering—reflecting the essence of the cultural entrepreneurial approach underlying the accelerated strategy.

A senior vice president explained the math behind how executives used the surplus online tuition revenues to finance bonds that generated superprofits:

> Bonds allow us to capitalize on low interest. . . . If we've got $10 in bonds and those $10 mature in 5 years, I only have to pay back $13. Then I can take $10 I would have spent on it and make $20 or $30 elsewhere. My rate of burn is less than my rate of income. It does not make sense to use your investment money over there [in construction]. The reason we did bonds was that we have the cash. We were *accelerating*.

By financing the money used to overhaul the campus through public bonds, Ardmore leaders created a gap between the millions they borrowed and the millions more they could make by investing their online tuition surplus elsewhere. The gap was used to generate additional profits on existing profits—superprofits. A second senior vice president stressed that the financialization approach would be "a huge positive for the next hundred years" of the university—not in terms of the mission, but in terms of financial return:

> Why spend money that you made when you can borrow and make 10 times more? Ask me for $1 million, I'll give you the $1 million, but that's all you are ever going to get from me. But ask me for $1 million, where I give you $100,000 each year and you take out the loan for $1 million over 10 years. . . . At the end of 10 years, a businessman will have $2 million because that $900,000 is going to keep making money.

According to its president, Ardmore's innovative approach that coupled financialization and margin capitalization permitted leaders to accelerate profits in a manner that catapulted its organizational wealth into a category that rivaled elites. He reminisced: "When we went to Wall Street to issue bonds a few years ago, the financial wizards commented that . . . most of the schools that they're used to dealing with have been the same schools since the early 1900s." He continued, pointing out their surprise: "Now to see a new one come on the scene building the same type of financial strength that you see in a lot of the Ivy Leagues . . . to see that take place in such a short amount of time, it's usually the type of thing that takes generations to occur."

The combined financialization and margin capitalization approach delivered truly unimaginable results. "We've got enough money in the bank that we can live without consequence for decades," an academic dean commented with an awestruck tone. A senior leader similarly boasted, "The financial strength of this university is very unique. There are not many schools around the country that have the strength we do right now." Yet lost in the pursuit of superprofits was a sense that profits were not an end in themselves, but the means to the mission, perhaps reflecting the biblical notion that you cannot serve both "God and mammon."[22] And if administrators thought they bought themselves time to then do God's work, they soon realized their embrace of the accelerated strategy had caught the eye of more than just Wall Street. Amid the innovative approach to amplify profits, other universities were diligently working to accelerate aspects of their organization, and Ardmore leaders soon found themselves hard at work laboring to keep pace with their accelerated competitors.

Advancing Among the Accelerated

Within a decade of implementing the accelerated strategy, Ardmore underwent a seismic financial turnaround from more than $100 million in debt to an excess of $1 billion in cash on hand. Ardmore leaders painstakingly accepted that their initial approach of leveraging church fundraising nearly shuttered the institution. The lesson they took from the experience was not to mimic elite institutions, but rather to reject that approach entirely: "Higher education culture seeps into everybody but us," a vice president offered. On reconsidering Ardmore's near-death era, its provost commented,

> Exclusivity is only working as a business model for a very tiny minority of institutions. But there are literally hundreds attempting to practice that business model to their eventual demise. . . . One of the key differences for Ardmore is we don't practice that business model at all.

The solution lay hidden in the prior experiences executives possessed scaling an affiliated call center formerly used to generate millions of dollars in donative revenues. The decision to apply this knowledge in a new context to scale their online market provided Ardmore leaders with surplus tuition revenues in the hundreds of millions annually that were used to transform the residential campus (through margin capitalization) and establish a lucrative endowment (through margin philanthropy). The scope of the financial turnaround was truly a testament to what neoliberal policies were designed to provide for institutions willing to adopt them in their purest market form.

Other universities also implemented the accelerated strategy and experienced similar financial success. Ardmore's leaders were aware of competing institutions that employed the same strategy. "A state institution that comes this close to practicing what we practice business model-wise is Arizona State . . . instead of saying 'We don't want you,' they say, 'We'll take you,'" the provost acknowledged. Ardmore leaders identified other accelerated schools they viewed as direct competition, including online competitors Capella University and the University of Phoenix, less familiar schools like Georgia State University and Southern New Hampshire University, and name-brand schools like University of Florida, Pennsylvania State University, and Ohio State University.

Despite Ardmore's religious distinctiveness, university administrators viewed these schools as direct threats to their bottom line, and they worked relentlessly to remain at the forefront of this innovative tier of institutions—not by highlighting their mission, but by continuing to innovate their revenue generation schemes. "Our speed to market with new products is vastly superior than our competitors," one leader boasted. They drew on data practices from Fortune 500 companies that leveraged operational analytics to generate new products and services. Unlike the competition that developed corporate partnerships to sell existing degrees, Ardmore leaders partnered with technology firms to create new degrees for the workforce of the future. As competition among accelerated institutions took a combative turn, Ardmore executives adopted a commandeering approach, taking clandestine steps to poach customers, data, and ultimately margins from their competitors. In a remarkable understatement, the president offered this summation of Ardmore's attempts to stay at the front of the pack when it came to schools embracing the accelerated strategy: "I would say we are probably more aggressive than most schools."

Yet a curious thing happened on the way to maintaining accelerated growth. Engrained in the Ardmore community's embrace of their divine mission was a refusal to concede defeat. A senior vice president explained that the institution possessed a "never-give-up, get-it-done type of culture . . . a sort of spiritual entrepreneurialism!" he proclaimed. But left behind in the supercharged entrepreneurial mindset was the reason the university sought growth in the first place: the mission. As Ardmore's leadership adopted more and more business practices, they moved further and further away from the school's transformative vision of changing students, leaving their own executives questioning whether they had ultimately forsaken the mission for a mess of pottage. "I did not say I think he is a great president," a professor confided, "but I think he is a really good businessman":

> At faculty orientation we kept talking about how blessed we are. . . . We've got incredible construction projects. We don't have to worry about where our paychecks are coming from. But if those are the blessings we list first, then we've got a problem.

The accelerated strategy set Ardmore on a parabolic trajectory at a pace its leaders were resolved to sustain, come what may. As a senior-level administrator admitted, "The president is not backing the foot off the pedal . . . he's just not." Nor was this approach covert; as another administrator at a network school divulged, "I'm not even sure Ardmore has a brake."

Data as a Commodity

Ardmore leaders readily understood that data functioned as a vital source of innovation in a highly competitive field where financial resources were predominantly governed by student choice. Unlike pioneer leaders who perennially kept their gaze fixed on the horizon for the next big thing, Ardmore administrators saw the data they already had as a commodity having high economic value (similar to raw materials) because of its vital role in production processes. In a remarkable admission of how passé the goal of educating students had become, a vice president confidently conveyed the outlook at Ardmore: "What we do best is data."

As a knowledge-producing field, higher education is awash in data, with colleges and universities generating large amounts of information to monitor their academic research, educational assessment, and student records. Most of this information is retroactively examined to draw conclusions about a given area, for example, the quality of education or accuracy of student information. Institutions have entire divisions that oversee annual assessments and detailed reporting to governments, foundations, accrediting associations, and other external agencies.[23] But rather than use information solely for reviewing snapshots of the past, Ardmore leaders processed data with an eye toward the present and future, emphasizing real-time or predictive analytics.

Integrating data and information as a central part of institutional processes is a practice known as *operational analytics*, whereby data are imbued with the capacity to shape decisions, products, and services, and in many instances they function as a catalyst for their innovation.[24] At the outset of the big-data craze in the early 2010s, leaders at Ardmore and other accelerated universities (along with many large corporations) embraced operational analytics.[25] Taking their cues from the corporate sector, Ardmore executives established key positions in "business intelligence," which quickly developed into a robust department.[26] "Our business intelligence office at Ardmore rivals Fortune 500 companies," assured one vice president. Rather than looking to the horizon for the next thing, the specialized group of business intelligence officers looked inward to mine large volumes of data for innovation. The provost shared with pride that,

> This last year we created an analytical team and came up with 11 elements on the academic side of the university we figured would benefit from careful analysis. Four of those projects yielded $10 million in additional income since last May.

Two innovative data discoveries were made in enrollment management and course registration. For decades, generating admissions leads traditionally focused on purchasing lists of prospective student information from academic testing companies, including the College Board (SAT data), American College Testing (ACT data), and Educational Testing Service (GRE data). Understanding that data could be predictive in nature, Ardmore leaders pivoted from purchasing test-list data to generating "tapestry data," an admissions emphasis one vice president described as "very aggressive in reaching out ... trying to find those that would be interested in coming here." A senior leader explained this critical enrollment management change the university adopted:

> You profile a student and say, "This is a suburb of Philly where I'm getting a bunch of students from." Then you start doing a profile, you get data [like] geodemographics: this is how much money they're making, this is the kind of job they have, these are the catalogs they subscribe to, this is the places they spend their money. You can buy all that data.

He explained that the various types of data are aggregated to build a student profile the university has been able to successfully recruit or wanted to recruit. Once a profile had been established, it could be used to locate similar types of online and residential students at substantially cheaper rates:

> So now you say, "This is a small cluster. Where can I find other clusters like this, like the neighborhood outside Philly?" Now you're doing microspending, not just spending on data lists. You are saying, "I want suburbs like this around Dallas." Then, when you go to list rental companies, you know exactly what you want ... and you make a lot more money because you're not spending as much. So that was a big thing, that was very innovative.

Using the tapestry data approach to admissions lead generation, Google and Microsoft—technology giants with endless volumes of fine-grained user data—quickly replaced the College Board and ACT as the highest annually paid independent contractors for Ardmore.[27]

Using operational analytics, Ardmore leaders made a second innovative discovery in the area of course registration—one that widely impacted every student and faculty member on campus and online. "We did an analysis of enrollment in online sections between when the sections are populated and the end of Drop/Add [2 weeks into the course]," a senior leader explained.

> Our self-imposed standard at Ardmore is that we fill a section at 25 students online. But we found the reality was that [2 weeks later] at the end of Drop/Add on the undergraduate side we had an average of 17 and on the graduate side we had an average of 19.

With this discovery, Ardmore leaders used operational analytics techniques to develop a course registration system that functioned with the same real-time overbooking processes as an airline reservations system. A faculty member explained the process from the vantage point of the end user:

> If I have a class that averages 6 students dropping out, I end up with 19 by the end of the course. So, they increased the cap size on that course in that semester to 31, just expecting there to be 25 in the class by the end [of Drop/Add] . . . which in turn allowed them to hire less professors and fill the classes up more.

According to the senior leader who oversaw the initiative, the results were astounding: "By consciously overbooking, we made another $4 million this fall that we wouldn't have made otherwise, just like an airplane flight." Although the switch to operational analytics enabled Ardmore to establish innovative products and services by embedding data within its processes, a vice president stressed that the move was essential if Ardmore was to keep pace with the competitive data practices of other accelerated institutions: "All the other biggies do the same thing."

The Corporate Shell

In the early 2010s, as the economy began to recover from the Great Recession, major American companies established partnerships with colleges and universities as part of employee retention and training initiatives. Accelerated institutions were among the first to announce partnerships with large corporations: Arizona State University joined with Starbucks, Southern New Hampshire University joined with McDonalds and Chipotle, Western Governors University joined with Nationwide, and the University of Florida joined with Walmart. The corporate–university partnerships afforded companies with workforce training and universities with an exclusive enrollment pipeline that could be scaled to accommodate thousands of students. The online mode of delivery with its high financial margins backed by enrollment volume that came with corporate partnerships made these initiatives lucrative for colleges and universities. The corporate enrollment market space became saturated to the point where institutions that wanted to enter this space had to locate a company without an existing partnership—or they had to innovate.

Rather than selling existing degree programs in a crowded corporate market, Ardmore leaders established an innovative approach rooted in a debate regarding the relevance of curriculum in a changing professional environment. Ardmore leaders differentiated themselves in the crowded corporate enrollment market space by emphasizing the possibilities their online shell could create. A senior leader summed up the position Ardmore leaders took regarding "typical" curriculum content and development:

> Business is changing like crazy! Technology is changing like crazy! Then you throw in the normal cycle of development where we spend 6–12 months building a class, put it into production, leave it there for several years, bring it up for re-dev. That's our typical thing. That's not going to work—it's not going to work at all.

Instead, Ardmore created curriculum development models "where we can say it's iterative, it's applicable, it's relevant." One faculty member expressed the complexity of the solution: "It's not a matter of just adding a few more classes and posting more curriculum somewhere in the catalog. I mean, we're talking about major changes . . . to make the curriculum really relevant." Another professor connected it not just to the curriculum but also to the degree itself.

> The outcome 10 years ago, if you got a degree, you got a job, right? But now, everybody has a degree. We need to figure out what's going to set you apart. What can we give you, what cognate, certification, or experience can we add on that makes you more employable?

Whereas before a discussion centered on what constituted an education, now it was taken as a given that the educational end game was about employment. As the senior-most academic officer put it, "Our customer isn't our student. Our customer is our students' future employer . . . we're trying to build for the future, and we're trying to build for someone else."

The solution Ardmore administrators arrived at came as a result of taking their viewpoint directly to industry leaders. A senior administrator shared,

> We're looking at some interesting potential partnerships with some of these major companies . . . we brought them to campus and said, "What is the workforce that you need? What is it that you're looking for there and saying it doesn't exist?"

"We've got these kinds of conversations going with Apple, Adobe, Cisco, Aruba, Oracle, [and] Microsoft. . . . At very high levels they are incredibly intrigued with what Ardmore is trying to do." The corporate representatives expressed a critical need for thousands of employees with data science and information analytics competencies, noting an existing shortage and employee retention challenges. "They cannot find the workers. . . . And when they can find them, they're easy to pluck from someone who will give them six plus," a faculty participant recalled of the corporate conundrum.

The solution that emerged from the campus visits was joint corporate–university collaborations to scale a nonexistent curriculum with the aim of mass-producing a not-yet-existent workforce. An IT administrator explained:

> They're working with Ardmore to say, "What if we backed up and de-engineered what those skills need to look like and try to actually *on a large scale*—which Ardmore can deliver—and on a remote basis—which Ardmore can deliver—come up with a way *to mass produce* this workforce that does not exist?"

The manifestation to scale the nonexistent curriculum for a not-yet-existent workforce came in the form of a synergistic partnership that blended Ardmore's curriculum shell with corporate personnel training retreats. An administrator mentioned that the idea came about when someone asked one of the Silicon Valley firms, "Can we take what you normally push out through either training or through workforce development 'boot camps' and package it in an 8-week class?" He explained it transformed the approach from the typical corporate training boot camp where "you go for a week and just die in all-day-long learning classes and then try to take an exam" to one focused on "discussion, ethics, and academic pieces [to] teach over 8 weeks remotely." It was an altogether different approach to corporate training and education that could be scaled at an accelerated pace to benefit both parties. Ardmore engaged in the design process with three Silicon Valley firms to package their corporate training programs in Ardmore's standardized shell for remote delivery to thousands of global employees.

As one senior leader remarked of the initiative, "Whether it will take off or not, I don't know, but it's a unique, very unique partnership . . . the idea [is to] take this real-life stuff and make it the curriculum." Creating new academic programs for global corporations in a new format provided Ardmore leaders with a different niche to compete among the other accelerated institutions that had focused on corporate partnerships to increase enrollment with existing academic programs. The approach also enabled Ardmore leaders to garner the attention of a different type of corporation. While the other accelerated leaders had pursued companies like McDonald's, Ardmore executives used the new approach to pursue Apple, Adobe, Cisco, Aruba, Oracle, and Microsoft. One administrator overseeing the new corporate programs explained the underlying strategy: "We're going to continue to push the envelope and try to move ahead of the market and not just be reactionary but be proactive." And from his perspective, the early returns were quite positive: "We met with a company president last month. They're bringing us in and saying, 'You're the experts, we want to be with you. You're winning higher education online.'"

Outsourcing the Curriculum

With colleges and universities outsourcing more of their services,[28] it was only a matter of time before institutions began outsourcing the knowledge content function of their faculty—the very feature deemed to be the purpose for which a school is said to exist. In online course design processes, IT personnel are traditionally responsible for developing the shell, whereas faculty are responsible for developing the content. The product in the storefront had always been built by faculty, even when delivered in innovative ways. However, by combining outsourcing and standardization, Ardmore leaders bypassed faculty in the knowledge creation process and searched for new content beyond the ivory tower to put into a shell and sell.

In looking for additional online products for the storefront in his vision, the provost at Ardmore found two—conversational foreign languages and life coaching. Ardmore administrators swiftly cut faculty out of the content development process and outsourced it through a partnership with a well-known language company. The provost explained that the partnership with Competent Conversationalist provided the university with rapid product expansion and enrollment growth for the program. "We went from offering 4 foreign languages to 27 and increased the number of students by 600% or something. We made $3.5 million this fall alone teaching foreign conversational language."

Members of the Ardmore community were at pains to point out the self-marketing feature of the partnership. As one professor explained, "When students come in to take classes, they think, 'Hey, Competent Conversationalist. I've heard about this on the radio. This is wonderful!' It kind of does its own marketing since it's a well-known product." To further leverage brand recognition, university publications and its website were strategically affixed with the slogan "Powered by Competent Conversationalist." One professor highlighted how the outsourced partnership impacted student enrollment and student interest:

> I think they choose Competent Conversationalist not necessarily for the content, [but] because it's something that's going to bring in students. And it does. Students come in and they make these initial comments about their introductions and how excited they are that they're going to be using Competent Conversationalist at Ardmore.

His emphasis stressed the brand familiarity for both organizations, which seemed to complement one another. Instead of hiding the fact that their curriculum was not developed by their professors, Ardmore championed it. But according to one professor, quality took a backseat: "A lot of it is market driven. If people will buy the courses, we will sell them to them, whether or not they are the best courses imaginable."

Ardmore leaders established a similar partnership with another company, the National Counseling Association and its training division called Bright University. It is now commonplace for companies like Apple, Disney, and Oracle to brand their professional development divisions with the term *college* or *university* to engender a sense of legitimacy. According to one academic dean, select university executives served as senior administrators at both Ardmore University and Bright University, which provided Ardmore an opportunity to capitalize on an outsourcing partnership for its curriculum. "It's almost as if the two of them are parallel organizations," remarked one professor. A colleague of hers extolled the partnership with palpable enthusiasm: "I was very, very excited when Ardmore was developing a coaching program . . . especially when I found out that their whole curriculum was a curriculum that had been purchased from another organization." Ardmore established coaching programs using the purchased curriculum, which—like the foreign language programs—substantially bolstered enrollment with students. It also had an added advantage, according to the professor: "There's a lot of money in life coaching because you don't have to have all the degrees to teach it."

Both programs reflected a different approach to innovation. Previously, the conversion of in-person to online courses resulted in similar content but two different learning experiences through *product innovation*. The approach provided the university with a new type of online product to sell, moving from selling individual courses to full degree programs ("strings" or "tracks" of courses). But now, when Ardmore leaders combined standardization and outsourcing processes, they developed two new academic programs to sell that entirely bypassed the residential courses and faculty through *process innovation*. Once leaders purchased the fixed content from external companies, they embedded it within shells using standardized course design processes. One professor contrasted the old approach with the new:

> You don't get to pick your books anymore. You don't get to make the tests anymore. You don't get to select the topics for your paper.... In other words, you stop teaching. There's no creativity involved.... I cannot change anything... they took all of that away.

Although Ardmore professors were still used to administer the predominantly automated courses to students, they had been "innovatively" removed from the design process entirely.[29]

The outsourced programs provided Ardmore with burgeoning student enrollment, but its success came with what would have traditionally been seen as considerable downsides. As one foreign language professor explained, most of the work was completed online through the outsourced company. "The bulk of their grade comes from their work in Competent Conversationalist ... in fact, the student has to download his output or grade and then submit that to the professor to record." Faculty in the coaching program also expressed concern that the purchased curriculum did not align with professional standards—standards that in their view influenced job placement. As one professor confided, "Nothing in the curriculum was true coaching. It was counseling... just a [company] of counselors who wanted to capitalize on the coaching craze." But from the perspective of Ardmore's leadership, these were assets, not liabilities. Ardmore's bottom-line approach capitalized on student interest in these areas, as both programs became "bestsellers" in the academic marketplace.

Ultimately, outsourcing had a broader impact on the university than just the two academic programs developed for the online "storefront." The effort reinforced a broader mindset of efficiency and expansion that came to pervade both the online market and the residential campus. "It's very efficient. You know we can get a lot done very quickly. And that's a good thing," an academic dean shared. "What's not a good thing is that we have a collection of 3,000 faculty members who are smart people, who have a lot to say, who care deeply, and who don't have a voice." This predominant need-to-know style of communication seemed to reflect the wholesale embrace of market logic by senior leaders, as one professor explained:

> They tell us what we're doing, but that happens like once or twice a year. That's the only real information that we get about where we're going as a university and why

we're doing it. It's almost like a military model as opposed to the normal academic model. We operate more like a business than we do like a university.

Previously, when the online curriculum grew out of the residential offerings, the accelerated strategy meant the scaled product—online classes—would ultimately be the driver. In a rare moment of critique, one leader caustically observed,

> It's having a profound impact on the residential side of things. . . . They say they want high quality, but they're not putting the money towards that in terms of classes. Rather than building an institution of higher learning, it feels like they're building an empire.

Or, as another leader revealingly put it, "It feels like a Ponzi scheme."

Taking From the Competition

As explained in chapter 1, federal education policies rooted in economic reasoning have strategically organized the American system of higher education around the notion of competition. Limited financial resources are allocated to institutions based on principles of market competition, whereby funding is distributed to colleges and universities by way of individual students empowered to "shop" across institutions in search of a quality product. One IT administrator explained that leaders are readily aware of the pervasive competition but, more important, know exactly which schools are "direct competitors," as was the case among accelerated schools:

> One day last spring, I remember sitting here laughing because all of a sudden within a 2-week time period I personally had been approached by Penn State, Ohio State, I want to say Georgia State, [and] University of Florida. All these major schools were contacting me about something and wanting to know what Ardmore was doing with it. . . . They were looking and [asking], "What's going on over there [at Ardmore]? They've been successful with it. Let's figure out what they're doing."

Ardmore leaders explained the competitive environment was changing as others launched new educational products: "The new realm with massive open online courses and badgification and gamification and nanodegrees. . . . It's so much more competitive! We need to combat it!" a senior leader asserted in an apprehensive, yet aggressive tone. The competition among accelerated institutions had evolved into combat for students: "If Ardmore is doing 3 years from now what we were doing 3 years ago, we're old news. Most of the industry that's in our competitive group would say the same thing," an administrator asserted. Executives decided to take aim at their direct competitors with the goal of taking their customers, their data, and even their margins.

Technological advances in Internet marketing enabled accelerated institutions to target prospective students of their competitors. A vice president explained the method centered on keywords: "[There is] more heat coming up. Southern New Hampshire University is turning the model on its head because they're spending beaucoup dollars. . . . They're advertising in our niche. Phoenix is advertising in our niche. They buy words!" The keywords method was part of pay-per-click marketing, where advertisers pay a fee to purchase the advertising space at the top of Google and Microsoft search engines. In the instant a prospective student types in an education-related search term, an algorithm-controlled auction takes place that computes multiple variables, including the size of the financial "bid" a university pays, advertising campaigns, landing pages, and multiple types of targeting (e.g., device targeting, location targeting, day and time targeting, and demographic targeting). The algorithm decides on a "winning" university, which is advertised at the top of the search engine results. If a prospective student clicks on the advertisement, the institution successfully "purchases" another visit to its website.

The Ardmore vice president explained that the practice was commonplace among the accelerated schools: "We all do pay-per-click." However, Ardmore took the bidding wars to a new level. He explained the school's different approach, which aimed to take the customers of competitors by identifying the keywords unique to other institutions while increasing the financial bid on them to win the prominent spot on the search results. The Ardmore vice president confided, "We're spending a minimum of $4 or $5 million, which isn't a number you want to publish since our competitors won't tell us theirs. They lose a competitive advantage if we know what they're spending." Secrecy was an essential element in the effort to covertly acquire these students.

To combat the competitive pressures of other accelerated institutions, Ardmore leaders explained how they also developed a clandestine method of taking their competitors' data. One senior-level administrator boasted she had a team of stealth-like employees tasked with this objective. "It's pretty neat. We're currently doing some guerilla competitive research." The "guerilla research" had two distinct data emphases—one public and one private. For the first, "we analyze IPEDS [Integrated Postsecondary Educational Data System] data and a whole bunch of stuff" derived from public sources, databases, and websites, while the second employed "professors and other students" that either teach or attend other accelerated schools. "We pay to get information," she admitted, describing the specific outcomes of their "innovative" guerilla research: "We can get screenshots of other schools, what they're doing, see how the process goes, see how the communication flow goes, how quick they're hitting people, how quick the call center calls back, how long the wait is." Taking data from competitors allowed leaders to refine their own metrics, processes, and products to strengthen their competitive advantage. The senior leader referred to it as "competitive benchmarking" before she pointedly acknowledged a deeper truth: "I mean, we're a business at the end of the day. I think that's one of our—speaking back to core values—that's one of our things: we don't do education without looking at business outcomes."

Ardmore also hoped to update an old adage and convince its competition that if they could not beat them, then they should join them. As part of his annual administrative update, the provost explained to the faculty that Ardmore had begun a new initiative to sell its online services to other colleges and universities interested in establishing new online markets. In essence, the university aspired to turn competing institutions into clients by functioning as a paid partner, becoming an online program manager for other schools. And like paid partners, Ardmore was positioned to receive a percentage of the tuition revenues their competitors-turned-clients generated. By reconceiving what they sold—services rather than degrees—the arrangement made it possible for Ardmore to take a portion of the margins from competing institutions. Leaders established formal arrangements to provide online services to two other schools that lacked the financial capacity to establish online programs from the ground up. And Ardmore executives knew that if they could successfully scale this approach, they would establish a new form of superprofits by harnessing the tuition margins of students at competing institutions.

Conclusion

Having taken education to scale, the accelerated strategy left Ardmore awash in abundant cash. Unlike the traditional, pioneer, and network leaders who were forced to search for the next sustainable strategies, Ardmore leaders arrived at a lucrative self-sustaining strategy resting on market logic principles. The unfathomable financial turnaround allowed them to realize a billion-dollar campus transformation (funded by margin capitalization) and continually compound superprofits (funded by margin philanthropy). Yet the model of what constitutes sustainable success looks radically different than the customary values and conventional practices in capitalizing the core. If a neoliberal "edu-business" approach is the portrait of success in higher education, then a reckoning with educational ideals certainly looms as well.

Ardmore's leaders understood it was imperative to undercut the prestige structures that buttressed the elite model of higher education where selectivity rather than scalability reigned. At the same time, they were keenly aware of the rampant competition in their market niche and kept their gaze fixed on other accelerated institutions. Accelerated schools like Arizona State University and Georgia State University trumpeted that they were more innovative than even Massachusetts Institute of Technology.[30] To maintain their enrollment advantage, Ardmore's competitive practices took a more "aggressive" turn that emphasized methods appropriated directly from the market logic innovations of Wall Street, including operational analytics, launching initial public offerings, outsourcing core products, pay-per-click marketing, and "guerilla competitive research."

The compounding competitive pressures ultimately resulted in a trade-off where leaders seemingly forsook their founding focus of "for God" to maximize the monetary motto "In God We Trust." Many within the Ardmore community were distressed at this change, with one leader taking aim at the family firm model: "You cannot keep calling this a ministry. We don't cultivate an environment that's family focused." Amid the metamorphosis, the mission was hard to discern. "In an operation this size it's easy to think about the buildings rather than to think about our mission," one leader acknowledged, while a colleague observed, "We've grown too fast at the expense of our founding." The transformation even prompted administrators to question the essential underpinnings of their own "blessing." "I don't think God looked at us and said, 'Ya'll are doing a great job and I'm going to bless you,'" one academic dean posited. "I hope that we're not going to be an example that is instructive for others later in a bad way." Another academic dean even began to critically question who might be bearing the burden of the blessing:

> We don't think about where the prosperity is coming from. Like how many adjuncts are not making a lot of money? How many students are taking on massive debt? How much would it help students if we could increase the scholarship pool?

One administrator was certain they would soon become the negative example others feared: "You cannot drive faster and faster and faster and at some point not hit a tree."

Just as intensifying competition among all postsecondary institutional types had compelled other leaders to look for greater market-centric strategies, Ardmore leaders were already trying to ascertain what was next. A new motivating factor emerged among executives: "What if federal funding is cut?" This terrifying possibility compelled senior leaders to maximize their pursuit of student loans while they still flowed freely. At the same time, one senior vice president explained the university had already made efforts to finance its future by adopting measures to simultaneously focus on generating additional tuition revenue and making shrewd investments with existing margins: "We're preparing ourselves for the day we no longer have student aid funding . . . we're already working towards a strategy that will make that not matter. If all student loans go away, we can self-fund."

The accelerated strategy provided Ardmore with "more money than God," but leaders were now determined to unlock a multiplied version of scaling up—a type of "superscaling" that would magnify superprofits by (in the words of a tech-savvy administrator) "spinning up new markets":

> What if Ardmore bought another school? What if Ardmore took off with 200,000 Chinese students? We have to be ready, and we have to think about dynamic growth. Maybe it's through outsourcing of services, maybe it's through the way we cluster things. . . . Whatever it is, we have to think about what if we had to double this place in a month. What does that look like? And that's very much in our thinking.[31]

The Ardmore leader with the framed enrollment elbow on her wall put it this way: "If you took the chart that's on my wall and not just extrapolate where does it go next," her finger traced upward to signify future enrollment growth, "but pull it this way and see *another* curve for K–12 and *another* curve for certificates and *another* for overseas and some of those other verticals." Ardmore leaders remained determined to confront this highly competitive context in the same entrepreneurial manner they overcame their near-death experience. As one administrator summed matters up, "The story the last 10 years at Ardmore has been growth, and I don't think that story is over. But I don't think that is the story today. I think the story today is innovation." For Ardmore executives, market logic dictated that the next innovation would be the convergence of the accelerated and network strategies in an altogether new model—accelerated networks.

Notes

1. Cultural entrepreneurism differs from social entrepreneurism and value entrepreneurism in that it takes cultural resources and processes as its object of focus. It is "the process by which actors draw upon cultural resources (e.g., discourse, language, categories, logics, and other symbolic elements) to advance entrepreneurship or to facilitate organizational or institutional innovation." Lounsbury, M., & Glynn, M. (2019). *Cultural entrepreneurship: A new agenda for the study of entrepreneurial processes and possibilities.* Cambridge University Press, p. 3.
2. Leaderman, D. (2019, December 17). The biggest movers online. *Inside Higher Ed.*
3. A common trope among Protestants is that many institutions of American higher education—like the nation itself—were founded with a religious emphasis. For example, a Presbyterian school, the College of California, faced severe financial challenges and merged with a state institution to form what is today the University of California at Berkeley. Marsden, G. M. (2021). *The soul of the American university revisited: From Protestant to postsecular.* Oxford University Press; and Burtchaell, J. T. (1998). *The dying of the light: The disengagement of colleges and universities from their Christian churches.* W. B. Eerdmans Publishing Company.
4. "Pastor" or "founder" is used to refer to the Ardmore founder and "president" to refer to the founder's son.
5. The family business model is common in non-Western nations. Anderson, R. C., & Reeb, D. M. (2003). Founding-family ownership and firm performance: Evidence from the S&P 500. *The Journal of Finance, 58*(3), 1301–1328; Chen, S., Chen, X. I. A., & Cheng, Q. (2008). Do family firms provide more or less voluntary disclosure? *Journal of Accounting Research, 46*(3), 499–536.
6. It was common for interviewees to express discomfort when responses focused on explaining the functionality of the family firm. For example, one academic dean replied, "I am not going to tell you that one. It is all in the family. Blood is thicker than water."
7. Bjork-James, S. (2021). *The divine institution: White evangelicalism's politics of the family.* Rutgers University Press.
8. For example, see Anne Graham Lotz, Sarah Jakes Roberts, and Sarah/Naomi Zacharias. Bowler, K. (2020). *The preacher's wife: The precarious power of evangelical women celebrities.* Princeton University Press.
9. The idea that "all the world is a stage, and all the people are players" takes a contemporary form in the work of Erving Goffman, which uses dramaturgy as a central organizing frame where life is like a stage full of actors.
10. Lounsbury, M., & Glynn, M. A. (2001). Cultural entrepreneurship: Stories, legitimacy, and the acquisition of resources. *Strategic Management Journal, 22*(6–7), 545–564; Lounsbury, M., Cornelissen, J., Granqvist, N., & Grodal, S. (2019). Culture, innovation and entrepreneurship. *Innovation, 21*(1), 1–12.
11. This practice was common to religiously affiliated universities, but many have since abandoned the approach because of competing financial priorities for host denominations. Brigham Young University remains one of the few institutions that receives generous subsidies from its host denomination. Its three campuses (Utah, Hawaii, and Idaho) rank in the *U.S. News* least expensive colleges because of the substantial subsidies from the Latter-Day Saints church.

12. A series of controversies in the late 1980s involving three different multimillion-dollar religious broadcasting organizations garnered national media attention that included Jim and Tammy Faye Bakker, Jimmy Lee Swaggart, and Oral Roberts. The scandals contributed to a national distrust in "televangelists" that followed. Schultze, Q. J. (2003). *Televangelism and American culture: The business of popular religion.* Wipf and Stock Publishers; Lyon, D. (2013). *Jesus in Disneyland: Religion in postmodern times.* John Wiley & Sons.
13. Toutkoushian, R. K., & Lee, J. C. (2018). Revisiting economies of scale and scope in higher education. In M. B. Paulsen (Ed.), *Higher education: Handbook of theory and research* (pp. 371–416). Springer; Zhang, L. C., & Worthington, A. C. (2018). Explaining estimated economies of scale and scope in higher education: A meta-regression analysis. *Research in Higher Education, 59*(2), 156–173; Deming, D. J., Goldin, C., Katz, L. F., & Yuchtman, N. (2015). Can online learning bend the higher education cost curve? *American Economic Review, 105*(5), 496–501.
14. While the definitive set of innovation types continues to be debated, product innovation remains one of the three primary types that include product, process, and business model innovation. Keeley, L., Walters, H., Pikkel, R., & Quinn, B. (2013). *Ten types of innovation: The discipline of building breakthroughs.* John Wiley & Sons.
15. The elements of product bundling focus on structing order and choice, submitting a solution, generating value that is greater than the sum of its parts, eliminating redundant or unnecessary components, and provoking new interest. Reinders, M. J., Frambach, R. T., & Schoormans, J. P. (2010). Using product bundling to facilitate the adoption process of radical innovations. *Journal of Product Innovation Management, 27*(7), 1127–1140.
16. Panopticon refers to the building, institution, or system that monitors the masses without the observation of any singular individual. The panopticon was derived by Jeremy Bentham, an 18th-century philosopher, who designed circular prisons with a centralized guard tower whose windows were obscured so a prisoner was uncertain if they were being specifically observed.
17. CRM refers to customer relationship management software used to manage marketing campaigns, streamline admissions processes, and monitor employee performance.
18. Jessop, B. (2017). Varieties of academic capitalism and entrepreneurial universities. *Higher Education, 73*(6), 853–870.
19. Krippner, G. R. (2005). The financialization of the American economy. *Socio-economic Review, 3*(2), 173–208.
20. Karwowski, E. (2019). Towards (de-)financialization: The role of the state. *Cambridge Journal of Economics, 43*(4), 1001–1027.
21. Engelen, E., Fernandez, R., & Hendrikse, R. (2014). How finance penetrates its other: A cautionary tale on the financialization of a Dutch university. *Antipode, 46*(4), 1072–1091; Eaton, C., Habinek, J., Goldstein, A., Dioun, C., Santibáñez Godoy, D. G., & Osley-Thomas, R. (2016). The financialization of US higher education. *Socio-economic Review, 14*(3), 507–535.
22. Matthew 6:24.
23. The evolution of the field is mapped in Brown, J. T. (2017). The seven silos of accountability in higher education: Systematizing multiple logics and fields. *Research & Practice in Assessment, 11*, 41–58; Brown, J. T. (2018). Leading colleges & universities in an age of education policy: How to understand the complex landscape of higher education accountability. *Change: The Magazine of Higher Learning, 50*(2), 30–39; Cowhitt, T.,

Brown, J.T. & Antonio, A.L. (2024) The emergence and evolution of ambiguous ideas: an innovative application of social network analysis to support systematic literature reviews. *Scientometrics.* https://doi.org/10.1007/s11192-024-05144-7.

24. Davenport, T., & Harris, J. (2017). *Competing on analytics: The new science of winning.* Harvard Business Press.
25. Webber, K. L., & Zheng, H. (2020). *Big data on campus: Data analytics and decision making in higher education.* Johns Hopkins University Press.
26. Drake, B. M., & Walz, A. (2018). Evolving business intelligence and data analytics in higher education. *New Directions for Institutional Research, 178,* 39–52.
27. The IRS requires nonprofits to annually report the top five paid independent contractors in the Form 990.
28. See "Paid Partners" in Chapter 3.
29. Although they facilitate the individual courses for students, Ardmore faculty members remain unlisted in websites and promotional materials for the conversational foreign language and life coaching programs.
30. As reported annually by *U.S. News & World Report.*
31. The question, "What if we bought another school?" was the strategy taken by Purdue University in 2018 when it purchased Kaplan University and by the University of Arizona when it purchased Ashford University in 2020. Upon doing so, Purdue instantly amassed 30,000 additional students and Arizona immediately acquired 35,000 new students (notably, both institutions were purchased for the rock-bottom price of $1).

5
A Sector of Schools

"We're Here to Make Money"

Introduction

The stories behind the strategies of the entrepreneurial schools are a reflection of the emergent practices in higher education as well as a harbinger of the pervasive sector-wide norms to come. While such practices might be thought to be common at for-profit schools like the University of Phoenix, Capella University, and Strayer University, the fact that they have penetrated so deeply into nonprofit and religious school sectors has ominous implications for the future of education. Whereas all these schools were forerunners and first movers with respect to these strategies, today the impact of market-minded practices in higher education is unavoidable. "We are all participants in the commodification of education. Even the University of Virginia has commodified education—and Harvard," an Ardmore dean contended.

As a parable, these schools highlight the degree to which market competition has come in time to influence the daily practices in American higher education. It is embedded throughout the organization in everything from admissions and course design to product development, infrastructure design, and maximizing investments. Most institutions selectively adopt market-centric practices, but when an institution like Ardmore leverages the logic of the market in toto—throughout all its practices—it serves as a forerunner and ideal type of the matter-of-fact ways market-centric institutions will operate as standard practice. Or, as an Ardmore director put it more bluntly, the university "is not an educational organization—it's a 'We're here to make money' organization."

Market-minded practices have even breached the walls of elite institutions with the prevalent use of online program management, lucrative margins from executive education, and widespread financialization of endowments.[1] Many elite business schools, such as the University of Pennsylvania, Stanford University, and the University of Oxford, maintain profitable executive education programs that generate enough marginal tuition revenues to autonomously sustain the school itself (as is the case with the University of Virginia) and substantially contribute to the broader university coffers (as is the case with Harvard University).[2]

Neoliberalism strategically injected competition into higher education by design, bringing about a constant state of rapid change that higher education leaders continually grapple with. It forces an upward momentum across the field, one that left leaders who embraced the pioneer strategy laboring to diversify markets, those who made the leap to a network strategy figuring out how to scale markets, and administrators at schools that adopted an accelerated strategy determining how to multiply scaled markets. This relentless competition across all institutions of higher education has resulted in a continually changing environment characterized by uncertainty and possibility: "When there is change, there is danger. And when there is change, there is opportunity," the Ardmore provost intoned. Yet the kind of change that came about was quite unexpected. Ardmore's students did not change the world as much as they changed the school's bottom line. Market policies did not change customer choice as much as they changed institutional mission. And competition did not change educational quality as much as it changed educational strategy (Figure 5).

Each of the four strategies—traditional, pioneer, network, and accelerated—provides a unique glimpse into the diverse approaches leaders took toward sustaining their universities, but when taken as a collective whole, these eight tuition-dependent institutions highlight how colleges and universities operate in a context of limited financial resources. If lawmakers continue to withdraw public support of higher education, public colleges and universities will increasingly rely on entrepreneurial strategies to locate marginal tuition revenues—some more quickly than others. For example, the recent decision of Arizona state legislators to entirely defund their major community college systems instantaneously made the colleges completely tuition dependent—in practice, no different than the schools discussed in *Capitalizing on College*. When systems are structured on market principles, anyone in need must turn to the market. Indeed, the leaders of the various schools asserted the turn to rely on market logic solutions was not exclusive to them. A Winchendon administrator observed that "everyone is trying to figure out how to grow enrollment," while a Lansdale senior leader went further:

> Everybody is taking a hard look at efficiency, the cost of education, the return on investment.... Everybody is looking at it—public, private, everyone—*all* higher ed!

It is fitting in this concluding chapter to then examine these eight schools together, rather than as individual types of cases, to highlight the approaches

Figure 5 Revenue Sources for Sustaining the Core

they collectively employ toward policy innovation, the crisis they collectively feel regarding their identity, and ultimately the fate of the residential core. To gain a competitive advantage, leaders at these schools focused on latent opportunities embedded within the interpretive and ambiguous elements of the market-oriented policies themselves. But in their relentless pursuit of enrollment advantages, everyone revealed their fears regarding an erosion of their identity, encapsulated in one Boxborough professor's remark: "You should be able to see the mission in the balance sheet." In the end, leaders ironically gravitated to an enrollment philosophy that squarely took aim at an identity rooted in the residential core—abandoning the raison d'être for the various strategies they pursued in the first place.

Policy Innovation in Higher Education

Like a building or an airplane, a system of higher education is a strategically built entity, engineered to meet the educational needs of a diverse national population. Since the mid-20th century, the policies used to structure the system have increasingly relied on market-oriented premises, or what some refer to as neoliberalism. By design, these policies have successfully achieved widespread competition for student tuition dollars across all types of postsecondary institutions. But they have also had the unintended consequence of having produced competition within and among the policies themselves. Leaving no revenue stone unturned, innovative actors focused on the interpretive and ambiguous characteristics of policy to give them a competitive advantage in the enrollment marketplace. The new approach executives took toward policy innovation sheds light on the tenuous reality that confronts university administrators in their ongoing search for enrollment markets and the valuable financial resources that market-oriented policies incentivized them to pursue.

Competition and Choice Trumping Cooperation

From campus to campus and across interviews, one of the inescapable themes on the minds of administrators and faculty alike was what the Pepperell provost pointedly described as an "incredible competition." In the narratives that university leaders offered, competition was never static, but always on the move as an unseen and ever-burgeoning force: "Competition has heated up" was a phrase frequently bandied about, only to be replaced by phrases like "Competition has exploded." The thrust of competition was the underlying force that compelled university leaders to continually modify their strategy in search of new students, taking some leaders to the ends of the earth. "The market is really hard... you have to work to get the students. I need to search for students all over the world," a Winchendon leader wearily remarked. As a Lansdale academic dean highlighted, the threat of competition took other leaders into new markets at a bewildering pace: "I would describe it as a frenzy to create these programs." Even the devout Stoneham nuns readily acknowledged the omnipresent impact competition had on their institution. As one sister confessed, "There's a real sense of being in competition with schools, that there's no time to waste, and that we always have to be a little ahead of everybody in the game."

Despite its pervasive and powerful influence over institutions, competition yielded exactly what policy makers had intended for students—choice. Time and again, leaders underscored the primacy of student choice. "The finances are key for a kid to make a choice here," a Pepperell coach mentioned, while a Lansdale leader observed, "Our brand is strong, especially for the kind of student who wants to choose us." The Malvern chief financial officer opined that "there's a lot of competition ... and students have a lot of choice."

Competition and choice intersect by design in higher education through market-oriented education policies, which emphasize that competition brings about increased choice, and choice brings about improved product quality. The Lansdale provost explained that their institutional survival lay at the confluence of both: "In today's market, to be competitive you have to have some distinctive, something that people would say, 'This is why I want to go there,'... a distinct identity that tends to help people be part of the reason they choose you." Winchendon's president echoed the sentiment in even franker terms: "The Hispanic population is growing, and we are their number one choice—period."

However, for some at these schools, policies stemming from economic reasoning were not just shoals to be navigated but also frameworks that distorted the entire enterprise of higher education. A Stoneham professor pointed out that "the logic of business or capitalism left to itself leads to monopoly and low wages for workers, which is why we have been trying to temper it since the 19th century." A faculty member at Boxborough was similarly vexed by the pervasive market tension at his school and looked to prior eras for contemporary sense-making: "It is not just about inserting ethics into our transactions; it is about changing the underlying production processes so that they are humanizing." He went on to explain what he meant:

> We have to have a paradigm shift to solve our sustainability issues going forward.... [If] we can work in *cooperation* with and in service to others to bring down our inborn egocentricity ... if we develop economics on that basis—cooperation rather than competition—then we get a whole different view of the economy.

What was the Boxborough faculty member suggesting? Many thinkers have described the foundation of modern society as possessing two dichotomous logics in tension with one another—an economic sphere and a social sphere. Competition remains the organizing framework at the core of the economic sphere, promoting individual initiative, choice, and efficiency, whereas cooperation is the organizing logic of the social sphere and promotes community, ethics, and reciprocal commitment.[3] Situated between these two spheres is an arena for the exchange of goods and services known as the market, which exists as both an economic and a social institution. Colleges and universities reside in this space, and broader structures like government agencies or policies directed at higher education draw on the central organizing ideas in both spheres. But as systems and the organizations embedded within them evolve over time, the original balance between these dichotomous logics can shift.[4]

The change in American higher education from viewing it as a "public good" to a "private good" underscores how policies strategically grounded in economic reasoning by design cumulatively shifted the focus of an entire system away from its social dimensions.[5] Just like the divine mission of Ardmore could not in the end constrain the growth mindset of the accelerated strategy, it is not surprising to find the notion of the public good falling to the wayside when encountering the same strategy at public institutions of higher education.[6]

This evolution leading to the dominance of neoliberalism is rooted in a widespread trust that the market is the most effective means of fairly distributing valuable resources to individuals and organizations. But the presence of a public good in one sector poses an ideological threat to neoliberal governance in another sector—if water can be fairly distributed through cooperation rather than market means, the same might be true of other social sectors. While the widespread trust in the social value of higher education enabled it to remain more resilient against neoliberal encroachment than other sectors (e.g., what has happened with land, healthcare, welfare, and transportation[7]), the persistent erosion is such that many "public" institutions currently receive paltry sums of public support—or have given up the idea of being holdouts and turned entirely to privatized forms of financial support.[8]

The high degree of public trust also permitted individual colleges and universities to pursue market-centered strategies whose emphasis would be deemed profit-seeking absent their connection to a social logic. As others have explained, the greatest financial gains are often made possible with the presence of some type of human connection to exploit.[9] The specific changes in higher education financial policies during this era—per-student funding and student loans—were rooted in notions of individualism and competition that derive from the economic sphere and essentially exploit the notions of cooperation and reciprocity found in the social sphere. They promise a type of freedom and future opportunity while deliberately shifting the burden of cost from the organization to the individual consumer. When these market-centered policies are taken to their fullest extreme, they ignore the humanizing aspects of education and incentivize quite opposite practices. As one Ardmore dean confessed,

> The call centers by their very nature are dehumanizing. . . . I think we forget about the humans in the process. . . . I think we forget what is supposedly a core belief of ours, that we are image-bearers, and no matter what people do, whoever they are, they have value.

Interpretation as Innovation

But economic reasoning did not merely create competition between schools to find new educational markets or offer new educational products. The embrace of market-based competition ultimately drove universities to innovate with respect to the interpretation of the neoliberal policies themselves.

Policy innovation is customarily understood as the development of specific policies separate and independent from the innovations that aim to catalyze innovation in a given sector or industry to solve complex social issues.[10] Within this understanding, the central innovation of economic reasoning is to resolve issues by establishing a marketplace to govern the allocation of public resources. But the executives of the entrepreneurial schools turned policy innovation on its head.

While policy makers may have intended to create an educational marketplace where universities competed for students and resources, university leaders acted innovatively toward the actual policies themselves to give their institutions a competitive advantage. Hidden within the ambiguous wording of education policy were latent opportunities administrators could competitively leverage and exploit by interpreting them in entrepreneurial ways to innovatively secure more money.[11] Competition thus did not solely occur in the marketplace that neoliberal policies strategically attempted to engineer, but also manifested as a result of actual policy verbiage. In an ultimate form of embracing market-based reforms, university leaders pulled neoliberal education policies into the very market the policies governed.

One area of policy innovation that the leaders of entrepreneurial schools openly embraced involved "enrollment threshold" funding associated with underrepresented students. With funding allocated on a per-student basis, leaders were incentivized to search for new types of students in new markets. An Ardmore official put the matter bluntly: "All colleges are basically trying to find ways of accepting all students, because the government is handing out the money [on a per-student basis]." If leaders could innovatively combine enrollment-based policies through novel interpretations of the wording, they could secure even further federal funding. The additional federal funding available was linked to "dynamic" characteristics of an institution (i.e., enrollment), differing in kind from the funding associated with the "static" characteristics of an institution (i.e., the fixed historical designation of historically Black colleges and universities).[12] If the total student enrollment for a college or university surpassed 40% Black, it could achieve the designation of a predominantly Black institution; if student enrollment surpassed 25% Hispanic, it could achieve the designation of a Hispanic-serving institution; if student enrollment surpassed 10% Asian American, Native American, or Pacific Islander, it could achieve the designation of an Asian American and Native American Pacific Islander–serving institution.[13] Colleges and universities with these designations received additional federal funding when their total student enrollment met these diversity thresholds. In short, while an institution cannot become a historically Black college or university, neoliberal incentives encourage colleges and universities to become a predominantly Black institution if they can enroll enough Black students.

Entrepreneurial leaders were readily aware of the valuable financial resources made available at these thresholds. The diminishing supply of traditional-aged college students incentivized leaders to not only establish new markets, but also consider how to innovatively leverage the enrollment-based policies to secure further funding. With a lower enrollment threshold to achieve than predominantly Black institutions and a surging national population among Hispanics, many entrepreneurial institutions fixed their ambitions on becoming Hispanic-serving institutions.[14] "Demographics are changing; you have to be able to go where there is growth, which is Latino and first-generation students. A traditionalist [approach] is an uphill battle," the Pepperell provost observed.

To gain an advantage amid increased competition, many school leaders had begun to pivot their attention toward the dynamic aspects of enrollment policies and come to realize a new admissions paradigm was within reach for their institutions—to enroll more of a certain *type* of student was to secure even more money. It did not matter whether the school had a tradition of serving such students or even catered to their particular needs: "Hispanic-serving institutions are basically a federal designation based on enrollment," a senior Winchendon leader clarified, and then knowingly remarked, "But what does it *really* mean to be a Hispanic-serving institution?" The answer was spelled out unambiguously by a Lansdale vice president: "We are *this* close to the 25% mark," he smiled, holding up his thumb and forefinger. From a perspective of economic reasoning, serving underrepresented students was strictly a numbers game.

The impact of interpretation on neoliberal enrollment threshold policies nominally intended to support diversity emerges most clearly when contrasting Winchendon with Pepperell. Winchendon leaders worked for years to bolster Hispanic student enrollment and were ultimately rewarded with additional federal funding for surpassing the 25% enrollment threshold. Pepperell leaders also enrolled a substantial number of ethnically diverse students—an unmistakable feature of their campus population, but not one recognized by neoliberal policies. As one exasperated leader explained, Pepperell's diversity "does not come out in the numbers because [the enrollment policy] counts Middle Eastern students as White! . . . if you look at our diversity numbers, we are not considered that diverse, which is completely fucking ridiculous!" Despite serving a substantially high percentage of Middle Eastern students, Pepperell administrators were not beneficiaries of the diversity funding available to other institutions because of the way the enrollment policy interpreted diversity. Another Pepperell leader put the matter bluntly:

> Our diversity calculations are misrepresented. . . . People do not consider socioeconomic and religious diversity. They just always look at race. And if they are just looking at race, *there is no box* for Middle Eastern, so you click White. Diversity gets lost.

While some schools were able to successfully innovate and draw underrepresented populations to them to reap financial rewards, others were comparatively penalized despite being "organically" diverse. Despite their commitment to local Middle Eastern students, Pepperell leaders were not rewarded the way other entrepreneurial schools were because they were unable to reinterpret the market logic of enrollment policies centered around racial categories. The Pepperell administrator offered a succinct summation of the neoliberal approach to diversity: "I think it's total bullshit."

The Challenge of Compliance

Making the enrollment numbers come out right to receive federal funding became an increasingly expensive proposition at these schools. By accepting federal monies, an institution also accepts the policy scheme that dictates how federal financial resources will be distributed (i.e., per-student funding and financial aid), as well as oversight regarding that distribution (i.e., accreditation and compliance). With a twist of wit, a Stoneham nun who oversaw policy compliance referred to it as "the golden rule"—"whoever has the gold makes the rules." She conceded that,

> [Policy makers] have a right to track the money and make sure it is not being abused. If you are going to accept federal money so that students get their Pell and their Stafford loans, then that is big bucks. The money that flows through this place is unbelievable!

But the increasing complexity of the policy environment and the many new regulations associated with federal financial aid led senior leaders at entrepreneurial schools to describe following the policy scheme as "challenging," "complicated," and "risky." The legal labyrinth taxed the mettle of administrators: "We're trying to deal with this assessment monster," one Pepperell dean expressed in a tired tone. "Three or four years ago I had zero compliance officers, but now I have four just for us to stay on top of government regulations," the Pepperell president griped. "The government is complaining about the cost of college. Well, that is four salaries I had to pick up because you came out with 25,000 new rules."

But worries about the negative impact compliance could have on the bottom line extended far beyond having to pick up just a couple additional salaries. The Boxborough provost recalled how one change in particular resulted in crippling financial losses for the college. "Before the government changed the compensation rules, companies would pay their people 80% of tuition to come here. It was the gold star," he stated with a nostalgic tone. The senior-most academic official explained how Boxborough leaders strategically leveraged aspects of the compensation policy to establish a dominant competitive advantage throughout the region: "We had a cache that nobody else had—liberal arts, value-based education, where we were going to get you out into the community [and] live in solidarity with others. We couldn't be touched, and we did it really well!" But in describing the change, a forlorn look came over his face and his voice cracked. "And then the rules changed [to] a commodity-market, and we didn't have any value proposition to beat everybody else." Undone by a change in federal compensation policies, Boxborough's market niche quickly evaporated. The market-centered policy changes brought about lower prices and increased competition, stripping Boxborough of its ability to continue to deliver community-centered programs fundamentally grounded in the humanizing characteristic of cooperation.

Administrators were therefore quick to exploit policy loopholes before they closed. For example, ambiguities existed in accreditation policies with regard to faculty workload, allowing schools to save on labor costs. The Winchendon chancellor explained how professional accreditors required certain facilities, salary levels, and administrative staffing, but regional accreditors did not specify similar resources for the undergraduate level:

> You start a professional school and the accreditor is going to tell you exactly how many full-time faculty you are going to have and not one less. They are going to say you cannot have any adjuncts. But we can have undergraduate schools with only one dean, one secretary, and way more students [per faculty member] than there are in the professional school. But we can cut corners here because the regional accreditor is not going to say how many [employees] to have. They don't care . . . we've grown the numbers of students until they are just hanging off the ceiling.

Even policy changes in domains other than education could have unintended consequences for schools. Malvern leaders described the impact of one such policy change regarding employee compensation and benefits. "The Affordable Care Act squashed our model because we didn't really have any restrictions on how many courses adjuncts could teach in a year's time," an academic official pointed out. "When they said what qualifies as full-time, we had to really take a hard look at that because we couldn't afford to offer them all benefits. So right now, what we've come up with is they can teach one course at a time." Administrators "innovatively" responded to the policy: whereas before they might have a select number of adjuncts working "part-time" teaching large numbers of courses, they now spread their course coverage needs across a larger pool of adjuncts so that they did not have to absorb the cost of providing them healthcare—a social provision based on cooperation.

A poignant exchange with a senior vice president at Winchendon highlights how administrators navigated the challenge of compliance.

> I had an evaluation with another staff member, and I told him, "You are the registrar, and I need you to be the registrar, but this year I want you to be 'the Registrar of Yes.' I don't want to hear a 'No' out of your mouth."

The senior leader grinned and proceeded with how she explained to the registrar that they could "innovatively" utilize policy ambiguity to the school's advantage:

> I know you have to say "No" because accreditation says you cannot do everything. You have to follow regulations, but what I want to hear you say when you are talking with students, the faculty at large, and myself, instead of "No," say, "The regulations say we have to do it a certain way, but let's see how we can fit this within the regulations." Which is a way of saying "Yes" as opposed to "No." I don't want to hear about what the accreditors say. I want to hear about what we can do that falls within the legal guidelines.

The senior leader then made air quotes: "There are regulations and then there are 'regulations.'" She used her finger flutter to pivot her narrative from a registrar who needed to learn to locate the "yes" within policy to the director of financial aid who embraced the possibilities inherent in interpreting ambiguous policy by going after every single possible federal funding dollar:

> I'm not advocating doing anything to break the rules. I want us to be ethical. I want us to be responsible. My financial aid director is not bucking authority. He is very creative and looks within the guidelines, understanding they are a template—a baseline to go by. As long as you do not violate that, there is nothing wrong with painting outside the lines.

The interpretive and ambiguous aspects of policy provided opportunities for university executives to embrace market principles and leverage neoliberal policies in innovative ways to give them a competitive advantage in the very marketplace the policies espoused. Policies do not create a theoretical market "out there" solely guided by the invisible hand of competition; the market can also be guided by the hands of entrepreneurs themselves. The competitive nature of a market left to its own devices possesses few limits—not even the policies that provided its genesis are deemed sacred. Once created, markets themselves are subject to their own pressures. But in pursuit of the almighty enrollment dollar—to the point that schools were willing to exploit economic reasoning in changing their institutional character—what got left behind was an identity tied to mission and purpose.

Identity in Higher Education

One of the unparalleled strengths of the American system of higher education is the wide diversity of institutions that were established to educate an equally diverse population of people. The identity of each institution, rooted in an educational mission and collective values, propelled schools forward from one generation to the next.[15] Yet the contemporary shift toward market-oriented education policies incentivized institutional leaders to locate new financial resources by pursuing enrollment growth. To navigate the increased competition for financial resources, university executives explained it was imperative that they remake and rebrand their identity to distinguish themselves from competitors and attract students. Determined to survive, university leaders set out to simultaneously emphasize both money and mission in their dogged pursuit of growth. Yet the approach created competing identities within the schools, and growth came at a cost that no balance sheet could accurately capture.

An Identity Paradox

As university leaders canvassed the future resource landscape for their institutions, they described an environment filled with "contradictions," "tensions," "a serious divide," and "two roads." The question was a pressing one: "How do we continue our economic success, but without becoming a corporate entity?" a Stoneham professor asked. There were no easy solutions on the horizon for most schools: "Winchendon has two paths in front of it, and it is not clear to me which one it will go down," its chancellor expressed with concern. The chasm seemed clear, but in an unseemly way the two sides were also curiously connected: "You know, you need some margin for mission," a senior Boxborough leader stated while holding out her left hand, but then extended her right hand as she continued, "and you need some mission to be able to get the margin."

The tensions between institutional finances and identity—or "margin and mission," as many framed the issue—certainly had troubled leaders of the past. And yet present-day institutional leaders faced an intensified resource challenge brought about by neoliberal policies that allocated financial resources on a per-student basis, making the margin–mission connection further contingent on enrollment growth. "Like it or not, we've got to sell ourselves, we've got to develop that Boxborough brand. And if we don't do that, it impacts everything else, because at the end of the day it is a numbers game," a vice president asserted. "'No Money, No Mission' holds true in a lot of cases." Remarks by the Pepperell provost were representative of how university leaders thought about this seemingly inescapable tension: "I don't think the fiscal is ever going to get back to the point of where it was," he lamented of the long-past golden age in higher education.

The market logic approach ensured that more money was available to institutions to achieve their mission—via more students. Looking to the horizon, a senior Boxborough leader commented, "Once we get the consistent and reliable enrollment numbers and some growth, then we're going to have more resources to support the objectives which we need to be able to pursue our mission and to distinguish us from competitors." But the inescapable tie between margins and mission troubled university leaders. "How do we continue to feed the growth so that we serve the population and do it consistently with who we are, what our identity is?" the Malvern president asked, while his contemporary at Lansdale posited, "How does a place like Lansdale continue to be who we are and yet not be cut off from federal funds?" Growth was the only path forward to acquire valuable financial resources, but it was also the path that put institutional identity at risk.

Rather than a fork in the road where one divergent path must be chosen over another, leaders chose to move forward as though these were parallel tracks to be used in tandem. Executives resolved to be distinct yet dynamic, creating an identity rooted in their school's past, but one that simultaneously evolved in search of new markets. But the relentless competition among institutions for students all but ensured leaders remained challenged to balance the pervasive tension between maintaining a distinct identity that remained true to their values while having to continually reshape their schools in dynamic ways to set them apart. "Like other institutions, we're continuing to try and brand, rebrand, *and* keep our feel on the question of identity—to maintain who we are as Pepperell," one professor thoughtfully explained. An academic official at Winchendon similarly described the dichotomy: "Winchendon has tried to maintain who we are, maintain our identity, *but also* redefine it a little bit. The powers that be thought that they have needed to redefine who we are to become more attractive to society." Boxborough leaders described the attempt to rebrand and focus on establishing new enrollment options for working-class students this way: "We are on the cusp of reclaiming our identity . . . we are reframing ourselves *and* starting to re-believe we are about the students." Within this highly competitive reality, university leaders expressed that their institutional identity had to be simultaneously staid yet constantly remade.

Leaders commonly spoke of identity when describing the "ethos" or the "culture" of the institution using the same succinct phrase: "It is who we are." Those with strong ties to their university frequently intertwined personal and institutional identities, like one long-serving leader at Lansdale who seamlessly described "the identity of who I am and who we are." The notion of identity was so vital that many universities formally established offices of mission and identity headed by an administrator who reported directly to the president. Having previously served in the role at another institution, the Boxborough provost underscored that these identity administrators were tasked "to get the mission inclusive" and ensure it remained "grounded" in communal values, while the same officials at Lansdale were charged with having to "codify and clarify its identity to the world." "The Lansdale president contended it was imperative that the university address what is about Lansdale that is 'going to make a difference in a very large pool of institutions, because it is starting to become a bit of an issue.'" With an unmistakable look of concern, he drew on a metropolitan motif: "We're basically a freeway university. There are 15 million people [in the area]. That's a good place to be, but you still need to have an identity, a reason for people to take your off-ramp."

While leaders attempted to simultaneously pursue both margin and mission, achieving a balance between the two paths remained elusive. The approach created competing identities within the schools, as one Ardmore academic dean acknowledged: "Because we've always been in a growth mode, it makes it tough to nail down the identity." The universities became bigger and grander as they secured larger margins and built more buildings. But in looking back, leaders acknowledged undertones of uncertainty and fear. "Growing pains" was a term frequently heard. "People are a little afraid that the growth is too quick, and we've not addressed some of the issues that come with growth," was how a Winchendon board member put it.

Time and again, executives stated that the impetus to remake and rebrand the identity of the institution derived from the need to compete for valuable financial resources. Based on policies, more resources demanded the acquisition of more students, ultimately causing leaders to question the impact of growth. "The desire to expand, to grow, and yet still retain the ethos and the values of the culture... how big can you get before you lose that?" a Boxborough administrator asked. When asked whether Lansdale achieved balance during his leadership tenure, the president pensively admitted, "I think we chased growth." Continuing in a tone of nostalgia, he said, "I remember when we were one of the smaller colleges when I was a student here... our default [during my tenure] has been 'Let's grow!' And that has brought new opportunities, new challenges, and new problems." Even at a school like Ardmore, whose leadership had seemingly whole-heartedly embraced growth over identity, administrators confessed how these conflicting interests resulted in an unmistakable imbalance:

> We tried so hard to identify things that could become traditions that would help to give Ardmore an identity tied to the students and tied to the activities of the students, whether it be their academics or whether it be their sports—that there would be something that would connect them. But the problem was that over the years there was not a whole lot of interest in tradition. The interest was more in growing the university. And marketing really took over.

A Change in Composition

Powerful tropes in American society about attending college have shaped the establishment of institutions and their development over time. For generations, it has been understood that young adults leave home in a coming-of-age ritual to attend college in person on a residential campus adorned with stately buildings, manicured grounds, and established educational histories. This widespread social understanding about attending college on a physical campus has influenced the centrality of the residential experience and was woven into the identity of institutions. "When I came here 30 years ago, we were almost exclusively perceived to be an undergraduate residential institution. That was our identity," the Lansdale provost shared. Maintained by elite institutions, the residential model has remained the foremost legitimate form of higher education, despite its high cost of delivery. Despite being vexed by the seemingly inseparable tie between identity and finances, administrators at tuition-driven institutions understood they needed to establish new models focused on bolstering both margins and mission if they were to overcome the mounting resource challenges associated with maintaining a residential core.

The stories in this volume highlight the innovative strategies institutions developed to sustain their residential core and the identities that emerged within institutions as they pursued new forms of enrollment growth. Leaders remained adamant their efforts were influenced by the connection between identity and finances: "The identity thing continues to be a factor . . . ultimately it will be a factor in terms of branding and how it plays out in the way you recruit students," the Lansdale provost noted, while a Boxborough vice president contended, "We are trying to build an identity thinking 10 years out because there will be a lot of schools that are underendowed, not being very strategic, and will be closing." A Malvern administrator took care to explain that identity must be addressed with each new market they established: "The identity needs to be worked out in terms of structure, priority, and academic programming."

Yet for the entrepreneurial schools, the strategies they adopted radically changed the institutions. Working adults soon outnumbered traditional undergraduates at Malvern, Winchendon jettisoned its sole identity as a women's college, ethnic minorities became the majority at Lansdale, and Pepperell maintained near-equivalent Muslim and Catholic student enrollments. Executives deliberately pursued multiple identities to achieve growth. "I think we will reconsider the composition of the university so that our traditional face-to-face undergraduate population will probably be identified and limited," a Lansdale senior vice president explained. "It will continue to be a core part of our identity, but we will continue to extend and expand some of these other identities." Other leaders were decidedly pessimistic about overcoming the mounting resource challenges associated with maintaining a residential core. "If the world continues to question the cost–benefit analysis of a college education," a Lansdale professor contended, the debate between "cost and identity" will not end well for the school. Nor did schools have to look far to see their potential futures: online enrollment at Ardmore eclipsed its residential population by 10-fold.

The emergence of multiple identities within each institution required leaders to manage conflicting and competing identities that existed simultaneously. The Winchendon chancellor cautioned that despite all the advancements in their enrollment growth, "You will see there are conflicting narratives about who we are and what our identity is." Malvern leaders pointed to persistent tensions between the main and satellite campuses: "There is real confusion on who we are . . . people have noted that we cannot be two separate institutions, though in some ways I think we functioned better when we ran like two separate institutions." One leader skeptically described it as a "tug of war" occurring within Lansdale: "You want to keep bringing people in because you are a good school, but if you keep bringing people in, things start to break apart a little bit."

One telling example of how entrepreneurial universities tried to resolve these tensions could be found in how—as they began their nascent foray into online markets—they physically established the new digital divisions of employees far from the residential campus. One division was located miles away in an old high school, another was two towns over in a vacated factory, and a third was trying to locate adequate commercial property in Las Vegas to relocate its online division—nearly 2,500 miles away from campus. The millions of dollars in funding needed to sustain the core were increasingly generated nowhere near it.

As they conveyed their institutional narratives, leaders took care to point out that many peer institutions were also contending with competing identities brought about by organizational transformations. The Stoneham president explained that state policy makers had recently converted all public 2-year institutions in his state to 4-year institutions to boost enrollment and revenues to strategically offset the reduction in state allocations. A Havertown leader lamented how another university in the state "just went off the deep end" regarding student consumerism to pursue a $1.5 billion building spree predominantly funded through loans: "They are a niche market. . . . They did what they thought they needed to do from a marketing perspective to get students, but I don't think they have retained who they are." Many public universities have recently pursued large enrollment increases in markets beyond their residential core. Institutions like Pennsylvania State University, University of Maryland, Washington State University, Colorado State University, and University of Illinois have enrolled thousands of students online in "global campuses," while other institutions like Purdue University, University of Arkansas, University of Idaho, University of Massachusetts, and University of Arizona purchased outright entire for-profit universities to quickly acquire tens of thousands of new enrollees.[16] With satellite and online enrollments that rival or exceed their residential core enrollment, these public institutions possess competing identities and hybrid organizational forms that resemble those described in this book.

Leaders labored relentlessly to manage the internal competition between multiple identities while navigating the intensifying external competition with peer institutions in the marketplace. At Boxborough, leaders were "pushed to attract more and more highly affluent students . . . that shifted the culture," which prompted a concerned vice president to ultimately ask, "So then what does that mean about mission?" Havertown leaders themselves were pushed, as an academic official confided:

We knew who we were. And I'm just hoping that for the glitzy purposes we're not moving too fast for ourselves.... But I am seeing a lot of stress, and they cannot push us that much more!

In some instances, executives pushed the dynamic nature of the institution's identity too far and had to work to recapture rather than rebrand. "The institution for a period of time was kind of moving away from their identity," a Lansdale vice president explained. "The president is trying to pull them back, but it's difficult to pull something back once it starts to move."

Selling Your Soul

The simultaneous pursuit of margins and mission skewed heavily toward market interests as university leaders worked tirelessly to balance competing institutional identities and blended others to further reduce costs. The relentless rebranding and never-ending pursuit of growth left many administrators feeling aimless. A Havertown dean asked in an exasperated tone, "We are struggling with our identity a little bit. What are we going to be?" Without mincing words, the Winchendon chancellor confided, "All of this growth has been challenging to our identity—to who we want to be, who we think we are." One of her colleagues described it as "a general kind of murmur" among the faculty who were imploring, "Who are we? How do we define ourselves? Is it okay to define ourselves in many different ways? How do we embrace that?" The widespread spirit of uncertainty seemed inaccessible, reminiscent of when the hookah-smoking caterpillar asked Alice lost in Wonderland who she was, and she replied, "I hardly know, Sir, just at present—at least I know who I was when I got up this morning, but I think I must have been changed several times since then."[17]

At the same time, in this strategically designed policy system, university leaders were readily aware that if growth stagnates, so do the valuable financial margins needed to sustain the residential core. As the Winchendon chancellor shared,

We have been growing faster than all the rest of the privates, [but] there may be a wall coming. We did not make our freshman number this year and we were stable last year. You could say stable or stale, I am not sure which.

He continued in a cynical tone, "The president has the idea that we are just going to keep growing like a meteor going forward." At the opposite end of the country, Malvern leaders were confronted with a similar lull in enrollment growth: "We are in a crucial time because we are at a place where enrollment has plateaued and maybe even declined a little bit," an academic dean elucidated with alarm. She, too, highlighted that the focal matter was ultimately about revenues:

> Just a little drop, 1% or 2% of 15,000 students is a lot of revenue, and that is crucial! We have to focus over the next few years on finding a way to *not* let it drop any more... a healthy university is one that is *not* declining in enrollment.

Amid the emphasis on growth, university leaders experienced a type of decay, what some referred to as "erosion of identity," "compromising our identity," and, most frequently, "an identity crisis." The downward trajectory in mission ran opposite enrollment growth: "We are very much a growth model [which] is 'Take everyone you can get who is willing to pay,'" one academic official candidly conveyed, "and we desperately need to transition because I think we will completely lose who Stoneham is if we stick with the growth model indefinitely." At Malvern, the metamorphosis was near-instantaneous: "The growth was fast, so fast and furious we came out on the other side of it saying, 'We do not recognize ourselves anymore,'" one professor proclaimed, while a senior leader recalled how institutional qualities that should never have been forgotten had become lost during the years of expansion:

> We started shooting higher and that's when we started to lose our identity. That's when we started to forget.... We forgot who we were that got us here and we've been trying to change to something that is already out there, and that's not really who we are.

An academic official at Lansdale felt like important qualities of her institution had also been lost. "People that had been here for a long time felt like the ethos of the place was changing, that it was losing its identity, and that has been a constant tension," she said with a sigh. A Pepperell professor similarly lamented, "It's more of a business than an educational institution from the perspective of those who run it. In fact, the academic mission is not even secondary anymore. I think they've totally forgotten about it."

For some, an undercurrent of discomfort persisted amid the growth-only strategies, like the Stoneham provost who inquired in a distressed tone, "How much more? How much bigger can a person grow before they get too big?" before he conceded, "It's the mantra of the Industrial Age. It's the mantra of capitalism." Despite the persistent efforts of its mission and identity officers, these worries persisted at Boxborough. "It's losing sight of the mission. It's forgetting what makes us who we are and letting the financial pressures sort of win the day," a professor explained. Even an Ardmore academic dean voiced worries about identity erosion: "What traditions will remain intact if we have any, in terms of our identity? And will our identity change, remain consistent?" The Boxborough provost confided that university administrators were increasingly concerned about the emergence of "an identity through rhetoric." As one of the university's board members confided, "Some people seem happy enough if things are on pieces of paper that they can point to and say 'This is our identity.'" Or as a Malvern senior administrator bluntly emphasized, "You see all these new buildings? *This* is who we are."

Like their geologic counterparts, these "erosions" occurred over time, but unlike the thousands of years it took to produce the Grand Canyon, the winds of neoliberal change took only decades to carve a seemingly unbridgeable chasm through the mission of these schools. As one professor at Lansdale sagely pointed out, the changes resembled slow transformations in other industries where the intent initially seemed to be to preserve the mission at all costs: "As institutions create their growth . . . they metamorphose into these quasi-clumsy organizations that lose their spirit—not because they wanted to lose it." With the endless pursuit of resources, institutional emphases shifted. An unforgettable visual of mission decay occurred when a Pepperell vice president handed me a new piece of stationery she had recently designed. "I had never heard this statement before connected with our school. That is our school motto." She pointed to the embossed crest and continued, "Everybody forgot. That was a problem. We all forgot."

What remained clear to university leaders at the highest levels is that the simultaneous pursuit of margins and mission risked impacting the integrity of the institution. A Boxborough board member explained:

> Those two things fight each other. If all we wanted to do was to be deeply mission conscious and make sure our students have wonderful experiences, things would spiral out of control rapidly and we would be out of business. Or we could just decide, "To hell with that and let's take the steps needed to batten down the financial hatches and sacrifice the mission stuff." And then we would lose our soul.

When university administrators turned to the one remaining funding source available to them—those governed by public policy rooted in economic reasoning—it set them on a path that rewarded the market values of growth and competition alone. As one Ardmore manager noted, "The irony is that it was not secularism that altered the soul of these institutions. It was the market." There is not an inbuilt incentive in market logic to maintain mission or pursue cooperation—or, to put it biblically, one cannot serve mission and mammon.

University leaders painfully discovered it is impossible for an organization to maintain a balance between margins and mission when it is dependent on the distribution of financial resources governed by market principles. In the face of increased competition, leaders in due time came to see themselves as having traded the spirit of the institution for financial margins. "One thing that concerns me is that we have grown too fast at the expense of our foundation," an Ardmore administrator related, and an academic dean echoed those sentiments: "Our success is notable . . . there is a danger that we are proud." Some could feel the erosion at work in palpable ways. "Their focus on growth is pulling them away from the goal of educating people," a Pepperell academic official lamented.

A Malvern professor contended their institution was not alone in the exchange and that most institutions were facing a similar trade-off: "A lot of places are going to be tempted to move away from their mission to chase the market. I hate to use a gambling metaphor, but I keep thinking, 'Let's double down on our mission!'" A senior vice president solemnly mentioned, "We've lost our way. We've had at least two board discussions the last 5 years because three books basically [said] Lansdale lost its identity." Similarly, one of its faculty members offered this unvarnished summation:

> You say you care about mission, and you say you care about these students and yet it seems like everything you're doing is undermining that . . . the only way I can make sense of the decisions that are made here and the rhetoric is to say, "Oh, the rhetoric is just bullshit . . . it's all just about money."

Hollowing the Core

History reminds us that the core residential model of higher education has encountered many cycles of financial challenges throughout the past century. Colleges and universities contracted during the Great Depression and World War II, only to be followed by a period of explosive growth and support during the golden age of higher education.[18] Leaders explained that their institutions responded to a contemporary cycle of financial threats in the final decades of the 20th century by developing strategies to sustain the core that differentially leveraged two tools—endowments and enrollments. Yet, as they discovered, their innovative uses of these tools were blunted in the face of intense competition that ultimately brought about skewed institutional identities and considerations of cannibalizing the core itself.

Unsustainable Margins

The common approach across the four diverse strategies administrators devised—traditional, pioneer, network, and accelerated—is that they pursued resources beyond the core itself to subsidize the costs of the core residential model. Indeed, it was understood that the core required monetary imports. Traditional leaders subsidized the core with endowment margins generated from investment interest, while executives of the entrepreneurial schools subsidized the core with tuition margins generated from periphery enrollment markets. For most institutions in American higher education with limited financial resources, the recent past and present tell a tale of the tuition margins of nontraditional students being used to subsidize the costs of residential students in the core.

Yet financing the residential core faced two seemingly inescapable challenges. First, in the words of the Stoneham provost, the core fundamentally functioned on "arithmetic growth."[19] Additional students brought additional revenues, but they also brought greater costs in the form of physical buildings and infrastructure. Two hundred new students required an additional residence hall, 300 a new dining facility, and 400 a new academic building. The approach plagued most administrators, as one Malvern senior leader explained:

> Not long ago, I attended a conference [where] we are all having the same general conversations on our campuses, amazed at how consistent they are: financial, enrollment, technological, and facilities challenges. How do you stay ahead of the curve and build campuses that are hard to afford once you have put them up?

The arithmetic growth inherent to the residential core restricted leaders from ever getting "ahead of the curve" in ways the elusive "geometric growth" would have financially provided with its generous tuition margins.

The second inescapable challenge in financing the core was the need to maintain enrollments in order to maintain buildings. Once an institution erected a new building, it required tuition revenues from the same number of students to maintain it over time. An Ardmore academic dean took care to describe the conundrum of the core:

> Spending hundreds of millions of dollars to tear down the old and build the new is a wonderful thing if you see growth continuing at the same rate into the future. However, stuff falls apart. Costs increase.... Eventually the furnaces are going to go, and the roofs are going to need to be repaired, and the floors are going to be redone, and the lab equipment will get broken and old. The cost of maintaining

programs is extraordinary over time. If you have a continually ever-growing money stream, that's not a problem. But if you do not . . .

Leaders were explicit in their belief that if tuition-driven institutions did not change their financial models to overcome these challenges, the outcome would be disastrous. Their very survival was brought into question because, as a Malvern vice president candidly offered, they "could not afford the campus they built. Enrollment didn't grow, didn't sustain the buildings they built—the financial model didn't work."

These two challenges, combined with increased competition in periphery markets over time, ultimately resulted in the realization that an alteration in course was needed. The Stoneham provost did not mince words on the urgency of the matter: "We have *got* to change." But rather than merely change strategies to generate new subsidies beyond the core, what came into focus is the need for a transformation of the core itself. A Malvern administrator set the stage for the changes ahead when he conceded, "We have to become a *completely* different entity!"

The End of History

What kind of change to the core did the future portend? While there were differences in the envisioned outcomes, almost everyone agreed that the days of the traditional core were numbered. Perhaps as a result of their school's identity being in flux, what was remarkable was that instead of arguing for one more push to preserve the traditional core, school administrators were poised to bury it. Some, like the Winchendon president, embraced its hybridization. "We are blending 10% of the full-time undergraduates into online education," he pointedly stated. "That will become larger and larger, because that also will drive the cost down." Academic leaders at Pepperell were also questioning whether the blending approach was achievable in their future: "Is there a way to have some kind of blended format where we can raise the number of undergraduate students on campus? If we don't figure this out, we're going to be competing for more and more students." Malvern's senior vice president seemed to channel its prior first-mover ways as she considered future possibilities for blending:

> We cannot continue doing what we've been doing, even recruiting, even the structures that we have as a university; all those are going to have to be rethought at this point. We've got to start thinking creatively now. The question I'm trying to raise

to our school is, "Is there a way for us to do residential but extension at the same time, the combination of both? How do we come along and give students the feel of a residential campus, of a community, without having to be here for 4 years?"

In other instances, leaders were already questioning which aspects of the traditional core experience were truly essential. One Lansdale senior leader forecasted,

A day is coming where a residential student—an 18-year-old—shows up on our campus and says, "I want to step foot in a classroom, but only a few times in my 4 years. I want the residential life experience to play athletics and feel the community, but I don't necessarily want to hear somebody lecture on something I can Google."

Questioning the essential elements of the residential core was motivated by trying to find solutions to control the cost of the core, but in the end, the sacredness of the residential model was also up for grabs. Another Malvern leader openly confessed,

There has to be a creative way for us to look at the future of education, and finances are going to play a big part of it. . . . The idea of continuing to build structures on a property . . . I am not really sure that is the direction that higher education should be going or will be going.

For a select few individuals, to lose the traditional core was to lose history and the embodiment of the institutional mission. A Stoneham historian shared, "I hope this place never moves away from the brick-and-mortar campus. It has the heart and soul of the place. I hope it does not go towards the least common denominator kind of a situation." But for an accelerated institution like Ardmore, an academic dean claimed that market-oriented policies instead of the past dictated their response:

Henry Ford said history is bunk. Like the typical entrepreneur, we are always looking forward. This place has never had much of a memory.

Despite whatever remaining pull history, tradition, and even mission had with these schools, with revenues in periphery enrollment markets declining as result of competition and costs of the core marching upward, the hybridization of the core was seen as seemingly inevitable. A senior vice president at Landsdale was pointed in predicting the demise of a "single pathway" through the residential core:

> I don't think we're going to be able to say to students in 10 years' time, "Give us 4 years of your life [and] spend the price of half a house. We will tell you what you need to learn, how you need to learn, what secrets you will learn, and what hours you will learn it in, and then we will tell you whether you are successful or not." I just don't think students in 10 years' time are going to say, "That's absolutely fine with me."

Pepperell's president boldly ventured that the residential core was on its way to becoming an outlier option among the many emergent models that would soon be more dominant. "It is going to be a whole new world. There will be outposts like Pepperell that will continue to have residence halls because that is important." Yet even in offering the residential option, the president asserted it must be a blended experience: "Our focus might be more on providing a residential experience, but also tapping into the latest technology."

As the Pepperell president continued, he clarified that the changes would also be driven by increased competition across sectors of higher education: "The community colleges are going to replace us in the freshman and sophomore years . . . so we will become the junior and senior programs." Another Pepperell senior administrator even envisioned that the "dissolution" of the core would trickle across national boundaries:

> You will also see huge interactions between American institutions that survive and international institutions. We have five American colleges that are partnered across America where students can start a degree here and end up in Houston and finish it there. That is starting for Chinese students . . . we have an alpha group here right now. You are going to find a lot of us partnering with institutions we never would have partnered with before where we recognize faculty, programs, credits, joint list our courses so you can take a course here and next week you can be in New York and take another course. It is going to be a dramatic change.

Leaders at Malvern had similar notions of establishing intrastate partnerships with multiple "sister" institutions for services in their residential core, such as shared libraries, human resources, and technology. "Could we combine our resources so an in-state school and Malvern, which have already signed articulation agreements, work with each other instead of against each other to try and maximize the resources that we have?" Every aspect of the residential model seemed up for negotiation. "It might mean we are actually in the business of residential housing while offering courses online—and that is how we deliver education," envisioned a Lansdale vice president. University administrators were unambiguously clear that competitive market forces were driving the emergent models of the core. Nor were they sanguine about the outcomes. "A lot of institutions are going to get hurt," the Pepperell president concluded.[20]

As campus leaders were looking to the future and hastily establishing blended models, the natural bent of the market that incentivizes financial margins was already at work. Not unlike what happened with policy innovations and threshold enrollments, schools began to locate and leverage the hidden tuition margins within the latent policy ambiguities of what it meant to be a residential student versus an online student. An academic official at Ardmore explained how the recent blending approach already provided senior executives with the opportunity to create new tuition margins in the residential core that they had previously only been able to establish in their scaled online program:

> A lot of our residential students are taking online classes . . . that are cheaper. But when students are coming here, they are paying full tuition, and even if it is just one class, are they getting a discount on their tuition? Do the parents even know students are taking half of their classes online and sitting around in their dorms? Do the taxpayers who are footing the bill through student loans know that the students are paying tuition, room, and board at the taxpayer's expense to sit around and take classes online that they could be doing at home? . . . I have visions of this place being a ghost town someday because the chickens come home to roost, or the government finds out.

Conclusion

As university leaders turned their gaze inward and commenced with the once-unthinkable process of cannibalizing the core, it appeared that their intention to provide educational opportunities to the marginalized in affordable ways was becoming more and more elusive. According to one Lansdale academic administrator, these ambitions withered amid their relentless attempts to survive the market competition that had come to dominate higher education. The administrator became visibly despondent as she described the aspiration to achieve this noble but seemingly out-of-reach educational goal:

> There is more to our lives than being little productive capitalist machines. There is something wonderful about cogitating beautiful thoughts and having conversations that produce nothing and go nowhere . . . thinking, talking, and reading about profound things and looking at art for its own sake. People that don't have that in their lives are missing something really important. How, then, does one make

those opportunities authentically available, given the harsh economic realities of our world and the fact that this was always and only ever available to a few? If you really want to bring it to everybody, how does one do that?

The reality of equality—that all persons might have an opportunity to receive a meaningful education—is that it happens within "the harsh economic realities of our world." Higher education policies rooted in a neoliberal outlook are designed to reward market-based behavior (i.e., competition) rather than equality-based behavior (i.e., cooperation), further skewing inequitable outcomes. The academic administrator, still visibly distraught, went on to highlight how the market-oriented policies offered little to her students:

> These students feel the weight of their parents' sacrifice and want to give back to their communities financially. Plus, they've got to provide for themselves, they've got to pay for all this, right? How can they do it and not basically have pissed away their parent's sacrifice, have tremendous debt with nothing to show for it, and not be able to give back to their communities?

If faculty and students were questioning the purpose and value of higher education, college and university leaders were left pondering how to finance institutions that no longer appeared poised to offer a traditional college experience. A remarkable example of this occurred mid-interview with the Lansdale president, when the doors to his executive suite unexpectedly flung open. Standing at the threshold was the board chairperson. "Do you have a moment?" he asked. A startled president looked back at me, saying, "Will you please excuse me for a minute?" and then hastily exited.

I stood up to stretch my legs and was drawn to a discolored aerial photograph of the university taken in the early 1970s when the president had arrived as a first-year student. The aging image of a much smaller campus with paltry facilities testified to the scope of the institutional transformation that occurred during his tenure. Other presidents had similar images on display in their offices: at Pepperell it was a charcoal sketch by a faculty member of the original stately building the 19th-century monks built—one the president later razed to pave the way for new construction projects. In conversation with the artist of the sketch, the professor shared his reservations and admiration for the president and university leadership:

> As much as I have thought the president of our university has made some bad mistakes in terms of decisions, especially tearing down our grandfather building, the man is a visionary. He has built this place. I can honestly say that I could not have

done what he did, sort of a conceptual artist on a grand scale. Years ago, when I was drawing that building, knowing that it was going to come down, he was here on a Sunday planting trees. He was planting trees on campus to make it beautiful.

Still waiting for the president to return, I took note of enrollment projections written on a whiteboard adjacent to the window. Handwritten scribbles in green sketched out enrollment possibilities for both the periphery and the core. Earlier in the day, one of the vice presidents had stressed, "*Everyone* is cut-throat, fighting against each other to gain [enrollment] because high school graduates are diminishing." As he well knew, although enrollment declines have gradually advanced over the past decade, what looms on the horizon for all colleges and universities is a demographic "enrollment cliff" of college-aged students that will fall nationally by an estimated 15%–20% beginning in 2025.[21] Since 2025 is imminent, I wondered what future institutional transformations would look like. Would schools like Lansdale quickly attempt to employ a network strategy and establish multiple new periphery markets like those envisioned in green on the whiteboard? Or would they follow the recommendations of one Boxborough senior leader who advocated "leapfrogging" straight to the accelerated strategy? What would happen when the leaders of these schools realized that school leaders who embraced the accelerated strategy were plotting to adopt a strategy consisting of accelerated networks? Whatever the decision, it had become clear that a common theme spanning all the schools was cannibalizing their core to remain competitive, shifting their focus toward "hybridizing," "blending pathways," or becoming "residential outposts." I imagined what it would be like to be in the shoes of this president—to have achieved what he did, but now face an uncertain future with far fewer resources at hand.

When the door reopened nearly 30 minutes later, the president re-entered and apologetically explained that he and the board chairman had to address an urgent financial issue. As he talked, he walked to his panoramic window that overlooked the golden foothills, placed both hands on the ledge, and let out a transitory exhale: "Where were we?" "The future of higher education, sir," I replied. After a second exhale, he began, "I think disruptive change is *really* going to happen this time. It will be a different model that either displaces or exists alongside the current model. And it will be *so* much more than just online."

He paused, and then resumed his analysis, his voice growing in conviction:

The different model is something that absolutely addresses affordability, accessibility, and, as much as higher ed does not like this word, employability, or the vocational route. It may be that this thing dies and something else is reborn. And it *may* be reborn or rebirthed without federal dollars in certain areas.

He turned from the idyllic scene outside his window. "I think the next 10 years are going to be absolute game-changers. I really do. My stress level goes up, but it doesn't scare me, though it causes me great pause." As he ushered me to the door, the president concluded our conversation as if handing off the baton for the final leg of a track relay:

> I mean, those younger, like you, it will be interesting to see what you see, right? Someday, when I'm dead and in the grave, remember you had a conversation with that guy at Lansdale who said the future isn't so doom and gloom. Education has always been the footstool to culture and society becoming better.

Notes

1. Doh, J. P., & Stumpf, S. A. (2007). Executive education: A view from the top. *Academy of Management Learning & Education, 6*(3), 388–400; Haskins, M. E., Centini, L., & Shaffer, G. R. (2017). Ideas for growing executive education revenue: Codification and catalyst. *Journal of Management Development, 36*(4), 581–597; Cheslock, J. J., Kinser, K., Zipf, S. T., & Ra, E. (2021). Examining the OPM: Form, function, and policy implications. *EdArXiv*. https://doi.org/10.35542/osf.io/py3sz.
2. Amdam, R. P., & Benito, G. R. (2022). Opening the black box of international strategy formation: How Harvard Business School became a multinational enterprise. *Academy of Management Learning & Education, 21*(2), 167–187.
3. Collier, P. (2018). *The future of capitalism: Facing the new anxieties*. Harper; Foley, D. K. (2009). *Adam's fallacy*. Harvard University Press.
4. Thornton, P. H., & Ocasio, W. (1999). Institutional logics and the historical contingency of power in organizations: Executive succession in the higher education publishing industry, 1958–1990. *American Journal of Sociology, 105*(3), 801–843.
5. Labaree, D. F. (2016). An affair to remember: America's brief fling with the university as a public good. *Journal of Philosophy of Education, 50*(1), 20–36.
6. Kezar, A., Chambers, A. C., & Burkhardt, J. C. (2015). *Higher education for the public good: Emerging voices from a national movement*. John Wiley & Sons.
7. Harvey, D. (2007). Neoliberalism as creative destruction. *Annals of the American Academy of Political and Social Science, 610*, 22–44.
8. In the case of the University of Virginia, a discussion of its privatization is in "Mr. Jefferson's 'Private' College," in Kirp, D. L. (2003). *Shakespeare, Einstein, and the bottom line*. Harvard University Press.
9. Han, B. C. (2021). *Capitalism and the death drive* (D. Steuer, Trans.). Polity; Han, B. C. (2017). *Psychopolitics: Neoliberalism and new technologies of power* (E. Butler, Trans.). Verso Books.

10. Edler, J., & Fagerberg, J. (2017). Innovation policy: What, why, and how. *Oxford Review of Economic Policy, 33*(1), 2–23.
11. The wording of education policies (and public policies more broadly) is crafted with language that is substantively vague yet procedurally specific to adequately represent a diverse array of interest groups and produce a policy that is "agnostic" regarding the particular course of action. This is a common characteristic in policymaking where the policy structure engineered uses such language and is further buttressed by the social and economic foundation on which it rests. VanSickle-Ward, R. (2014). *The devil is in the details: Understanding the causes of policy specificity and ambiguity.* State University of New York Press; Stone, D. (2002). *Policy paradox: The art of political decision making.* W. W. Norton & Company.
12. For a discussion of the dynamic versus static characteristics, see Brown, J. T. (2022). The evolving missions and functions of accessible colleges and universities. In G. Crisp, K. R. McClure, & C. M. Orphan (Eds.), *Unlocking opportunity: Broadly accessible four-year colleges and universities,* 65–81. Routledge/Taylor & Francis Group.
13. See "Buildings and Bodies" in Chapter 3 and corresponding policy references. Johnson, A. (2020). *The history of predominantly Black institutions: A primer.* Rutgers Center for Minority Serving Institutions; Garcia, G. A. (2019). *Becoming Hispanic-serving institutions: Opportunities for colleges and universities.* Johns Hopkins University Press; Nguyen, M. H., Espinoza, K. J., Gogue, D. T.-L., & Dinh, D. (2020). *Looking to the next decade: Strengthening Asian American and Native American Pacific Islander serving institutions through policy and practice.* National Council of Asian Pacific Americans.
14. Enrollment strategies related to race and ethnicity have also been highlighted in public institutions. Salazar, K. G. (2022). Recruitment redlining by public research universities in the Los Angeles and Dallas metropolitan areas. *The Journal of Higher Education, 93*(4), 585–621.
15. Rine, J., Brown, J. T., & Hunter., J. M. (2021). How institutional identity shapes college student recruitment: The relationship between religious distinctiveness and market demand. *American Journal of Economics and Sociology, 80*(1), 133–159; Rine, J. & Brown, J. T. (2023). Shifting environments, emerging norms: How changes in policy, technology, data, and market competition affect college enrollment management processes. In Braxton & Reason (Eds.), *Improving College Student Retention: New Developments in Theory, Research, and Practice,* (p. 258–283). Sterling: Stylus.
16. Brown, J. T., Kush, J., & Volk, F. (2022). Centering the marginalized: The impact of the pandemic on online student retention. *Journal of Student Financial Aid 51*(1), 1–24. https://doi.org/10.55504/0884-9153.1777; Cheslock, J. J., & Jaquette, O. (2021). Concentrated or fragmented? The US market for online higher education. *Research in Higher Education, 63*(1), 33–59.
17. Carroll, L. (2016). *Alice's Adventures in Wonderland and Through the Looking Glass.* Bloomsbury Publishing. (Original work published 1965)
18. Labaree, D. F. (2017). *A perfect mess: The unlikely ascendancy of American higher education.* University of Chicago Press.
19. See "Supporting the Mission" in Chapter 2.
20. The global COVID-19 pandemic expedited decisions regarding innovation and competition as many institutions now pursue approaches in scaling, online education, artifi-

cial intelligence/analytics, and workforce alignment. Gallagher, S., & Palmer, J. (2020, September 29). The pandemic pushed universities online. The change was long overdue. *Harvard Business Review.* https://hbr.org/2020/09/the-pandemic-pushed-universities-online-the-change-was-long-overdue.

21. The beginning of this population "pullback" will occur in 2025 and continue for a generation. Grawe, N. D. (2018). *Demographics and the demand for higher education.* Johns Hopkins University Press.

Outtakes

"These Are Things I Wish I Could Tell Somebody Someday"

In the same years the colleges and universities discussed in this book were developing innovative educational products and financial practices to sustain their futures, an independent film company named Pixar Animation Studios was developing innovative approaches of their own, adding "outtakes" to their early feature films following their conclusion. Whereas movie-goers had previously rushed out of the theater when credits appeared, the newly added outtakes enticed many to remain and continue to emotionally engage.

In a similar spirit, I have included an outtakes section to close this book. The selected quotes briefly highlight the rich humanity involved in the on-site research where stories are pursued in person (i.e., sole to sole) and verbally deposited from one person to another (i.e., soul to soul) in an approach I refer to as "sole to soul." I hope the addition of this section not only inspires readers to linger in the narrative for a few additional moments, but also influences future researchers, journalists, and authors to consider including outtakes as well.

> If you resonate with what the school is about, and fall in love with it, that is what we ask. Because you cannot serve what you do not love. You cannot sacrifice for what you do not love. You cannot believe that you must work to all ends for the school to survive if you do not love it.
>
> —**President, Havertown College**

> In my role, basically, I am head of the sales force.
>
> —**Vice president of admissions, Boxborough College**

> Our executive vice president has a lot of sayings, stories that help make a complicated situation very simple, like "It is easier to breathe life into the living than to raise the dead." In other words, focus on retention: work with the individuals who are already with you, because it is very costly to recruit new students.
>
> —**Vice president, Pepperell University**

When they see the monks and habit, it is a visual. . . . I am in ecclesiastical garb because it is not about me, it is about being a symbol for the community. I think we are a community of symbols, and we need to see that.

—**Campus priest, Stoneham University**

The Catholic Church doesn't give sisters a dime. You know the idea that Rome and the Roman Catholic Church pays sisters a salary is utter fantasy. They don't support sisters and nuns; we are completely on our own. Since monks are allowed to be ordained, they get stipends for saying mass, and the sisters never get those. It makes a huge difference.

—**Campus sister, Stoneham University**

I think at our core, what our core values are—other than being a Christian university and faith-based—is speed and the culture of speed to delivery. A speedy mean time to resolution in IT terms is something that we brag about and we hold dear, and it is the reason we have had, one of the reasons other than the direct blessing of God, that we've had our success. . . . Speed is everything.

—**Vice president, Ardmore University**

Branding is always a positive with the NCAA. The blue disc carries a lot of weight in the world of intercollegiate athletics.

—**Athletic director, University of Malvern**

I believe in this place. I believe that higher education can be transformative for students. I believe that transformation can impact the world through what students go out and do. I am driven by those commitments . . . and if I left here and went to do something else, I would leave a part of me [here].

—**Vice president, Boxborough College**

Two weeks ago in Texas, a provost looked me right in the eye and said, "How in the world are you going to successfully teach a young Hispanic student who barely speaks . . ." these are his exact words, ". . . he barely speaks any English, how to appreciate Shakespeare if you are teaching them online?" And I am looking at the guy and said, "So why are you teaching a young Hispanic who barely speaks any English, making him learn Shakespeare at all?" He looked at me like I had, you know, . . . prostituted the process.

—**Provost, Ardmore University**

The president was about 80 at the time; he did not understand the youth that were coming to Havertown, and we were not growing. We were in a meeting, and he told us, "Boys, you need to just forget those computers. You need to make sure you got paper and pen because that is just a fad that's going out!"

—Vice president, Havertown College

I am always looking for new income sources. Because everybody is now in the adult market, I have got a new certificate program for intergalactic space travel when the first aliens land!

—President, Pepperell University

When you are under threat, the natural tendency is to make yourself bigger and stronger. Look at the animal kingdom. How do animals protect themselves? It is just a natural reaction. Our way forward is to get *better*. Because I think the better we are, what we do, the more people will seek us out. . . . Let's not worry about getting bigger right now, let's worry about getting better.

—President, University of Malvern

We had national coverage on *ESPN Game Day*. We were playing the number one school in the country. We got our asses kicked, but we got great press!

—President, Winchendon University

We will reach out to people in Honduras quicker than we will reach out to the next street over. It becomes almost like a commodity to go to Nicaragua or Honduras because it is exotic and far away, yet we cannot do the things we preach in the neighborhood next door.

—Professor, Boxborough College

Student-wise we've seen kind of a shift in demographics. A part of it comes with the competition obviously. When we were the only name in town, basically, we got the cream of the crop. Now that they're spread out, we're seeing much more academically challenged students that need a lot more help. That's been a challenge for us.

—Vice president, University of Malvern

The biggest part of learning is not in the answers; it is in finding the answers.

—President, Pepperell University

It concerns me that I do not experience the emotional quality of the vision for the future. I hear a good speech [from leadership] and I say, "Oh, that is interesting," but it does not grab me. We are in a lull. And if we are in a lull, you pay a price. You just hope that price won't be too big.

—Professor, Lansdale University

When I worked with Lou Holtz, he said, "To be successful you have to have a vision, you have to have a plan," and I bought it until I came here. Then I realized you have to have a vision, you have to have a plan, but you have to have money to make the plan work.

—Athletic director, Ardmore University

Buddhism has helped me to reconnect with my desire to be compassionately nonattached. I am to care very deeply, to look out for others, but not attached to the outcome. . . . The fighting over where is money going—is it going to buildings, or people, or help? You can be committed, you can fight the fight, but at the end of the day, you just let it be. Or you can start holding on to it and say, "I hate that fucker. . . . That person is an asshole"—and now you are attached to it.

—Provost, Boxborough College

God used Balaam's ass. I am sure He can use all those administrators at Ardmore.

—Professor, Ardmore University

I am not sure it sinks in that internationalization does not mean we are going out into the world and we are saving it, which is such an American thing. . . . I think the world has a lot to offer the United States. Internationalization has to be an exchange—let's talk—which means understanding somebody's culture, opening your head, not just your door.

—Professor, Boxborough College

One of the bad words around here that the board does not like and faculty do not like is being elite. This is a place that would never say, "We want to be an elite." They would consider that to be countercultural for us. Anything you do that starts to smack of that, the defenses go up. And it was a place that prided itself on being open to people who wanted a higher education but maybe could not get access because of finances or other things in any other place.

—President, University of Malvern

I came here for pragmatic reasons, but I actually buy into it now. . . . In the *Shawshank Redemption*, Tim Robbins says to Morgan Freeman, "You know, the ironic part is I had to come to prison to learn how to be a crook." I had that same kind of epiphany here.

—Academic dean, Ardmore University

I do not like the term *access*. I prefer *opportunity* because access just means you open the doors and let people in. Any institution can do that and that is a question of money. Opportunity, on the other hand, is your commitment to see them to graduation. Are you providing the support services . . . are you recognizing the needs of that person?

—Department chair, University of Winchendon

I think there have been enough people hurt by the organization that at some point someone is going to say, "I don't give a shit!" They are going to be so hurt and wounded by what has taken place that they will [speak up]. There is going to be a trickle-down effect, others will jump on board, and you are going to see all sorts of things coming out about the university.

—Professor, Ardmore University

Do not complain about admissions not bringing in the smartest students. [Instead] bring students that are not so good and put expectations higher for them to reach. I am one of those people. I did not become a Julliard graduate because I started out as a prodigy. For heaven's sakes, I had to work my butt off! I still did not believe it and had to let other people build me up.

—Vice president, Pepperell University

These are things I wish I could tell somebody someday, and maybe I will, but maybe I won't.

—Academic dean, Ardmore University

Methodological Appendix

"I Am Probably Being Too Candid Here"

Introduction

Studying "the missing middle" of higher education policy and finance required the use of different tools than did prior analyses, which predominantly focused on the "bookend" crises of higher education: surging student debt at one end and diminishing government support at the other. By emphasizing the middle and "going inside" institutions to offer the organizational perspective, *Capitalizing on College* provides insights about previously unknown elements of a societal narrative that relies on market paradigms to allocate financial resources in higher education.

The foundation of this book rests on a case method approach that compares multiple organizations to uncover and highlight common themes.[1] In his interview, the Pepperell provost unwittingly summarized the reasons for adopting this approach: "If I compare and contrast Pepperell with other universities, there are some distinct differences. But if you whittle away and get down to the ground level, you find a common end goal, but maybe how they get there is different."

This appendix covers both the *science* that serves as the backbone of the book and the *strategy* with which its findings are presented. It explains a mixed methods approach to social science that intertwines the study of cases, interviews, archival analysis, and ethnographic techniques.[2] It also details the distinct narrative strategy that uses story arcs, sidebars, and visuals to put forth a compelling grand narrative about contemporary American higher education. This chapter pulls back the research curtain to provide the reader with the science behind this previously untold story.

The Science of Mixed Methods

Capitalizing on College employs a mixed methods analysis to understand the impact of market-oriented policies on organizational leaders seeking to sustain missions of educational access and opportunity in an era of resource constraint. It differs from customary quantitative policy studies that examine the technical pre/post differences of an implemented policy or those that assess its economic impact (often explained as a change in Y outcome for every X dollar spent).[3] The rationale for pursuing this approach was nicely summed up by a Stoneham professor at the close of his interview: "Your questions took on new weight for me. If you were doing something quantitatively it would have been a lot less illuminating. Not asking questions like these is like being an electrician and never knowing where power comes from."

Sampling Across and Sampling Within

Selecting which institutions to study is important because it shapes what a researcher will find and how the findings can be generalized more broadly. Choosing schools with similar characteristics allows one to control for the natural "noise" that occurs because organizations are embedded in different environments. A Malvern professor keenly emphasized the impact of variation in environments when he posed a series of hypothetical questions when imagining comparisons: "What about other colleges in the state? What about other colleges in our conference? What about the others that we might kind of benchmark?" But the challenge comes from the fact that colleges and universities are dynamic entities whose characteristics and relationships with other institutions change over time. As the Boxborough president highlighted, this dynamic feature of colleges is an important facet in making an organizational comparison:

> Twenty years ago, Allerton University was one of our main enrollment competitors; now they hardly are at all. There's a little bit of competition with kids from Granby who want to stay up there, but it's not like we are competing for kids from anywhere else that want to go to Allerton. Something happened to us institutionally in the 20 years that I've been here such that we do not compete with Allerton anymore.

Sampling is a "snapshot" of a limited set of dynamic organizations at a specific moment in time that researchers use to understand a societal phenomenon they could not feasibly study if it required going to all organizations of a given type.

In many senses, sampling strives to create an equal starting line by which to compare institutions on specific factors. Whether the comparison is quantitative or qualitative, many higher education researchers rely on the Integrated Postsecondary Education Data System (IPEDS) government database to identify similar characteristics among colleges and universities.[4] In fact, the leaders in this book commonly referenced their own strategic use of IPEDS. One administrator at Ardmore described how IPEDS augmented their "guerilla competitive research," while at Winchendon the provost highlighted how it offered the necessary variables to compare their approach with that of others:

> We had a project a few years ago where the deans were feeling like they were at their wit's end with no infrastructure. And by infrastructure, I mean we could use more people in the Registrar, in the Business Office, and in all of these offices. It seems like everybody is overworked. We turned to IPEDS and studied a bunch of schools similar to us and their full-time-equivalent administrators. It turns out we had the highest ratio of anybody we could compare ourselves to.

Following the same comparative approach, the sample was selected across the population of colleges and universities that self-identified as Catholic or Protestant in the IPEDS database ($n = 873$). For inclusion in the sample, institutions had to have reported enrollment data on the "unduplicated headcount" variable to calculate the overall change in enrollment growth from 2000 to 2014.

I used the unduplicated headcount enrollment variable to calculate institutional growth rather than the full-time-equivalent enrollment variable to account for all forms of revenue-generating students within institutions. Full-time equivalence is a measure of student enrollment that only accounts for those students who can attend a college or university in a traditional "full-time" manner (12 or more credit hours per semester for undergraduates; 9 or more hours for graduate students). It is an exclusionary measure that overlooks many nontraditional students pursuing other forms of credentialing and lifelong learning, such as part-time students, students in certificate programs, students pursuing executive education, university employees, and continuing education students. The unduplicated headcount variable is a more accurate enrollment representation of student activity at tuition-driven institutions.

To establish an equal starting line in calculating the rate of change in student enrollment from 2000 to 2014, the sample of institutions was restricted on three factors: institutional type (doctoral and master's universities), selectivity (SAT, 25th percentile), and starting enrollment (more than 3,000 students). These controls eliminated the possibility of unequal resource comparisons that pose alternative explanations for growth, such as contrasting the University of Notre Dame ($18 billion endowment/12,600 enrollment) with the Franciscan University of Steubenville ($57 million endowment/3,300 enrollment). These controls reduced the sample to 75 institutions, which were then divided into four categories of enrollment growth: high (+100%), medium (60%–99%), low (1%–59%), and negative (<0%). The intent in choosing cases with different growth approaches was to reduce bias in the results, or what researchers call "sampling on the dependent variable."[5] Studies designed to solely examine one approach or type (i.e., high growth) descriptively emphasize *what* occurred, whereas studies designed to comparatively examine multiple approaches (i.e., high, medium, low, negative growth) can assess *why* leaders differentially acted in the same environment.

After considering organizational age, geography, demographic diversification, and site access, a final set of Catholic/Protestant matched cases were selected within each growth quadrant. The eight universities in their matched-pair sets are presented in Table 1.

Table 1 Interview Counts by Institutional Growth Type

Organization and Growth Type	Interviews
High growth (+100%)	
Pepperell University[1]	17
Ardmore University[2]	21
Medium growth (61%–99%)	
University of Winchendon[1]	19
University of Malvern[2]	20
Low growth (1%–60%)	
Stoneham University[1]	20
Lansdale University[2]	19
Negative growth (<0%)	
Boxborough College[1]	18
Havertown College[2]	17
Total	151

Note: 1 = Catholic; 2 = Protestant.

In addition to sampling *across* institutions by growth rate and religion, I also pursued a targeted sampling strategy *within* each institution by employee and rank. Sampling employees from multiple levels of the organization was used to gauge "saturation," or the pervasiveness of themes within the institution that emerged in the data.[6] In some instances, a topic arose at a "lower" level of the organization, where an employee would highlight the presence of a theme but refer to persons at "higher" levels for specificity. For example, an executive director at Lansdale mentioned, "The institution was financially stressed . . . some other administrators, if they feel they can talk about it, can give you details." In other instances, I encountered competing narratives within the organization, and having interviews from multiple levels within the institution helped identify differences between perceptions by faculty and vice presidents. This was the case at Ardmore, where competing narratives arose about which leader (the founder or his son) had initiated the explosive growth. One senior administrator explained the various interpretations of the dramatic enrollment "elbow" moment:

> There have been a number of attempts to revise history and lots of different ways people have described the way things evolved or happened. The truth is, and there is verifiable proof in this, plenty of witnesses who would verify my version of the truth. . . . [The elbow] did not happen in '08 or '07. I mean, go to the executive vice president for enrollment and get him to show you the charts. It happened in '04 and '05. It is there and you can see the graph . . . people that knew how that really happened, people like the chief information officer, the vice president for enrollment, the vice president for admissions, I'd think of a few more, but those boys were there.

Without strategic sampling within an institution, it becomes challenging for the researcher to identify competing narratives that arise, particularly those that pertain to the attribution of organizational success (or failure).

I strategically initiated interviews with individuals from across four hierarchical levels of the organization. The executive level consisted of anyone serving as a member of the board, chancellor, president, or provost ($n = 19$). The cabinet level was composed of leaders who held roles in the president's senior administrative team or cabinet, which included vice presidents, chief information officers, chief financial officers, and athletic directors ($n = 48$).[7] The middle manager level consisted of various university department leaders, including executive directors, directors, and associate directors ($n = 16$). Finally, the faculty level contained faculty members serving at all levels of self-governance: deans, chairs, professors, associate professors, and assistant professors ($n = 68$). To keep the project focused on persons in decision-making positions, I did not interview employees below the middle management level or students.

Access and Arrival

In selecting a set of schools, the researcher essentially says, "I approve of you," but for an interview-based project to advance beyond mere design, the school must reciprocate and say of the researcher, "We approve of you." Thus, a notable and challenging gap resides between selecting a school for a sample and securing a school for a sample.[8]

To gain access to each of the eight universities in the study, I identified a cabinet-level administrator willing to function as a point of contact. The individual (usually a vice president) functioned as an "ambassador" who aided in navigating the culture and unfamiliar processes of the organization.[9] In many instances, these ambassadors temporarily loaned me their social capital as their social network temporarily became my social network. An academic chair at Winchendon reminded me of this point when she said, "The personal relationships are what move this place forward. You're sitting here now because the vice president asked."

The ambassadors provided information regarding interviews, archives, lodging, tours, publications, dining, and other important details about the institution that I needed to establish a 1-week site visit. The precise dates for each visit were determined according to the availability of both the university president and the provost in the same calendar week, an effort that required 2 months of notice, on average.[10] Once the coinciding appointments with these two highest-ranking administrators were confirmed, I spent a little over 1 month scheduling the week-long site visit. Research activities included conducting 18 to 21 one-hour interviews, collecting archival records, securing copies of all university magazines and course catalogs between 2000 and 2015, and participating in an official admissions tour. In addition to planning these standard research activities for each university in the study, I was the beneficiary of the generous hospitality extended to me by each school—which added a myriad of unplanned events to my schedule that helped me further understand the university community and its specific culture.

Despite my extensive preparation, with each new campus visit I felt an immense sense of anxiety about finding everything I sought. During his interview, one Boxborough professor inadvertently yet aptly described the challenge I felt:

> E. F. Schumacher has a book called *A Guide for the Perplexed* in which he talks about when he was lost in St. Petersburg (which at the time was Leningrad). There was a beautiful church in front of him that he couldn't find on the map. So, he asked this guard, "Where's this church on the map?" And the guard says, "We don't put churches on maps, we label them as museums." Schumacher says, from that point, he realized that all the maps of knowledge that he had been given in his life were maps of knowledge that were missing the most important things that he could experience and see for himself but were not on his maps of knowledge.

His words reminded me that I was arriving at each university to see and experience the missing middle—the part of higher education that has been left off the map. Finding what I sought would require experiencing new worlds and seeking to listen, observe, and understand the university leaders describe in their own words how they strove to uphold educational access and opportunity in the face of declining resources.

I began practicing listening to religiously infused cultures 1 year prior to the site visits, when I started voluntarily attending both a Protestant and a Catholic church in my local community. These visits helped me gain a familiarity with and further understanding of cultural elements that could impact my ability to conduct interviews, such as language, symbols, stories, leadership, and traditions. I knew these cultural elements would likely surface in meaningful ways, and with campus visits compressed to 1 week, I wanted the off-site preparations to complement on-site data collection for each religious tradition. There were numerous times when my preparations paid off; for example, there was the time when an academic dean discussed the recent launch of the new branch campus a dozen states away and he mentioned how faculty costs were impacted by the bishop. "The theology professor is tenure track," he explained. "The bishop insisted on that. Most of the other faculty are going to be what's called 'clinical,' with 5-year contracts, but not tenure. But the bishop insisted the theology professor be tenure track." Having attended the local Catholic parish for a year, I had become accustomed to hearing about the regional authority of the bishop, which prompted me to ask, "When a Catholic school bridges geographic boundaries, do they have to deal with two bishops, or one?" The academic dean clarified that each bishop had a role depending on the geographic location of the specific campus and was keen to explain the degree to which each "has his fingers in our pie." This was but one example of the many instances where attending the local Protestant and Catholic churches prior to the site visits helped prepare me to be more attuned to the cultural factors at play at each university campus.

I would arrive on campus early on a Monday morning, having traveled to the school over the weekend. En route to meet my ambassador, the grounds of the school and its newly overhauled campus infrastructure always stood out. Shortly after connecting with my host, I began with the official university tour provided by admissions. Each tour was as distinct as the university itself: the Lansdale tour began in a private movie theater with booming surround sound, the Havertown tour with fresh popcorn and a personalized golf cart, and the Pepperell tour with university swag and a caffeinated student guide.

In hindsight, completing the tour prior to beginning the archival and interview research provided me with a valuable infusion of cultural knowledge to help me navigate throughout the week. When leaders used localized language like "the barn" or "the island" to refer to places, or phrases like "when the monks led" to refer to time periods, I understood them because they had been explained to me by the admissions guide. On a more practical level, the tours also oriented me to the dozens of buildings and facilities across the campus, highlighting both long-standing campus landmarks and newly constructed student unions and residence halls. This proved invaluable not only when discussing campus infrastructure, but also when I had to speedily navigate the grounds during my jam-packed days to ensure my timely arrival to interviews.

In-Person Interviews

At the heart of *Capitalizing on College* are 151 strategically sampled interviews with college and university leaders. The structure of these was intentionally designed, following standard social science practices that included institutional review board approval, signed confidentiality statements, pre-interview questionnaires to collect demographics (e.g., gender, race/ethnicity, religion, years of employment, degrees), and digital recordings to generate transcripts.[11] Unless the interviewee requested otherwise, most interviews occurred within the sanctuary of their own office.

Interviews with university leaders were guided by a list of 20 questions that focused on three primary areas—culture, change, and connection. Every interview began with the same question, the dual aim of which was to get the person comfortable in sharing their story: "Can you describe what brought *you* to this university?" Immediately following the opening question, I pivoted to a group of questions about the culture of the university. Examples included:

- If I were to work at [insert university], what is the most important thing I would need to know?
- Can you describe the culture of [insert university]?
- What factors, people, or events do you feel contributed to the development of this culture?

The nature of these questions attempted to ask persons to identify the present organizational culture as well as to describe its historical origins or development over time. Many respondents explicitly connected the university culture to people or characteristics from the founding era, like an Ardmore director who mentioned, "I think the founder is most responsible for the culture here," or a Winchendon professor who explained, "We are still very committed to the idea of service and justice. If we ever changed that, then we're no longer living the legacy of the sisters."

The second group of interview questions focused on organizational change. I asked participants to consider the period between 2000 and 2015 and to describe changes that occurred during these initial years of the 21st century. Examples of such questions include:

- What challenges did the organization face during this period and how did it respond?
- How (or where) do you feel the organization has focused most of its resources during this period?
- What are the important factors that contributed to the success of the organization during this era?

The nature of these questions sought to encourage persons to pinpoint change as well as the drivers of change. Quite unexpectedly, many leaders rooted the need for change in a prior era of survival and the incentive for change in broader national policies that emphasized market-oriented means of allocating financial resources. Typical was the response of a long-serving Malvern vice president, who recalled,

> It really was not a beautiful campus at all. None of the buildings we have were here . . . and enrollment was a struggle. Basically, there came a time when we realized . . . that if a university or college did not reach 1,000 students, they were going to run into financial problems and may not even survive.

Most important, the entrepreneurial financial practices uncovered in *Capitalizing on College*—margin capitalization and margin philanthropy—were first revealed in the responses leaders provided to this set of questions.

The third group of interview questions focused on the connection between the employee and the university. Some questions focused on assessing the presence of an emotional or affective connection to the institution, while others sought to gauge the extent to which an individual felt they were part of the broader success of the university. Examples of the connection-themed questions include:

- Can you describe the extent to which you have been able to contribute to the innovation of this organization?
- In what ways has the trajectory of the organization conflicted with your personal beliefs?

The nature of these questions attempted to gauge the impact of organizational change on individuals themselves. Many persons found the self-reflective quality of these questions to be challenging, like the Winchendon vice president, who responded with a tension-filled laugh, "Gosh, that's a tough question! You ask me how self-aware I am of myself." The questions triggered deep emotions in others, like an academic dean at Ardmore who described the personal transformation he underwent during the school's transformation:

> At first, I would get up every day thinking, "How can I make Ardmore University a better place?" And I really thought that I would be heard. Then I discovered that's not the way it is . . . and a little disillusionment set in. What I advise people (based on how I coped) is to find something else to do while teaching here. I've told people, "Don't make this your sole reason for getting up."

This set of questions was often not only the most emotionally laden portion of the interview, but also where the interviewee was most transparent. Many offered remarks, like the academic chair, who after sharing a particularly revelatory admission added, "I am probably being too candid here."

In the same manner that every interview opened with a primer question, each ended with a future-oriented question of closure: "I have spent the majority of this interview asking about the past decade at [insert university]. Would you be willing to offer your thoughts on the next decade?" Respondents typically emphasized the impact of trends occurring in the broader society as they related to higher education and their school in particular. "I think because of the economic situation in the United States, a lot of families will strongly encourage their young people to go into professional fields," one Winchendon professor observed. "They all buy the idea that the way to succeed is to get a business degree. . . . We're going to see fewer and fewer students in the humanities, and that scares me." Alternatively, respondents stressed the competitive trajectory the institution or higher education as a whole was on, as a Lansdale director emphasized:

> I would see that we continue to push the educational boundaries of how we can award college-level credit to help a student earn a degree and what does it mean to have a degree in terms of education. Is it just sitting in class and submitting assignments and you

accumulate 120 units? I think the competency-based learning would be a direction that we're going... there's institutions that are doing that now.

Overall, the interviews generated different unforeseen cathartic responses from leaders—a president who laughed with regret about not recruiting more aggressively, a vice president who suggested a closing hug, or the executive director who yelled from his office as I exited, "That felt so damn liberating!" Participants conveyed their personal stories and raw emotions in a manner that routinely closed with explicit postscripts that acknowledged the confessional nature of their story: "Please don't tie me to this because I could get in all kinds of shit," a Winchendon vice president confided, while a Boxborough senior leader conveyed similar sentiments: "If I said that publicly, I'd probably get hung."

In interview-based studies, it is common practice for researchers to conduct *member checking*, a process whereby participants are asked to review results for accuracy.[12] Because of the unanticipated emotional responses and candor with which university leaders engaged me, I did not pursue a member-checking approach; rather, my approach focused on emotional closure with participants at the time of the interview and immediately thereafter.[13] Following my departure from campus, I wrote a personal letter to each individual, thanking them for their gift of time and confidential engagement, and provided my contact information. In response, I received many emails from university leaders thanking me for the opportunity to reflect and have their perspective considered. No one asked for their confidential remarks not to be used.

All methods of inquiry possess limitations. For example, quantitative studies often fail to highlight the rationale or sense-making of why a phenomenon develops, whereas qualitative studies typically cannot identify specific units of difference, such as the previously mentioned "change in Y outcome for every X dollar spent." Despite strategic attempts in sampling, a notable limitation in conducting interview research that aims to provide a snapshot of an organization at a given point in time is that it is biased by those individuals who remained. An academic dean at Pepperell explained how his presence contributed to this bias:

> I'm sure there are institutions that wish they had been able to expand along the lines that Pepperell has been able to expand, in terms of adding additional [enrollment] legs to the stool that we've done under the president's leadership. To some extent, I guess I have been complicit because I served as dean. I have done stuff. *I have stayed.*

Because this project was heavily reliant on the stories of leaders "who stayed," I incorporated a mixed methods analysis that emphasized the triangulation of data to mitigate the natural bias inherent in an interview-based approach.

Mixed Methods: A Focus on Triangulation

The mixed method research design for *Capitalizing on College* drew on interviews and triangulated them with site visits and archival analyses that allowed for concentrated cultural immersion. Every host institution added unplanned aspects to my site visits. These ran the gamut from administrators spontaneously asking, "What are you doing after this interview—would you like to go to lunch?" to a vice president at Malvern insisting that I tour the student-run coffee shop as an example of the pervasive entrepreneurial spirit. One Winchendon leader even drove me to the side of the city known as "the barrio" so I could understand the impoverished socioeconomic status of their Hispanic students by seeing their neighborhoods. The concentrated immersion of the site visits was an important component of the triangulation process where I connected cultural aspects I was able to see and experience for myself with those aspects leaders explained in interviews as essential to understanding their community and their past.

While completing each week-long site visit and schedule of interviews, I also worked with librarians to secure digital copies of four types of data from 2000 to 2015: university magazines, course catalogs, financial reports, and IRS Form 990 records. Although I did not formally interview any librarians, upon hearing about my project, more than one archivist was quick to volunteer additional personnel and resources to complete the collection of historical and financial records. Indeed, most librarians continued to send digital records weeks after I departed campus. When explaining the characteristics of the university in prior eras, leaders routinely referenced historical volumes about the institution that included scholarly histories, autobiographies of presidents, and commemorative volumes marking special occasions in the school's history. I included the historical volumes as part of the set of archival records from each school to corroborate strategies and provide clarity regarding the origins of strategies the leaders described.

My analytic strategy for the interview data followed the approach that emphasized a three-part process of data reduction, data display, and triangulation.[14] In contrast to other qualitative approaches, I chose this approach because it allowed for the generation of conceptual frameworks based on emergent codes and themes while also focusing on finding the sequences and regularities that link phenomena.[15] The systematic coding across digital document types (course catalogs, university magazines, and interview transcripts) was facilitated by the qualitative analysis software NVivo 11.

The process of analysis began with *data reduction*, whereby the data were reduced to a manageable state through the writing of summaries, analytic memos, and coding. I used first- and second-cycle coding to transform documents to key themes and patterns within and across cases. I looked for similarities and differences within and across the Catholic and Protestant organizations with regard to their attention to priorities, identity, and legitimization. In the second stage of analysis, *data display*, I summarized data that emerged from second-cycle coding in visual form for the purpose of illustrating what the data showed regarding financial sources (i.e., endowments and enrollments) and innovative financial practices (i.e., margin capitalization and margin philanthropy). During the final stage, *triangulation*, I advanced the data from visual displays to confirmation and meaning. For example, when university leaders explained how they developed innovative financial practices in face-to-face interviews, I triangulated information in the codes "margin capitalization" or "margin philanthropy" with historical spending patterns as reported in IPEDS and IRS Form 990 data.

Triangulation is a process of confirming a theme or phenomenon across multiple sources using mixed methods of analysis. The process is important when comparing multiple cases to draw inferences about a broader social phenomenon.[16] Triangulation is also important when conducting organizational research, given the tendency for some organizations to "hide" aspects of their story or to offer competing narratives, which often occur amid intense periods of organizational change. It was important to use triangulation processes to better understand historical and cultural themes. For example, at Winchendon the responses by the president describing the lock-step uniform agreement he achieved when pursuing organizational change ("Save yourself a lot of time and read my book. It tells you the whole history, every step that we took together along the way") conflicted with what was in a less well-known volume that one of the sisters alerted me to ("He had a little, you know, tussle with faculty senate back some years ago. You can read about it in the book").

The Strategy of Narrative

One of my mantras in quantitative education assessment is, "How the data *look* in their presentation (charts and graphs) is just as vital as the data themselves." In writing this book, I have come to discover the same holds true in qualitative education research: "How the data *read* in their presentation (narrative) is just as vital as the data themselves." More important, most people do not typically reconsider the dominant narratives of society because they happen across the findings of a regression model or advanced statistical technique. Rather, people more frequently reconsider taken-for-granted ways of knowing when they experience an equally compelling narrative, one they can see themselves within in some way and eventually retell to others.

Writing the Narrative

Many early challenges I encountered with the manuscript were the result of trying to write a book in the same manner in which I had been trained to write an academic article. My approach was analytically precise, key terms were empirically supported, and the contribution to the literature was clearly articulated. As a result, I had placed the social structure and scientific jargon in the foreground and relegated narrative to an off-stage prop. The pages seemed lifeless until I decided to bring the narrative to the fore—something that I had been reminded to do by numerous interviewees and the oft-repeated refrain, "Don't forget the story of X—it is essential for understanding this school."

The systematic approach to writing the narrative of this book relies on three central features—the story arc, sidebars, and visuals. Each empirical chapter presents a story arc that chronicles the development of a specific financial strategy established by a set of universities to sustain their mission. The arc is grounded in the many responses leaders provided to interview questions on organizational culture, change, and connection. Time and again, leaders began their story about the 21st century by prefacing it with the founding of the institution or an explanation of enrollment crises they encountered in the final decades of the 20th century.

These patterned responses informed the story arc used for each chapter, which begins with a brief origin account of each institution and moves to explain their past and present environments as composed of a key cultural disposition and an organizational one. The dual dispositions forge a specific trait that I found enshrined at each school from one generation to the next, such that when entrepreneurial leaders encountered their financial crisis in the late 20th century, the strategies they adopted were informed in a manner rooted in the past. For example, an Ardmore senior leader argued that their accelerated growth remained true to their founding emphasis: "We've always been focused on growth that emanated from the founder ... when you have a numeric mindset, bigger is always better," while a Pepperell president contended that the university founding was "not a one-time event but rather an ongoing process whereby 'modern-day founders' are needed as much as the original ones ... with high energy, vision, and passion for what might be." Similarly, Winchendon leaders identified multiple enrollment markets that aligned with their past: "Our newest thing is a medical school. That is part of the sisters' original mission," explained one senior leader. A colleague in a different interview added, "Healthcare education really strikes at our roots ... the truth of it is I think where we're heading is very timely in terms of the mission." In sum, their culture predisposed their strategic focus and response.

From its historical base, the story arc "ascends" to explain how leaders established strategies that enabled them to differentially pursue new student enrollment markets. While each strategy succeeds for a season, despite what market logics might suggest, increased competition leads to factors that result in the gradual failure of each strategy (highlighted in the "descent" of the story arc). At key moments during the ascent, I allude to future entanglements captured in the descent phase (for example, the description of the pioneer strategy closes with the excerpt of a nun euphorically proclaiming she believes they have discovered the model for financial sustainability for colleges and universities, only to be followed by, "Little did she know... faith alone would not be sufficient to withstand the oncoming market competition").

In writing the narrative, I made an important decision to "weave" excerpts rather than merely drop them into the text. Some qualitative studies explain Phenomenon A and follow it with a large block quote that illustrates Phenomenon A in a manner that resembles how a numerical data table is abruptly dropped into a quantitative study at the close of a paragraph. When the dropping approach is used with qualitative data in the form of large block quotes, it often privileges the vantage point of the researcher who collected the data and possesses the advantages of context, time, and connection with the interviewee. In contrast, weaving excerpts emphasizes the vantage point of the reader, where an author labors to unveil the narrative piece by piece. Additionally, it often necessitates that the author triangulate multiple excerpts about a phenomenon and weave them into a comprehensive narrative, using some details in the excerpt as context and other details as quoted material.

With the narrative unveiling of each story arc came certain contextual information important for readers. Stories about financial demise and new markets do not necessarily make sense without unveiling the complex context in which a narrative occurs. Organizations are embedded in systems that are important to understand for their own sake, as well as for how they might compel leaders to act in certain ways. Momentarily pausing in the narrative and adding "sidebars" provides important information to the reader—an essential detour on an otherwise straight road. The sidebar in Chapter 1 highlights how student loans are used to incentivize financial margins ("Revolution in Student Loans"), while Chapter 2 introduces how colleges use margins to capitalize their infrastructure ("Margin Capitalization"). Chapter 3's sidebar explains how colleges rely on outsourcing to maximize margins ("Paid Partners"), and in Chapter 4, I describe how when margins are taken to scale, it enables a new form of philanthropy that relies on student loans ("Margin Philanthropy").

I rely on the use of visual illustrations as a third feature to aid in unveiling the narrative. If the story arc is the trajectory and the sidebar a tangent, then the illustrations serve as a map (complete with a key) for navigating the specific strategy. The illustrations act as an anchor for describing a complex social context in ways that visually reinforce the concepts, enabling readers to quickly recall a newly explained phenomenon (particularly when additional layers to the narrative are added). Like sketches in classic children's stories, these illustrations promote sense-making through a visual paradigm that adheres to the educational adage of "using the known to explain the unknown." The illustrations depict the many strategies that emerge through the various combinations of essential components and their differential uses.

Conclusion

Culture produces a powerful bonding element between persons, and in studying the organizational culture of universities, I became reeled in to that force eight times over. At each campus, the intense week of activities, long hours, and candid conversations yielded a concentrated cultural experience that compelled me to want to say goodbye to the institution in a meaningful way. But when studying an organization, to whom does one say goodbye? This feeling I experienced before departing the grounds was akin to the close of summer camp or the final day of high school, when the reality sets in that returning to this community and experiencing these same bonds will likely never occur. What I have since come to discover is that, in part, I was unable to say goodbye when I left each campus because I was still carrying foundational elements of the institution inside me, and in some instances its darkest secrets.

Despite the time that passed since sitting with these university leaders, I have remained unable to fully convey the gravitas of the many stories they shared. Time and again, the interviews thrust me into an unexpected role whereby I was entrusted with heretofore unspoken elements of a person's story, which left me carrying the burden of these confessions. In committing them to the page, my goal has not been to scurrilously gossip about the past or condemn these schools for attempting to ensure their future. Rather, it has been to honor their stories in a way that is congruent with their deepest beliefs—bringing to light the way policies rooted in an economic style of reasoning are systematically undermining educational access and distorting the missions of these schools.

One interview in particular has echoed in my ears. It was during my visit to Pepperell where I met a priest about my age. He had just been elected to a leadership role by his elderly colleagues and, like me, felt the weight of responsibility in being tasked to carry their stories into an uncertain future. At the end of our time together, he escorted me to the door and placed a kindly hand on my shoulder. I turned to look at him. He met my gaze. After a pause, he smiled and offered these parting words: "God bless with the project. I hope it bears 'good fruit.'"

Time will tell.

Notes

1. Eisenhardt, K. M. (1989). Building theories from case study research. *Academy of Management Review*, *14*(4), 532–550; Yin, R. (1984). *The case study as a research method*. Sage.
2. Parker-Jenkins, M. (2018). Problematising ethnography and case study: Reflections on using ethnographic techniques and researcher positioning. *Ethnography and Education*, *13*(1), 18–33; Ingold, T. (2014). That's enough about ethnography! *Journal of Ethnographic Theory*, *4*(1), 383–395.
3. Delaney, J. A., & Kearney, T. D. (2016). Alternative student-based revenue streams for higher education institutions: A difference-in-difference analysis using guaranteed tuition policies. *The Journal of Higher Education*, *87*(5), 731–769; Furquim, F., Corral, D., & Hillman, N. (2019). A primer for interpreting and designing difference-in-differences studies in higher education research. *Higher Education: Handbook of Theory and Research*, *35*, 1–58; Belfield, C., Crosta, P., & Jenkins, D. (2014). Can community colleges afford to improve completion? Measuring the cost and efficiency consequences of reform. *Educational Evaluation and Policy Analysis*, *36*(3), 327–345.
4. Jaquette, O., & Parra, E. E. (2014). Using IPEDS for panel analyses: Core concepts, data challenges, and empirical applications. In L. W. Perna (Ed.), *Higher education: Handbook of theory and research* (Vol. 29, pp. 467–533). Springer.
5. This refers to selecting cases on a specific phenomenon or criteria and then employing those cases as evidence the phenomenon or criteria exists: Flyvbjerg, B. (2016). The fallacy of beneficial ignorance: A test of Hirschman's hiding hand. *World Development*, *84*, 176–189.
6. Glaser, B. G., & Strauss, A. L. (1975). *Chronic illness and the quality of life*. Sociology Press.
7. I use the terms *executive* and *leader* interchangeably to refer to persons in the executive and cabinet levels.
8. Only one institution of the proposed eight universities declined to participate in the study. In this instance, I shifted to the second-choice university in the specific matched-pair set (+100% growth rate). The alternative institution accepted the offer to participate, which yielded an initial institutional acceptance rate of 87.5%.

9. Mikecz, R. (2012). Interviewing elites: Addressing methodological issues. *Qualitative Inquiry, 18*(6), 482–493; Hertz, R., & Imber, J. B. (1995). *Studying elites using qualitative methods.* Sage Publications.
10. Interviews with the president and provost of each institution were an essential characteristic of the study. All eight presidents and provosts completed in-person interviews.
11. Ostrander, S. A. (1993). "Surely you're not in this just to be helpful": Access, rapport, and interviews in three studies of elites. *Journal of Contemporary Ethnography, 22*(1), 7–27. All but three interviews were recorded. In these instances, I took detailed notes while interviewing and completed a reflective memo immediately thereafter.
12. Lincoln, Y. S., & Guba, E. G. (1985). *Naturalistic inquiry.* Sage Publications; Motulsky, S. L. (2021). Is member checking the gold standard of quality in qualitative research? *Qualitative Psychology, 8*(3), 389–406.
13. Hallett, R. E. (2012). Dangers of member checking. In W. Midgley, P. Danaher, & M. Baguley (Eds.), *The role of participants in education research: Ethics, epistemologies, and methods* (pp. 29–39). Routledge.
14. Data reduction and data display are the first of two steps in a qualitative analysis approach advocated by Miles and Huberman. I have replaced their third step—conclusion drawing and verification—with my emphasis on triangulation. Miles, M. B., & Huberman, A. M. (1994). *Qualitative data analysis: An expanded sourcebook.* Sage Publications.
15. Strauss, A., & Corbin, J. (1994). Grounded theory methodology: An overview. In N. K. Denzin & Y. S. Lincoln (Eds.), *Handbook of qualitative research* (pp. 273–285). Sage Publications.
16. Flick, U. (2004). Triangulation in qualitative research. In U. Flick, E. Von Kardorff, & I. Steinke (Eds.), *A companion to qualitative research* (pp. 178–183). Sage Publications.

Bibliography

Abbott, A. (2014). *The system of professions: An essay on the division of expert labor*. University of Chicago Press.

Acosta, A., McCann, C., & Palmer, I. (2020). *Considering an online program management (OPM) contract: A guide for colleges*. New America.

Amdam, R. P., & Benito, G. R. (2022). Opening the black box of international strategy formation: How Harvard Business School became a multinational enterprise. *Academy of Management Learning & Education, 21*(2), 167–187.

Anderson, R. C., & Reeb, D. M. (2003). Founding-family ownership and firm performance: Evidence from the S&P 500. *The Journal of Finance, 58*(3), 1301–1328.

Archibald, R. B., & Feldman, D. H. (2006). State higher education spending and the tax revolt. *The Journal of Higher Education, 77*(4), 618–644.

Barrow, C. W. (1990). *Universities and the capitalist state: Corporate liberalism and the reconstruction of American higher education, 1894–1928*. University of Wisconsin Press.

Bea, D. W. (2004). *Modernizing higher education administration: How market and economic factors are changing small college and university business operations* [Unpublished doctoral dissertation]. Claremont Graduate University.

Belfield, C., Crosta, P., & Jenkins, D. (2014). Can community colleges afford to improve completion? Measuring the cost and efficiency consequences of reform. *Educational Evaluation and Policy Analysis, 36*(3), 327–345.

Berman, E. P. (2022). *Thinking like an economist: How efficiency replaced equality in US public policy*. Princeton University Press.

Bitektine, A. (2011). Toward a theory of social judgments of organizations: The case of legitimacy, reputation, and status. *Academy of Management Review, 36*(1), 151–179.

Bjork-James, S. (2021). *The divine institution: White evangelicalism's politics of the family*. Rutgers University Press.

Blumenstyk, G. (2018). One way to set up liberal-arts majors for success: Focus on skills. *The Chronicle of Higher Education, 5*(1), 1–14.

Bornstein, D., & Davis, S. (2010). *Social entrepreneurship: What everyone needs to know*. Oxford University Press.

Bowler, K. (2020). *The preacher's wife: The precarious power of evangelical women celebrities*. Princeton University Press.

Boyne, G. A., & Meier, K. (2009). Environmental change, human resources and organizational turnaround. *Journal of Management Studies, 46*(5), 835–863.

Breneman, D. W., Pusser, B., & Turner, S. E. (2006). The contemporary provision of for-profit higher education. In Breneman, David W., Brian Pusser, and Sarah E. Turner (Eds.), *Earnings from learning: The rise of for-profit universities* (pp. 3–23). State University of New York Press.

Bromley, P., & Powell, W. W. (2012). From smoke and mirrors to walking the talk: Decoupling in the contemporary world. *Academy of Management Annals, 6*(1), 483–530.

Brown, D. K. (2001). The social sources of educational credentialism: Status cultures, labor markets, and organizations. *Sociology of Education, 74*, 19–34.

Brown, J. T. (2023). The ethical poverty of dorms for the rich. *The Chronicle of Higher Education*. May 2.

Brown, J. T., Volk, F., & Kush, J. M. (2023). Racial and economic stratification on campus: The relationship between luxury residence halls, race, and academic outcomes. *Journal of College Student Development* 64(1), 108–113.

Brown, J. T., Volk, F., & Kush, J. M. (2023) *Equality and a built environment of differences: Towards more equitable residential life experiences.* Columbus, OH: Association of College and University Housing Officers – International (ACUHO-I).

Brown, J. T., Volk, F., & Spratto, E. (2019). The hidden structure: The influence of residence hall design on academic outcomes. *Journal of Student Affairs Research & Practice*, 56(3), 267–283.

Brown, J. T. (2017). The seven silos of accountability in higher education: Systematizing multiple logics and fields. *Research & Practice in Assessment*, 11, 41–58.

Brown, J. T. (2018). Leading colleges & universities in an age of education policy: How to understand the complex landscape of higher education accountability. *Change: The Magazine of Higher Learning*, 50(2), 30–39.

Brown, J. T. (2021). The evolving missions and functions of accessible colleges and universities. In G. Crisp, K. R. McClure, & C. M. Orphan (Eds.), *Unlocking opportunity: Broadly accessible four-year colleges and universities* (pp. 65–81). Routledge.

Brown, J. T. (2021). The language of leaders: Executive sensegiving strategies in higher education. *American Journal of Education*, 127(2), 265–302.

Brown, J. T., Kush, J., & Volk, F. (2022). Centering the marginalized: The impact of the pandemic on online student retention. *Journal of Student Financial Aid*, 51(1), 1–24.

Brown, W. (2015). *Undoing the demos: Neoliberalism's stealth revolution.* MIT Press.

Burt, S., & Sparks, L. (1997). Performance in food retailing: A cross-national consideration and comparison of retail margins. *British Journal of Management*, 8(2), 133–150.

Burtchaell, J. T. (1998). *The dying of the light: The disengagement of colleges and universities from their Christian churches.* W. B. Eerdmans Publishing Company.

Carey, K. (2019, April 1). The creeping capitalist takeover of higher education. *The Huffington Post.* https://www.huffpost.com/highline/article/capitalist-takeover-college/

Carroll, L. (2016). *Alice's Adventures in Wonderland, Through the Looking Glass and Alice's Adventures Underground* (J. Tenniel, Illus.). Bloomsbury Publishing. (Original work published 1985)

Chen, S., Chen, X. I. A., & Cheng, Q. (2008). Do family firms provide more or less voluntary disclosure? *Journal of Accounting Research*, 46(3), 499–536.

Cheslock, J. J., & Gianneschi, M. (2008). Replacing state appropriations with alternative revenue sources: The case of voluntary support. *The Journal of Higher Education*, 79(2), 208–229.

Cheslock, J. J., & Jaquette, O. (2021). Concentrated or fragmented? The US market for online higher education. *Research in Higher Education*, 63(1), 33–59.

Cheslock, J. J., Kinser, K., Zipf, S. T., & Ra, E. (2021). *Examining the OPM: Form, function, and policy implications.* EdArXiv. https://doi.org/10.35542/osf.io/py3sz.

Clark, B. R. (2017). *The distinctive college: Antioch, Reed, and Swarthmore.* Routledge.

Collier, P. (2018). *The future of capitalism: Facing the new anxieties.* HarperCollins.

Collins, J. (2001). *Good to great: Why some companies make the leap and others don't.* HarperCollins.

Collins, R. (2019). *The credential society: A historical sociology of education and stratification.* Columbia University Press.

Cottom, T. M. (2017). *Lower ed: The troubling rise of for-profit colleges in the new economy.* The New Press.

Cowhitt, T., Brown, J.T. & Antonio, A.L. (2024) The emergence and evolution of ambiguous ideas: an innovative application of social network analysis to support systematic literature reviews. *Scientometrics.* https://doi.org/10.1007/s11192-024-05144-7

Curs, B. R., & Jaquette, O. (2017). Crowded out? The effect of nonresident enrollment on resident access to public research universities. *Educational Evaluation and Policy Analysis, 39*(4), 644–669.

Davenport, T., & Harris, J. (2017). *Competing on analytics: The new science of winning.* Harvard Business Press.

Deephouse, D. L. (1996). Does isomorphism legitimate? *Academy of Management Journal, 39*(4), 1024–1039.

Deephouse, D. L., & Carter, S. M. (2005). An examination of differences between organizational legitimacy and organizational reputation. *Journal of Management Studies, 42*(2), 329–360.

Deephouse, D. L., & Suchman, M. (2008). Legitimacy in organizational institutionalism. In R. Greenwood, C. Oliver, K. Sahlin, & R. Suddaby (Eds.), *The Sage handbook of organizational institutionalism* (pp. 49–77). Sage Publications.

Dehne, G., & Small, C. (2006). The dilemma of the tuition-driven college. *Trusteeship, 5*(6), 13–18.

Delaney, J. A., & Doyle, W. R. (2011). State spending on higher education: Testing the balance wheel over time. *Journal of Education Finance, 36,* 343–368.

Delaney, J. A., & Kearney, T. D. (2016). Alternative student-based revenue streams for higher education institutions: A difference-in-difference analysis using guaranteed tuition policies. *The Journal of Higher Education, 87*(5), 731–769.

Deming, D. J., Goldin, C., & Katz, L. F. (2012). The for-profit postsecondary school sector: Nimble critters or agile predators? *Journal of Economic Perspectives, 26*(1), 139–164.

DiMaggio, P. J., & Powell, W. W. (1983). The iron cage revisited: Institutional isomorphism and collective rationality in organizational fields. *American Sociological Review, 48*(2), 147–160.

Doh, J. P., & Stumpf, S. A. (2007). Executive education: A view from the top. *Academy of Management Learning & Education, 6*(3), 388–400.

Douglass, J. (2016). *The new flagship university: Changing the paradigm from global ranking to national relevancy.* Springer.

Drake, B. M., & Walz, A. (2018). Evolving business intelligence and data analytics in higher education. *New Directions for Institutional Research, 178,* 39–52.

Duffy, E. A., & Goldberg, I. (1998). *Crafting a class: College admissions and financial aid, 1951–1994.* Princeton University Press.

Eaton, C. (2022). *Bankers in the ivory tower: The troubling rise of financiers in US higher education.* University of Chicago Press.

Eaton, C., Habinek, J., Goldstein, A., Dioun, C., Santibáñez Godoy, D. G., & Osley-Thomas, R. (2016). The financialization of US higher education. *Socio-Economic Review, 14*(3), 507–535.

Edler, J., & Fagerberg, J. (2017). Innovation policy: What, why, and how. *Oxford Review of Economic Policy, 33*(1), 2–23.

Eisenhardt, K. M. (1989). Building theories from case study research. *Academy of Management Review, 14*(4), 532–550.

Eisenhardt, K. M., & Graebner, M. E. (2007). Theory building from cases: Opportunities and challenges. *Academy of Management Journal, 50*(1), 25–32.

Faulkner, D. O., & Campbell, A. (Eds.). (2006). *The Oxford handbook of strategy: A strategy overview and competitive strategy*. Oxford University Press.

Flick, U. (2004). Triangulation in qualitative research. In U. Flick, E. Von Kardorff, & I. Steinke (Eds.), *A companion to qualitative research* (pp. 178–183). Sage Publications.

Flyvbjerg, B. (2016). The fallacy of beneficial ignorance: A test of Hirschman's hiding hand. *World Development*, *84*, 176–189.

Fort, E. (Ed.). (2013). *Survival of the historically Black colleges and universities: Making it happen*. Lexington Books.

Freeland, R. M. (1992). *Academia's golden age: Universities in Massachusetts, 1945–1970*. Oxford University Press.

Fryar, A. H. (2012). What do we mean by privatization in higher education? In J. C. Smart & M. B. Paulsen (Eds.), *Higher education: Handbook of theory and research* (pp. 521–547). Springer.

Fuller, M. B. (2014). A history of financial aid to students. *Journal of Student Financial Aid*, *44*(1), 42–68.

Furquim, F., Corral, D., & Hillman, N. (2019). A primer for interpreting and designing difference-in-differences studies in higher education research. *Higher Education: Handbook of Theory and Research*, *35*, 1–58.

Gallagher, S., & Palmer, J. (2020). The pandemic pushed universities online. The change was long overdue. *Harvard Business Review*, *29*.

Garcia, G. A. (2019). *Becoming Hispanic-serving institutions: Opportunities for colleges and universities*. Johns Hopkins University Press.

Gasman, M., & Bowman, N., III. (2013). *Engaging diverse college alumni: The essential guide to fundraising*. Routledge.

Gehman, J. (2021). Searching for values in practice-driven institutionalism: Practice theory, institutional logics, and values work. In M. Lounsbury, D. A. Anderson & P. Spee (Eds.), *On practice and institution: Theorizing the interface*, Vol. 70 (pp. 139–159). Emerald Publishing Limited.

Gehman, J., Grimes, M. G., & Cao, K. (2019). Why we care about certified B corporations: From valuing growth to certifying values practices. *Academy of Management Discoveries*, *5*(1), 97–101.

Geiger, R. L. (2019). *American higher education since World War II*. Princeton University Press.

Gerber, L. G. (2014). *The rise and decline of faculty governance: Professionalization and the modern American university*. Johns Hopkins University Press.

Glaser, B. G., & Strauss, A. L. (1975). *Chronic illness and the quality of life*. Sociology Press.

Gleason, P. (1967). American Catholic higher education: A historical perspective. In R. Hassenger (Ed.), *The shape of Catholic higher education* (pp. 182–220). Chicago University Press.

Goldrick-Rab, S. (2021). *Paying the price: College costs, financial aid, and the betrayal of the American dream*. University of Chicago Press.

Grawe, N. D. (2018). *Demographics and the demand for higher education*. Johns Hopkins University Press.

Greene, H., & Greene, M. W. (2010). *The hidden Ivies: 50 top colleges—from Amherst to Williams—that rival the Ivy League*. HarperCollins.

Hallett, R. E. (2012). Dangers of member checking. In W. Midgley, P. Danaher, & M. Baguley (Eds.), *The role of participants in education research: Ethics, epistemologies, and methods* (pp. 29–39). Routledge.

Hamilton, L. T., & Nielsen, K. (2021). *Broke: The racial consequences of underfunding public universities*. University of Chicago Press.

Bibliography 281

Han, B. C. (2017). *Psychopolitics: Neoliberalism and new technologies of power* (E. Butler, Trans.). Verso Books.

Han, B. C. (2021). *Capitalism and the death drive* (D. Steuer, Trans.). Polity.

Harvey, D. (2007). *A brief history of neoliberalism*. Oxford University Press.

Harvey, D. (2007). Neoliberalism as creative destruction. *Annals of the American Academy of Political and Social Science, 610*, 22–44.

Haskins, M. E., Centini, L., & Shaffer, G. R. (2017). Ideas for growing executive education revenue: Codification and catalyst. *Journal of Management Development, 36*(4), 581–597.

Hertz, R., & Imber, J. B. (1995). *Studying elites using qualitative methods*. Sage Publications.

Hillman, N. W. (2016). Geography of college opportunity: The case of education deserts. *American Educational Research Journal, 53*(4), 987–1021.

Hsu, G., & Hannan, M. T. (2005). Identities, genres, and organizational forms. *Organization Science, 16*(5), 474–490.

Hughes, R. T., & Adrian, W. B. (1997). *Models for Christian higher education: Strategies for survival and success in the twenty-first century*. Wm. B. Eerdmans Publishing.

Iloh, C. (2016). Exploring the for-profit experience: An ethnography of a for-profit college. *American Educational Research Journal, 53*(3), 427–455.

Ingold, T. (2014). That's enough about ethnography! *Journal of Ethnographic Theory, 4*(1), 383–395.

Jack, A. A. (2019). *The privileged poor: How elite colleges are failing disadvantaged students*. Harvard University Press.

Jaquette, O., & Curs, B. R. (2015). Creating the out-of-state university: Do public universities increase nonresident freshman enrollment in response to declining state appropriations? *Research in Higher Education, 56*(6), 535–565.

Jaquette, O., & Parra, E. E. (2014). Using IPEDS for panel analyses: Core concepts, data challenges, and empirical applications. In L. W. Perna (Ed.), *Higher education: Handbook of theory and research* (Vol. 29, pp. 467–533). Springer.

Jessop, B. (2017). Varieties of academic capitalism and entrepreneurial universities. *Higher Education, 73*(6), 853–870.

Johnson, A. (2020). *The history of predominantly Black institutions: A primer*. Rutgers Center for Minority Serving Institutions.

Karabel, J. (2005). *The chosen: The hidden history of admission and exclusion at Harvard, Yale, and Princeton*. Houghton Mifflin Harcourt.

Karwowski, E. (2019). Towards (de-)financialization: The role of the state. *Cambridge Journal of Economics, 43*(4), 1001–1027.

Keeley, L., Walters, H., Pikkel, R., & Quinn, B. (2013). *Ten types of innovation: The discipline of building breakthroughs*. John Wiley & Sons.

Kerr, C. (1982). *The uses of the university*. Harvard University Press.

Kezar, A., Chambers, A. C., & Burkhardt, J. C. (2015). *Higher education for the public good: Emerging voices from a national movement*. John Wiley & Sons.

Kindel, A. T., & Stevens, M. L. (2021). What is educational entrepreneurship? Strategic action, temporality, and the expansion of US higher education. *Theory and Society, 50*(4), 577–605.

Kirp, D. L. (2003). *Shakespeare, Einstein, and the bottom line*. Harvard University Press.

Kraatz, M. S., Ventresca, M. J., & Deng, L. (2010). Precarious values and mundane innovations: Enrollment management in American liberal arts colleges. *Academy of Management Journal, 53*(6), 1521–1545.

Krippner, G. R. (2005). The financialization of the American economy. *Socio-Economic Review, 3*(2), 173–208.

Labaree, D. F. (1997). Public goods, private goods: The American struggle over educational goals. *American Educational Research Journal, 34*(1), 39–81.

Labaree, D. F. (2016). An affair to remember: America's brief fling with the university as a public good. *Journal of Philosophy of Education, 50*(1), 20–36.

Labaree, D. F. (2017). *A perfect mess: The unlikely ascendancy of American higher education.* University of Chicago Press.

Lemann, N. (2000). *The big test: The secret history of the American meritocracy.* Macmillan.

Levinthal, D. A., & Wu, B. (2010). Opportunity costs and non-scale free capabilities: Profit maximization, corporate scope, and profit margins. *Strategic Management Journal, 31*(7), 780–801.

Leyshon, A., & Thrift, N. (2007). The capitalization of almost everything: The future of finance and capitalism. *Theory, Culture & Society, 24*(7–8), 97–115.

Lieberman, M. B., & Montgomery, D. B. (1988). First-mover advantages. *Strategic Management Journal, 9*(S1), 41–58.

Lincoln, Y. S., & Guba, E. G. (1985). *Naturalistic inquiry.* Sage Publications.

Loss, C. P. (2012). *Between citizens and the state: The politics of American higher education in the 20th century.* Princeton University Press.

Lounsbury, M., Cornelissen, J., Granqvist, N., & Grodal, S. (2019). Culture, innovation and entrepreneurship. *Innovation, 21*(1), 1–12.

Lounsbury, M., & Glynn, M. (2019). *Cultural entrepreneurship: A new agenda for the study of entrepreneurial processes and possibilities.* Cambridge University Press.

Lucas, C. J. (2016). *American higher education: A history.* Springer.

Lyon, D. (2013). *Jesus in Disneyland: Religion in postmodern times.* John Wiley & Sons.

Marglin, S. A. (2008). *The dismal science: How thinking like an economist undermines community.* Harvard University Press.

Marsden, G. M. (1996). *The soul of the American university: From Protestant establishment to established nonbelief.* Oxford University Press.

McClure, K. R., Barringer, S. N., & Brown, J. T. (2020). Privatization as the new normal in higher education: Synthesizing literature and reinvigorating research through a multilevel framework. In L. W. Perna (Ed.), *Higher education: Handbook of theory and research* (Vol. 35, pp. 589–666). Springer.

McDonough, P. M. (1997). *Choosing colleges: How social class and schools structure opportunity.* State University of New York Press.

Mikecz, R. (2012). Interviewing elites: Addressing methodological issues. *Qualitative Inquiry, 18*(6), 482–493.

Miles, M. B., & Huberman, A. M. (1994). *Qualitative data analysis: An expanded sourcebook.* Sage Publications.

Miller-Bernal, L., & Poulson, S. L. (2004). *Going coed: Women's experiences in formerly men's colleges and universities, 1950–2000.* Vanderbilt University Press.

Morphew, C. C. (2002). "A rose by any other name": Which colleges became universities. *The Review of Higher Education, 25*(2), 207–223.

Motulsky, S. L. (2021). Is member checking the gold standard of quality in qualitative research? *Qualitative Psychology, 8*(3), 389–406. https://doi.org/10.1037/qup0000215.

Muniesa, F., Doganova, L., Ortiz, H., Pina-Stranger, Á., Paterson, F., Bourgoin, A., Ehrenstein, V., Juven, P. A., Pontille, D., Saraç-Lesavre, B., & Yon, G. (2017). *Capitalization: A cultural guide.* Presses des Mines.

Nguyen, M. H., Espinoza, K. J., Gogue, D. T. -L., & Dinh, D. (2020). *Looking to the next decade: Strengthening Asian American and Native American Pacific Islander serving institutions through policy and practice.* National Council of Asian Pacific Americans.

Ostrander, S. A. (1993). "Surely you're not in this just to be helpful": Access, rapport, and interviews in three studies of elites. *Journal of Contemporary Ethnography, 22*(1), 7–27.

Parker-Jenkins, M. (2018). Problematising ethnography and case study: Reflections on using ethnographic techniques and researcher positioning. *Ethnography and Education, 13*(1), 18–33.

Posecznick, A. (2017). *Selling hope and college: Merit, markets, and recruitment in an unranked school*. Cornell University Press.

Reinders, M. J., Frambach, R. T., & Schoormans, J. P. (2010). Using product bundling to facilitate the adoption process of radical innovations. *Journal of Product Innovation Management, 27*(7), 1127–1140.

Rine, J. & Brown, J. T. (2023). Shifting environments, emerging norms: How changes in policy, technology, data, and market competition affect college enrollment management processes. In Braxton & Reason (Eds.), *Improving College Student Retention: New Developments in Theory, Research, and Practice*, (p. 258–283). Sterling: Stylus.

Rine, J., Brown, J. T., & Hunter., J. M. (2021). How institutional identity shapes college student recruitment: The relationship between religious distinctiveness and market demand. *American Journal of Economics and Sociology, 80*(1), 133–159.

Rizzo, M., & Ehrenberg, R. G. (2004). Resident and nonresident tuition and enrollment at flagship state universities. In C. M. Hoxby (Ed.), *College choices: The economics of where to go, when to go, and how to pay for it* (pp. 303–354). University of Chicago Press.

Rudolph, F. (2021). *The American college and university: A history*. Plunkett Lake Press.

Ryan, H., & Hamilton, M. (2019, June 6). Online degrees made USC the world's biggest social work school. Then things went terribly wrong. *Los Angeles Times*. https://www.latimes.com/local/laffnow/la-me-usc-social-work-20190606-story.html

Salazar, K. G. (2022). Recruitment redlining by public research universities in the Los Angeles and Dallas metropolitan areas. *The Journal of Higher Education, 93*(4), 585–621.

Santos, F. M., & Eisenhardt, K. M. (2009). Constructing markets and shaping boundaries: Entrepreneurial power in nascent fields. *Academy of Management Journal, 52*(4), 643–671.

Schultze, Q. J. (2003). *Televangelism and American culture: The business of popular religion*. Wipf and Stock Publishers.

Sherlock, M. F., Crandall-Hollick, M. L., Gravelle, J., & Stupak, J. M. (2015). *College and university endowments: Overview and tax policy options*. Congressional Research Service.

Shermer, E. T. (2021). *Indentured students: How government-guaranteed loans left generations drowning in college debt*. The Belknap Press of Harvard University.

Stensaker, B., & Norgård, J. D. (2001). Innovation and isomorphism: A case-study of university identity struggle 1969–1999. *Higher Education, 42*(4), 473–492.

Stevens, M. L. (2007). *Creating a class: College admissions and the education of elites*. Harvard University Press.

Stevens, M., & Kirst, M. W. (2015). *Remaking college: The changing ecology of higher education*. Stanford University Press.

Stiglitz, J. E. (2013, February 16). Equal opportunity, our national myth. *New York Times*, (p. SR4).

Stone, D. (2002). *Policy paradox: The art of political decision making*. W. W. Norton & Company.

Strauss, A., & Corbin, J. (1994). Grounded theory methodology: An overview. In N. K. Denzin & Y. S. Lincoln (Eds.), *Handbook of qualitative research* (pp. 273–285). Sage Publications.

Suarez, F. F., & Lanzolla, G. (2007). The role of environmental dynamics in building a first mover advantage theory. *Academy of Management Review, 32*(2), 377–392.

Suchman, M. C. (1995). Managing legitimacy: Strategic and institutional approaches. *Academy of Management Review, 20*(3), 571–610.

Tandberg, D. A. (2010). Politics, interest groups and state funding of public higher education. *Research in Higher Education, 51*(5), 416–450.

Taylor, B. J., & Cantwell, B. (2019). *Unequal higher education: Wealth, status, and student opportunity*. Rutgers University Press.

Thelin, J. R. (2004). *A history of American higher education*. Johns Hopkins University Press.

Thornton, P. H., & Ocasio, W. (1999). Institutional logics and the historical contingency of power in organizations: Executive succession in the higher education publishing industry, 1958–1990. *American Journal of Sociology, 105*(3), 801–843.

Thornton, P. H., Ocasio, W., & Lounsbury, M. (2012). *The institutional logics perspective: A new approach to culture, structure and process*. Oxford University Press.

Toutkoushian, R. K., & Lee, J. C. (2018). Revisiting economies of scale and scope in higher education. In M. B. Paulsen (Ed.), *Higher education: Handbook of theory and research* (Vol. 33, pp. 371–416). Springer.

Tuchman, G. (2009). *Wannabe U: Inside the corporate university*. University of Chicago Press.

Turner, J. K., & Pusser, B. (2004). Place matters: The distribution of access to a state flagship university. *Policy Futures in Education, 2*(2), 388–421.

VanSickle-Ward, R. (2014). *The devil is in the details: Understanding the causes of policy specificity and ambiguity*. State University of New York Press.

Volk, F., Brown, J. T., Gibson, D. J. & Kush, J. (2023). The anatomy of roommate change: Residence hall design, academic performance, and differences in race and socioeconomic status. *Journal of College and University Student Housing, 49*(2), 48–65

Walshe, K., Harvey, G., Hyde, P., & Pandit, N. (2004). Organizational failure and turnaround: Lessons for public services from the for-profit sector. *Public Money & Management, 24*(4), 201–208.

Webber, D. A. (2017). State divestment and tuition at public institutions. *Economics of Education Review, 60*, 1–4.

Webber, K. L., & Zheng, H. (2020). *Big data on campus: Data analytics and decision making in higher education*. Johns Hopkins University Press.

Wekullo, C. S. (2017). Outsourcing in higher education: The known and unknown about the practice. *Journal of Higher Education Policy and Management, 39*(4), 453–468.

Wilde, M. J. (2018). *Vatican II: A sociological analysis of religious change*. Princeton University Press.

Williamson, B. (2021). Making markets through digital platforms: Pearson, edu-business, and the (e)valuation of higher education. *Critical Studies in Education, 62*(1), 50–66.

Wilson, E. H. (1988). *For the people of North Carolina: The Z. Smith Reynolds Foundation at half-century, 1936–1986*. University of North Carolina Press.

Yin, R. (1984). *The case study as a research method*. Sage Publications.

Zaloom, C. (2019). *Indebted: Student loans, fragile families, and the future of the middle class*. Princeton University Press.

Zhang, L. C., & Worthington, A. C. (2018). Explaining estimated economies of scale and scope in higher education: A meta-regression analysis. *Research in Higher Education, 59*(2), 156–173.

Index

Figures are indicated by an italic *f* following the paragraph number

For the benefit of digital users, indexed terms that span two pages (e.g., 52–53) may, on occasion, appear on only one of those pages.

academic programs
  with credentialism, 58–59
  Havertown credentialism investment of, 58–59
  Lansdale and Malvern unorthodox settings of in-person, 99
  Stoneham military base in-person, 99–100
academic services, as paid partner, 140–141
academic standards
  Boxborough and Havertown reputation of high, 33, 35, 36–38
  economic connotation of high, 76 n.2
academic testing companies
  ACT, 211–212
  Educational Testing Service, 140, 211–212
  SAT, 140, 211–212
accelerated networks, 223, 228
  neoliberalism impact on, 228
accelerated strategy, 23–25, 24*f*, 177–193.
  See also Ardmore University
  advancement in, 208–221
  Boxborough movement toward, 255
  competition and, 219–221
  corporate shell, 213–216
  cost containment in, 202–205
  curriculum outsourcing, 216–219
  data as commodity, 210–213
  direct competition knowledge, 219–220
  family firm management approach, 177, 179, 181–183, 256 n.6, n.9
  of Grand Canyon University, 118
  grand narrative of cultural change, 183–185
  Internet marketing for prospective student target, 220
  margin capitalization use in, 193
  overcoming double hundreds, 185–188
  pursuit of, 193–208
  scaling up in, 193–196
  store with two products, 196–199
  superprofits of financialization, 205–208
access and arrival, for methodological approach
  ambassador as point of contact for, 267–268
  institution tour and, 267–269
  off-site preparations for, 268
  research activities for, 267–268
accreditation policies, ambiguities in, 237
ACT. *See* American College Testing
adult education
  at Malvern, 243
  pioneer strategy and, 113–114
  tuition-driven schools innovative, 11–12
Alpha Consulting, as paid partners with Winchendon, 141–142, 163
  AI use for prospective student identification, 174 n.10
ambassador, as point of contact, 267–268
American College Testing (ACT) academic testing company, 211–212
Amherst College, 35–36
Ardmore University. *See also* online education market, of Ardmore
  accelerated strategy of, 23–25
  assumption of $110 million debt, 186–187
  on blended approach, 253
  call center services-at-scale for student service support, 200–202, 209, 233
  call center workplace panopticon, 201, 257 n.16
  church subsidizing of through donation fundraising, 185–186, 257 n.11
  competitive benchmarking of, 220–221

Ardmore University (*Continued*)
  cultural entrepreneurism of, 177, 179, 183–185, 189, 192–195, 256 n.1
  curriculum development models of, 214
  data as commodity at, 165, 210–213
  distance-learning periphery market, 197
  faculty removal from curriculum design process, 218
  family firm management approach, 177, 179, 181–183
  financial crisis of, 187–188
  on golden age of higher education, 179–180
  guerilla competitive research of, 177–178, 220–222
  guided by God disposition, 179–181
  on identity paradox, 241
  knowledge of direct competition, 219–220
  land acquisition for residential campus, 180
  large philanthropist giving at, 188–189
  lucrative self-sustaining strategy with market logic principles, 222
  margin capitalization at, 208–209, 221–222
  margin philanthropy and, 24, 188–194, 209, 221–222
  as market-centric institution, 227
  mission of, 210, 222, 232
  national religious scandals damage to, 186–187
  neoliberal edu-business approach, 221–222
  neoliberal funding policies of, 192
  operational analytics at, 211–213, 222
  pay-per-click marketing of, 220, 222
  on per-student funding, 234
  physical campus transformation, 206
  process innovation at, 217–218
  product innovation of, 196–197, 217–218
  public bonds generation of superprofits at, 207
  religious outlook of, 178–179
  on residential core model, 251
  residential enrollment increase attempts, 205–206
  scaling up at, 194–196
  technological infrastructure of, 196–197
  as university for God, 177–180, 222

  vision of large student numbers, 184
arithmetic growth
  in enrollment growth, 249
  scaling up and, 195
Arizona State University, 209, 213, 222
Ashford University, 226 n.31
Asian American and Native American Pacific Islander Serving Institutions (AANAPISI), 175 n.18, 234
aspiring Ivies
  Boxborough and Havertown following of, 32–33, 76 n.1, 35–36
  endowment revenues of, 53
  Malvern, Lansdale, Stoneham and, 95–96
athletic programs
  Boxborough investment in, 57–58
  Power Four athletic conferences, 156, 175 n.21
auxiliary services, as paid partner, 140–141

baby boom
  adulthood and enrollment decrease, 41–42, 87, 128, 140
  neoliberal policies for funding higher education, 79
Bakker, Tammy Faye, 186–187, 257 n.12
Big Three universities, of Harvard, Princeton, Yale, 14–15, 51, 184
  prestige and uniqueness of, 178
  residential campus at, 97–98
blending approach, to residential core, 255
  Ardmore on, 253
  Malvern on, 250–251
Bluefield State University, 175 n.18
bonds
  Ardmore financialization for superprofits generation through public, 207
  institutional loans and, 61
  margin capitalization funded through, 12–13
  periphery enrollment markets for payment of, 149–150
Boston College, 35–36, 51, 57
Boxborough College, 231–232
  accelerated strategy movement by, 255
  aspiring Ivies followed by, 32–33, 76 n.1, 35–36
  athletic program investment by, 57–58
  attempts to increase residential enrollments, 69

buildings funded through donations, 38
campus physical transformation at, 54–56
commitment for community higher education, 34–35, 37–38
community opportunity importance, 33, 37–38
competition response from, 67–68, 71–74
customized financial aid packages of, 44
deliberate decision-making at, 20
on discount pricing in competition, 45
endowment growth at, 46–47, 50–53
endowment revenues of, 19–20, 39, 50–53, 77 n.18
enrollment growth for federal tuition revenue, 41
enrollment of unprepared students, 70
faculty and staff reductions, 70–71
federal financial aid compliance efforts, 236–237
financial aid packages undercut at, 68–69
financial crisis at, 64–65
fundraising initiatives at, 52–53, 59–61
fundraising limits at, 63–64
in golden age of higher education, 41–43
heritage philosophy strategy, 46, 73
historical emphasis on quality, 36
on identity paradox, 239–240
impoverished region location of, 33
in-person communal approach at, 50
institutional fund for impoverished students, 38
institutional loans and bonds, 61
on mission, 32, 228
movement toward accelerated strategy, 255
online education market and, 49–50, 68, 72
professional norms and decision-making, 66–67
professional programs emphasis, 49
reputation of high academic standards, 33, 35, 36–38
reputation to uphold of, 35–38, 76 n.3
residential enrollment attempts, 46–47
successful alumni of, 37
traditional philanthropy for endowment revenue, 20, 51–52, 60, 62–63
traditional strategy ineffective at, 20, 62–64, 67, 74–75
traditional strategy of, 19–20, 37–38

on tradition importance, 37–38
on tradition of residential enrollment, 48–49, 73
tuition dependence of, 52–53
tuition discounts subsidized by endowments, 50–51
branch campus model
financial resources through enrollment growth, 111–112
global network in, 152–155, 168–169
Brigham Young University, 111–112, 257 n.11
Brown University, 175 n.16
buildings, 38
margin capitalization and renovations and, 12, 102, 149–150
network strategy periphery enrollment markets revenue for, 149
of Pepperell and Winchendon funding of new, 150
residential core model for maintenance of, 249–250

cabinet level in institutions, 267–268
call center
Ardmore workplace panopticon, 201, 257 n.16
margin capitalization funds generated from, 206
services-at-scale of Ardmore University, 200–202, 209, 233
of universities, 201
Capella University, 227
Carleton University, 35–36
cathartic response, from interviews, 271
Catholic populations
of Pepperell and Winchendon, 128, 243
religious college admissions of, 14–15
centralization, for accelerated strategy cost containment, 202–203
change, interview focus on, 269–270
choice
competition and student, 231
market-oriented education policies and competition with, 231
market principle of, 25
trumping competition, 230–233
Colby College, 35–36
College Board (SAT) academic testing company, 211–212

College of the Holy Cross, 53
Colorado State University, 244
commodity-market rules, for federal financial aid, 237
community
  Boxborough and Havertown commitment for higher education in, 34–35, 37–38
  Boxborough and Havertown on opportunity in, 33, 37–38
  of need, Pepperell and Winchendon in, 128
comparative marketing, Lansdale on, 117, 228
Competent Conversationalist, Ardmore outsourcing foreign conversational language to, 216, 218
competition
  accelerated strategy and taking from, 219–221
  accelerated strategy on knowledge of direct, 219–220
  Ardmore guerilla competitive research, 177–178, 220–222
  Ardmore online, 209
  Boxborough and Havertown response to, 67–68, 71–74
  Boxborough on discount pricing, 45
  choice trumping cooperation and, 230–233
  COVID-19 pandemic impact, 31 n.37
  between economic and social spheres, 232
  educational strategy change from, 228
  external with peer institutions, 244
  from for-profit institutions, 113
  increase due to traditional-aged students decline, 27, 41–42
  Lansdale on, 230–231
  Malvern and resource cuts, 120
  market-oriented education policies and choice intersection with, 231
  market principle of, 25
  network strategy to saturate periphery enrollment market, 159
  from nonprofit college and universities, 113
  Pepperell and Winchendon internal, 161, 165–166
  Pepperell and Winchendon swift response to, 157–158
  Pepperell on incredible, 230–231
  physical facilities and student enrollments correlation, 53–54, 56
  pioneer strategy efforts to lead, 112
  within and among policies, 230
  Stoneham and staffing adjustments, 120
  Stoneham nuns on impact of, 230–231
  student choice primacy, 231
  Winchendon on threat of, 230–231
compressed education timeline, of pioneer strategy, 114
connection, interview focus on, 269–270
corporate enrollment market, 213
  corporate training and education approach, 215
  for curriculum for needed workforce, 215
  discussion for needed corporate workforce, 214
  online shell for, 213–214
  remote online delivery to global employees, 215
corporate shell
  accelerated strategy and, 213–216
  corporate-university partnerships, 213
corporate-university partnerships, 213
  of Ardmore, 214–216
corporations
  expression of need for data science and information analytics competencies, 214–215
  university partnerships for employee retention and training initiatives, 213
cost containment, in accelerated strategy, 202–205
  centralization for, 202–203
  standardization for, 205
  wage containment for, 203–205
course registration system, operational analytics development of, 212–213
COVID-19 pandemic, 31 n.37
credentialism
  academic programs with, 58–59
  nontraditional students and, 97–98
CRM. *See* customer relations management
cultural entrepreneurism, of Ardmore, 177, 179, 183–185, 189, 192–195, 256 n.1
culture, 268–269
curriculum outsourcing, at Ardmore, 216–219, 222

curriculum design bypassing faculty, 216, 218
for foreign conversational languages, 216, 218
for life coaching, 216–218
product innovation for, 217–218
curriculum shell, of Ardmore, 215–216
customer relations management (CRM), at Ardmore, 201, 257 n.17
customized financial aid packages, 44

data as commodity, at Ardmore, 210–213
    data aggregated of student profile for recruitment, 211–212
    operational analytics, 165
    tapestry data admission emphasis, 211–212
data display, 77 n.14, 272
data reduction, 77 n.14, 272
Davidson College, 62
decision-making
    Boxborough and Havertown deliberate, 20
    family firm management approach focused, 182
    Havertown and Boxborough professional norms and, 66–67
    pioneer strategy value emphasis in, 108
DePaul University, 14–15
distance-learning periphery market, of Ardmore, 197
dramaturgy
    of Ardmore founder and family, 182–183
    Goffman and, 256 n.9
Drexel University, 111–112
Duke University, 15, 52–53, 175 n.16

early adopter, 103–104, 112, 124
economic reasoning, 8, 30 n.19, *See also* market logic; market-oriented; neoliberalism
    central innovation of, 233
    component of margin capitalization, 160
    created competition, 19, 233
    driver of scaled fundraising, 190
    financial aid packages products of, 44
    frameworks of, 231–232
    governs financial resources, 247–248
    impact on underrepresented students, 235
    intended outcomes of, 113
    organized system of higher education, 219, 232
educational access, mission of, 28
educational products, tuition-driven schools innovative
    adult education, 11–12
    entrepreneurial schools, 11
    satellite campuses, 11
Educational Testing Service exams
    ACT, 211–212
    GRE, 140, 211–212
    SAT, Praxis, and TOEFL, 140
elite universities, 3–8
    endowment revenues of, 51, 53
    endowments funding expenses from residential core, 4–5
    financial aid at, 5
    funded approach to competition through endowments, 46
    large philanthropic giving for, 188–189
    marginalized populations scholarships and in-kind support, 5
    market-minded practices at, 227–228
    Oxbridge tradition and, 3
    partnering with private firms, 30 n.30
    residential core model and, 3–4
    tuition 25% of revenue stream for, 4–5
    tuition-schools emulation of, 3–4
Elon University, 35–36
Emory University, 62
endowment revenues
    of aspiring Ivies, 53
    Boxborough and Havertown expansion of, 19–20, 39, 50–53, 77 n.18
    of elite universities, 51, 53
    traditional philanthropy for, 20, 51–52, 60, 62–63
    traditional strategy to subsidize, 19
endowments, 1, 4–5
enrollment
    baby boomer adulthood and decrease in, 41–42, 87, 128, 140
    Boxborough and Havertown unprepared students, 70
    financial resources through growth in, 111–112
    growth of mission-centered schools, 106
enrollment growth
    arithmetic growth in, 249

enrollment growth (*Continued*)
  cost of student housing and feeding with, 9
  downward trajectory of mission with, 246
  federal financial aid with, 5, 7–8
  Malvern concern about, 245–246
  needed for funds increase, 1
  neoliberalism and pursuit of, 239
  poorer student recruitment for, 1
  to secure financial resources, 15, 43
  Stoneham and Boxborough concern about, 246–247
  in tuition-driven religious schools study, 16
  Winchendon on, 228
enrollment management divisions, at universities, 8
enrollment services, as paid partner, 140–141
enrollment threshold funding, 234
entrepreneurial approach. *See also* cultural entrepreneurism; social entrepreneurism; value entrepreneurism
  of network strategy, 145–146, 160, 173
  physical locations for online market, 244
  structural change in university from, 243
  within tuition-driven schools, 11
entrepreneurial schools, 11, 227, 249
executive level in institutions, interviews with, 267

faculty and staff
  Ardmore curriculum outsourcing bypassing, 216, 218
  reductions at Boxborough and Havertown, 70–71
faculty level in institutions, interviews with, 267
family firm management approach, 181, 256 n.6
  American Protestantism university examples, 181–182
  of Ardmore, 177, 179, 181–183
  authority with founder and family members, 181
  dramaturgy of, 182–183, 256 n.9
  focused decision-making in, 182
  of S&P Fortune 500 firms, 181
federal financial aid. *See also* student loans
  absence before 20th century, 7
  Boxborough compliance efforts, 236–237
  challenge of compliance with, 236–239
  commodity-market rules for, 236–237
  distribution oversight for, 236
  with enrollment growth, 5, 7–8
  guaranteed student loans, 6, 44
  margin capitalization and reliance on students with, 92
  minority student funding, 151, 175 n.18, 234–235
  parent loans, 44
  Pell Grants, 6, 236
  per-student funding, 40–41, 76 n.7, 233–234, 236, 240
  university compliance officers for, 236
financial aid packages
  customized, 44
  undercutting of Boxborough and Havertown College, 68–69
financial bid, in Internet marketing, 220
financial crisis, for universities, 1, 87
  at Ardmore, 187–188
  at Boxborough and Havertown, 163–164
  mission-driven schools and money necessity, 2
  at Pepperell and Winchendon, 137
  policy debates and policy solutions to solve, 27
  tuition increase to resolve, 1–2
financialization
  accelerated strategy superprofits of, 205–208
  by leveraging wealth of existing financial assets, 206–207
  public bonds for superprofits generation, 207
financial surplus, nonprofit institutions reinvestment of, 91
first mover, 103–105, 111–112
  criticism of, 104
  description of, 103–104
  Lansdale, Stoneham and Malvern as, 20–22, 79–80, 95–96, 103
  Malvern, Lansdale and Stoneham erosion of, 121–123
  Malvern and blending approach to residential core, 250–251
  in periphery education markets, 114

per-student federal education policies and, 104
flagship institution
  described, 125 n.2
  Malvern, Lansdale and Stoneham as, 79–80, 96–97, 101
foreign conversational language, Ardmore outsourcing to Competent Conversationalist, 216, 218
for-profit institutions
  competition from, 113
  practices penetration into nonprofit and religious institutions, 227
  pursuit of maximizing margins, 91
  university purchase of, 244
Fortune 500 firms. *See* S&P Fortune 500 firms
funding
  of elite expenses and residential core model, 4–5
  enrollment threshold, 234
  indirect on per-student basis, 40–41, 76 n.7
  minority student, 151, 175 n.18, 234–235
  neoliberalism mechanisms for, 40–41, 76 n.6, 79
  per-student, 40–41, 76 n.7, 233–234, 236, 240
  tradition, at Boxborough and Havertown, 37–39
  of traditional strategy, 37–39
  tuition-driven schools solutions for, 25–27, 32, 75–76
fundraising, 35
  Ardmore subsidy by church donation fundraising, 185–186, 257 n.11
  initiatives of Boxborough and Havertown, 52–53, 59–61
  margin philanthropy as form of neoliberal, 190
  traditional strategy limits for, 63–66
Furman University, 62
future-oriented question of closure, for interview, 270

Georgetown University, 35–36, 53, 57
Georgia State University, 209, 219, 222
GI Bill. *See* Servicemen's Readjustment Act
global network, of branch campuses, 152–155, 168–169

God, Ardmore as university for, 177–180, 222
Goffman, Erving, 256 n.9
golden age of higher education, 8, 87
  Ardmore on, 179–180
  Boxborough and Havertown in, 41–43
  building boom of, 40, 53–54
  explosive growth during, 248
  Pepperell on, 240
  student enrollment rapid expansion and public support in, 40, 76 n.4, 248
  student loans at end of, 44
Google, tapestry data approach for admissions and, 212
Grand Canyon University, accelerated strategy of, 118
growth strategies, strategic management for, 18–19, 30 n.34
guaranteed student loans, 6, 44
guerilla competitive research, of Ardmore, 177–178, 220–222
guided by God disposition, of Ardmore, 179–181

Hampshire College, 35–36
Hampton University, 29 n.14
Hartly College, Pepperell purchase of, 169–170
Harvard University, 53, 175 n.16, 227–228
  as Big Three university, 14–15, 97–98, 179
  commodification of education at, 227
Haverford College, 35–36
Havertown College, 32–33
  academic programs with credentialism investment, 58–59
  attempts to increase residential enrollments, 69
  buildings funded through donations, 38
  campus physical transformation at, 54–56
  commitment for community higher education, 34–35, 37–38
  community opportunity importance, 33, 37–38
  competition response from, 67–68, 71–74
  customized financial aid packages of, 44
  deliberate decision-making at, 20
  endowment growth at, 46–47, 50–53

Havertown College (*Continued*)
  endowment revenues of, 19–20, 39, 50–53, 77 n.18
  enrollment growth for federal tuition revenue, 41
  enrollment of unprepared students, 70
  faculty and staff reductions, 70–71
  financial aid packages undercut at, 68–69
  financial crisis at, 64–65
  following aspiring Ivies by, 32–33, 76 n.1, 35–36
  fundraising initiatives at, 52–53, 59–61
  in golden age of higher education, 41, 43
  heritage philosophy strategy, 46, 73
  impoverished region location, 33
  in-person communal approach, 50
  institutional loans and bonds, 61
  multiple identities of, 244
  online education market and, 49–50, 68, 72
  professional norms and decision-making at, 66–67
  professional programs emphasis, 49
  reputation of high academic standards, 33, 35, 36–38
  reputation to uphold of, 35–38, 76 n.3
  residential enrollment attempts, 46–47
  successful alumni of, 37
  traditional philanthropy for endowment revenue, 20, 51–52, 60, 62–63
  traditional strategy ineffective at, 20, 62–64, 67, 74–75
  traditional strategy of, 19–20, 37–38
  on tradition importance, 33, 37–38
  on tradition of residential enrollment, 48–49, 73
  tuition dependence of, 52–53
  tuition discounts subsidized by endowments, 50–51
  tuition paid through bartering, 38
higher education
  change from public good to private good, 232
  financing changes in 1970s, 42
  identity in, 239–248
  market-minded practices in, 227
  missing the middle in policy and finance of, 28
  paid partnerships entrenched practice throughout, 143–144
  policy innovation in, 230–239
  twentieth century increased access and public support for, 8
Higher Education Act (1965)
  per-student funding for all citizens, 76 n.7
  student loan forgiveness in national defense fields, 76 n.8
hiring practices, pioneer strategy values and, 110–111, 118–119
Hispanic serving institutions (HSI), 1–2, 5–6, 175 n.18, 234–235
Hispanic students, degrees at Winchendon, 145–146, 150–151, 231, 235
historically Black colleges and universities (HBCU), 1–2, 5–6, 15, 43, 175 n.18, 234–235

identity, in higher education, 239–248
  collective values for, 239
  emergence of multiple, 243–244
  loss of mission and purpose in, 246
  in residential core, 228
identity paradox, in higher education, 239–242
  Ardmore on, 241
  Boxborough on, 239–240
  Lansdale on, 240–243, 246, 248
  Malvern on, 243, 246, 248
  on mission identity and economic success, 239, 246–247
  Pepperell on, 240–241, 248
  Stoneham on, 239
  Winchendon on, 239–241
immigrant school, Pepperell and Winchendon as, 130
impoverished regions, Boxborough and Havertown location in, 33
inclusion priority, of Pepperell and Winchendon, 129
indirect funding, of federal financial aid on per-student basis, 40–41, 76 n.7
innovation spirit
  of Malvern, Lansdale, Stoneham, 84–85
  of pioneer strategy through moving, 98–99
institution selection, 264–266, 266*t*, 76 n.8
institution tour, 267–269

institutional financial aid packages,
    scholarships from need based to merit based, 44
institutional loans and bonds, 61
institutional types. *See also* aspiring Ivies; Asian American and Native American Pacific Islander Serving Institutions (AANAPISI); Big Three universities; elite universities; flagship institution; for-profit institutions; Hispanic serving institutions (HSI); historically Black colleges and universities (HBCU); minority serving institutions (MSI); mission driven schools, non-profit colleges and universities; multiversities; predominantly Black institutions (PBI); public institutions; regional institutions; religious college; state institution; Tribal colleges (TC); tuition-driven schools; vocational institutions; women's colleges
institutions of higher education, enrollment solutions focus, 89
Integrated Postsecondary Education Data System (IPEDS), 265, 272
international template approach, of network strategy, 153–154
internet marketing
    financial bid for advertising and targeting types, 220
    pay-per-click marketing for Google and Microsoft search engines, 220, 222
interview data analysis
    data display, 77 n.14, 272
    data reduction, 272
    triangulation, 77 n.14, 272
interviews, 269–271
    cathartic response from, 271
    focus of, 269–270
    future-oriented question of closure, 270
    with institution levels, 267
    limitations in research through, 271
    member checking process, 271
    sampling by institutional growth type, 266, 266*t*
    social science practices for, 269
IPEDS. *See* Integrated Postsecondary Education Data System
isomorphism, 4, 104

Jewish populations
    elite schools limited admission of Jewish students, 14–15, n. 29
    large Jewish alumni base at DePaul from inclusionary admissions, 14–15
    similar admissions for Muslim students, 15
    strengthen Jewish identity at Winchendon, 131–132
Johns Hopkins University, 175 n.16

Kaplan University, 226 n.31

Lafayette College, 35–36
Lansdale University
    affiliated high school programs of, 80
    aspiring Ivies and, 95–96
    commitment to value of relationships, 79, 81, 82–83, 120–121
    on comparative marketing, 117, 228
    on competition, 230–231
    continuous organizational change at, 80, 84
    core values and hiring practices, 110
    elementary and high school programs of, 84
    enrollment plateaus at, 113, 121–122
    as first mover, 20–22, 79–80, 95–96, 103
    as flagship institution, 79–80, 96–97, 101
    Grand Canyon University as primary competitor of, 118
    on identity paradox, 240–243, 246, 248
    innovation spirit at, 84–85
    in-person academic programs in unorthodox settings, 99
    marginalized populations mission of, 79, 95–96, 105, 124
    as mission-driven school, 105–106
    mission-oriented focus with commitment to values, 80–81
    multisite organizational form of, 96–97, 102
    name changes of, 84
    need for strategic enrollment growth, 88
    periphery enrollment markets and, 93, 100, 243
    pioneer strategy, 20–22
    pullback intensity at, 121–122
    on relationship with particular family, 81–82

Lansdale University (*Continued*)
  relocation of, 84
  residential campus relocation, 80
  on residential core model, 251
  on student choice, 231
  value entrepreneurism, 20–21, 79, 80–81, 126 n.6, 85–86, 90, 95–96, 111
  on values emphasis in periphery locations, 109–110
legitimacy, 3–5, 9, 18, 25, 76 n.2, 93, 104, 127 n.18
life coaching, Ardmore outsourcing to National Counseling Association, 216–218
Look to your left, look to your right orientation phrase, 69, 78 n.21

Malvern. *See* University of Malvern
marginalized populations
  elite universities scholarships and in-kind support for, 5, 29 n.10
  Malvern, Lansdale and Stoneham mission for, 79, 95–96, 105, 124
  religious college focus on, 14–15
  at Winchendon, 135–136
marginal tuition revenues
  entrepreneurial strategies for, 228
  periphery enrollment markets to strengthen, 20–21, 23
margin capitalization, 12, 24, 124–125, 139
  accelerated strategy use of, 193
  of Ardmore, 208–209, 221–222
  buildings and renovations, 12, 102, 149–150
  criticism of, 102
  described, 92–93
  entrepreneurial form of, 173
  funded through donations or bonds, 12–13
  funds generated from call center, 206
  Malvern emphasis on financial benefits of, 94–95, 101
  margin described, 90–91
  of network strategy, 142, 144, 160, 172, 191
  Pepperell residential campus support through, 158–159
  periphery enrollment markets marginal revenues for, 12–13, 92–93, 149–150
  of pioneer strategy, 90–95
  reliance on students with federal financial aid, 92
  in residential core model, 144
  tabletop model imagery, 147–148
  through tuition and federal financial aid, 12–13
margin capitalization and philanthropy, 270
margin philanthropy, 12
  of Ardmore, 24, 188–194, 209, 221–222
  from current students, 177–178
  as form of neoliberal fundraising, 190
  margins to build endowment, 189
  scenario example of, 190
  through tuition, 13, 189, 190
margins
  described, 90–91
  for-profit institutions pursuit of maximizing, 91
market approach, to university finances, 7–8
  customized financial aid packages, 44
  guaranteed student loans and, 6, 44
  higher education increased access and public support, 8
  parent loans, 44
market-centric institutions, 227
market-oriented, 30 n.19, 140–141, 230, 239, *See also* economic reasoning; market logic; neoliberalism
  framework for resource allocation, 18
  impact on student loans, 44–45
  practices of, 27, 91
  prioritizes competition, 17, 28
  role in paid-partners, 140–141, 159
  tension between purpose and profit, 15
market-oriented policies, 228–230, 233
  allow students to shop across schools, 68–69
  competition and choice intersection through, 231
  incentivized institutional leaders, 239
  inequitable outcomes in, 254
  influence at Ardmore, 251
  shape indirect funding, 104
  university leaders response to, 28
market logic, 25–27, 30 n.19, 141, 240, *See also* economic reasoning; market-oriented; neoliberalism
  driver of accelerated networks strategy, 223

embraced by Ardmore leaders, 25, 221–222
innovation of Wall Street, 222
policies, 25–27, 43, 89, 235–236
role in paid partnerships, 141-38
role in privatization, 113
role in race based enrollment policies, 235–236
securing university funding, 15, 144
solutions of, 228
style of communication, 218
market principle, of choice, 25
Massachusetts Institute of Technology, 222
member checking process, with interviews, 271
merit-based scholarships, 44–45
methodological approach. *See also* interviews; mixed methods research
access and arrival in, 267–269
introduction to, 264
Microsoft, tapestry data approach for admissions and, 212
middle manager level in institutions, interviews with, 267
military
academy for boys at Stoneham, 84
Stoneham in-person academic programs at base, 99–100
minority serving institutions (MSI), 1–2, 5–6
minority student funding, through federal financial aid, 151, 175 n.18, 234–235
missing the middle, in higher education policy and finance, 28
mission-driven schools
enrollment growth of, 106
Lansdale and Malvern as, 105–106
Malvern as, 106
nonprofit colleges and universities as, 91
revenue necessity for, 2
Stoneham as, 106
tuition-driven schools as, 5–7
mission-oriented focus with commitment to values, of Malvern, Lansdale and Stoneham, 80–81
missions
of Boxborough and Havertown, 32, 228
downward trajectory with enrollment growth, 246
of educational access, 28
identity paradox of economic success and, 239, 246–247
limited financial resources for sustaining, 15
lost identity tied to, 238–239, 246–247
to marginal population by Malvern, Lansdale and Stoneham, 79, 95–96, 105, 124
tuition-driven schools emphasis on unique, 5–6
mixed methods research, 264–272
narrative strategy, 272–274
triangulation in, 77 n.14, 271–272
Mormon populations
branch campus model for Brigham Young campuses, 111–112
Brigham Young schools ranked least expensive by US News, 257 n.11
universities in the western US, 14
Mount Holyoke College, 35–36
multidivisional form, 145–146, 156–157, 165–166
multiple identities, of universities, 243–244
internal competition between, 244
organizational transformations for, 244
of Stoneham, Havertown, 244
multisite organization form, of Malvern, Lansdale and Stoneham, 96–97, 102
attempts for mission unification, 107–108
management of, 100–103
multiversities, of network strategy, 128–129, 174 n.2, 145–146, 160–161, 176 n.23
multiversity organization form, of Pepperell and Winchendon, 145–146
Muslim populations
Pepperell graduates of, 145–146, 175 n.17, 150–151, 175 n.19, 235, 243
religious college admissions of, 14–15

narrative strategy, 272–274
National Counseling Association, Ardmore outsourcing life coaching to, 216–218
National Defense Education Act (1958), 7–8
student loan forgiveness in national defense fields, 76 n.8
need-based scholarships, 44–45
neo-entrepreneurialism, for pioneer strategy, 125

neoliberal edu-business approach, 233–234
    of Ardmore, 221–222
neoliberalism, 8, 30 n.19, *See also* economic reasoning; market logic; market-oriented
    accelerated networks impacted by, 228
    approach to diversity, 235–236
    described, 76 n.6
    evolution leading to dominance of, 232–233
    federal education policies and competition, 219, 228
    funding mechanisms of, 40–41, 76 n.6, 79
    margin philanthropy fundraising form of, 190
    market-based competition interpretation of policies of, 233
    paid partner as innovation of, 140–141
    pursuit of enrollment growth, 239
    student loans transformation by, 43
    tuition-driven schools funding solutions and federal policies of, 25–27, 32, 75–76
network strategy, 22f, 22–23, 128–129, 172–173, 228. *See also* paid partners, in network strategy; Pepperell University; University of Winchendon
    access for all, 183
    broad access for all, 133–136
    buildings and bodies, 149–152
    commissioned to care, 129–144
    competition within and without, 165–167
    complex enrollment network monitoring difficulties, 169–170, 172–173
    diversity dilemma, 160–172
    entrepreneurial approach of, 145–146, 160, 173
    global network of branch campuses, 152–155, 168–169
    inclusion priority, 129–132
    international template approach of, 153–154
    living on edge, 161–165
    of margin capitalization, 142, 144, 160, 172, 191
    multiversities of, 128–129, 174 n.2, 160–161, 176 n.23
    neoliberalism impact on, 228
    passing the torch, 136–139
    periphery enrollment markets in, 22–23, 128–129
    portfolio balance, 169–172
    programmatic diversity in, 22, 159–160
    pursuit of, 95–97
    residential core expenditure fluctuations, 171
    to saturate new periphery enrollment market, 159
    shared governance in, 155–157
    social entrepreneurism and, 22, 128, 129, 134–136, 144–145, 174 n.1
    social problems addressed at Pepperell and Winchendon, 135
    speed and saturation, 157–160
    stable leadership and, 129–130, 132–133
    students-as-resources mentality, 163
    tabletop model, 144, 146–149, 156–157
New York University, 160–161
nonelite universities
    endowments limited at, 5
    financial aid at, 5
    student loans at, 5
nonprofit college and universities, 29 n.8
    competition from, 113
    financial surplus reinvestment, 91
    for-profit school practices penetration into, 227
    as mission-focused institutions, 91
    philanthropy focus on donations, 189
nontraditional students
    credentialism of, 97–98
    tuition-driven schools pursuit of, 9
Northwestern University, 14–15

off-site preparations, for access and arrival, 268
Ohio State University, 209, 219
Ohio University, 111–112
Omega Services, as paid partners with Pepperell, 141, 164–165, 170
ongoing founding phenomenon, of Pepperell, 174 n.3
online education market, 215
    of Boxborough and Havertown, 49–50, 68
    entrepreneurial approach on physical locations for, 244
    network strategy online program managers, 142–144, 174 n.11
online global campuses, 244

Pepperell periphery enrollment market through paid partner for, 150
online education market, of
　Ardmore, 23–24, 177–178, 191, 197, 243
　aggressive embrace of online education, 191
　competition of, 209
　online enrollment explosion, 199–200, 205–206
　online shell and corporate enrollment market, 213–214
　product innovation of enrollment periphery market, 197
　sale of online services to other universities, 221
　technological infrastructure for mobility and standardization, 197–198
online program managers, 143–144, 174 n.11
operational analytics, at Ardmore, 211, 222
　course registration system developed through, 212–213
Oxbridge tradition, elite universities and, 3, 29 n.2

paid partners, in network strategy
　academic services, 140–141
　of Alpha Consulting with Winchendon, 141–142, 163
　of auxiliary services, 140–141
　Educational Testing Service exams, 140, 211–212
　of enrollment services, 140–141
　neoliberal innovation of, 140–141
　of Omega Services with Pepperell, 141, 164–165, 170
　of online program managers, 142–144, 174 n.11
　periphery enrollment market interaction with, 150
　of student services, 140–141
　tuition revenue sharing with, 143
　for turnaround in management process, 174 n.12
panopticon, Ardmore workplace, 201, 257 n.16
parent loans, 44
partnerships. *See also* paid partners
　corporate-university, 213–216

Malvern on intrastate, 252–253
3 + 1 between university and community colleges, 159, 175 n.22
pay-per-click marketing, Ardmore use of, 220, 222
Pell Grants, 6, 236
Pennsylvania State University, 209, 219, 244
Pepperell University
　access for all provision of, 128, 135
　buildings funded at, 150
　as Catholic institution, 128, 243
　clergy as faculty and administrators at, 132–133
　clergy supply drop-off and payroll cost increase, 136–137
　coed residential model, 136, 150–151, 175 n.16
　in community of need, 128
　comparison to University of Notre Dame, 161
　diversity commitment of, 131–132, 151–152, 235
　entrepreneurial layperson as president, 138–139, 146
　federal financial aid compliance officers at, 236
　global network of branch campuses, 152–155, 168–169
　on golden age of higher education, 240
　Hartly College purchase by, 169–170
　historical narrative of, 130–131
　on identity paradox, 240–241, 248
　as immigrant school, 130
　inclusion priority of, 129–131
　on incredible competition, 230–231
　internal competition within, 161, 165–166
　international template approach of, 153–154
　likelihood of closure, 138
　multiethnic and multireligious student populations, 129
　multiversity organization form of, 145–146
　Muslim graduates at, 145–146, 175 n.17, 150–151, 175 n.19, 235, 243
　network strategy of, 22–23
　Omega Services paid partnership with, 141, 164–165, 170
　ongoing founding phenomenon, 174 n.3

Pepperell University (*Continued*)
  online periphery enrollment market through paid partner, 150
  periphery enrollment markets and, 22–23, 147, 148–149, 171
  racial tensions at, 137
  residential campus support through margin capitalization, 158–159
  on residential core model dissolution, 252
  second campus for, 167–168
  social entrepreneurism of, 22, 128, 129, 134–136, 144–145, 174 n.1
  stable leadership, 129–130, 132–133
  on student choice, 231
  swift response to competition, 157–158
  3 + 1 partnerships of, 159, 175 n.22
  top-down governance of, 157
periphery enrollment markets
  Lansdale and, 93, 100
  of Malvern, 97, 100
  marginal revenues for margin capitalization, 12–13, 92–93, 149–150
  for payment of bonds, 149–150
  of Pepperell and Winchendon, 22–23, 147, 148–149, 171
  pioneer schools dramatic enrollment increases, 93
  revenues for buildings, 149
  to strengthen marginal tuition revenues, 20–21, 23
  values role in, 106, 108, 109–110
  Winchendon on sale of sites for, 168
per-student funding, 40–41, 233, 236, 240
  Ardmore on, 234
  GI Bill for veterans only, 76 n.7
physical campus. *See also* buildings
  Ardmore transformation of, 206
  Boxborough and Havertown transformation of, 54–56
  competition and correlation with enrollments and, 53–54, 56
  entrepreneurial approach for online market locations for, 244
pioneer strategy, 20–22, 21f, 79–80, 124–125, 228. *See also* Lansdale University; Stoneham University; University of Malvern
  adult education and, 113–114
  challenge to values, 115–118
  compressed educational timeline of, 114
  connection importance, 81–83
  core values and hiring practices, 110–111, 118–119
  culture of change, 83–84
  efforts to lead competition, 112
  enrollment markets for residential core sustenance, 124–125
  financial consequences, 111–123
  first movers of, 20–22, 79–80, 95–96, 103–105, 114
  innovation spirit, 84–87
  innovation through moving, 98–99
  inspired evolution of, 80–111
  lack of viability in, 123
  marginal tuition revenue of, 112
  margin capitalization, 90–95
  mission-centered growth, 106–109
  mission support, 87–90
  money as great priority for, 119
  multisite form management, 100–103
  neo-entrepreneurialism for, 125
  neoliberalism impact on, 228
  new types of periphery markets, 124–125
  opportunities to reconceive place, 97–99
  periphery enrollment markets and, 93
  pullback perils, 121–123
  pursuit of, 95–97
  relationships taxing, 118–121
  residential core sustenance strategies, 20–22, 96f, 101–102, 112, 124–125
  residential students recruitment, 101–102
  satellite campuses in, 20–21, 105
  social stigma of, 105
  tuition margins in, 101
  two-front defense, 112–115
  value emphasis in decision-making, 108
  values across space, 109–111
  values-oriented student experience and, 109
policy
  ambiguities in accreditation, 237
  competition within and among, 230
  debates and solutions for financial crisis of universities, 27
  innovation utilizing ambiguity in, 238
  leverage and exploitation in interpretation of, 234
  market-oriented premises for, 230

student loans and changes to federal, 40–41
policy innovation, in higher education, 230–239
Pope, (the Pope), 144–145
Power Four athletic conferences, 156, 175 n.21
predominantly Black institutions (PBI), 175 n.18, 234–235
prestige-focused resource approach, 62
Princeton University, as Big Three university, 14–15, 97–98, 175 n.16, 179
private college education, student loans and, 43
privatization, 126 n.8
　individual consumer expense from, 42, 77 n.10
process innovation, at Ardmore University, 217–218
product bundling, at Ardmore, 199, 257 n.15
product innovation, at Ardmore University, 196–197, 257 n.14, 199, 217–218
　of online enrollment periphery market, 197
professional programs, Boxborough and Havertown emphasis on, 49
programmatic diversity, in network strategy, 22, 159–160
Protestants, institutions with religious emphasis, 179–180, 256 n.3
public good, higher education change to private good, 232
public institutions, state appropriations decline in 1970s, 42, 126 n.8
public support
　for educational access, 40–41
　in golden age of higher education, 40, 76 n.4, 248
pullback in enrollment growth, pioneer strategy and, 121–123
Purdue University, 226 n.31, 244

regional education, 11, 23, 93, 97, 111–112, 120
regional institutions, 1–2, 5–6, 11, 68
relationships

Malvern, Lansdale and Stoneham commitment to value of, 79, 81, 82–83, 120–121
　pioneer strategy taxing, 118–121
religious college, 30 n.26
　Ardmore religious outlook, 178–179
　Catholic, Muslim admissions at, 14–15
　for-profit school practices penetration into, 227
　marginalized populations focus of, 14–15
　study selection of, 14
religious scandals, Ardmore impacted by, 186–187, 257 n.12
reputation of high academic standards of Boxborough and Havertown Colleges, 33, 35, 36–38
　economic connotation of, 76 n.2
reputation to uphold, in traditional strategy, 35–38, 76 n.3
research. See also mixed methods research
　interview limitation for, 271
　site visit and activities of, 267–268
residential core model, 3–4
　at Big Three Universities, 97–98
　blending approach to, 250–251, 253, 255
　Boxborough and Havertown growing, 48–49, 69
　for building maintenance, 249–250
　composition change for, 242–245
　elite funding expenses from, 4–5
　endowments and enrollments to sustain, 248
　financial margins to sustain, 245, 249
　identity in, 228, 243
　Lansdale on, 251
　Malvern on intrastate partnerships in, 252–253
　Pepperell on dissolution of, 252
　questioning essential elements of, 250–251
　Stoneham and Ardmore on, 251
　tabletop margin capitalization in, 144
　tuition-driven schools innovative ways to pay for, 9–14
residential core sustenance strategies accelerated, 23–25, 194*f*
　network strategy, 22–23, 145*f*, 149
　pioneer strategy, 20–22, 96*f*, 101–102, 112, 124–125
　revenue sources for, 26*f*, 229*f*

residential core model (*Continued*)
  traditional, 19–20, 47f, 114–115
Roberts, Oral, 257 n.12

St. John's University, 111–112
sampling, 264–267
  institution comparison, 265
  across institutions by growth rate and religion, 266, 266t
  institution selection, 264–266, 266t, 76 n.8
  IPEDS on similar characteristics for, 265, 272
Santa Clara University, 62
Sarah Lawrence College, 175 n.16
SAT. *See* College Board
satellite campuses, 11
  of Malvern, 95–96
  in pioneer strategy, 20–21, 105
scaling up
  accelerated strategy of rapid, 193–196
  at Ardmore University, 194–196
  arithmetic growth or expansion, 195
  equal attention to growth and cost in, 202
  GI Bill and, 195
scholarships
  of elite university for marginalized populations, 5
  institutions change from need-based to merit-based, 44–45
sector of schools, 227–230
  challenge of compliance, 236–239
  change in composition, 242–245
  competition and choice trumping cooperation, 230–233
  end of history, 250–253
  hollowing the core, 248–253
  identity in higher education, 239–248
  identity paradox, 239–242
  interpretation as innovation, 233–236
  policy innovation in higher education, 230–239
  selling your soul, 245–248
  unsustainable margins, 249–250
Servicemen's Readjustment Act (1944) (GI Bill), 7, 29 n.16
  per-student funding for veterans by, 76 n.7
  scaling up with, 195

shared governance, in network strategy, 155–156
shell
  Ardmore standardized for global employees, 215
  corporate, 213–216
  corporate enrollment market of Ardmore and online, 213–214
  corporate-university partnerships and corporate, 213
  curriculum of Ardmore, 215–216
sidebars, in narrative writing, 273–274
site visit, 267–268, 271
Skidmore College, 35–36
Smith College, 35–36
social entrepreneurism, of Pepperell and Winchendon, 22, 128, 129, 134–136, 144–145, 174 n.1
social science practice, for interviews, 269
social stigma
  of Entrepreneurial leaders, 11–12
  of network strategy, 161–162
  of pioneer strategy, 20–21, 96–97, 104, 105, 124
Southern New Hampshire University, 209, 213, 220
S&P Fortune 500 firms, 37, 177–178, 181, 209–211
stable leadership, of Pepperell and Winchendon clergy as faculty and administrators, 129–130, 132–133
standardization, for accelerated strategy cost containment, 205
Stanford University, 15, 84–85, 227–228
state
  state funding, 7, 27, 28, 42, 126 n.8, 184, 244
  state institution, 15, 20–21, 97–98, 120–121, 135, 209, 244, 252–253, 256 n.3
  state legislatures, 27, 42, 98, 228
  state demographics, 2, 48, 151–152
  state policy, 126 n.8, 244
Stoneham University, 231–232
  acute enrollment strain, 88
  affiliated high school programs of, 80
  aspiring Ivies and, 95–96
  commitment to value of relationships, 79, 81, 82–83, 120–121

competition and staffing adjustments, 120
continuous organizational change at, 80, 84
core values and hiring practices, 110–111
enrollment plateau at, 113, 121–122
as first mover, 20–22, 79–80, 95–96, 103
as flagship institution, 79–80, 96–97, 101
on identity paradox, 239
innovation spirit at, 84–85
in-person academic programs at military base, 99–100
marginalized populations mission of, 79, 95–96, 105, 124
military academy for boys at, 84
as mission-driven school, 106
mission-oriented focus with commitment to values, 80–81
multiple identities of, 244
multisite organizational form of, 96–97, 102, 244
name changes of, 84
nuns on competition impact, 230–231
outside agency for student recruitment, 116
pullback intensity at, 122
on residential core model, 251
on university as educational business, 90
value entrepreneurism, 20–21, 79, 80–81, 126 n.6, 85–86, 90, 95–96, 111
on values emphasis in periphery locations, 108–110
story arc, in narrative writing, 273–274
strategic management, 18–19, 30 n.34
Strayer University, 227
student loans, 7–8, 233
  at end of golden age of higher education, 44
  federal policy changes and, 40–41
  forgiveness in national defense fields, 76 n.8
  guaranteed, 6, 44
  neoliberal transformation of, 43
  at nonelite universities, 5
  private college education costs and, 43
  students-as-resources strategies recruitment and, 10–11
  traditional strategy revolution of, 43–46
  university survival and, 5, 8
students

Boxborough and Havertown enrollment of unprepared, 70
choice from competition, 231
enrollment growth and recruitment of poorer, 1
financial liability 20th century shift to, 7
margin philanthropy from current, 177–178
Stoneham outside agency for recruitment of, 116
tuition-driven schools diversity of, 1–2
university competition due to decline in traditional-aged, 27
students-as-resources strategies
  recruitment of students with student loans, 10–11
  student with higher tuition rate enrollment, 10–11
student services, as paid partner, 140–141
Swaggart, Jimmy Lee, 257 n.12

tabletop model, in network strategy, 144, 146–149
  margin capitalization imagery, 147–148
  top-down governance of, 156–157
tapestry data admissions emphasis, at Ardmore, 211–212
  Google and Microsoft for, 212
technological infrastructure, of Ardmore University, 196–197
  in call center, 200–202
  distance-learning periphery market, 197
  online enrollment mobility and standardization, 197–198
3 + 1 partnership between university and community colleges, 159, 175 n.22
top-down governance, 156–157
traditional-age students, competition increase due to decline in, 27, 41–42
traditional philanthropy, for endowment revenues, 20, 51–52, 60, 62–63
traditional strategy, 19f, 19–20, 47f, 32–33, 228. *See also* Boxborough College; Havertown College
  absence of speed in, 66–68
  building and renovations in, 53–56
  challenge for, 40–42
  challenge to catch up with competition, 71–74
  community opportunity, 33–35, 37–38

302 Index

traditional strategy (*Continued*)
  end of, 250–253
  endowment revenues increase to subsidize, 19
  enrollment cliff, 68–71
  funding of, 37–39
  fundraising limits, 63–66
  heritage influence on, 32–46
  overhaul of offerings in, 56–59
  pursuit of, 46–62
  reputation to uphold in, 35–38, 76 n.3
  residential core growth, 48–53, 114–115
  stewards of opportunity, 59–62
  student loans revolution, 43–46
  university endowment expansion, 50–53
  wage of prestige, 62–74
triangulation, in mixed methods research, 271–272
  interview data analysis, 77 n.14, 272
Tribal colleges (TC), 1–2, 5–6, 15, 175 n.18
Trinity College, 35–36
tuition. *See also* marginal tuition revenues
  Boxborough and Havertown Colleges dependence on, 52–53
  decrease and cost-saving mechanisms, 6
  elite institutions 25% of revenue stream, 4–5
  increase to resolve university financial crisis, 1–2
  margin capitalization through federal financial aid and, 12–13
  margin philanthropy through, 13, 189, 190
  margins in pioneer strategy, 101
  pioneer strategy marginal revenue of, 112
tuition-driven religious schools study
  enrollment growth in, 16
  schools strategized for, 17–27
  selection of, 14–17
tuition-driven schools, 228
  competition and choice market principles, 25
  elite universities emulated by, 3–4
  enrollment and changes in environment, 6–7
  entrepreneurial schools within, 11
  federal neoliberal policies and new funding solutions for, 25–27, 32, 75–76
  first-generation, underrepresented students at, 1–2
  innovations to pay for residential core model, 9–14
  innovative adult education, 11–12
  innovative educational products of, 9–14
  as mission-driven schools, 5–7
  nontraditional student enrollment pursuit, 9
  religious college study selection, 14
  student diversity in, 1–2
  unique mission emphasis of, 5–6
tuition revenues, paid partners shared, 143
Tuskegee University, 29 n.14

universities. *See also* financial crisis
  call centers of, 201
  compliance officers for federal financial aid, 236
  customized financial aid packages of, 44
  enrollment management divisions at, 8
  enrollment needs for funds increase, 1
  enrollment solutions focus of, 89
  federal financial aid through enrollment growth, 5, 7–8
  for-profit institutions purchase by, 244
  leaders response to market-oriented practices, 28
  student loans and survival of, 5, 8
university for God, Ardmore as, 177–180, 222
University of Arizona, 226 n.31, 244
University of Arkansas, 244
University of California, Berkeley, 256 n.3
University of Chicago, 14–15, 51
University of Connecticut, 111–112
University of Florida, 209, 213, 219
University of Idaho, 244
University of Illinois, 244
University of Kentucky, 111–112
University of Malvern
  adult education at, 243
  affiliated high school programs of, 80
  aspiring Ivies and, 95–96
  commitment to value of relationships, 79, 81, 82–83, 120–121
  commitment to values, 117
  competition and resource cuts, 120
  continuous organizational change at, 80–81, 84
  core values and hiring practices for, 110
  enrollment plateaus at, 113, 121–122

as first mover, 2, 21–22, 79–80, 95–96, 154
as flagship institution, 79–80, 96–97, 101
on identity paradox, 243, 246, 248
innovation spirit at, 84–85
in-person academic programs in unorthodox settings, 99
on intrastate partnerships in residential core model, 252–253
marginalized populations mission of, 79, 95–96, 105, 124
on margin capitalization financial benefit, 94–95, 101
as mission-driven school, 105–106
mission-oriented focus with commitment to values, 80–81
multisite organizational form of, 96–97, 102
name changes of, 84
need for strategic enrollment growth, 88
new neo-entrepreneurialism of, 125
periphery enrollment markets of, 97, 100
pullback intensity at, 122–123
reinvestment of financial surplus, 91
relocation of, 84
residential campus relocation of, 80
satellite locations of, 95–96
on student choice, 231
value entrepreneurism, 20–21, 79, 85–86, 90, 95–96, 111, 126 n.6
on values emphasis in periphery locations, 109–110
University of Mary Washington, 175 n.16
University of Maryland, 244
University of Massachusetts, 244
University of Massachusetts, Amherst, 35–36
University of Notre Dame, 36, 57, 95–96, 160–161
　Pepperell comparison to, 161
　Winchendon on, 172
University of Oxford, 227–228
University of Pennsylvania, 15, 227–228
University of Phoenix, 209, 227
University of Richmond, 35–36
University of Virginia, 69, 146, 227–228
University of Washington, 160–161
University of Winchendon
　access for all provision of, 128–129, 135

Alpha Consulting paid partnership with, 141–142, 163
buildings funded at, 150
as Catholic institution, 128, 243
clergy as faculty and administrators at, 132–133
clergy supply drop-off and payroll cost increase, 136–137
coed residential model, 136, 150–151, 175 n.16
in community of need, 128
deteriorating core campus at, 137
diversity commitment of, 131–132, 151–152
on enrollment growth, 228
entrepreneurial layperson as president, 138–139, 146
financial crisis of, 88
global network of branch campuses, 152–155, 168–169
Hispanic student degrees at, 145–146, 150–151, 231, 235
historical narrative of, 130–131
on identity paradox, 239–241
as immigrant school, 130
inclusion priority of, 129–131
internal competition within, 161, 165–166
international template approach of, 153–154
levels of risk in leadership approach, 161–163
likelihood of closure, 138
multiethnic and multireligious student populations of, 129
multiversity organization form of, 145–146
network strategy of, 22–23
orphanages established at, 134
periphery enrollment market revenues for buildings, 149
periphery enrollment markets and, 22–23, 147, 148–149, 171
second campus for, 167–168
social entrepreneurism of, 22, 128, 129, 133–136, 144–145, 174 n.1
stable leadership, 129–130, 132–133
swift response to competition, 157–158
on threat of competition, 230–231
top-down governance of, 157

University of Winchendon (*Continued*)
  on University of Notre Dame, 172
  women college identity change, 243
US News & World Report, 9, 257 n.11

value entrepreneurism
  as benefit and burden, 118, 124
  described, 125 n.1
  of Lansdale, Stoneham, and
    Malvern, 20–21, 79, 80–81, 126 n.6,
    85–86, 90, 95–96, 111
  pioneer strategy and values-oriented
    student experience, 109
  quickly evolving enrollment and
    adaptation, 115–116
values
  collective for university identity, 239
  emphasis in pioneer strategy
    decision-making, 108
  Malvern, Lansdale, Stoneham
    mission-oriented focus of, 80–81
  Malvern, Lansdale and Stoneham
    commitment to relationship, 79, 81,
    82–83, 120–121
  Malvern commitment to, 117

pioneer strategy hiring practices and
  core, 110–111, 118–119
role in periphery enrollment
  markets, 106, 108, 109–110
Vanderbilt University, 15
Vassar College, 175 n.16
Vatican, 136–137, 175 n.17
Villanova University, 62
visuals, in narrative writing, 273–274
vocational education, 1–2, 5–6, 11, 23,
  92–93, 98, 124–125, 147, 255
vocational institutions, 1–2, 5–6, 11, 23, 59,
  255

wage containment, for accelerated strategy
  cost containment, 203–205
Wake Forest University, 62, 83
Washington State University, 244
West Virginia State University, 175 n.18
Western Governors University, 213
Winchendon. *See* University of Winchendon
women's colleges, 1–2, 15, 43, 175 n.16, 243
writing, of narrative, 273–274

Yale University, as Big Three
  university, 14–15, 95–98, 179, 184